Yale Agrarian Studies Series

James C. Scott, series editor

THE AGRARIAN STUDIES SERIES AT YALE UNIVERSITY PRESS seeks to publish outstanding and original interdisciplinary work on agriculture and rural society—for any period, in any location. Works of daring that question existing paradigms and fill abstract categories with the lived experience of rural people are especially encouraged.
—James C. Scott, *Series Editor*

James C. Scott, *Seeing Like a State: How Certain Schemes to Improve the Human Condition Have Failed*
Steve Striffler, *Chicken: The Dangerous Transformation of America's Favorite Food*
James C. Scott, *The Art of Not Being Governed: An Anarchist History of Upland Southeast Asia*
Timothy Pachirat, *Every Twelve Seconds: Industrialized Slaughter and the Politics of Sight*
James C. Scott, *Against the Grain: A Deep History of the Earliest States*
Loka Ashwood, *For-Profit Democracy: Why the Government Is Losing the Trust of Rural America*
Jonah Steinberg, *A Garland of Bones: Child Runaways in India*
Hannah Holleman, *Dust Bowls of Empire: Imperialism, Environmental Politics, and the Injustice of "Green" Capitalism*
Johnhenry Gonzalez, *Maroon Nation: A History of Revolutionary Haiti*
Christian C. Lentz, *Contested Territory: Điện Biên Phủ and the Making of Northwest Vietnam*
Dan Allosso, *Peppermint Kings: A Rural American History*
Jamie Kreiner, *Legions of Pigs in the Early Medieval West*
Christian Lund, *Nine-Tenths of the Law: Enduring Dispossession in Indonesia*
Shaila Seshia Galvin, *Becoming Organic: Nature and Agriculture in the Indian Himalaya*
Michael Dove, *Bitter Shade: The Ecological Challenge of Human Consciousness*
Japhy Wilson, *Reality of Dreams: Post-Neoliberal Utopias in the Ecuadorian Amazon*
Aniket Aga, *Genetically Modified Democracy: Transgenic Crops in Contemporary India*
Ruth Mostern, *The Yellow River: A Natural and Unnatural History*
Brian Lander, *The King's Harvest: A Political Ecology of China from the First Farmers to the First Empire*
Jo Guldi, *The Long Land War: The Global Struggle for Occupancy Rights*
Andrew S. Mathews, *Trees Are Shape Shifters: How Cultivation, Climate Change, and Disaster Create Landscapes*
Francesca Bray, Barbara Hahn, John Bosco Lourdusamy, and Tiago Saraiva, *Moving Crops and the Scales of History*

For a complete list of titles in the Yale Agrarian Studies Series, visit yalebooks.com/agrarian.

Moving Crops and the Scales of History

Francesca Bray

Barbara Hahn

John Bosco Lourdusamy

Tiago Saraiva

Yale UNIVERSITY PRESS · NEW HAVEN & LONDON

Published with assistance from the foundation established in memory of
Philip Hamilton McMillan of the Class of 1894, Yale College.

Copyright © 2023 by Yale University.
All rights reserved.
This book may not be reproduced, in whole or in part, including
illustrations, in any form (beyond that copying permitted by Sections 107
and 108 of the U.S. Copyright Law and except by reviewers for the public
press), without written permission from the publishers.

Yale University Press books may be purchased in quantity for educational,
business, or promotional use. For information, please e-mail sales.press@
yale.edu (U.S. office) or sales@yaleup.co.uk (U.K. office).

Printed in the United States of America.

Library of Congress Control Number: 2022934331
ISBN 978-0-300-25725-0 (hardcover : alk. paper)

A catalogue record for this book is available from the British Library.

This paper meets the requirements of
ANSI/NISO Z39.48-1992 (Permanence of Paper).

10 9 8 7 6 5 4 3 2 1

To Alina, Dagmar, Danyang, and Jon,
our heartfelt thanks

Contents

Acknowledgments, ix

List of Abbreviations,   xiii

Orientations. Cropscapes and History, 1

1 Times, 25

2 Places, 59

3 Sizes, 95

4 Actants, 134

5 Compositions, 172

6 Reproductions, 207

Epilogue. Beyond the Grain, 248

Notes, 253

Bibliography, 285

Index, 325

Acknowledgments

Moving Crops has been on the move over a period of about four years. Along the way we have gathered varied and pleasant debts of gratitude. Our foremost thanks go to the Max Planck Institute for the History of Science, Berlin (MPIWG). We thank its director and one of our biggest well-wishers Dagmar Schäfer, not only for seeding the project as part of Department III of MPI and hosting us generously for almost a dozen meetings, but also for enabling us to tap into one of the most precious attributes of MPIWG—one marked by a great deal of mobility and connectedness: the opportunity to meet with numerous scholars from around the globe, drawn to the institute as long- and short-term fellows or visitors. We have immensely profited in particular through our interactions with BuYun Chen, Emily Brock, Jonathan Harwood, Lisa Onaga, On Barak, Tamar Novick, Tim LeCain, and Yubin Shen.

We owe a special debt of gratitude to Alina Cucu, our intellectual coordinator at MPIWG, who provided us with astute criticism, creative suggestions, strong coffee, tasty snacks, and jazz evenings during our Berlin meetings.

Our travels to Berlin and our deliberations there would not have been as enjoyable and fruitful as they turned out to be without the precious roles played by the invariably cheerful and helpful MPIWG staff—in particular Danyang

x Acknowledgments

Zhang and her office, Gina Grzimek, Shih-pei Chen, Verena Braun, and the librarian Esther Chen.

Apart from hosting us regularly, MPIWG very generously brought to Berlin a set of scholars from around the world exclusively to brainstorm about our project in its very early days. Our warmest thanks go to the following scholars who attended the 2016 workshop and offered valuable feedback—so crucially needed at that early stage: Sarah Besky, Peter Coclanis, Sterling Evans, Jonathan Harwood, Susanna Hecht, Prakash Kumar, Peter Magee, Rebecca Marsland, Marcy Norton, Marcus Popplow, Augustine Sedgewick, Grace Shen, and Norton Wise.

For our part, we too moved the project around by way of dedicated sessions in various conferences, including the SHOT (Society for the History of Technology) meeting in 2017 and the World Economic History Conference, ICOHTEC (International Congress of History of Technology) and SHOT meetings in 2018. As a culmination of our efforts, toward the very end of the project we held our own exclusive workshop-cum-conference, *Republic of Plants 2019,* hosted by the Indian Institute of Technology Madras in December 2019. In exploring how they might apply the cropscape perspective to their individual or group works, the nearly forty workshop participants provided valuable help in testing the concept further. Among the contributors to the long-term conversation we wholeheartedly thank Abhigya, Jonas Albrecht, S. Jesudoss Arokiam, Sandipan Baksi, Cristiana Bastos, Dominic Berry, Puran Bridgemohan, Tad Brown, Helen Anne Curry, Rebecca Earle, Deborah Fitzgerald, Anabel Ford, Courtney Fullilove, Maria do Mar Gago, Elaine Gan, Anne Gerritsen, Dominic Glover, Hélène Guetat, Hong Xuedong, Ke Hu, Julie Jacquet, J. John, Mini Kachumbron, Lawrence Kessler, Aleksandra Kobiljski, Diwakar Kumar, Richa Kumar, Elena D. Kunadt, Frédéric Landy, Ernst Langthaler, Gabriela Soto Laveaga, Pamela O. Long, Harro Maat, Marta Macedo, Gergely Mohacsi, Biswamohan Mohanty, Timo Myllintaus, Sudha Nagavarapu, Lalitha Narayanan, Madhu Narayanan, Vishala Parmasad, Ines Prodoehl, Preeti Edakunny Ramanathan, Taniya Sah, Madhumita Saha, Thamarai Selvan, Jayeeta Sharma, Sam Smiley, Jenny Smith, Ramesh Subramanian, Franziska Torma, Sita Venkateswar, Wang Siming, Marisa Wilson, and Yuan Yi.

We thank Marta Macedo and Jeyakumar P for making some very fine illustrations for this book, Jim Nations for kindly providing the milpa photo, and Selin Kara, who went to the Topkapi on our behalf.

Our sincere thanks to our respective institutions (the departments, administrative offices and libraries) for the varied support rendered to us over the past four years as we worked on the book.

Yale University Press has been enormously supportive during the entire course of the making of the book. We wish, in particular, to thank James C. Scott and

Jean Thomson Black for all the timely advice, clarifications, and above all encouragement, as well as the six anonymous readers for their very constructive suggestions.

Finally, a very special thank-you to our near and dear ones, who bore with us for the hours, days, or weeks we had to be away from them as we kept moving ourselves, others, and the project along.

Abbreviations

ANT	actor-network theory
CNSL	cashew nut shell liquid
DOC	Controlled Designation of Origin (Portuguese)
EIC	East India Company (British)
FAO	Food and Agriculture Organization of the United Nations
FDA	Food and Drug Administration (United States)
FSR	farming systems research
GDP	gross domestic product
GIAHS	Globally Important Agricultural Heritage Systems
GM	genetically modified
GR	Green Revolution
IAHS	Important Agricultural Heritage System
IR8	International Rice Research Institute variety 8 (one of the most important so-called miracle rices of the Green Revolution)
IRRI	International Rice Research Institute
PRC	People's Republic of China (1949–)
SS	Schutzstaffel (Protective Echelon)

xiv Abbreviations

STS	science and technology studies
VIR	All-Union Institute of Plant Industry (Soviet)
VOC	East India Company (Dutch)
USDA	U.S. Department of Agriculture

Orientations Cropscapes and History

Among the products of human work whose flows are the stuff of global history—from silver, oil, or raw cotton to silk brocades or steam engines—crops are a very special category, life-forms literally rooted in their local environment. Crops are artifacts with attitude, plants subjected to intense human discipline but with an irrepressible propensity to slip free. A crop may be a weed in the making; weeds in a new place or time may become crops. Inseparably natural and social, inescapably material yet inherently symbolic, at once rooted and mobile, controlled and uncontrollable, crops are ideally suited to developing new and richer histories of global flows and interactions that are both rooted and rhizomatic.[1]

Human efforts to move crops from one place to another have been a key driving force in history. Crops have been on the move for millennia, from wildlands to fields or from heartlands to borderlands, from one imperial colony to another or from the lab to places across the world. They have moved in flows or circuits spanning scales from the local landscape to intercontinental trade routes, in rhythms or time spans ranging from annual crop rotation to the centuries of flow, convergence, and exchange that went into producing modern varieties of "world crops" like wheat, rice, and oranges. But there is no guarantee that a crop will either survive uprooting or prosper if transposed to a new environment, nor that it will fill its original role in its new home. Moving a crop is no simple matter, nor is the outcome predictable.

In the late 1830s the British East India Company smuggled tea seeds, tea bushes, and skilled workers out of China to set up rival tea gardens or plantations in Assam, where they lavished care and attention on the delicate transplants. Yet by the 1870s British planters and botanists had savagely turned on the precious "China stock," once so hopefully and lovingly tended, declaring it a "curse" to be uprooted, burned, and replaced with indigenous Assam bushes (discussed further in chapter 2, "Places"). The crop became a weed! In Aztec gardens, shrines, and cemeteries, marigolds, flowers that spoke to the souls of the dead, were ubiquitous and became successful if almost invisible travelers in the Columbian Exchange. It took just a few years for Mexican marigolds to root successfully a hemisphere away in India, where their glowing colors and spicy scent guaranteed them a welcome place on altars and in ritual garlands. Yet it took them four centuries to reach neighboring North America, a territory that they eventually invaded not as holy flowers but as cheap and cheerful bedding plants (see chapter 5, "Compositions"). Manioc (or cassava), imported from South America, was successfully grown around the slaving ports of Portuguese Africa from around 1500. Although manioc flour (*farinha*) soon became an indispensable staple for the urban poor of all races, in the interior manioc was typically just one garden crop among many. Then, after four hundred years of near dormancy, in regions like northern Mozambique manioc replaced millets and sorghum as "food" almost overnight: the sudden change of staple was a desperate response by African smallholders to a 1915 government policy obliging them to cultivate cotton ("Compositions").

Transplanting a crop successfully to a new place entails formidable efforts, social and symbolic as well as material; plant, planters, and place all change in the process of mutual adaption. Records of these struggles and metamorphoses, in a dizzying variety of formats from ancient Chinese bronze inscriptions and Ottoman miniatures to genomic analysis and workers' songs, span the histories and geographies of almost the entire world. This vast spatial and chronological span of experience and records not only encompasses a huge diversity of crops and contexts but also reveals many unexpected actors, human or nonhuman, and surprising connections or patterns. This prompts us to step back, set aside assumptions, and think more imaginatively about what kinds of history happened and what kinds of history we can write. The ubiquity of crops, their mutability and the flexibility of the very category, points at ways to write more liberated forms of history.

Moving Crops and the Scales of History is an experimental work in this vein, a contribution to "decolonizing" history. As we explain below, we consider multiple dimensions of movement: movements in space and in time, expansions or contractions, organic or social metamorphoses, and shifts in association or significance. Our cases include the travels of date oases across the ancient Sahara and the moving cocoa frontier of modern Ghana; the cotton and wheat exchanges of the United States and the tea exports of medieval China; the lineages of seemingly timeless milpa gardens in the Maya forests and of the high-tech Svalbard Global Seed Vault. As well as the crops themselves and the farmers who cultivated them, our historical actors include the spirits of long yams and the spirits that halt the fermentation of port wines; the Black American agronomist George Washington Carver and the imperial Chinese agronomist Xu Guangqi; elephants, drops of water, and the future.

Exploring the dual nature of crops as rooted and movable things that reconnect local and global, microscale and macroscale, daily routines and events and the *longue durée,* we exploit the exciting profusion of materials on crops to propose a method for writing new and richer histories of the dynamics of material worlds. The span and variety of our sources, their harmonies and dissonances, spur us to break out of the familiar periodizations and geographies, the conventional scales, boundaries, and directionalities that still structure much global or comparative history. Our reframings seek to counter teleological or determinist narratives that justify today's geographies of power and inequality.[2] We hope to give visibility to ignored historical agencies and neglected geographical linkages.

Our arguments unfold through a series of contrasting crop histories carefully structured to play with scales of time, space, and agency. We focus on movement but choose crops as our prism precisely because they are rooted living organisms. The fact that crops must be uprooted from a local ecology in order to move them requires us to take rootedness and places of origin as seriously as mobility and destinations. And as things shaped by human technical intervention that are also life-forms with their own agency, crops oblige us to reckon seriously with the specifics of their materiality—its affordances, its resistances, and how these affect agency, movement, growth, and the creation or loss of meaning as crops move in various ways—or as they stay in place. We use crops to develop our arguments but contend that the method is applicable to any of the other material artifacts or commodities that are the stuff of rooted global history.

INTRODUCING THE CROPSCAPE

Crops are the product of specific environmental conditions and human intervention, including cultivation techniques, modes of production, needs and values, tastes and ideals. An assemblage or coalition of human and nonhuman actors must be brought together to produce and reproduce a crop, and when humans seek to transplant such assemblages they may single out separate elements: the crop species itself, the associated mode of cultivation, institutional form, motivating ideology, patterns of consumption, and so on. To address these complex and evolving entanglements we propose the *cropscape,* both as a concept to encompass the constellation of elements that are brought together to make a specific crop in a specific place and time, and as a tool to analyze the sum of movements and forces that produce and reproduce the working set of elements, as well as the capacity or incapacity of crops and their assemblages to travel.

We define the cropscape, then, as an *assemblage formed around a crop:* the heterogeneous elements or actors brought together in a specific place and time that make and grow that crop. Our cropscape assemblages comprise plants, people, weather, markets, ideas, desires, and *histories*—not only the unfolding history within which a cropscape or crop is embedded but also the histories or narratives that they have been used to tell in the past, and that they are used to tell today. Cropscapes operate at multiple spatial and temporal scales, from a crumb of soil to a global trading network, from the life span of a plant to the unfolding of the Green Revolution. Each engages different sets of actors, human and nonhuman, material and institutional. The same cropscape will look quite different to a farmer, a locust, a futures trader, or a tax inspector. In other words, we propose the cropscape not as an object with strictly defined boundaries and components but as a way of seeing and of looking, a multifocal, multiscale framing device—and thus a powerful instrument for investigating movement and change.[3]

Our idea of cropscape draws inspiration from the refashioning of landscape as an analytical tool. The approach originated with French studies of the *paysage* as a composite product of history and geography, beginning with Paul Vidal de La Blache and developed by members of the Annales school.[4] Classic studies by Annales historians linked the ways of life, political forms, social relations, and ways of thinking generated within a particular rural landscape to its material milieu and environmental setting. Annales studies operated at multiple scales in time and in space, many intensely local, others explicitly global in scope. They demonstrated the profound historical impact both of global climatic shifts and of such apparently trivial changes in farming practice as a shift from two-year to three-year fallows.[5] As interdisciplinary researchers drawing upon the resources of economics, sociology, psychology, climatology, and other sciences, the reflexive question of framing was at the core of their project. As Marc Bloch wrote in *The Historian's Craft,* "As a coherent unit (*unité*), the landscape (*le paysage*) exists only in my consciousness": different disciplinary (or personal) perspectives perceive different landscapes, differently framed and analyzed in different terms.[6]

When it came to the dynamics of change, Annales historians were materialists, though not historical materialists in the Marxist sense. The radicality of their approach in the 1930s was to shift attention from the court to the landscape, from political history peopled with Great Men to ordinary people, everyday lives, and mountains. Although the economic and material base were fundamental to their analysis of social formations, tensions, and historical change, the concepts of class struggle or contradictions in the mode of production were not—they deemed such approaches narrow.[7] It was Raymond Williams's cultural-Marxist critique of the romance of rural England, appearing in 1973, that brought Marxist sensibilities into the study of the landscape. Williams's contentions have both reflexive and methodological implications. First, as creatures of our own age we need to acknowledge and examine how our historical interpretations of a landscape are inflected by the structures of feeling, the social and material conditions of existence that direct and define our gaze. Second, a landscape is neither timeless nor natural: it is built from struggle over resources, a continuously shifting compound of intrahuman power relations, of changes in how wealth is produced and controlled, of how labor and expertise, and the usefulness or aesthetics of different kinds of land, are defined. Furthermore, rural and urban are mutually constitutive: the country has been penetrated by the city since farming began.[8]

While treating the influences between humans, their material practices, and their environments as reciprocal, both the Annales paradigm and Williams's cultural Marxism still maintained a categorical, ontological distinction between humans and the world of nature and artifacts that they inhabit. In the 1990s landscape studies took on a new lease of life. Post-processual archaeologists associated with the emerging field of material culture studies, most notably Barbara Bender and Christopher Tilley, sought to retrace the phenomenology of landscapes and the "ontological groundings" of their occupants. They supplemented Williams's cultural materialism with a more robust and systematic attention to matter and why it matters.[9] Their integrating this strong materialism into their analyses aligned their perspective more closely than Williams's with the Annales approach. But in tune with Williams the archaeologists systematically mobilized the multivocality of landscape as a tool to disrupt the linearity and homogeneity implied in prevailing archaeological models of socio-technical-environmental sequencing, such as the progression from hunter-gatherer band to horticultural tribe to pastoral chiefdom and agricultural state.[10] "Rather than offering a smooth sequence-oriented narrative, the

6 Orientations

evidence is reworked *along a number of different axes* in an attempt to elucidate the many different ways in which people engaged with and experienced their material (and often immaterial) worlds."[11]

Landscapes thus conceived enter the realm of historical analysis as contested and continuously evolving fields of action: dense webs of places, things, and people competing or collaborating. Such landscapes are inherently multivocal and multifocal. Framing thus becomes a consciously political as well as epistemological choice: different boundaries or axes put different actors and factors in the limelight, and produce different stories. Confronting or superposing the different framings of a given landscape unsettles established accounts and calls into question assumptions about scale and scope, the relative significance of different actors, directions of flow, linearities of change, or patterns of causation. Because topographies of power are an inherent dimension of this conceptualization of landscape, it is not surprising that "scapes" have been enthusiastically adopted by globalization theorists as a device to map and explicate flows through global fields of migrants, ideas, money, and so forth.[12]

Nonlinearity, strong materialism, multivocality, reflexivity: our concept of cropscape mobilizes all these critical features of landscape studies to develop new, critical approaches to global history, its boundaries, dynamics, and mechanisms. In focusing attention on how cropscapes take shape, we highlight how, along with the crop plants they favor, particular forms of power are materialized and rooted, and transferred across space and time. Since crops are life-forms resulting from human intervention within specific material affordances or constraints, the cropscape encourages an approach to historical process and regimes of power that is more strongly materialist yet less teleological than most conventional analyses of technology in world or global history.

If the cropscape, like the landscape, draws us into rooted global histories, in pushing us to ask how its elements are assembled or travel, the cropscape nests histories of place within entangled, rhizomatic histories. A landscape is a walled garden; a cropscape sprawls. Land, as Tania Murray Li remarks, is a strange object precisely because "it is not like a mat: you cannot roll it up and take it away."[13] As an assemblage, a landscape is a place of convergence. But crops, like mats, can be materially detached from the ground—indeed, one key characteristic of crops is that as harvests or seeds they are routinely detached and removed from the land upon which they grow. The boundaries and potential axes of the cropscape are thus more elastic than those of the landscape, or indeed of global history. We can play with the scale, with what to include and what to foreground. Each choice of framing and inclusion tells a different but complementary story. To understand how U.S. cotton contributed to world history, for

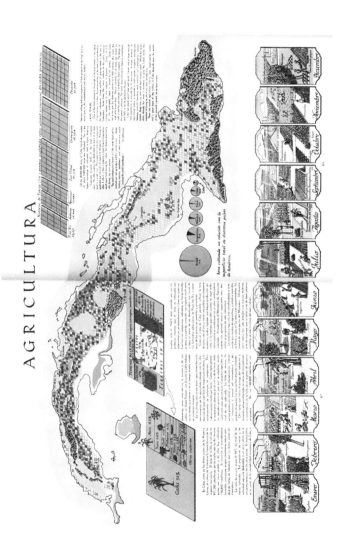

Agricultura, from *Atlas de Cuba*. Using experimental cartographic methods, the atlas was intended for use by the general public as well as the scientific community. *Agricultura* highlights the preponderance of sugarcane plantations in the Cuban cropscape and farming calendar. *Atlas de Cuba*, 1949, Gerardo Canet and Erwin Raisz, pp. 42–43. Courtesy of Raisz Landform Maps.

8 Orientations

example, we not only consider the impact of Liverpool cotton brokers upon the well-being of African American sharecroppers but also include in our consideration the thickets surrounding the cotton fields, where weevils fresh in from Mexico overwintered. Significant actants fashioning this Southern cotton-scape included seeds, plant physiology, the preferences of insect pests, climate, prices, wars, and entomological science as well as farming methods and labor regimes (see chapter 4, "Actants").

As a conscious framing device, the cropscape pushes us to question both the stories told about crops and history and why we, or our historical actors, like to tell them that way. As an example of reading history through cropscapes, let us compare two accounts of Cuba, both produced in the 1940s before Batista's coup.

In 1949 the Cuban geographer Gerardo Canet published a sixty-four-page, thirty-four-map bilingual *Atlas de Cuba,* created in collaboration with the pioneering Harvard-based cartographer Edwin Raisz. In high modernist mode, to assemble their data Canet and Raisz worked with the Cuban Navy, which organized a series of flights across the island for them, allowing them to take numerous aerial photographs in color.[14] The graphic style, incorporating the Isotype (International System of Typographic Picture Education) style of pictorial statistics created in the 1930s by Otto Neurath, was an experiment in conveying both the dynamics and the scales of Cuba's resources and engagement with the world. "This Atlas," Canet declares, "is more than an attempt to describe Cuba. Our aim is not only to present the setting in which the drama of Cuban life is played but to show how this life itself changes its own setting, creating new problems and new adjustments to them."[15]

Agricultura is the twenty-third of thirty-four maps. It depicts the island's farming zones, surrounded by small charts showing the distribution of *fincas* (farms), land uses, and the percentage of land devoted to Cuba's main crops—the vast majority (52 percent) under sugarcane, with tobacco (Cuba's other most important export) coming sixth, at 2.9 percent, after maize, cassava (*yuca*), coffee, beans, and bananas. Beneath the main map the page is bordered by twelve vignettes of monthly farming activities—evoking the rustic calendar of the medieval French book of hours *Les très riches heures du duc de Berry,* but with the chimneys of the sugar factory, smoking from February to May, replacing castle turrets in the background. In January farm workers cut cane and harvest tobacco and beans (*frijoles*); in February they cut cane and harvest aubergines and oranges; in March they cut agave fiber (*heneguen*), plant cassava, and vaccinate livestock. And so on. *Agricultura* shows Cuba as a diverse cropscape, a patchwork of subsistence and commercial crops, smallholdings and estates, dominated by cane plantations. Selected crops get their own maps, *Sugar* and *Tobacco* coming first. Each contains an ingenious diagram illustrating, in different graphic formats, Cuba's leading place in world exports and its heavy dependence on U.S. markets and prices.[16]

The *Atlas* presents a holistic view of Cuba in which sugar and tobacco feature clearly as the dominant players in the cropscape and economy, combining to tie the island nation into a risky dependency on the United States.[17] Although historically informed (see below), Canet's cropscape is basically future oriented, framed by political economy and agronomy to outline plans for policy action. "Our approach," writes Canet, "is as follows: 1. What are the facts?, 2. What are the essential problems?, 3. What will be their effects in the future and what may be done about them?" In the text insets of individual maps, Canet proposes mechanization to improve conditions for farm and factory workers, and to restore competitivity to Cuban tobacco products; tenurial reform to help smallholders, thus encouraging crop diversification and reducing the nation's dangerously high export dependency; and negotiations with the U.S. government for better terms for Cuban sugar exports.

The *Atlas* presents a diverse Cuban cropscape disequilibrated by the dominance of both sugar and tobacco; *Cuban Counterpoint: Tobacco and Sugar,* as the title suggests, eliminates all the secondary characters from the stage. Written by the criollo intellectual Fernando Ortíz and published first in Spanish, in 1940, and then in English, in 1949, the study presents Cuban society as riven between two opposing moral economies and their corresponding cropscapes.[18] The cultivation of tobacco and sugar serve Ortíz as metaphors for the qualities of an independent and a dependent Cuban society. Don Tobacco duels with Doña Sugar for the soul of the nation: "Liberty and slavery; skilled and unskilled labor; hands versus arms; men versus machines; delicacy versus brute force. The cultivation of tobacco gave rise to the small holding; that of sugar brought about the great land grants. . . . The native versus the foreigner. National sovereignty as against colonial status. The proud cigar band as against the lowly sack."[19]

Canet too notes that tobacco is grown on smallholdings, adding that a key factor in the excellence of Cuban tobacco is "the traditional skill of the Cuban tobacco growers, who hand down from father to son the essential techniques required by Havana tobacco"—but unlike Ortíz he confers no intrinsic virtue on either skill or tradition.[20] Canet's maps too trace the racial and political history that configured the rise of sugar plantations and tobacco smallholdings in Cuba. But Canet wishes to be dispassionate, to convince with numbers, to persuade with graphics.[21] Ortíz gives us passion and poetry, the subtle history of a melting pot of classes, races, and cultures forever on the boil. Ortíz's cropscapes are vividly material, sensory, and social, saturated with entangled histories and creolized cultures. To understand Cuba and its dilemmas in 1940, Ortíz insists, we must learn the ritual and social heritage of tobacco smoking that began with the Tainos, we must acknowledge that Africans were ground like cane in the rollers of the sugar mill, we must discern what new spice or texture each wave of migration added to the peppery stockpot of Cuban society.

Ortíz devotes two hundred pages to unfolding the historical processes of what he calls *transculturation,* a process in two steps: deculturation (in our more agronomic terms, uprooting) and neoculturation (the outcome of grafting or hybridization). The same processes can be read in filigree in Canet's *Atlas,* but very differently framed, expressed, and evaluated. The atlas contains three historical maps (conquest, colonial Cuba, and revolutionary Cuba) with timelines, laying out much of the same history Ortíz invokes, but necessarily in very concise format. In *Population* Canet gives us a pie chart showing that three-quarters of the Cuban population are white, one-quarter "black and mestizo"; the accompanying text on "racial integration" states: "Part of the original population of Cuba died out and part was absorbed by the Spanish conquest. Most of the present negroes are of mixed blood and they are gradually being absorbed into the population. . . . Cuba has much less of a racial problem than some of its neighbors. The 5% of foreigners in Cuba added a great deal of stimulus to the life of the country": in an atlas designed for schools and government offices, this sanitized version hints in palatable terms at the violent, passionate encounters that drove transculturation.[22]

"The more Ortíz tells us about tobacco and sugar," says the anthropologist Fernando Coronil in his introduction to a new edition of *Cuban Counterpoint* published in 1995, "the more we feel we learn about Cubans, their culture, musicality, humor, uprootedness. . . . Imperceptibly, we likewise begin to understand the social forces that have conditioned the ongoing construction of Cuban identities within the context of colonial and neocolonial relations."[23] The *Atlas of Cuba* is an equally rich mine of information about how the cropscapes of tobacco and sugar evolved, shaping Cuban lives, cultures, and politics. But its arguments are framed not as an explicit critique of imperialism but in the idiom of political economy and geographical science, expressed in maps, graphs, and understated snippets of text. Ortíz argues through metaphor, assuming the role of his nation's bard. Canet's rhetorical tool is the supposed neutrality of facts, skillfully deployed to press the case for reducing Cuban dependency in the moderate, reasoned terms of liberal governance.

So what has thinking with cropscapes achieved here? First of all, it inspired us to compare the *Atlas* and *Cuban Counterpoint,* hitherto never considered together, as distinctive but complementary accounts of how and why Cuban society came to be dominated by sugar and tobacco and tied into dependency on the United States and international capital. Second, contrasting the elements, formats, and styles of persuasion that Canet and Ortíz marshaled to frame their arguments draws our critical attention not only to the constitution of the cropscape itself but also to the processes and techniques of representation, the strategies of persuasion and, by extension, the different audiences for whom specific cropscape stories are composed. Finally, these contrasting yet overlapping pictures of entanglement suggest the rich opportunities that cropscapes can offer to global historians tracking the movements of people and things.

Here, a word about our historiographical choices is in order. Readers may be surprised that we chose to confront Canet and Ortíz's formulations of a Caribbean cropscape without mentioning Mintz. *Sweetness and Power* is familiar to many of us: a pioneering classic of global history that vividly portrays how the output of Caribbean sugar plantations fueled the rise of industrial modes of production and consumption, transforming diets and desires along the way. From a cropscape perspective, *Sweetness and Power* has been an inspiration throughout our study, offering a compelling illustration of the global articulations and multiple materialities of the Caribbean sugarscape. Furthermore, Ortíz was one source of inspiration for Mintz, even if he evokes the concept of transculturation only in the final paragraph of his book.[24] If in this chapter we deliberately omitted Mintz as an obvious theoretician of the Cuban cropscape, it is because we have sought, wherever possible, to be more attentive to different historical traditions than is often the case in the largely anglophone field of global history, both in our choices of crops and through the sources, debates, and conceptual frameworks with which we engage.[25] Here we have set in dialogue two Cuban formulations of the politics of their national cropscape; in chapter 1, "Times," we engage with Khaldunian as well as Braudelian philosophies of history; in chapter 5, "Compositions," we contrast the scaling principles of monoculture with those of the seventeenth-century Chinese statesman and agronomist Xu Guangqi and play with the cropscape of the Caxoeira plantation in the São Paulo interior, building on the work of Brazilian historians of capitalism. Our framing of the history of cinchona (chapter 4, "Actants") responds to Spanish and Latin American sources and historians; our section "Port" (chapter 6, "Reproductions") is immersed in Portuguese materials and arguments; our discussion of Washington Carver's reclamation of wasteland ("Reproductions") invokes the Black radical tradition exemplified by W. E. B. Du Bois; in "Tulips" (chapter 2, "Places") we present debates among Turkish historians. This strategy has not been possible in every case. The challenges included the limits of our

ON MOVEMENT AND STAYING IN PLACE

Global history emphasizes the creation of meaning and being, and of new associations, skills, and knowledge, through movement. But movement is by no means a simple or singular phenomenon, and here again crops are special. Plants perfectly illustrate Aristotle's four distinct but typically overlapping types of motion, of which change of place is just one, along with changes over time (growth and decay) and change of form (metamorphosis).[27] Growth and decay are of course intrinsic to all life-forms, including plants, and metamorphosis occurs within and across generations, as seeds germinate and fruits form, or as plants adapt to new environments. Movement across distances and periods small or large is an inherent element of all plant reproductive strategies. Pollination, seed dispersal, and rhizomatic spread all contribute to the spatial mobility essential to their natural survival. External disruptions to the regular annual or perennial cycle of reproduction can be overcome when seeds lie dormant or fallen trees send up new suckers. But these spontaneous movements are not limitless; they are circumscribed by the climatic, hydrological, or soil tolerances of the plant, the presence of new pests or predators at the point of arrival, the possibility of recreating equivalent co-dependencies with other plants or life-forms (pollinators, mycorrhiza) to those at the point of origin, and so on.

Let us mention just a few examples of how our cases engage different modes of movement and change. Our initial examples of tea, marigolds, and cassava illustrate the interplay of crop-plant movements in both space and time. Growth, decay, and metamorphosis all feature vividly in the case of cocoa (chapter 1, "Times"), which shows how an advancing cultivation frontier wove together the life cycles of trees, farms, and farmers, generating social and technical change as it progressed. The case of rice (chapter 1, "Times," and chapter 3, "Sizes") shows how the microscale of the rhythms of the plant ties into long-term macroeconomic change, while highlighting how different geographical and chronological framings by historians generate stories of civilizational decay or progress. As humans moved eucalyptus to new continents (chapter 4, "Actants"), it acquired formidable powers to change its environment that eluded human control.

Movement is inherent in the growth, survival, and evolution of individual plants and plant communities: with or without human intervention, plants are continuously on the move through space and time. Crops are plant species or varieties deliberately selected and located in sites chosen by humans. Yet like all life-forms that humans seek to control, they have their own preferred patterns of spatial and temporal behavior and innate propensities to vary; they are endowed with their own agency and capacities for resistance. As historians of such fundamentally human constructs as agriculture, technology and science, economy, and global systems, we cannot afford to sideline human agency to the radical extent proposed in some post-humanist critiques. But our *Moving Crops* project by its nature requires us both to reject nature-human dichotomies and to pay significantly more analytical attention than is characteristic of most history of technology or of agriculture to the agency of nonhuman actors—and to the fact that many of our historical human actors drew the boundaries between humans and nonhumans, and their forms of agency in very different ways from ourselves.[28]

Making a plant into a crop, that is to say, a regimented plant form with features useful to humans, that will yield sufficient output to make production and distribution of it worthwhile, and that can be reliably reproduced from one year to the next, is a struggle requiring continual inputs of resources and ingenuity, attention, and systems of discipline that range from brutal to tender. Taking a familiar crop to a new place and making it thrive there is even more challenging, and may likewise involve considerable material or symbolic violence, or love. By love, we denote a spectrum stretching from the attentions of bees or the human care that goes into cultivating a field, to the passionate attachment of human and nonhuman actors to a crop itself, or to the kind of cropscape that it promotes. Love and violence are often the opposite sides of the same coin. The love of the Spanish conquistadores for their familiar, Christian wheatscape led to extreme violence when they recreated it in their American colonies. The loves of nonhuman actors on the move can be equally devastating. As the boll weevil followed the expansion of cotton regions through the southeastern United States in the early twentieth century, its "dark secret love" for the cotton boll, like that of Blake's "invisible worm that flies in the night in the howling storm," destroyed its object of desire, if not as a plant, at least as a salable commodity, thus undermining its own survival (see chapter 4, "Actants").

When humans began domesticating plants and turning them into crops, one tactic was to restrict movement: selecting, for example, for cereal varieties that did not shed their seeds and segregating the preferred plants spatially—thus creating weeds (chapter 5, "Compositions"). But at the same time, they wanted their crops to be mobile: they wanted to plant them in new fields, different ecozones, or newly conquered territories and to exchange them with trading partners.

Throughout their history humans have persisted in their efforts to move crops into new niches and new places, whether to secure subsistence, expand empire, generate wealth, or support the growth of cities and states, industries, and institutions. Crops are thus perfect things with which to think simultaneously in all three of Fernand Braudel's orders of historical time, to confront histories at the scale of hours, days, or years with histories at the scale of decades or millennia, and likewise to confront the scale of field, farm, or village with that of regional or cross-continental dispersions or transfers.

This is well illustrated by the coming into being of American wheat (chapter 2, "Places"). The hard "Russian" or "Turkish red" winter wheat that by 1890 had enthroned the American Midwest as the world's chief breadbasket was the product of centuries of movement and exchange. The "red" wheat's lineage derived from a centuries-long sequence of interactions between Caucasian peasant farmers, Tatar pastoralists-cum-farmers, the expanding tsarist state, "model" yet vulnerable Mennonite farmers on their trail from Germany to Russia and thence to Kansas, U.S. railroad companies, displaced native peoples and eradicated prairie plants, the Chicago Stock Exchange, the research facilities of a newly established U.S. Department of Agriculture, and an ideal of manifest destiny.[29] American wheat's pedigree is by no means unusual in scale, either historically or geographically. Furthermore, it vividly illustrates the effects of differentials of power between actors, whether human or nonhuman.

Over the roughly ten millennia since plants were first domesticated as crops, hunter-gatherers, nomads, migrants, plantation owners and slaves, states and peasants, empires, colonial and postcolonial governments, and transnational agribusinesses have all been in the business of moving crops. When it comes to successfully implanting a crop in a new environment, clearly the agency of an enslaved African woman hoping to grow familiar foodstuffs on the margins of a Caribbean plantation differs from that of Frederick the Great of Prussia directing his peasantry to adopt the potato as a staple. Yet, as Alfred W. Crosby's pathbreaking study of the Columbian Exchange first demonstrated, outcomes cannot be predicated on the power of human actors alone.[30] Crop histories can usefully contribute to today's concern with "subaltern (im)mobilities" by illustrating the differential agencies of humans while also integrating material resources and nonhuman agencies more fully into the story.[31]

The history of moving crops to other places is littered with failures and unintended consequences, but also with spectacular transformations of landscapes, populations, and lifestyles. In explaining the history of the early modern and contemporary worlds alone, historians have identified crop movements as a key foundation and trigger of economic development and geopolitical transformation. Examples include the quick-ripening Champa rice varieties introduced into eleventh-century China, the Columbian Exchange, the role of sugar, cotton, tea, and rubber plantations in building colonial empires and industries for Spain and Britain, the Netherlands, and Japan, and the worldwide Green Revolution launched in the 1960s that has been judged by many, whether proponents or critics, as "the era's most significant phenomenon."[32]

Twentieth-century scientific crop-breeding programs have been particularly optimistic that breeding the right variety and providing the right technical inputs will allow a universal dissemination of desirable crop types, transforming, enriching, and modernizing the world as they go (see chapter 6, "Reproductions"). As development sociologists, farming systems researchers, agroecologists, and other critics pointed out, this seed determinism unfortunately ignores the fact that crop seeds are the product of complex sociotechnical contexts, encapsulating political agendas and social struggles as well as adaptation to and collaboration with a range of human and nonhuman actors in the local environment.[33] But what is important to note is the long-standing and pervasive belief that around a seed not just a crop but a whole social landscape, a realm of values or memories or proper social relations, will sprout. Catholic monks hewed out fields of wheat and vines along the coasts of New Spain as terroirs fit to nourish the true faith. Enslaved Africans or destitute European peasants tucked seeds or slips of familiar food crops, tastes of home or tastes of freedom, into their bundles as they boarded ship for the Americas. Medieval Chinese emperors, Japanese daimyo, French colonial governments, and Green Revolution scientists all shared the conviction that promoting intensive rice farming would trigger a whole process of civilizing the indigenes and making them into productive citizens. In our terms, these projects were intended not to move individual crops but rather to reassemble desired cropscapes.[34]

How far does studying movements between far-flung places, over unusual time spans, or featuring unexpected actors, actually unsettle the historiographical status quo? Global history follows flows and encounters, knowledge, and materials in motion, while history of science and technology are now increasingly interested in the mobility of knowledge systems, focusing on transfers and the resulting processes of transformation and appropriation.[35] Where the study of mobility goes hand in hand with postcolonial or decolonial critique, as it so often does in these fields, it offers a powerful tool for "provincializing" or "decentering" the West. Such approaches have enabled historians of the colonial and postcolonial world to refute claims for Western exceptionalism and to show the trajectories of modernity as truly global processes. Yet inevitably, as long as historians are operating within the time span of the early modern to the contemporary, that is to say, within the framework of an era understood as leading up to and on from Western colonial domination and the rise of industrial capitalism, then the dynamic appears inevitable, the future is foreclosed. It is difficult to challenge, let alone to bracket out, the teleologies, concepts, and categories of the modern world order. In consequence, Eurocentric frameworks prove remarkably resistant, while other histories are difficult either to retrieve or even to imagine.[36] In *Moving Crops,* it is through expanding the historical as well as the geographical scale of inquiry while moving the spotlight from the back histories of modern industrial commodities to the more universally valued category of crops that we have been able to spill out of preset chronologies or associations, and thus open new windows and trace some new patterns. Date palms and tulips supporting different strands of Islamic capitalism are one example ("Times," "Places"). Other examples include the long but largely invisible history of slash-and-burn farmers' contributions to shaping to regional and world commodity markets ("Actants"); the historical looping represented by the recuperation as heritage of ancient cropscapes such as Chinese millet farming ("Times" and "Reproductions"); or the "patchiness" revealed in even the most severe monocropping landscape when viewed in close-up ("Compositions").

Another question is whether focusing primarily on travels and transfers, however sophisticated the framework of analysis, can do full justice to all the types or forms of mobility and transfer prompted by human agency that have significantly reshaped the world. Can we satisfactorily account for mobility if we do not also explicate staying in place? One of the problems about focusing on the motion of things between places is that we tend to lose sight of the places themselves, of the complex material-cultural embeddedness of things that have to be loosened or pried out of their original matrices in order to set them in motion, and of the domestic changes that result when a local thing is launched into the wider world.

Unlike unique objects like the Koh-i-Noor diamond, when technical artifacts or practices travel they do not leave an aching void at their place of origin. They continue to exist and evolve in their local matrix. Following things as they move from one place to another can distract attention from their parallel trajectories of remaining. A focus on travels and destinations inclines us to dehistoricize a thing at its point of origin, to neglect the processes of "moving on the spot" through which a thing takes shape and stays in place ("Tobacco" in "Sizes"). No doubt because the end point of so many flows studied by global historians is the adoption of useful exotics by Western societies, more attention has been paid to how artifacts are reconfigured or reembedded, and meanings selectively translated or redefined, at the point of arrival than at the point of departure. As

Pamela Smith puts it: "The *routes* that materials, practices and knowledge take [have become] more important than their *roots* or origins."[37]

The impact of a thing's movement upon the assemblage of origin merits closer attention than it is often given. Once again, crop plants are excellent to think with here. In considering all the modalities of crop movement, we can better address how cropscapes emerge and evolve, grow, change, and decay "at home" as well as how they travel (or fail to travel) through space and through time. For example, histories of the spectacular late nineteenth-century success of the tea industry in British India, launched by the importation of Chinese plants and techniques, tend to imply that the rise of the Indian industry essentially eliminated China from global tea markets. But this is just the view from Britain concerning which flows count. A more comprehensive study of the structures and scope of the post-1890 Chinese tea industry shows that Indian competition, far from destroying it, prompted a vigorous reorientation toward other markets ("Places"). The long history of tulips in the Ottoman Empire is another excellent example of the rewards of inquiring what changes when things stay in place ("Places"), while the story of coffee mosaics in Ethiopia ("Sizes") asks what happens when not the crop but the historian stays in one country to retrace the longue durée history of a global commodity.

THICKNESS AND THINGNESS:
MORE-THAN-HUMAN HISTORIES

Whether staying in place or traveling, historians now like to think of technologies, artifacts, and commodities in terms of "thick things," "a phrase meant to invoke the multiple meanings ascribed to particular material artifacts, even those apparently subject to the thinning regime of modern science."[38] Artifacts are entangled in a local web of meaning, and moving them to another cultural regime without changing their significance is therefore a challenge. They are also embedded in material and social assemblages. This too hampers their ability to travel, if in a more prosaic fashion. The failure of artifacts, skills, or knowledge to travel successfully was, of course, a central focus of development theory and studies of post–World War II technology transfer, revolutionized by the insights of actor-network theory (ANT) scholars like Madeleine Akrich.[39] The study of things that do not travel, with all that such refusals or failures hint about never taking mobility for granted, is now gaining ground in history. Marcy Norton's study of how chocolate was translated in its travels from Mexico to Spain is a pioneering work of how and why a commodity can be sticky in some respects and very fluid in others. In her investigation of why one of the most refined signifiers of Chinese elite culture, the inkstone, failed to travel beyond the sinophone world, Dorothy Ko offers an exemplary study of how matter and meaning are enfolded within these symbolically powerful objects, and why the density of their significance made them too "sticky" to travel.[40]

In sum, the local assemblages in which an artifact like a plough, a field of wheat, or an ideal of the plantation are embedded will never travel in their entirety. Movement is a process of shedding some associations and building others. A thing in one place becomes another thing elsewhere. In *Moving Crops* all our actors and all our "things"—the tobacco plant, or cinchona, for instance—are treated as instantiations of historical processes ("Times," "Actants").

Environmental history has illuminated the historical relevance of many nonhumans: rivers, cattle, mosquitoes, wheat, or corn are obligatory presences in narratives of settling the West of the United States, expanding slavery into the Caribbean, incorporating the steppes into the Russian Empire, or coping with European colonialism in the Ovambo floodplains in the Angola/Namibia borderlands.[41] But those nonhumans are not stable historical entities. It is not only that organisms have an evolutionary history but also that humans held very different understandings about what nonhumans they were engaging—or even where the boundaries, if any, between human and nonhuman lay. It matters historically that Andean healers and Spanish merchants of the seventeenth and eighteenth centuries saw the febrifuge powers of the cinchona tree as lodged in its bark, while French, Dutch, and British colonialists of the nineteenth century explained those same properties through the presence of a chemical compound, quinine, which, once its composition was known, could be purified or even synthesized. Hence the making of the cinchona bark into a medical commodity under the monopolist control of the Spanish Crown was very different from the later Dutch monopoly of quinine in the nineteenth and twentieth centuries ("Actants"). Ascribing historical importance to cinchona only because of its quinine content misses the rich history of engaging with the plant before the alkaloid was isolated by chemists—or, better said, before quinine existed.

It follows from treating the cropscape as an assemblage that, as in science and technology studies (STS), we relativize without discounting the place of humans as actors. Humans figure in an environment they have helped create, but the cropscape can be observed, framed, and analyzed from many different perspectives or vantage points, not all of which place humans at the focal point or even in the foreground. We have generally resisted the temptation to make our crop plants into heroes of bildungsromans, or to anthropomorphize pests and pesticides beyond the bounds of reason. Yet it can be productive to consider our crops and other nonhuman actors in some of the roles attributed to humans.

Eucalyptus colonizes new lands ("Actants"); maize, beans, and squash live together as sisters ("Compositions").

It might be objected that in attributing agency to nonhumans we risk erasing power from our analysis.[42] But crops are both place makers and place extenders. Rooting a new crop in the soil is as often an act of violence as a fact of nature; keeping a "traditional" cropscape going invariably involves the exercise of power. Introducing nonhuman actants, treating our cropscapes as more-than-human worlds, in no sense erases power or denies human agency. On the contrary, it offers a method of delving more deeply into the affordances and barriers that shape or channel human agency, reframing geographies and topographies of power while revealing unexpected but significant ways in which human power is exercised.[43]

In tune with new materialist and post-humanist histories, we treat crops as "things" rather than "objects," "not as inert and passive, but rather as animated, animating and effective." This approach imputes "excessiveness" to things: they have "modes of being," impulses, affinities, and dynamics that escape human attention, elude control, and affect the outcomes of human designs and activities.[44] Crops, as living beings, are particularly headstrong and slippery things, and they act on us as we act on them—many scholars have pointed out that domestication is a mutual process ("Actants"). Humans have put huge efforts into accommodating and understanding crops, adapting to what they understand as crops' needs and drives as well as bullying them into submission. We look closely at these material negotiations, not forgetting that often our human actors explicitly attributed combinations of being, consciousness, agency, or power to cropscapes and their denizens. The worms in the yam gardens of Papua New Guinea superintend the gardeners' morality ("Actants"); the architects of the Green Revolution claimed that adopting miracle seeds and their technological packages would transform ignorant peasants into modern entrepreneurs ("Sizes"); historians of East Asia dispute whether intensive rice cultivation brought the region's history to a halt or propelled it into a distinctive modernity ("Times").

Today we like to think that our impressive advances in scientific knowledge have perfected the human capacity to tame life-forms and strip them of independence. Yet still our carefully bred and regimented crop varieties may go rogue and turn feral. The slide of self-seeded genetically modified rape into an invasive species is just one example.[45] So the struggle to reconcile the aspirations of humans with the propensities of their crop plants endures—in other words, examining these interspecies negotiations is a transhistorical project.

It is also a project that requires us to take the materialities of cropscapes seriously, as key factors driving the technological choices of our human actors.[46]

Matter matters—but how do we grasp it? The materiality of historical things is still an experimental theme for historians of science, environment, and the global. Post-humanist and new materialist studies show the importance, and difficulties, of working between a prosaic scientific recognition of the ostensibly stable physical or biological properties and propensities of material *stuff*, on the one hand, and, on the other, a historical or cultural critique that unsettles fixities, emphasizing *things'* enmeshment and agency, and the complexities of their becoming.[47] Recent critical studies of the Anthropocene—our current geologic age, in which humans are changing Earth's climate—are a good example of how working between these two distinctive ways of seeing and knowing materiality challenges us to write new histories: about the things themselves as they come into being or move through space and time; about the ways in which our historical actors made, used, and understood these things or were, in turn, remade by them; and—at a more reflexive level—about the ways in which we ourselves build those ways of seeing, doing, and knowing into social theory or historical explanation.[48] We likewise take the materialities of cropscapes, and their meshing of stuff and things, as a key reference point for exploring how specific crops become rooted in place, how they moved, how they were understood, and how they were, and are, used to tell stories or histories.

CROPSCAPES AT WORK

Moving Crops mobilizes the cropscape concept to rework the evidence from crop history along six axes, time, place, size, actants, compositions, and reproductions, each representing one dimension or register of mobility that plays a key role in theorizing the impact of crops on history. Within each of those rubrics, our tactic is to counterpose a set of intriguing cases, deliberately contrasting cropscapes from different periods and of different scales. We may choose to look at a crop and the cropscape in which it is embedded at the spatial scale of the field, the state, or the market. We may select a timescale of plant, pest, or human life cycles, the passage of months, or the passage of centuries. Each perspective, each choice of scale, engages different sets of actors, human and nonhuman, material and institutional, highlighting often unconsidered trends, unexpected oscillations or tensions, and counterintuitive shifts. Playing with cross-cutting scales thus helps subvert established narratives and spotlights the theoretical or ideological assumptions woven into different choices of scale and boundary setting.

How have we selected our cases? Rather than aiming at exhaustive coverage, we have chosen cropscapes to illustrate unexplored historical scales or connections, unexpected dynamics or constellations. Many were chosen to unravel the interplay of "empire, power, and political contestation."[49] We interrogate "racist-imperialist" categories and hierarchies of crops, cultivation systems, human livelihoods or interspecies relations not only in "colonial-modern-contemporary" contexts but also in less familiar non-Western empires. While we may not always explicitly invoke postcolonial or decolonial theory, issues such as the discursive constructions of the non-Western world, erasures and epistemological asymmetries, agencies denied and achieved are sustained themes. Most of our stories carry diverse perspectives and do not unfold on expected lines. We seek out continuities or resurgences that challenge standard dichotomies like that of the modern and the nonmodern (the sections "Dates" and "Cocoa" in "Times," "Coffee" in "Sizes," "Waste" in "Reproductions") and, wherever our materials allow, we invite readers to see non-Western phenomena in their own right rather than in the light of Western standards.

Our cropscapes feature not only acknowledged global crops like wheat, tea, and cotton but also oranges and cashews, dates, marigolds, and yams, cases chosen sometimes to highlight how a plant takes shape and evolves as a crop, sometimes to explore how it accrues or imparts meaning in its site of origin and as it travels through space and time. It is not uncommon for global historians to ask how a market or a taste affects what we call a cropscape, its scale, organization, and geographic distribution. By including cases that shift the viewpoint to that of nonhuman actors like elephants, boll weevils, or weeds, who also seek to make cropscapes in which they can thrive, we explore how their practices intersect, shape, or conflict with the competing efforts of humans. The juxtapositions between supposedly major and minor crops (the latter more typically studied by anthropologists or cultural historians than by economic or global historians) prompt us to consider the cosmological, symbolic, or social powers of even such a disenchanted crop as hybrid wheat and how these potencies and meanings travel. They encourage us to reflect more deeply upon the role of crops or cropscapes in the formation of political or religious authority, or upon the nesting of nonmonetary circuits of exchange within capitalist formations.

We considered drawing a comprehensive set of maps and time lines to guide the reader through chapters and through the book, but after several experiments we realized that each cropscape would require at least one map. (We found it necessary to refer to almost every one of the thirty-four isotypic maps in Gerardo Canet's *Atlas de Cuba* to reconstruct the cropscape of Cuban sugar as Canet saw it.) In the end we included only four maps, of single crops following rather simple trajectories: the advancing cocoa frontier in Ghana ("Times"), the linkages between the world's main wheat export regions ("Places"), the tea regions of India ("Places"), and the location of ersatz rubber plantations in the Nazi empire ("Reproductions"). We apologize to our readers for leaving it to them to identify sites in an atlas or on Google Maps.

CROPSCAPES AT PLAY

Moving Crops is experimental in form, organized in the structure of improvisational jazz, with chapters as sets and cases as riffs. Our chapter titles and subheadings indicate the playful conversation we wish to initiate. A riff entitled "Seeing Like an Elephant" studies tea plantations but also puns on James C. Scott's classic *Seeing Like a State*. "Dates," our opening riff in chapter 1 ("Times") traces the history of the fruit to introduce a set of variations on periodization. Images have been selected not only to illustrate but also to evoke moods and metaphors (an Ottoman celebration of tulip culture, an anonymous caricature of the Irish nationalist O'Connell as "the Great Agi-Tater"). The book lays out a serious historiographical critique, but we hope it will be fun to read.

Moving Crops is also an experiment in collective writing. This was not simply a matter of dividing up chapters or sections between the four coauthors. Not only did we plan the work collectively, we sat down together (thanks to the generosity of Dagmar Schäfer at the Max Planck Institute for the History of Science) and collaboratively wrote and rewrote every element and every level of the book. Our collective expertise covers a wide range, coinciding in the history of agriculture, history of technology, and global history. Francesca Bray is an anthropologist and historian of East Asia; if she had to name her totemic crop, it would be rice. Barbara Hahn is an Americanist, a historian of capitalism as well as agriculture and of the Industrial Revolution; she has written extensively on tobacco and cotton. John Bosco Lourdusamy is a historian of science, engineering, and medicine in colonial and contemporary India; the tea industry and the tea gardens or plantations of South Asia are his emblematic cropscapes. Tiago Saraiva's focus of attention has been reproduction technology: breeding to understand fascism, cloning to understand racial capitalism in America and the Global South. Wheat, potatoes, and oranges are among the crops his research considers. Our diversity of interests has influenced the selection of crops and the framing of cropscapes in the text, but to surprise our readers we first needed to surprise ourselves. For most of our cases we have ventured out of our familiar territories. To do so we have relied on the research of other scholars (which we hope we have rendered or synthesized responsibly). These forays have been a source of great delight and instruction, and sent us back to our own familiar cropscapes with newly opened eyes. The result of our experiment is, we hope, as enjoyable and surprising as the lively arguments that went into our cowriting.

To conclude, crops and cropscapes offer a novel, indeed experimental, approach to the writing of global histories because they are at once inherently local, a concrete product of a specific time and place, and ineluctably mobile, whether in their components and spaces shifting over time or their travels into new niches or across the globe. A cropscape is never static: it is constituted of living elements that may or may not prosper, of flows and associations that are always in flux. The maintenance, reproduction, and transposition of a given cropscape are never guaranteed. So much for the timeless traditions of peasants! Instead, cultivation requires from human and nonhuman actors alike considerable work, energy, ingenuity, and adaptability. At this rooted scale, the historiography of cropscapes generates what Kapil Raj calls microhistories of the global, intimate histories that provide a corrective to global history's emphasis on flows largely removed from their original roots or matrices, an emphasis that tends in consequence to neglect key factors like place making and reproduction.[50]

What we propose in *Moving Crops* is both an argument and a method. We propose the cropscape not as an object with strictly defined boundaries and components but as a way of looking, an infinitely adjustable framing device to help illuminate shadowy presences, change scale or focus, survey at global level, or dive underground among the roots and worms. While the cropscape focuses attention on crops and agriculture, it offers a method and a breadth of vision that open new perspectives for global history more generally, providing effective new tools for writing histories of the material world.

The cropscape serves us here as the vehicle for an experimental approach to writing the history of complex systems. We use the concept as a device to link microhistories and macrohistories of change, movement, and connection, and to explore assemblages that connect human and nonhuman actors, environment, materialities, passions, and institutions in complex and often surprising entanglements. Rooted in an intense engagement with the local, individual cropscape histories may also unveil long-distance connections in time and space.

Our claim, then, is that the cropscape method breaks open the straitjackets of period, geography, direction, who and what matters—it opens the historical imagination. Our cases are deliberately selected and connected to challenge both the linearities and the principles of inclusion or exclusion of much global history, including global histories of technology and of agricultural commodities. Looking at contemporary Californian date orchards in the light of Saharan oases reveals the traditional dimensions of modern agribusiness and the capitalist sophistication of medieval long-distance commerce. Elephants loom through different cropscapes as both builders and destroyers of colonial plantation techno-dreams. We show that the choice to pinch out or not to pinch out the tobacco leaf has historical consequences. We demonstrate that the circuits of exchange of yams or manioc in Oceania and Amazonia, invisible in global histories because tubers were not commoditized and the societies that grew them were presumed to be primitive backwaters cut off from the circuits and temporal dynamics of global capitalism, have, thanks to that very Otherness, generated social theories that have been at the core of arguments about the characteristics of modern industrial society and how the modern global economy emerged.

Finally, cropscape as method focuses conscious attention on how we make choices about selecting cases, scale, and frame. As an explicit framing device, the cropscape forcefully draws our attention to the politics of historiographical choice and pushes us to reflect upon the genealogies of our own ways of knowing.

Chapter 1 Times

In "Times" we use the concreteness of cropscapes and the elasticity of their histories to question and experiment with timescales, periodizations, and temporalities. Time, as Henri Bergson famously argued, is not something out there, independent of who perceives it. The French philosopher urged his readers to reconsider their notion of time so they could fully appreciate the nature of change and "the perpetual creation of possibility."[1] Bergson drew a distinction between time (*le temps*), an essential tool for science in that it treats time as linear, homogeneous, and thus measurable—what we might call chronometric or historical time—and duration (*la durée*), a multiple, heterogeneous, and subjective experience, an essential dimension of consciousness inseparable in its weight and meaning from context and relationships—what we might call a sense of time, or time consciousness.

The following riffs look at the interplay of time and sense of time from the perspective of humans, plants, and historians. In the spirit of Braudel and his *Annales* colleagues, our key theme is how short-term and long-term temporalities, material exigencies, and social institutions fit together. Plants have their own rhythms, which humans modify when they grow them as crops. Crops in turn set many of the human rhythms of farming life. States, industries, and businesses all seek to discipline agricultural time yet must also accommodate the natural and social temporalities of the cropscape, which may shape the history of a society or even the ways in which that history is interpreted. Here the sense of time comes into play. We are interested in how a particular set of rhythms and a corresponding sense of time come into being within a specific cropscape, and in how these temporalities are construed, whether by denizens of the cropscape or by historians. We explore how these multiple temporalities interact to shape the histories and longevity of cropscapes, including their rhizomatic resurfacing in unexpected times or places. These novel perspectives on variations in time suggest intriguing possibilities for understanding and writing history.

DATES

Date trees are good things to think with when reflecting on time in global history. Date palms are one of the earliest domesticated tree crops. A staple of ancient Sumer and the Arabian Peninsula, dates were spread by Arab expansion into North Africa through the trans-Saharan oasis complex, transferred into the Americas by Spanish conquistadores, and then, in the twentieth century, brought into California by plant hunters of the U.S. Department of Agriculture. The ancient Near East, Arab expansion, the Columbian Exchange, and modern California are ingredients of a topical world-civilizations narrative in which the time lines are all well defined. But engaging with the date's history through date cropscapes suggests alternative ways of dealing with time, in which origin stories are challenged, societies don't evolve from nomadic into settled ones, premodern practices trouble chronologies of capitalism, modern practices demand engagement with medieval scholars, and obsessions with novelty and expansion are disturbed by an appreciation of ruins.

ORIGIN STORIES

Discussions about the place of domestication of the date tree point to the problems of writing origin stories for crops. Adding to the difficulty of distinguishing between the different species of the genus *Phoenix,* the genus to which the date palm (*Phoenix dactylifera* L.) belongs, it was not clear for a long time from which wild species the domesticated form derived. Did it descend from wild *Phoenix dactylifera* or from another species in the genus, such as *Phoenix sylvestris* or *Phoenix atlantica?* In the 1970s the possibility was even suggested that the domesticated form resulted from the hybridization of different species. Genetic analyses have nevertheless shown divergences between *Phoenix dactylifera* and other

Phoenix species that point to the domestication of the date palm from a single wild species. Researchers have therefore tried to locate remaining wild date palm populations to situate the domestication of the tree. They have found them across the entire area of the domesticated palm's distribution: the Sahara, the Arabian Peninsula, the Dead Sea basin, the Zagros Mountains (spanning Iran, Iraq, and Turkey) and Baluchistan (spanning Iran, Pakistan, and Afghanistan).[2]

To make things harder, fruit trees are characteristically subject to less intensive selection processes than other crops, and thus differences between wild and cultivated tend to get blurred. Specimens of date palms bearing small unpalatable fruits are classified as wild, but there's always the possibility that such trees are no more than descendants of abandoned cultivated palms or that they grew from seeds left in the soil after the fruit was eaten. And while archaeological vestiges from the late fourth millennium B.C.E. show that the tree had already been domesticated in the Middle East, this doesn't eliminate the possibility of additional independent areas of early domestication in North Africa (this is the case, for example, of the olive tree). The simple image of agriculture developing in the Fertile Crescent and traveling out from there to other regions of the world doesn't fit the complicated story of date domestication currently being produced by archaeologists and paleobotanists.

The history of the date palm oasis is particularly relevant to ideas about the diffusion of agricultural practices. There are multiple cuneiform texts of the third millennium B.C.E. from Mesopotamia mentioning irrigated orchards, which in addition to dates included figs, grapes, pomegranates, and apples. There are also references to vegetable gardens growing onions, garlic, and leeks between the fruit trees. These texts clearly differentiate between such orchards and the open fields where cereals, pulses, and flax were cultivated. But it is in the Arabian Peninsula that we find the first cropscapes totally dependent on date palm growing. Not just a cropscape with dates, where one finds date palms next to other things, but a date cropscape, viable only due to the presence of date palms.

The date palm tree can tolerate very long hot dry summers and is well adapted to sandy soils and saline conditions, making it a pioneer species in what are inhospitable lands for all other crops: desert areas. The date palm's canopy produces shade, favoring the cultivation of a new layer of other fruit trees, typically figs, almonds, or citrus, enabling their presence in areas whose arid climates would otherwise make it impossible. A third layer, closer to the soil level, is also made cultivable by the date tree's shade, producing wheat and barley to feed humans and livestock. To cultivate a date palm grove entails no less than settling the land. The emergence of agriculture in Arabia, at the beginning of the third millennium B.C.E. (some three thousand years after it had started in Mesopotamia) thus coincides with the emergence of the date palm oasis.[3]

Although growing in desert areas, the date palm tree demands abundant ground water and constant irrigation. No treatise on date cultivation omits the saying "[The tree] must have its feet in running water and its head in the fire of the sky." Trapping run-off water through terracing, building small dams, and simply digging wells were well-proven irrigation methods that could sustain date groves, but these became less effective when climate change circa 1000 B.C.E. increased the aridity of southeastern Arabia. Archaeologists have demonstrated that it was in response to these increasingly adverse conditions that in the Iron Age local populations developed the *falaj*, which tapped into deeper ground-water resources.[4] This irrigation technology—also known as *qanat*, *karez*, or *foggara*—taps aquifers in mountainous areas and transports the water via subterranean channels that may extend for several kilometers, assuring a constant supply to lower-lying cultivation areas in the piedmont and crucially overcoming the slow rhythms of rainfall in arid zones.

The falaj is a sophisticated piece of infrastructure. The slope of the underground canal must be carefully calculated and maintained to ensure a proper balance between efficient gravity flow of the water and excessive speed that erodes the structure. No less admirable are the systems of water distribution at the surface, still in place in date palm oases supplied by the falaj. While water flows in an oasis can be determined simply by spatial logic, in which adjacent plots of land are irrigated one after the other, the last one to get water being the one at the edge of the irrigation system, in some areas such as Oman the water is distributed through time slots. In this case, each irrigator has control of the water flow during a determined period of the day, and water might thus travel from one point of the irrigation system to a nonadjacent one in the opposite edge of the system, producing a more egalitarian distribution of the resource. The moving shade of a solar quadrant over a small-scale model of the oasis made of sticks and stones indicates the moment when an irrigator may move the sluices and conduct the water to his plot. During the night, the division of irrigation time is determined by stellar observations. While it can be argued that the falaj liberated oases dwellers from the constraints of natural rhythms of rainfall, it is no less true that it generated a social organization totally dependent on obsessive observation and division of time.[5]

The large investments involved in building and maintaining such infrastructures as well as the social complexity built around water distribution both contributed to the widespread belief that the falaj had arrived in Arabia from more civilized areas, namely, Iran. Although no archaeological record sustained such a claim, this was part of a grand narrative in which agriculture techniques were presumed to have originated in the great river civilizations in the Fertile Crescent, the Indus, or the Yellow River and to have spread out to more peripheral areas inhabited by uncultivated nomads, such as the Arabian Peninsula. The history of the falaj and the date cropscape in Arabia suggests instead how local populations outside those alleged cradles of civilization were also able to develop original solutions to major environmental challenges, such as climate change.[6]

CAMELS, TRADE, AND CAPITALISM

Date palm trees permitted humans to settle new places in apparently inhospitable environments. Yet the rooting abilities of date palms shouldn't obscure the long-distance connections they sustain. In other words, when engaging with date cropscapes it becomes clear that there is no neat separation between movement and rootedness or, in an alternative formulation, between nomad and settler. Indeed, oases are not self-contained worlds: the shade of the date trees is rarely wide enough to sustain large production of food crops, so exchanges with the outside world are indispensable. Conversely, oasis dwellers don't consume their entire production of dates, which they not only stock but also export, making dates a major object of trade relations. Structures such as the *madbasa*—a room coated with clay plaster and a floor of baulks and channels sloping gently to a tank lying below—specifically designed to extract juice from dates and dating at least from the mid-second millennium B.C.E., confirm the local abundance of fruits and their processing for commercialization.[7]

Domesticated camels, known in the Middle East since 3000–2500 B.C.E., constituted the other element needed to establish cross-desert communications.[8] Renowned for their efficiency as beasts of burden (their cost per ton-mile is considerably lower that of oxen or donkeys), camels put the date palm oases in contact with other areas of production. Nomadic camel herders and oasis dwellers developed a profitable symbiosis: with camels, new oases could be established, while the spread of oases increased demand for camels. Camel breeding spread steadily through Eurasia and North Africa, reaching Somalia in the first millennium B.C.E. and Morocco around 400 C.E., opening new possibilities for trans-desert trade. Arab expansion westward in the sixth and seventh centuries followed the road infrastructure previously laid out by the Roman Empire across North Africa's Mediterranean coastal plain, reaching Iberia in 711.

The novelty was that the main commercial cities on the Mediterranean under Muslim control were now able to sustain regular commercial relations with African polities south of the Sahara through the combination of camels and oases. The fabled trans-Saharan trade carried Mediterranean and Asian products (textiles, glassware, arms, ceramics, paper) as well as Saharan commodities (salt and dates) to Djenné, Timbuktu, and other great cities of el-Sudan, the savanna zone stretching from the edge of the Sahara south to the forests of the tropical belt. In el-Sudan the goods from the north were exchanged for slaves and gold. The caravans followed chains of date-grove oases offering rest and provision.[9] Camels carried the trade goods, along with the heavy, bulky palm offshoots required to replant the date groves. The date groves anchored the trade, sustaining the denizens of the oases, the caravans, and the slaves, who numbered some ten million between the ninth and twentieth centuries. No less consequential, the gold acquired in el-Sudan, around one ton per year between 800 and 1500, fueled the monetized economy of the Mediterranean while also enabling exchanges with India and China. It was through sub-Saharan gold that Arab merchants exerted their role as main connectors between west and east, between the Mediterranean and the Indian Ocean.

This interimperial trading system shared an intriguing number of features with modern colonial or capitalist commercial formations. Oases and their irrigation infrastructure were expensive endeavors, sustainable in scarcely populated desert areas only due to the high returns of the gold and slave trades.[10] New oases were built, and established date groves purchased, as speculative investments by merchants living far away in the great ports of the Mediterranean coast, such as the city of Cairo, described by geographers of the tenth century as "the wealthiest city in the world." Oases were colonial outposts of the caliphates, nodes in far-flung and sophisticated commercial networks that knit together an Islamic ecumene stretching well south of the Sahara. As in the European colonies established several centuries later, there was a chronic shortage of local labor to build and maintain the falaj and to tend the date palms. And as with the early European colonies, the absentee landowners and their local managers, usually connected by family ties, relied on continual inflows of slave labor to do the work.

Ibn Hawqal's work written in 977, *The Face of the Earth,* described the "huge profits" from "uninterrupted commerce with Sudan" he observed in Sijilmasa, the Moroccan commercial entrepôt located in the Tafilalt oasis, where date palms blanketed an area twenty kilometers long and fifteen kilometers wide, irrigated by water from the Atlas Mountains.[11] The celebrated traveler and chronicler also detailed the letters of credit he saw in Aoudaghost, another oasis town, at the southern end of a trans-Saharan caravan route in Mauritania, which reached forty-two thousand dinars, values he had never seen in the East. Business practices such as *commenda* agreements, in which an investor entrusted capital to a merchant to be used in commercial ventures, were also common in the trans-Saharan trade, beginning in the eighth century. Such assemblages of long-distance commerce, capital investment, and extractive regimes accreted around the date groves of the Saharan oases display many features that we usually claim for the early history of European capitalism and the role of Italian cities like Genoa and Venice.[12]

These were not just coincidences and parallels between premodern and modern periods but a case of intricate genealogy. While the European capitalism of Italian city-states was built on the previous Arab trade empire, the history of the date palm oasis in the trans-Saharan trade also suggests a longue durée history connecting it to Atlantic history. The Portuguese expeditions into Africa in the mid-fifteenth century that inaugurated European control of the Atlantic aimed precisely at tapping into the riches crossing the Sahara. The large majority of the first Black slaves arriving in southern Portugal were acquired on the coast of Mauritania, from camel caravans with access to the trans-Saharan routes connecting the Mali Empire and cities like Timbuktu to the Moroccan oases of the Atlas piedmont farther north, such as Sijilmasa. Navigating farther down the coast of Africa, the Portuguese hoped to get directly at the sources of gold and slaves, avoiding Muslim intermediaries. The (in)famous Elmina factory inaugurated in 1482 by the Portuguese on the Gold Coast (Ghana), and later occupied by the Dutch and British Empires, would become a major slave depot, exemplary of the importance of these new Atlantic trade routes that landed millions of slaves from sub-Saharan Africa, first in Europe and later, on a much larger scale, in the Americas up to the nineteenth century. While many of these slaves would be forced to work on Brazilian sugar plantations, many others would work in the silver mines in Peru and Mexico. Here, they produced the bullion sustaining European purchases in Asia, since European traders didn't have much more to offer to their Chinese or Indian counterparts. American silver thus took over the role of African gold shipped through Saharan date-palm oases, which had sustained the long-distance trade relations of Arab merchants.[13]

HISTORY, RUINS, AND NOSTALGIC GARDENS

While challenging Eurocentric chronologies of the rise of capitalism is certainly important, it is no less interesting to take clues from Muslim historical scholars on how to interpret the historical dynamics of the Mediterranean after North Africa came under Arab control in the seventh century. Instead of insisting on unidirectional capitalist expansion and imperial conquest, Ibn Khaldun (1332–1406) preferred to consider the cycles of history and its constant production of ruins. His masterpiece, *Muqaddimah,* has been praised as a major work in historical sociology that offered a model of cyclical rise and fall of dynasties: vigorous nomadic

32 Times

tribes conquered cities ruled by decaying elites, only to be seduced by the comforts of urban life and give up their place some four generations later to brisk nomadic tribes newly descended from the mountains.[14] To assess the significance of the model for historians, it suffices to note its major influence on Edward Gibbon's *History of the Decline and Fall of the Roman Empire* (1776) or on Arnold Toynbee's *Study of History* (1934), which both made intensive use of Ibn Khaldun's notion of historical cycles.[15] But Ibn Khaldun does not draw as sharp an opposition between nomadic barbarians and civilized city dwellers as most of his followers. The *Muqaddimah*'s account of historical change deals with nomadism and settlement as interwoven realities, with civilized settlements needing the periodic influx of nomadic experiences to strengthen the social fabric.[16]

As noted above, the date palm oasis is a space that invokes both movement and rootedness, nomadism and settlement. It is certainly no coincidence that Ibn Khaldun wrote part of his *Muqaddimah* while in the Biskrah oasis located in present-day Algeria. He arrived there fleeing from the coastal city of Bijayah, where the local leader, his patron, had been ousted from power. Instead of a glorious story of steady progress, Ibn Khaldun's personal trajectory points at permanent change, restlessness, and exile: a descendant of a line of Arab scholars from Seville who had fled to Tunis after the Christian Reconquista, he moved successively to Fez, Tlemcen, Granada, and Bijayah, always in search of a stable political situation and a reliable patron willing to employ his scholarly skills.

The Arab scholarly elite of Al-Andalus, from which Ibn Khaldun descended, had served the Umayyad rulers who arrived in the Iberian Peninsula in the aftermath of the Muslim expansion of the eighth century. But what modern world-history books register as imperial expansion was also lived as exile by Abd al-Rahman, the first Umayyad ruler of Al-Andalus, who crossed the Mediterranean as a refugee escaping his home city of Damascus after the slaughter of his entire family by the Abbasids. While the new Abbasid caliphate would move the center of Arab civilization east from Damascus to Baghdad, inaugurating the so-called Islamic Golden Age, Abd al-Rahman would transform Cordoba in the Iberian Peninsula, at what was then the western limit of Islam, into a living memorial to the Umayyad Damascus he had lost: Cordoba's mosque, bridges, libraries, and palaces were to reproduce in the West the magnificence of Damascus during the Umayyad caliphate. Back in Syria, the walled city of Rusafa, south of the Euphrates, had held a special meaning for the Umayyads, who made it into their family retreat. It was there that the Abbasids murdered the entire family; only Abd al-Rahman escaped. In Cordoba, the exiled prince built a new palace on the outskirts of the city, which would become legendary for its role as a botanical garden acclimatizing crops and trees from the Middle East into Al-Andalus. Abd al-Rahman named it Rusafa. And no other tree better materialized his longing for the lost home than a date palm to which he wrote the following poem:

> Noble palm-tree, you are also an exile to this soil.
> Mild winds of the West lovingly fondle your leaves;
> Your roots strike firm and deep into a fertile earth;
> And yet, like me, you grieve,
> If, like me, you remember!
> I have dewed with tears the palms
> Which bathe in the flood of Euphrates.[17]

The moving of the date palm doesn't here invoke empire, expansion, or capital investment. It suggests instead a different understanding of movement, as exile obsessed with the ruins left behind. After the Abbasids slaughtered the Umayyads, Cordoba became the new Damascus. Once Cordoba was ransacked by mercenary Berber troops in 1009, the new Al-Andalus leaders—the Almohads—would make Seville into the new Cordoba-Damascus. After Seville was lost to the Christian armies under Ferdinand III of Castile in 1248, Granada would become the new Seville-Cordoba-Damascus. The famous Alhambra gardens of Granada, which Ibn Khaldun would also know, were nostalgia materialized, evoking the luxurious gardens and the surrounding well-kept agricultural hinterlands of fabled ruined cities.[18] After Granada, the last bastion of Muslim culture in the Iberian Peninsula, was taken by the Catholic monarchs Ferdinand and Isabella in 1492, the city and its Alhambra gardens would in turn become a preferred mourning object for several generations of poets, a status it still holds today.[19]

CALIFORNIA: AGRIBUSINESS ROOTED

At first sight, nothing seems more detached from such nostalgic concerns with ruins than the highly commercialized date crop of California. The U.S. date industry had its origins in the 1880s. Keen both to develop substitutes for expensive imports and to expand the range and territories of American cropping, the USDA began looking for likely locations to grow dates on American soil, and in 1904 the Coachella Valley in California was identified as most suitable. Offshoots of prime date varieties were brought in from Algeria, Tunisia, Egypt, Iraq, and Baluchistan and tested. Commercial production began in 1905, with the first date-packing house opening in Coachella in 1912. The success story of transplanting date palm trees to California is indeed part of the wider late nineteenth-century project of transforming this region into the biggest supplier of Mediterranean produce—dates, figs, grapes, oranges—to the East Coast of the United States, supplanting southern Europe and North Africa.[20]

Popenoe, *Date Growing in the Old World*. American plant hunters who traveled in North Africa and the Middle East in order to transfer the date palm cropscape into California in the early twentieth century were also erudite orientalists. Reproduction practices learned from allegedly backward civilizations became the cornerstone of the modern date industry of the Far West. Popenoe, *Date Growing in the Old World and the New*, 1913, frontispiece.

The use of the very term "industry" when referring to the Californian date cropscape suggests the prevailing scale of American agricultural practice and aims, contrasting with allegedly traditional operations of the Old World. And the economies of countries of the Mediterranean basin would indeed suffer acutely from the rise of California and the subsequent loss of American markets. It has been less noticed how much the modern aligned rows of date palm trees of the Coachella Valley depended on reproduction practices developed in Arabian oases. The USDA scientists sent to the Middle East and North Africa tasked with transplanting the date cropscape to American soil insisted on the importance of reproducing the trees from the offshoots of the trunk and not from seeds as had been done, for example, in Mexico.

As Sarah Seekatz points out, few other Americans knew anything about the regions from which dates came, so the plant scientists became "experts in all things Arabian."[21] Pictures in American plant hunters' travel accounts of date growers in traditional Arab costumes holding huge chisels for detaching offshoots might have evoked Orientalist tropes of backward peasants, but they also asserted that asexual reproduction techniques (soon to be known as "cloning")[22] were essential to make dates into profitable commodities.[23] Cultivating date palm trees from offshoots and not from seeds not only guaranteed that new trees reproduced true to type and that fruit quality was stable but also gave control over the number of male and female trees. Considering the spatial constraints in oases limited by the reach of the irrigation infrastructure, maximizing the number of female trees, the only ones bearing fruit, was paramount. Profitable commercial date palm cropscapes relied on a few male trees to provide pollen manually inserted into female flowers. The industrial date palm orchards of the Coachella Valley of the twentieth century, bearing uniform fruit of a few commercial varieties (Deglet Noor and Medjool) and pollinated by a few selected males, resulted from moving to California the whole commercial method of reproduction used in Arab oases. While date palm trees had been present in the Americas well before the USDA plant hunters brought them to California, it was only by engaging with the reproduction techniques learned in North Africa and the Middle East that they became another epitome of American commercial prowess.

The Coachella date groves expanded from less than seven hundred hectares in 1930 to around two thousand hectares in 1950, which sounds like an industrial success story.[24] Ostensibly a modern agribusiness organized for expanding markets, the California date industry surprises with its many "premodern" features. Mechanization proved elusive: the techniques of Middle Eastern date workers were barely modified in the New World setting.[25] Work in the Coachella groves was year-round: the trees were—and still are—pollinated and trimmed by hand; the emerging fruit stems were manually thinned, bunched, and bagged; and finally the ripe fruits were handpicked, the Deglet Noor variety in whole bunches, the high-value, delicate Medjool individually as they ripened. All these skilled tasks took place at the crown of the tree and became increasingly dangerous as the trees grew up toward their full height of more than twenty meters or in windy conditions.

California date groves were, and remain, family-owned, labor-intensive operations. Growers organized into cooperatives to create solidarity and help promote and market their produce; equally important, once hired labor replaced family labor, cooperatives facilitated access to and control over workers.[26] During the first years of the Coachella date groves, when the palms were still low, it seems that the Anglo grove-owning families did much of the fieldwork themselves, wives and husbands together, hiring extra workers only at harvest time. But as the palms grew and the work became more dangerous, wives were relegated to the packing sheds, and finding labor to tend the groves became increasingly difficult.[27] And then came World War II, and the husbands were called up.

The Bracero Program of 1942 was a godsend to the date growers. Mexican *braceros* (field-workers) were typically regarded by employers as an unskilled proletariat, hands not heads, to whom they had few obligations, as work was only seasonal and braceros followed the harvests of different crops, returning to Mexico in the winter.[28] The date groves, however, required a dashing, fearless aristocracy of labor: the *palmeros* worked right through the year, it took at least three years to acquire the skills to perform delicate operations at great heights, and often palmero families would work at the same grove over two or more generations. Compared to other braceros, palmeros earned more and had enviable job security. For the date-grove owners, the difficulty of mechanizing meant palmeros were essential. When the Bracero Program was terminated in 1964, date growers used their cooperative clout to petition (unsuccessfully) for a special exception for their crop. Since 1964 there have been serial attempts to mechanize or digitalize the irrigation of date groves, to pollinate using helicopters, and to replace swaying ladders with mechanical hoists—but success has been limited. The palmeros are still there today, an essential but aging workforce whose demise threatens the survival of the "industry."[29]

American-grown dates retained a flavor of exotic Arabian luxury: the packets were designed with Oriental themes, and the Coachella Valley itself acquired the allure of Arabia as buildings in Moorish design sprang up and date festivals featuring Arabian Nights themes lured tourists to this East-in-the-West. Like the Old World date oases, the Coachella datescape was initially built by inward flows, of plants, skill sets, labor, and capital. But once established it became cut off. The Coachella dates themselves were originally intended for limited mobility, to stay within the United States as an import substitute; their relatively high price has excluded them from the main export markets.[30] As a site of production, the California date groves became a self-contained world: new palms are grown from local offshoots; highly specialized, date-specific cultivation skills tie labor to the locality; the family-owned date groves of Coachella and Yuma are not links in a chain sustaining a civilization but tiny enclaves at the margins of American agriculture. Nowadays Coachella is renowned for its music festival featuring the likes of Beyoncé, not so much for its dates. The town of Mecca, heart of the date business and for many years a sort of Middle East Californian theme park, has lost its glamour and no longer figures in postcards. Instead, its population is declining, and some 40 percent of its families live in poverty. To understand the dynamics at work in the datescape of California, one certainly needs to engage the history of expanding agribusiness and modern capitalism. But when the wind blows and dust from the fields and the nearby Salton Sea coats the whole town, one should probably also invoke Ibn Khaldun and his obsession with the ruins of history or, even better, Abd al-Rahman and the exiled date palm tree of Al-Andalus.

THE LIFE AND TIMES OF THE TOBACCO PLANT

A crop plant's seasonalities and life cycle may seem natural, but they are seldom the same as those of its wild ancestors. Whether it be manipulating its reproduction, as in the case of dates, or changing its seasonality from biennial to annual, as in the case of cereals, human intervention in a plant's temporalities is fundamental to domestication, and to moving it as a crop through space and time. Here we take tobacco as our exemplar for this process of adjusting the life cycle offered by the plant, one that invites us to play with different timescales, as we do throughout the book. The human manipulation of the tobacco plant's timescales provides a case to counter claims about natural causes of history. Scholars eager to avoid essentialism will heed the human inputs at the very start of the story—the construction of the plant as crop and the redirection of its own reproductive goals toward human purposes.[31]

There is a reason European colonizers and critics since King James have called tobacco a weed—prolific, abundant, maybe even invasive, tobacco is a perennial. A single plant can survive many years. It will bloom several times, and repeat and reproduce its life cycle through several seasons. Even within a single year, the tobacco plant has several cycles of growth: after its leaves have grown for a while, the plant produces a second set of smaller leaves ("suckers") that appear at the juncture of leaf and thick stalk on the plant. In addition, when the plant is cut down, new shoots ("ratoons") will appear, and from these will grow leaves, so the plant has a second life from the same roots.

All these "facts of the plant" were diminished or strengthened or manipulated when European colonizers started growing the plant for commercial purposes. In French Louisiana, the appearance of the little suckers meant the beginning of an extended harvest time, as first-growth leaves were removed and second growths were cultivated; while on the Spanish island of Cuba, tobacco was grown as a perennial, and ratoons had a market—as weaker, later growths, they were fine for smoking.[32]

In the case of British North America, tobacco had made Virginia a viable colony in the early seventeenth century and was cultivated specifically for its first-growth leaves. Inspection laws established by the colonial burgesses in the 1720s forbade the sale of second growths, in order to improve crop quality and produce leaves to a respectable standard. To meet that standard, colonists learned to civilize the plant into an annual cycle of production and reproduction. In addition, regimenting the plant from a perennial into an annual mobilized both legal and social power, including the legal distinctions between free and unfree labor, women's work from that of men, good wives from nasty wenches. Imposing order on the cropscape became associated with white male prerogatives that became the basis for broader political power, including laws elevating white males over other dependents, slaves, and servants, in an emerging colonial order.[33]

As a result of the regimentation of its reproductive cycle, Virginia tobacco follows a single, linear path after planting from seed: its flowers and suckers are treated as trash so that the first-growth leaves get big and strong and take all the activity of the plant's life cycle. When the leaves are harvested, any ratoons that may appear are cut down or plowed under. They are not part of the crop. In this way the periodizing power of the tobacco plant's life cycle becomes a secondary consideration to human needs and the laws and cultivation methods that express them. Yet this human-controlled life cycle of the plant creates harvest imperatives assumed by historical actors to be natural, dictated by the plant—as we discuss in future chapters.

The history of tobacco as a crop in colonial British Virginia thus provides an exemplar of how domestication reshapes the "nature" of a plant when making it into a crop. Only by understanding the malleabilities discussed here can we make sense of the more social histories of tobacco discussed later, where we learn (for example) how the cultivation calendar, the timing of tasks, is a human product, and thus could and did change in different historical periods. Changing cultivation cycles, each claimed to be the plant's natural life cycle, played an important role in changing the size of Virginia tobacco farms over time.[34]

Historians of agriculture often pay attention to time at this scale, at the level of the plant life cycle. Our goal is to introduce this manipulation of the plant to global history, to show how the movement of the crops depends on alterations that take place every season, every cultivation cycle—that cultivating a crop means making it something other than a plant. Adjusting the timing of its cycles to the needs of the cultivation system is crucial to the creation and maintenance of a cropscape. The riffs throughout this book always recognize that the crop's temporalities are not facts of nature. "The Life and Times of the Tobacco Plant" also indicates our role, as historians, in defining scales, both temporal and spatial, within each cropscape.

RICE: LIFE CYCLES AND DEEP HISTORIES

Like all the grasses from which human cereals were domesticated, the wild species of the Asian and African rices, *Oryza,* are typically perennial but were turned into single-crop annuals in the process of domestication.[35] This riff looks at further ways in which humans have manipulated the life or crop cycle of rice. Sometimes, as with ratooning, the cycle was extended. More often it has been abbreviated to increase the intensity of land use, a strategy shared by premodern states in China and Japan, and by the architects of the Green Revolution that transformed cropscapes worldwide in the 1960s and 1970s.[36] While the Green Revolution landscapes were celebrated as the triumph of modernization, Western social theorists of the Cold War era stigmatized earlier Asian ricescapes as involutionary and intrinsically incapable of development. Japanese historians, however, reframed the characteristics and longue durée evolution of East Asian ricescapes to propose an alternative path to industrial modernity: the "industrious revolution." In another equally surprising reframing, scientists are currently taking up the hitherto unregarded ratoon rices as crops with the potential to meet the challenges of the Anthropocene.[37] As with the datescape, historical ricescapes and the values assigned to them prompt us to reflect upon both the material and the intellectual lineages of "modern" systems of knowledge and practice.

QUICK-RIPENING RICES: RICE AS HISTORY, RICE AS SELF

As early as 300 B.C.E. the rice-growing cropscapes of Lingnan, "South of the Mountains" (now South China and northern Vietnam), were described by northern Chinese from dry-crop regions as places of natural plenty, the lands of fish and rice. As discussed in chapter 3, "Sizes," wet-rice fields, whether irrigated or rain fed, supported a diversity of useful plants and animals in addition to the rice itself: water chestnuts, fish, ducks, mulberries (which fed silkworms and supported silk production), and so forth. The surrounding higher, dry land accommodated villages, vegetable gardens, orchards, dry fields growing crops like cotton or beans, and rough grazing; then on the higher slopes farmers might grow bamboo (for food, paper, or construction), tea, more orchards, or timber trees.

A constellation of techniques for shortening rice's crop cycle and thus raising the output of the cropscape made these bounties possible. One key technique, transplanting, is first documented in the Lingnan region around two millennia ago.[38] The rice seed is sown in a well-fertilized nursery bed, and when it has grown to twenty or twenty-five centimeters high it is pulled up, trimmed, and replanted in well-spaced rows in the main field. Transplanting allows farmers to select the healthiest seedlings, encourages vigorous rooting and tillering (the producing of multiple stems and seed heads from a single plant) and facilitates weeding; all these increase the yield. An additional advantage is that transplanting reduces the time the crop spends in the main field by a month or six weeks, opening the way for a second crop.

Chinese references to double-cropping of rice in what is now Vietnam go back to around 100 C.E., and these early rices gradually spread north into southern and central China.[39] It was not for several centuries, however, that the Chinese state, habitually active in "promoting agriculture" (*quannong*), incorporated them into its policies.[40] Anxious to feed an expanding urban population and to provision its armies as the threat of invasion grew, in 1012 the Song dynasty government imported quick-ripening rice seed from Champa (southern Vietnam) into Jiangnan (the Lower Yangtze provinces, by then China's most productive agricultural region), allowing two crops of grain to be grown in a year.[41] In this new Jiangnan cropping system, summer rice was usually alternated in the fields with winter barley or wheat; farther south, two or even three crops of rice were grown annually in the same field. Short-period rices could also be grown in places where the climate was too capricious or harsh for traditional slow-ripening rices, or where there were risks of flood or drought. Although generally speaking the shorter the period the lower the yield, quick-ripening rices were so useful that Chinese farmers developed hundreds or even thousands of varieties; in one flood-prone part of Jiangsu province, sixteenth-century farmers succeeded in producing a "fifty-day" rice.[42]

The shortening of the rice plant's life cycle, through transplanting and the breeding of quick-ripening varieties, brought a quantum leap in rural productivity. It was not just that rice fields became more productive. Like the date oases, ricescapes supported multiple productive activities: commercial surpluses of rice along with other food crops, silk or cotton production, household and local manufactures (pickles, brewing), paper and book industries, commercial pig raising, and so on. These ricescapes were flexible and resilient: depending on markets, farmers might switch (short- or long-term) from rice to cotton and back, they might foreground paper making and background rice, growing just a little to pay rents and taxes or switching entirely, buying rice on the highly developed rice market that increasingly integrated all of Chinese imperial territory and its many trading partners.[43]

Over the centuries we observe a ripple effect as intensively farmed ricescapes moved out from early centers like Jiangnan and Guangdong, which increasingly backgrounded rice to foreground other commercial crops or manufactures, into hinterland river basins upstream. Here, in regions typically occupied by other ethnic groups, new frontiers of rice farming and of Han-style culture and social organization opened up. The ricescapes also spread across elevations, extending from easily managed river basins up into steep terraced hillsides or down into reclaimed land along the coast or in marshy floodplains, where continual pumping or the construction of seawalls might be necessary.[44]

These fertile, versatile ricescapes were idealized in official Chinese discourse and popular culture as an icon of fruitfulness and social harmony. The most famous celebration is a painted scroll produced in around 1134 by a Jiangnan magistrate, Lou Shu. The *Gengzhi tu* (Pictures of farming and weaving) is a set of forty-five paintings depicting the steps of rice cultivation and sericulture, each inscribed with a poem of the author's own composition. The work was presented at court a few years later. The delighted emperor praised and rewarded Lou, and gave orders for the scenes to be copied on the screen of the Inner Court with Lou's name on them—a signal honor. Lou Shu's work soon became famous among the ruling elite as a perfect medium for promoting agriculture. One of the fundamental priorities of the imperial state and its officials at every level, promoting agriculture was as much about inculcating social values as improving techniques. The *Gengzhi tu* reminds us that in Chinese understanding cropscapes were intrinsically gendered: in order to feed and clothe the people and—through tax payments—the state, the cropscape needed to produce textiles made by women as well as grain farmed by men.[45] Through the late imperial period and into the twentieth century, Chinese governments devoted huge efforts to propagating this cropscape: its material practices were presumed to inculcate properly Chinese moral values in backward villagers or newly conquered barbarians. Reflecting ingrained gender ideals and appreciation of diligence, the *Gengzhi tu* also had huge popular appeal, its scenes featuring on New Year prints, cheap painted pottery, or stone carvings on village gates.[46]

In late imperial China the versatile cropscapes built around shortening the reproductive period of the rice plant underpinned several centuries of impressive growth. Between 1400 and 1750 China stood as the world's largest producer and exporter of manufactured goods, along with India.[47] China became the sink for the silver of the New World and Japan, much of which was invested into the ricescape and its associated manufacturing economy.[48] Most global historians see 1800 as a tipping point—a moment of *divergence*—when Chinese growth faltered, soon to be fatally undermined by the dynamic industrializing economies of the Western colonial powers.[49] But another influential school locates the onset of decline much earlier, arguing that it was the long-term dynamics of the Chinese ricescape itself that curtailed Chinese progress and creativity.

INVOLUTION, INDUSTRIOUS REVOLUTION, AND THE TEMPORALITIES OF GLOBAL HISTORY

Many Enlightenment philosophers admired China's "enlightened despotism" and the prosperous society it sustained. But ever since Montesquieu another strand of European thought has stigmatized Asian civilizations as passive and unenterprising.[50] Marx theorized an Asiatic Mode of Production, arguing that Asian states were huge, overcentralized, absolutist monsters, essentially impervious to change; Weber elaborated a similar position on cultural rather than class grounds. In the early Cold War period, partly in reaction to Stalinism, Wittfogel rebranded Marx in his theory of "hydraulic societies" and "Asiatic despotism" (see "Muddy Waters" in "Sizes"), while in 1963 Clifford Geertz published *Agricultural Involution*, a study of colonial Java informed by Rostow's modernization theory.[51] Geertz argued that Asian intensive rice-farming systems lack the capacity to increase labor productivity. On the contrary, they support increasingly dense populations by absorbing labor, but with diminishing returns. Over time poverty grows, social relations involute, and the system cannot make the transition to a new form of industrial capitalist growth without external inputs and stimulus. Thus, Geertz argued, colonial Java involuted; late nineteenth-century Japan, however, leapt into modernity thanks to the decision of the Meiji (1868–1912) government to industrialize Western style, developing a chemical-fertilizer industry and other industrial inputs that could carry Japanese farming across the labor-productivity barrier and into a new era of development.

The concept of agricultural involution was eagerly applied by historians of China and comparative historians as a factor to explain what they saw as the economic and scientific decline of imperial China.[52] This interpretation reflected the prevailing modernist sense of time that understood continuity as inertia. Having identified the Song dynasty (960–1276) as a time of extraordinary cultural vitality and scientific as well as social innovation, seeing nothing technologically or institutionally innovative in the centuries of expanding prosperity that followed, struck by the rapid impoverishment and disintegration of Qing society after the Opium Wars of the 1840s, and by the stark contrast with the rise of Japan at the same time, scholars and social reformers initially blamed Confucianism and Chinese culture, then later added the supposedly involutionary nature of China's ricescapes, capable of sustaining growth for many centuries but incapable of the vital transition to capitalist, industrial development.

Geertz argued that Japan had broken out of what Mark Elvin later called the "high-level equilibrium trap" of "growth without development" by opening up to the West. This was of course a welcome message to the West and its allies at the height of the Cold War, when international development was getting into its stride. Yet when Geertz published *Agricultural Involution* in 1963 there was already a substantial body of Japanese research, made available in English in 1959 by the historian Thomas C. Smith, which refuted the Western-centered dynamics and periodization implicit in involution and related theories by demonstrating that the Meiji takeoff was firmly rooted in Tokugawa achievements.[53]

In the seventeenth century, under Tokugawa rule (1603–1867), the Chinese intensive and diversified ricescape and its associated agronomic ideals and expertise were imported to Japan.[54] Agricultural treatises proliferated, new varieties of rice and other crops were bred, fertilizing methods were improved and multicropping expanded, fueling the dynamic economic and manufacturing growth, the commercialization and urbanization that built the foundations for nineteenth-century modernization.[55] When the Meiji government was formed in 1868, in reaction to the threat of invasion by Western powers it determined to pursue a policy of rapid modernization, militarization, and industrialization mobilizing Western expertise. The platform for this takeoff, however, was the productive and versatile Tokugawa ricescape, not transformed but rather dynamized by Western agronomic science, commercial fertilizers, mechanized pumps, breeding programs, and the like.[56] The rise of Meiji Japan depended on national rice production. A ruthless regime of extraction from the rice-farming peasantry was veiled by an agrarian ideology extolling the small farmer as a loyal and productive citizen. It was the surpluses of food and labor extracted from increasingly immiserated rice farmers in Japan and its colonies of Taiwan and Korea that fueled Japan's rise as a military-industrial power.

Postwar Japanese sociologists, historians, and philosophers have elaborated the theory of Japan as a rice society in ways that fundamentally challenge Western-centered historical periodizations and geographies. For a start, they assert that the Japanese path to industrial modernity was rooted in ricescapes and thus was quite distinct from the path of the West. By the later Tokugawa, this argument goes, Japan had undergone an *industrious revolution* constructed around the demands and characteristics of intensive rice farming.[57] In Japanese models of longue durée history and paths to modernity, "industrious revolution" denotes an economic transformation based on the constellation of managerial, technical, and financial skills associated with the complex of small-scale rice farms, crafts, and manufactures that clustered in the early modern Japanese countryside. Starting in the seventeenth century, in a parallel trajectory to the rice regions of late imperial China, these characteristic resources led Japan, it is argued, on a rurally rooted, rice-based path of economic growth in which households increased both output and income by working harder; capital assets or inputs (machines, livestock) dwindled in importance as the quality of labor improved.[58]

In Japan the rural economy was not reactive to but constitutive of development trajectories. Furthermore, rural skills and creativity were not marginalized or displaced by Western-inspired technical expertise but mobilized and developed in the service of a characteristically Japanese repertory of modernizing techniques. There is a broad consensus among Japanese historians and social scientists that these deep-rooted resources and dynamics gave a distinctive shape to Meiji Japan's modernization and continue to shape the organization of the economy and of production in Japan today.[59]

The concept of industrious revolution and related analyses of how industrious Japan became industrial Japan soon attracted historians rethinking paths to modernity elsewhere. Among historians of Europe, Jan de Vries has been a particularly influential advocate of industrious revolution to explain how labor-intensive, mixed-occupation rural economies (for instance in the Low Countries) contributed to shaping the rise of industrial capitalism in Western Europe.[60] Akira Hayami objects that de Vries takes industrious revolution as the precursor to industrial revolution, whereas Hayami presented them as "opposing concepts."[61] But it is the linkages that the concept of industrious revolution suggests with national trajectories of modernization, or with global articulations of the emergence of capitalism, that other historians find seductive. Ravi Palat's recent study of rice economies in precolonial South India, for example, "draws upon the histories of societies based on wet-rice cultivation to chart an alternate pattern of social evolution and state formation; traces inter-state linkages and the grown of commercialization without capitalism: 'industrious revolution' in India, China, Japan and Southeast Asia."[62]

The long-term dynamics of Asia's ricescapes, their characteristic scale, the patterns in which they integrated rural communities into markets and manufacturing systems, the ways in which their typically dispersed and flexible networks of production and capitalization fed into world circuits of commerce, and their putative impact on national trajectories of modernization prompt a distinctive sense of time unfolding that unsettles conventional periodizations of global history. If we take the transition to a commercialized, diversified rural economy organized around a highly productive wet-rice cropscape as a significant marker, then for South India a rice era with very ancient roots takes shape in 1250. South China's rice era begins around 1000, to reach a zenith of prosperity and global impact around 1700. Japan was a relative latecomer on the scene, with its rice era beginning around 1600. But unlike the colonial collapse of rice-based economies in India and China, and the sense of civilizational rupture and failure which that collapse induces among historians, politicians, and the general public, in Japan the rice economy served as a springboard to successful modernization, and today it is claimed as one of the miracle ingredients that makes modern Japan exceptional. Japan's rice-centered historiography, though not intrinsically nationalist, is closely attuned to a broader public discourse of rice-as-self, where Japanese subjectivity, physiology, sociality, and aesthetics, as well as the terms of Japan's participation in transnational trade organizations, are molded by the farming and eating of Japanese round-grain rice. A popular mythology, kept alive in *anime* as well as imperial ritual, traces the roots of modern Japanese rice identity back to the Sun Goddess, who bestowed the precious grain upon the Japanese people before history began.[63]

FAST AND SLOW: GREEN REVOLUTIONS
AND SUSTAINABLE RATOONS

The long-term historical dynamics of great premodern Asian civilizations like South India, China, and Japan were closely entwined with the cropscapes generated by shortening the life cycle of the rice plant. Short-season rices were also a fundamental component of the technological packages devised to generate the spanking new cropscapes of the twentieth-century Green Revolution (and its socialist equivalents in the People's Republic of China and Vietnam). Although presented as "miracles," Green Revolution high-yielding rice varieties such as IR8, released by the International Rice Research Institute (IRRI) in 1966, were not bred de novo but made liberal use of earlier breeds, some dating back to late Ming or Tokugawa times, others derived from the national breeding programs set up around Asia in the early twentieth century.[64] The special traits of the "miracle" rice crops were high yields, combined with a short growing period to allow double-cropping. Although boosters spoke of "seeds of plenty," the new seeds were not in themselves sufficient to bring change. They were just one element in a "technological package": to achieve their genetic potential, they required irrigation, chemical fertilizers, and herbicides—in fact what turned out to be a radical transformation of the whole cropscape.

Many farmers found themselves unable to maintain the strict new forms of time discipline demanded by the Green Revolution regime. The miracle rices, double-cropped and dependent on water supply from large-scale irrigation schemes, imposed rigorous time constraints that were often hard to meet, and that had significant knock-on effects. In Kelantan, Malaysia, Green Revolution technologies and double-cropping were introduced in the 1970s. In order to keep up with schedules that typically required plowing for the new crop to begin just a few days after harvest, farmers had to abandon buffalo plows, sickles, and traditional labor exchanges in favor of tractors and reaping machines. Under the new time regime it became impossible to combine rice production with alternative and often more profitable sources of income such as market gardening or construction work, which could have helped pay for the inputs needed for the miracle rices to thrive. The flexibility of sharecropping contracts, which spread the risks of innovation and allowed farmers and landowners to divide up their responsibilities for cash and kind inputs in an almost infinite variety of ways, helped to smooth the path to adoption of the new technologies. Nevertheless, a number of farmers interviewed by Francesca Bray and Alexander Robertson in the late 1970s said they were giving up rice growing because the time constraints made their lives unmanageable.[65] The Green Revolution package was not intentionally designed to favor richer farmers with more land—in fact, one key rationale had been that it would reduce rural poverty and thus the risk of Red Revolution. Yet its time disciplines, along with its inbuilt economies of scale, triggered economic differentiation and a gradual exodus of poor farmers to towns.

A fierce debate about the merits of the Green Revolution developed in the 1970s. While economists and politicians welcomed the surge in cheap food for cities that the Green Revolution quickly generated, social scientists and activists were quick to criticize its negative impact on rural society, including in Asia's rice regions.[66] It was not long before an additional concern surfaced: the environmental damage caused by intensive chemical use, monoculture, and the use of heavy machines on fragile rice soils.[67] Curiously, an alternative strategy currently gaining popularity is to abandon short-cycle rice varieties and the cultivation complexes in which they are embedded and to seek both environmental and social sustainability by mobilizing the "natural" propensity of rice to ratoon.

Various domesticated rice varieties possess the capacity to ratoon, that is, to spring up from the dried-out roots of the old plant once or even twice. As with tobacco, ratooning rice was traditionally a low-labor, low-productivity system that raised output by extending the reproductive cycle of the rice plant to a second cropping season, basically by cutting the seed-bearing stems of the first crop and then leaving the plants to themselves until another crop ripened. In these cropscapes, the rice plant was typically grown in nonirrigated, rain-fed fields, including upland fields or fragile hillsides. Farmers might also choose to ratoon rices where mountainous terrain, or lack of draught animals or human labor, made conventional cultivation techniques too onerous, or when warfare or banditry made it dangerous to tend the fields. In modern times farmers in various parts of Asia, Africa, and the Americas have used ratooning to second-crop their rice fields, but it has remained a marginal practice.[68]

The contrast between the material characteristics and the historiographies of the cropscapes that developed around *shortening* and *lengthening* the life cycle of the rice plant could not be more striking. Low yields meant that ratoon rice was no more than a subsistence crop, nested within a mosaic of fields and gardens, forests, or marshes. The inhabitants of such cropscapes lived by various combinations of farming, gardening, gathering, livestock raising, and hunting. Trade with the wider economy usually involved high-value garden, forest, or animal products, not surpluses from the fields. These "Zomian" pockets of low population density and low cereal yields typically eluded the gaze and the reach of the state, its tax inspectors, and its agronomic experts—which is one reason why rice historians have found it difficult to trace in any detail the history of ratoon-rice cultivation, why ratoon rice was, until very recently, an "orphan crop" for scientific research, and why its capacity to support commercial activity was largely ignored.[69]

Recently, however, ratooning has attracted the attention of agronomists working on sustainable farming, under the auspices of national governments and transnational organizations including IRRI (the International Rice Research Institute) and the FAO (U.N. Food and Agriculture Organization). Ratooning plants have deeper roots than annuals, do not require chemical inputs, are better able to withstand drought, and ripen more quickly. Proponents argue that improved breeds of ratoon rice can help meet current global challenges of increased water scarcity, labor shortages, and expanding cultivation into fragile terrains.[70] As with millet, discussed below, here we see a system of great antiquity, surviving

THE SOCIAL LIFE OF COCOA

Having explored a spectrum of relations between plant time and cropscape time, we now ask how growing crops relates to growing families—naturally a matter of concern to most farmers. The case of cocoa in Ghana vividly illustrates a particularly intimate relationship between crop times and human times, where the life cycle of the cocoa farm is inextricably meshed with the life cycle of the farming household, and where the maturing of the cocoa trees reflects the maturing virtues of responsible adults. "As a lifetime project, the cocoa farm has acquired metaphorical significance in Ghana: for example, a civil servant may describe his career as his cocoa farm, likening it to a long-term enterprise in which good husbandry and family interests ultimately transcend notions of individual profit."[71]

Thick clusters of handsome ribbed pods, glowing gold in the dappled forest shade, adorn the branches of long lines of cocoa trees. For a century now this cropscape has been the chief source of wealth for what was once the colonial Gold Coast and is now independent Ghana. The golden pods sustain farming families, enrich their lineages, people the land, and (when world cocoa prices are high) bring prosperity to the nation. Twentieth-century histories of cash crops in Africa tend to assume a dark tone of land dispossession, forced labor, famines, and violence (chapter 5, "Compositions"). The history of cocoa on the islands of São Tomé and Principe, the main producer in the world of cocoa at the end of the nineteenth century, is an exemplary tale of plantation violence after the abolition of slavery.[72] But histories of Ghanaian cocoa, together with palm oil in coastal West Africa and coffee in the highlands of Tanganyika near Mount Kilimanjaro, speak instead of local peasant initiative and distributed prosperity.[73] In this vein but against the prevailing orthodoxy of colonial administrators and development economists, in the 1960s the economic anthropologist Polly Hill (niece of John Maynard Keynes) eloquently argued for understanding Ghanaian cocoa farmers not as peasants but as successful rural capitalists. You did not have to be a white settler to be on the right side of history. Hill's evidence came from detailed ethnographic and archival investigations of how family time, farm time, lineage time, and crop-frontier time related.[74]

Introduced in 1879 from Fernando Po, the cocoa plant was not native to Ghana but thrived in its new home.[75] Despite colonialists' claims to have

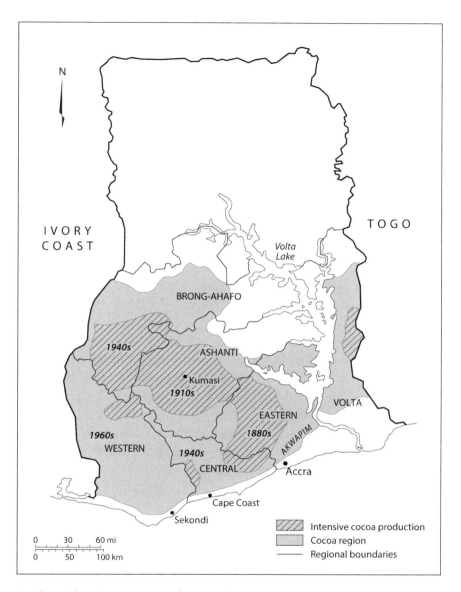

Southern Ghana's moving cocoa frontier. The expansion of southern Ghana's cocoa frontier from 1880 to 2010. William L. Nelson Maps, based on Robertson, *The Dynamics of Productive Relationships*, Map 2, p. 54, and Knudsen and Agergaard, "Ghana's Cocoa Frontier," Figure 1, p. 329.

introduced both the plant and the science needed to grow it, Ghanaian cocoa farming was an indigenous enterprise from the start, built up and expanded by powerful Akan lineages from Akwapim in the Eastern Region (southeastern Gold Coast) where cocoa was first introduced.[76] The British administration naturally claimed to have launched the new crop, but the financial innovations and social initiatives developed to cultivate cocoa were distinctively Akan (discussed below). The smallholder cocoa-farming techniques that spread through the forest zones were rooted in long-established patterns of forest fallow cultivation, owing nothing to the Caribbean-inspired "plantation paradigm."[77]

Starting in the 1890s, the Gold Coast "cocoa frontier" expanded steadily through the forests of the Eastern Region, reaching Ashanti in the 1930s and Brong-Ahafo and the Western Region, on the frontier with Côte d'Ivoire about three hundred kilometers to the west, in the 1950s and 1960s, respectively. The frontier advanced across Ghana by a process of leapfrogging. Once a farm matured, the owner would use the cash to purchase new forestland farther west. After the cocoa boom between 1950 and 1975, a sequence of fires and droughts in the 1980s drove many cocoa farmers to convert to maize farming. But recently many have converted their farms back to cocoa, arguing that even a low-yield cocoa farm brings better income than a high-yield maize farm, and, unlike annual crops, cocoa provides long-term security. "When you are into maize farming and you get old, you can't farm any more, but when you have a cocoa farm and you are old you can give it out for sharecropping."[78] Currently the world's second cocoa exporter after neighboring Côte d'Ivoire, Ghana today has more than eight hundred thousand smallholder cocoa farmers, spread across most of the country's forest zone; they typically derive 70 to 100 percent of their income from cocoa sales.[79]

The cocoa cultivation system has shown remarkable long-term resilience, no doubt because it is so well attuned to both social and environmental conditions.[80] Cocoa farms in Ghana were and still are small, typically three to four hectares; some forest is preserved for shade, and cocoa trees are planted three to eight meters apart.[81] Mature trees yield roughly 225 to 335 kilograms per hectare annually. Labor inputs for a mature cocoa farm are highly seasonal: a main harvest between October and December, and a minor harvest in May, with routine clearing, brush cutting, and application of pesticides or fertilizers in between. Beyond the annual cycle there are *four stages* in the development of the farm, and this is where crop time and family time mesh. A *new* farm, cleared from the forest, requires a substantial investment of labor and capital; it devours resources but offers no yield. The *young* farm starts bearing after three to five years, and the break-even point for investment comes around the twelfth year, by which time the trees are giving two-thirds of their mature yield. From fifteen to thirty-five years the *mature* farm is at full bearing, generating substantial profit, sufficient for the owner to invest in clearing new farms. After thirty-five years, yields decline steadily. At fifty years, the *old* farm is down to a sixth of its full yield. After five or ten years more, the derelict farm is turned over to other crops or replanted.

How does the life cycle of the cocoa farm mesh with human time? As documented at the height of the industry in the 1960s and 1970s, experienced cocoa farmers purchased forestland, using their own money often supplemented by capital borrowed from their lineage. They cleared the land and planted cocoa trees, hiring as weekly or monthly wage laborers migrants from the north or young relatives. Once the young trees were established, the farm needed a different kind of care, a low-cost, permanent presence on the farm. To provide this care, the owner would negotiate with a young man (sometimes a non-Akan migrant from the north, more often a relative), to take on the farm as an *abusa* man, a "caretaker" or sharecropper.[82] Today the funds to purchase a new farm are as likely to come from a sideline of shopkeeping as from a lineage loan, but the abusa system remains essentially unchanged: it is a highly successful system for implanting migrant stock, growing local communities as well as cocoa.[83]

Abusa, meaning one-third, was a long-standing Akan arrangement for usufruct, whereby in exchange for access to land a "stranger" farmer from outside the community gave the chief or landowner a one-third share of whatever came out of the land. In the case of cocoa farms, since the trees took so long to mature, the abusa arrangement grew with the trees. The new abusa man built up the farm, tending the young trees in exchange for provision of tools and inputs, and use of a subsistence plot for yams, plantains, and vegetables. The food plot was essential (see "Compositions"): it allowed the abusa man to marry, raise a family, and feed laborers—and thus provided the domestic and hired workforce to tend the cocoa trees, pluck the pods, and dry and ferment the beans. Initially, because the cocoa yields were small and labor inputs intensive, the abusa man would receive the full proceeds of the farm. As the trees matured, profits grew, and labor requirements fell, the amount the abusa man gave the owner rose, first to one-half and eventually to two-thirds of the proceeds.[84] At this point profits for both owner and tenant were high. The owner would typically start another cocoa farm. The abusa man, now established as socially mature and economically capable, would hope to move on from sharecropper to landowner status by acquiring his own cocoa farms, through purchase or inheritance, or sometimes by claiming ownership of part of the sharecropped land. Only slightly modified, the abusa system is still going strong today.[85]

The abusa man matures with his cocoa farm. Its growing income helps educate and establish his children. His old age coincides with the senescence of the trees, but by then, if his children or new farms are not sufficient to support him, he has at least acquired a recognized interest in the land sufficient to allow him to sublet the land for other crops or a newly planted cocoa farm.

The longevity of the cocoa farm matches the human life span and domestic cycle: the family grows in step with the cropscape. But cocoa farming is also a form of socialization. Children grow up helping with the harvest and turning the beans as they dry. Parents believe this is a necessary part of building character. Amanda Berlan writes, "Laziness is widely abhorred in Ghanaian society and parents told me that involving children in cocoa-farming was important as it would help them to become productive and hard-working individuals."[86] For a young Ghanaian man, access to a young cocoa farm as an abusa man allows him to begin his life as an independent adult, judged ready to marry and found a family. His family grows as the trees mature, matching the farm's expanding labor needs. Increasing profits allow farmers to act as responsible parents, feeding and educating their children, and eventually setting them up in their turn.

Beyond the farming household itself, abusa arrangements have historically built up shared and national wealth. Cocoa farmers contributed from their profits to lineage funds, community prosperity rose as towns grew up in the cocoa zones, and cocoa smallholdings (supported by cassava and yam gardens) became and remain a mainstay of the modern Ghanaian export economy. "When you look around the community, all the big houses you see . . . were built with cocoa money and also all the educated farmers in our communities are children or descendants of cocoa farmers."[87] The successful interlocking of crop and family rhythms, and the close match between the cocoa plant's requirements and established forest garden cultivation practices, have assured the continuity of this modern but specifically local cropscape over many decades.[88] Today, migrants from across Ghana continue to stream into the newer cocoa-growing regions, where both cocoa farming and the increasingly diverse livelihood opportunities that it supports are seen as offering a prosperous future.[89] "Cocoa is Ghana, Ghana is cocoa," goes the popular saying. The long history of millets in China offers a very different perspective on how a nation identifies with a crop.

MILLET IN CHINA: HEYDAY, AFTERLIFE, AND RESURRECTION OF A CROPSCAPE

Contrary to popular belief, millet, not rice, was the staple grain upon which Chinese civilization was founded. According to Chinese legend, it was Lord Millet (Hou Ji), a magical being conceived when his hitherto barren mother stepped in a footprint left in the soil by the supreme deity, who taught the ancient Chinese how to grow grain. The grains in question were millets, foxtail, and broomcorn (*Setaria italica* and *Panicum miliaceum*), spring-sown crops hardy enough to survive the semiarid climate of North China. From early Neolithic settlements dating back to 6000 B.C.E., through the early empires and dynasties and into the early modern period, *Setaria* and *Panicum* millets were the dominant staple of most of North China, shaping its cropscapes and farming practices (see "Muddy Waters" in "Sizes"), its cooking techniques (millet was prepared in characteristic tripod steamers), and its drinking patterns (glutinous varieties of millet were used for brewing). From the mountainous loesslands of Shaanxi province down to the Yellow River plains, the millet belt remained China's political, cultural, and economic core, the site of its capital cities and its principal tax base, until 1127 C.E., when the Northern Song government was defeated by Khitan armies and a new capital was set up south of the Yangtze River—after which rice supplanted millet as China's iconic cereal and cropscape.[90]

Millets provided the food and the taxes upon which China's early empires depended, and because millets can keep for years, especially if stored underground, they were particularly valuable as a fiscal base. Millet thinking also permeated the culture. Millet was the grain celebrated at the Altars of the Soil and Grain, central institutions of the state cult already well established in the Shang dynasty (ca. 1600–1042 B.C.E.). It was during the Shang that magnificent ritual bronze vessels became badges of the right to rule, used for the ritual preparation and offering of millet, meat, and alcohol to the deities. Prominent among these vessels were bronze tripods, refinements of the pottery millet steamers found in every household, whose three feet made them symbols of political stability. Lord Millet himself was said to have been a prominent minister of the Shang, and the ancestor of the royal house of Zhou (ca. 1042–771 B.C.E.), the succeeding dynasty to which Confucius attributed the foundation of China's core institutions and values. The interpenetration of good husbandry and good government was marked in early China. The canonical agronomic advice to plant millet in a checkerboard of straight ridges, allowing the farmer to maximize the resources of water and fertilizer while developing the crop's roots and facilitating the ruthless elimination of weeds, first appears in a third-century-B.C.E. treatise on political economy and government.[91] James C. Scott would no doubt appreciate this material metaphor for state legibility and control.[92]

With its tiny grains and symbolic heft, millet was also the perfect medium for early Chinese philosophical-mathematical treatises on measurement, which stipulated the number of millet grains corresponding to a particular weight, length, or capacity. The capacity of pitch pipes featured prominently here, for

Millet ritual in imperial China. The emperor ploughs the first furrow of spring in the sacred field outside the capital. 1530 edition of Wang Zhen's *Nongshu* (Treatise on agriculture) of 1313.

music, performed on exactly tuned instruments, was a key tool of early Chinese government: "With rites and music, [the Minister of Rites] adjusts the transformations of Heaven and Earth and the production of all the material things, so as to serve the ghosts and spirits, to harmonize the multitudinous people, and to bring all the material things to perfection."[93] The first dynastic history of China, the *Hanshu* (History of the Han dynasty), contains a section on calendars and pitch pipes, the tools for regulating time and tune, where the specifications for the exact dimensions of pitch pipes are given in terms of millet grains (the *huangzhong* size should fit twelve hundred grains of black millet).[94]

In concrete reality, millets steadily shifted from the center to the margins of the Chinese economy and diet over the imperial period. Starting in around the first century C.E., as milling techniques improved, wheaten noodles and breads became favorites with northern elites; by about 800 southern rice began to overtake northern millet as the biggest tax revenue; in around 1200 the Mongols introduced higher-yielding sorghums (*gaoliang*, "tall millet") to North China. By around 1600 millet had become a minor crop, food for the poor, in many areas where it had previously dominated the cropscape, although it remained the main cereal in rugged zones with harsh climates. Yet despite millet's reduced material presence, over the millennia Chinese reverence for canonical knowledge, values, and metaphors maintained its cultural presence (like biblical crops in Europe), while millets continued to be offered annually at the Temple of the Gods of Soil and Grain.

Millet in imperial China offers an excellent example of the long cultural and political afterlife of a crop and its cropscape, moving like a cultural capsule through time but stationary (or rather, contracting) in space. But with the fall of the Qing dynasty in 1911, dynastic cults and sacrifices to the Soil and the Grains ceased, while governments focused their attention on "major" grains, rice, wheat, and maize, that could be scientifically improved to feed the nation.[95] By these criteria millets were sidelined as what modern agronomists call "orphan crops." Yet millet survived in poor, remote regions, preserving a latent memory of a cropscape, its techniques, ecologies, and flavors. Today the millet cropscape is experiencing an unexpected cultural and material revival. The millions of city dwellers driving out into the villages in search of "peasant delights" (*nongjia le*—meals or homestays) enthusiastically consume millet porridge, formerly dismissed as coarse food (*culiao*) but now regarded as tasty and healthy.[96] Sigrid Schmalzer, a historian of postrevolutionary Chinese agriculture, recounts her visit in 2016 to Wangjinzhuang, a poor mountain village in the northern province of Hebei. Wangjinzhuang was recently designated a "Nationally Important Agricultural Heritage System," under a Chinese government program promoting U.N. global models for sustainable agriculture (discussed in "Reproductions"). In Wangjinzhuang the government subsidizes a mixed-farming system in which farmers grow millets and maize in rotation for subsistence, on narrow hillside terraces ploughed by donkeys, along with fruits, nuts, and medicinal herbs as cash crops. As Schmalzer notes, this confected neotraditional cropscape incorporates elements of Maoist legacy (including material infrastructure like terracing and epistemological hierarchies like acknowledgment of "peasant" expertise) into a refashioned "tradition" of donkey plows and low-input millets, repackaging a cropscape of toil and precarity as tourist-attractive sustainability.[97]

In imperial China the rice cropscape symbolized order, continuity, and plenty, but—unlike in Japan—there was no rice god or goddess in the Chinese imperial cult, and rice was not the grain that tied the Chinese to their mythological origins. It was the millet cropscape that symbolized the legendary roots of China's civilization, and that is currently being recuperated to symbolize both cultural authenticity and the frugal simplicity attributed to Maoist China.

In *Sweetness and Power,* published in 1985, Sidney Mintz made the argument, heretical at the time, that the seventeenth-century sugar plantations of the West Indies were an industrial system of production. The key was a particular form of time consciousness, dictated primarily by the nature of the sugar plant. The cane had to be crushed fresh from cutting, the juice needed to be boiled as soon as it was expressed, and it was believed that boiling the syrup was not to be interrupted until it had "struck." During the harvest season the sugar mills operated unceasingly, with coordinated teams working continuous shifts crushing the cane, boiling the juice, curing the molasses, drying the raw sugar, and distilling rum. Along with abundant slave labor and metropolitan capital, an essential element of the system was a "time-consciousness . . . dictated by the nature of the sugar cane and its processing requirements, [that] permeated all phases of plantation life and accorded well with the emphasis on time that was later to become a central feature of capitalist industry."[98]

In *Against the Grain,* James C. Scott makes a still more provocative claim for the power of crop times to shape history. As we domesticated cereals, Scott argues, so they domesticated us: wheat and barley, maize and rice were the seeds of civilization and its discontents. Scott argues that cropscapes organized around the seasonalities of cereals, which need planting and harvesting at one time and can be accumulated in bulk because they last well in storage, shaped the institutions and geographies, the regimes of discipline, extraction, and accumulation, the grand achievements, the violence, and inequalities of the early civilizations and—not least in significance—their classifications of humankind into the civilized and barbarian. The civilizing of cereals marked all subsequent human history, leaving indelible legacies in today's world.[99]

Scott challenges a widely held time consciousness that links the domestication of cereals not only to a Neolithic revolution and the rise of states and civilizations but also to a positive long-term history of human progress. Celebrating cereal domestication in this way assigns other human-plant relationships and temporalities (including gathering, for instance, or forest gardening, or cultivating crops like tubers, which mature year round and do not keep well) to a timeless existence outside history.[100] Our riffs have also connected the cyclical or rhythmic temporalities of crop production to longer-term patterns of social evolution, tracing the short- and long-term historical effects of crop choices. They offer more than simply different interpretations: they trace continuous threads across time spans, which in global history are typically divided into separate periods.

The datescapes of contemporary California agribusiness and eighth-century Saharan desert oases allow us to question such accepted divisions as wild-domesticated, nomadic-sedentary, and modern-premodern. The tobacco story brings us down to the microscale of plant biology, introducing the time of the plant and its reproductive rhythms as an important element of the narrative. As the "natural" life of the plant was redefined, markets, law, and labor regimes stabilized successive reformulations of tobacco's nature. The rice riff brings long-term and micro timescales together, braiding human manipulations of the life cycle of rice with the expansion of its cropscape, into the long history of the state in China, and, finally, with the rural transformations of the Green Revolution. In Ghana, we integrate human reproductive rhythms more explicitly. The springboard for the advance of the cocoa frontier was the intricate meshing of the life cycles of farmer, tree, and farm. The linkages between human and crop temporalities shape history in the short, medium, and long term—and not just in Ghana's cocoa belt, where the marriage between crop time and family time in the cocoa belt prospered. Elsewhere incompatibilities led to divorce: as noted in the rice riff, many Asian rice farmers found it impossible to keep up with the strict new timetables of the Green Revolution and in consequence gave up either rice or their farms.

In our studying time as one scale of cropscape analysis, history is part of the story. The history of Chinese millets is a story of cultural sedimentations and recuperations, a looping history of an ancient dominant cropscape gradually displaced to the margins, where it languished for several centuries only to resurface as an attractive candidate for today's landscape heritage revival, a theme to which we return.[101] The case of millet, like that of dates, reminds us that a cropscape is an assemblage, a bundle of materials, skills, and values that seldom travels entire.

Our riffs probe the connections among different scales of chronometric time—the life span of a plant, the seasonalities of a crop, the generational cycles of a family, or the grand eras of world history. We also seek to interweave not only the temporalities of plants, humans, and institutions but also the values or emotions thus evoked. This too can trouble modern preconceptions about which forces drive history, and which social institutions appear where on the march toward the modern.

This chapter reflects not only upon the temporalities of cropscapes but also upon their role in forming ideas about civilization and about the flows, eddies, and backwaters of history. The Annales historians proposed interweaving long, medium, and short timescales as a corrective to histories that privileged political events, crises, and ruptures, arguing that it was equally important to study continuity and how it was achieved. Our tactic of counterposing cases that explore differently intersecting temporal scales, from the short term of a rice plant's maturation to the millennial unfolding of the date palm's history as a crop, suggests novel ways to relate what Braudel calls the plural temporalities of history. Viewing the experience and politics of time from the perspective of plants as well as humans and their institutions, our riffs prompt general reflection upon how temporal practice and representation play out in a specific material context, thus identifying some surprising contrasts, echoes, and continuities. In asking how cropscapes make time, weaving periods together rhizomatically across the conventional cuts and seeking the meanings of time embodied in different cropscapes, this chapter sets the pattern for the book. In the next set, we turn to cropscapes and place making.

Chapter 2 Places

As crops move across space, new places take shape around them. "How," asks Hugh Raffles, "did this place I am interested in come into being? Pursuing this puzzle provokes ripples of association that shape interpretation like contour lines on a map, destabilize naturalized binaries, and shadow the unruly series of concentric circles through which a place is tied into multiple worlds."[1] Shifting constellations of relationships, time, affect, topographies of power, choices of frame and focus: in our introductory "Orientations" chapter we argued that cropscapes are places in precisely these terms and we laid out the analytical value of playing with how we frame those places in order to highlight different, perhaps unexpected, features or dynamics that raise new historical questions or insights.

Philosophers, historians, geographers, anthropologists, urbanists, and political activists have all delved into the nature of place making, analyzing places as "thick," local and textured, sites of continuous struggle teeming with associations and emotions.[2] On the one hand, places are products of habitus, practice, shared feelings and values, and everyday actions and interactions, consensual or contested—in this sense a place embodies the normalization of a sociospatial configuration, how it works and feels on the ground. On the other hand, places are dynamic; they are constantly being remade, fought over, transformed, and repositioned. These reconfigurations make the history of places, and of their connections. Furthermore, places are used to tell historical stories, and crops, it turns out, often figure as emblems in these narratives: tulips lock Amsterdam but not Istanbul into histories of capitalism; the yam gardens of the Trobriands are taken to exemplify places outside history. So each of our riffs asks how a particular place or constellation of places took shape around a crop, how they fit into history, and how their representations as a cropscape (immediate or retrospective, agreed or contested) have been used to tell world histories.

Crops make places, and places make crops, while the cropscape perspective also draws attention to how crops connect places. It is the processes of mutual shaping and identification, and their geographical and historical ramifications, that interest us here. The four riffs, on tulips, wheat, tubers, and tea, present contrasting cases of global commodities and local subsistence foods, of "useless" luxuries and "essential" staples, illustrating the complex historical and geographical impact of transplanting and naturalizing crops in new environments. The scales range from seventeenth-century walled gardens in Ottoman and Dutch cities to the global sprawl of wheatscapes in 1900, from isolated mountain plots in Highland New Guinea in the 1950s, supporting local circuits of war and exchange, to the equally isolated but vast tea estates of British India, shouldering their way into world markets.

BUBBLES, BULBS, AND OFFSETS:
TULIP PLACES IN THE HISTORY
OF CAPITALISM

Stories of moving tulips most often tell a tale about Amsterdam and its place in the history of capitalism. The well-known story fits easily into global-history narratives. The early modern Dutch are a usual (useful) suspect for an origin point in the story of the rise of the West, to which the tulip bubble of 1636–1637 (despite its foolish and unhappy ending) adds the development of clever financial instruments in futures trading—contracts for future delivery of a commodity at a set price.[3]

But the cropscape lets tulips tell a more complicated story. Dutch tulips grow from contingency and historical processes, as they grow from the offsets of bulbs. The well-known historical cropscape of Dutch tulips includes not only plants but also markets and financial instruments. The infamous tulip bubble shows also how taste and aesthetic preferences can shape finance, and how capitalism constructs morality. The bubble breaches the walls that divide taste from finance and finance from virtue. Studying tulips in terms of places, however, reveals an even more surprising offset from the history of capitalism—one that developed in a place outside the West, in Istanbul. A new history of tulips in terms of their cropscapes refines the history of global capitalism and adjusts assumptions about the rise of the capitalist West.

THE LONGUE DURÉE OF THE EPHEMERAL

The reproduction options of tulips shape these stories. To grow a tulip flower from seed can take five or ten years: the seed slowly matures into a bulb from which tulips may blossom every year. The seed stage can be bypassed, however, to cultivate flowers faster. Bulbs produce offsets—protrusions that can be pulled off and grown as bulbs themselves. Cultivating offshoot bulbs makes the plant produce tulips without the long wait. Each bulb still needs a period of chilling or vernalization each winter in order to flower. The patient winter months of dormancy are followed by a few weeks of blooming in the spring.[4] Taking offsets from bulbs, burying them for vernalization, and awaiting the glorious spring flowers, the cultivating of tulips from bulbs rather than seed gave the ephemeral flower a wider and more enduring attraction,.

TRADITIONAL TULIPS

They say tulips came to Amsterdam in 1594, although there are scattered reports from a generation earlier. The Flemish diplomat Ogier Ghiselin de Bousbecq, living in Istanbul as the Habsburg ambassador, sent bulbs and seeds of the flower, well known through Anatolia, Persia, and the Levant, to his countryman, the botanist Charles de l'Écluse (Carolus Clusius), who planted them in the imperial gardens in Vienna. Celebrated by historians of science for his role in incorporating plants from different geographic origins into general taxonomies, Clusius brought tulip bulbs with him to the University of Leiden, for teaching purposes and also for his own use. Raids on his personal stash cost him more than a hundred bulbs in 1596 and 1598. The thievery demonstrates how popular the plants would soon become in the Netherlands.[5]

From this easy story of east-to-west flower introduction, the tulip blooms, its brilliant blossoms provoking a turning point in the traditional history of capitalism. It becomes responsible for the "first financial crisis of note after the European 'discoveries' of the trading and exploitation possibilities in the rest of the world."[6] The tulip bubble grew during the dreary winter of 1636, when plague stalked Amsterdam. In the last months of the year, traders not ordinarily in the business of buying and selling flower bulbs paid outrageous prices for even common varieties.[7] By some accounts, at least one transaction for the future delivery of a single bulb surpassed ten times the annual earnings of a skilled craftsman. Just a few months later, however, in the first days of February 1637, the prices for bulbs collapsed rapidly and dramatically.

That bursting bubble has ever since functioned as a morality play about the dangers of rampant speculation and the financial innovation that enabled it. The timing of the bubble—during the winter months, when the bulbs lay dormant—meant that each transaction was a contract for future delivery. While such futures contracts became common in the exchange of agricultural commodities in the nineteenth-century wheat and cotton trades, in the early seventeenth century they were regarded with regulatory suspicion—a Dutch edict of 1610 forbade "windhandel," or "trading in the wind," which meant any transaction in items the seller did not then possess. Under this law, the financial innovation of futures trading (buying or selling a contract for future delivery of a commodity) was not prohibited as such, but contracts for nonexistent shares were simply unenforceable. Of course, futures contracts must trade interchangeable commodities, as the unseen article would be delivered later, and desirable tulips were anything but interchangeable. In fact, due to the Dutch law, at least one economic historian reads the situation as a game rather than a real commodity bubble.[8] No one went bankrupt from bad tulip trades, and the impact on the economy was actually minimal.[9] Yet the tulips' price pattern—inflation punctured, followed by sudden deflation—has often been used as a lesson against speculation in useless commodities. In the centuries since 1637, the tulip bubble has been the subject of numerous pamphlets and scholarly accounts as an example of the kind of irrational speculation that capitalism inspires, and a warning about what good, sober capitalists should avoid. In European allegorical art, the tulip went from a symbol of opulence to a symbol of vanity, and mortality.[10] Taken together, the events combined with the lessons made of them indicate how deeply tulips have traditionally rooted Amsterdam in the history of capitalism: tulips made Amsterdam, and Amsterdam made capitalism.

Of course, the timing is right too. The bursting of the tulip bubble coincides with the rise of the Dutch East India Company (Vereenigde Oost Indische Compagnie, VOC), founded in 1602.[11] The VOC is a key actor in the story of Europeans circumventing by sea the overland Silk Road that had long linked trade across Eurasia, in which Istanbul's Sublime Porte stood as the gateway between Asia and Europe. By sailing around the Cape of Good Hope and into the Indian Ocean, VOC ships gained access to the spices produced on Indonesian islands, and Dutch colonization of these places spurred new systems of world trade.[12] Like its French and English rivals, the VOC employed botanists to prospect for useful or interesting plants; they "sent regular cargoes of plants and seeds to botanical gardens and laboratories in Leiden and Amsterdam."[13] Dutch imperialists also played a role in the development of the plantation system that commodified so many cropscapes around the world. The VOC combined this well-known story of European imperialism with the institutional novelty of a public corporation that employed an impressive amount of capital raised from its 219 shareholders. The VOC also possessed from the Crown a monopoly on the Dutch trading business east of the Cape of Good Hope. Shares of colonial companies like the VOC were a large part of the paper traded on the Amsterdam stock exchange. The morality tales associated with the tulip bubble were therefore emblematic of a more generic embarrassment of riches produced by the speculative financial operations typical of Amsterdam's merchant capitalism.[14]

OTTOMAN TULIPS

But the place that matters depends on the story we are telling. Usually the analysis follows the tulips from Istanbul to Amsterdam, but let us linger in Istanbul for a little longer than is usual. The place of tulips in Istanbul is no mere origin point for the history of capitalist Amsterdam; instead, it suggests a different trajectory for the history of the world, including the history of capitalism.

First, and crucially, the Ottoman tulip was no wild plant from the East commodified by merchants in the West as they developed the capitalist system. In both East and West, the taste for tulips developed in the process of constituting what a tulip was—how it would grow, how it should look, and what it was worth, all combined in different ways as the tulipscape took shape in specific locations.[15] The fabled Orient had already commodified the plant, first by reproducing it from bulbs rather than from seeds. In the process, its physical appearance changed. The first tulips cultivated in Istanbul after its conquest by the Turks in 1453 were typically short and rounded, not too different from those found in the wild. But by the time that Suleiman the Magnificent came to the throne in 1520, the favored tulip form was characteristically almond shaped, generally considered a more delicate form. First found on the north shores of the Black Sea, these elongated tulips with needle-pointed petals were cultivated and reproduced by the vast cohort of gardeners of Suleiman's Istanbul, among whom we find the first experts dedicated exclusively to the cultivation of tulips.[16]

Second, this almond-shaped tulip form was also an important Ottoman design motif, widely reproduced on vases, tiles, and cloth.[17] Poets wrote verses about tulips. Europeans in their Dark Ages had disapproved of flowers, and representations of flowers too.[18] But now European elites were adopting both,

Tulip Courtiers Procession, Istanbul, 1533. Istanbul's courtiers celebrate the tulip in 1533, decades before the tulip's importation to Europe. The history of tulips in Istanbul moves the history of capitalism from Amsterdam to the Ottoman world. TSMK. H1344, fols. 199b–200a, *Tulip Courtiers Procession, Surname-i Hümayun*, Topkapi Palace Library. Courtesy of the Directorate of National Palaces, Istanbul.

through or from Istanbul. Both rare flowers and items decorated with their images were "part of an expanding repertoire" of "conspicuous consumption" across both the Middle East and Europe. Flowers were "displayed in festivals, tapestries, formal gardens, poetry, and the patronage of botanical sciences."[19] In this design repertoire, the tulip signified Ottoman culture as Europeans perceived it—the word for tulip derives from "turban," as headdress and flower had similar shapes.[20] The tulip's Islamic associations included peace and renewal, "spiritual turmoil and mystical intoxication, earthly power, and self negation."[21] On the other hand, the Turkish word for the flower, *lāle,* contains the same letters as *hilāl,* which means crescent, and thereby signifies Islam and Allah himself to Muslim mystics.[22] In both European and Ottoman culture, the flower carried meaning. The culture of flowers traded across Eurasia, as did the flowers themselves, but sometimes their meaning changed along the way.

In other words, the tulip did not travel to Amsterdam on its own, a clutch of bulbs for Clusius. It came as part of a cropscape that included decorative motifs and symbols of the exotic East. The Dutch tulip bubble, a foundational tale in the history of capitalism, thus also invites an opposite interpretation. It calls for an interpretation in which elements we now associate with capitalism are part of the tulip cropscape that moved from Istanbul to Amsterdam as the sixteenth century became the seventeenth.

After all, and as a third point, tulips had already been an article of commerce in Ottoman culture for a long time. In the fifteenth century, most tulips and other precious flowers were bred and grown in Ottoman royal gardens across the empire. Profits from sales of the flowers to ordinary people went to the treasury, and the state set up a flower institute to breed new types and set standards.[23] The ambassador Bousbecq (who sent the bulbs to Clusius half a century later), describing his travels through Turkey from 1554 to 1562, was fascinated by the flower business and flower culture, by tulips in particular. He offered a profusion of details about the sophisticated garden culture of Istanbul and was genuinely surprised by the conspicuous consumption of flowers he found in Turkey and the great sums of money spent on it.

One of Istanbul's characteristic products in the global marketplace was flowers. People came to Istanbul by sea to buy tulip bulbs as early as 1546.[24] Tulips were shipped from Istanbul markets to Vienna, Antwerp, Paris, and London as luxury exotic objects used and enjoyed by Europeans seduced by the Orientalist accounts of travelers, ambassadors, and merchants.[25] Although the Ottoman state attempted to preserve its own revenues by restricting the number of private flower sellers, by 1600 it had lost control: as in the Netherlands at almost exactly the same time, commerce had overtaken the world of growing as well as selling flowers.[26] In 1595 a decree had complained that the number of flower shops had increased illegally from five shops to two hundred, and efforts to keep the number down were unsuccessful.[27] By 1630, there were eighty flower shops and three hundred professional florists in the Ottoman capital.[28]

The blossoming of the flower trade and the way it burst free of state regulation indicate its capitalist nature—private enterprise overtaking government control and monopolies.[29] Before too long, and certainly by the time of the Dutch tulip bubble, demand was on the rise across Europe. Fashionable French women sometimes wore an array of tulips at the tops of their gowns.[30] Europeans sometimes associated Eastern culture with extravagance and luxury, but the consumption inspired by those associations also played an important role in the history of capitalism. Max Weber associated Protestantism and self-denial with capitalism, but the sort of sensual, sumptuous, indulgent ease that Europeans judged as Ottoman was also capitalist—long before Thorstein Veblen recognized the power of conspicuous consumption to mark socioeconomic differences and stimulate growth in developed capitalist societies.[31]

TASTE AND THE MARKET

Istanbul and Amsterdam have been assigned different associations in narratives of global history—lazy East, capitalist West.[32] But it was a specifically Dutch preference for a particular ornamental characteristic of some tulips that accounted for the inflation of the tulip bubble. The seventeenth-century Dutch loved best the tulips with streaky, flame-like patterns on their petals, such as the Semper Augustus tulip, whose bulbs commanded some of the highest prices during the bubble. The Dutch treasured streaky, stripy patterns in any material: jaspers and agates, marbled papers (which also happened to come from Turkey), and of course tulips. Centuries later, it turned out that the favored streaks and flames were not a trait bred into the plant itself—they originated not in the bulb or seed but instead in a mosaic virus that was unpredictable in its desired effects. Some buyers insisted on seeing a bulb they had bought in flower before it was lifted from the soil for delivery, to be sure it would produce the characteristics they had purchased. But the virus that made beautiful tulips could weaken or kill the plant, and although bulbs could survive for several years, the pattern was seldom repeated.[33] Without this particular Dutch taste for streaky patterns, another import from East to West, the history of capitalism and the financial instrument of futures trading might well have taken a different path.

Amsterdam during the 1636–1637 tulip bubble was not, however, a singular outpost in the rise of capitalism. Contemporary Istanbul was likewise a place where the expanding cult of tulips and other formerly rare flowers furthered the rise of a prosperous, cosmopolitan consumer society with dynamic markets. But the mechanisms and cultures of the Ottoman markets differed from those in the Netherlands, not least because the state engaged at different levels in the two cases.

The flower trade of Istanbul was shot through with flames of passion. Rich and poor all craved flowers. Some novel bulbs sold for such high prices that the state issued lists with price ceilings, frequently updated. In around 1700 the state established a flower council to judge and accredit new varieties; members had to have bred at least one new flower type. Breeders included men and women, courtiers and clerics, physicians, lumber merchants, and porters. These enthusiasts experimented not only with local almond-shaped tulips but also with the new Dutch varieties. They met for discussions and penned copious essays and articles, still preserved in the archives. Turkish historians have re-marked on the parallels between these aficionados and the naturalist circles of Renaissance Europe.[34]

The accreditation function of the Ottoman state flower councils combined with the labors of flower cultivators and endorsement by poets to establish norms, create flower brands, and diffuse a floral aesthetics that shaped industry as well as taste and commerce.[35] Tulips were prominent motifs on Iznik pottery wares and Bursa silks, two industries where workshops flourished by balancing court commissions against private orders for internal or export commodities. In addition to these sources of revenue, the Ottoman Empire, like the Dutch, drew much of its wealth from controlling key nodes in global networks of commerce. There too the Ottoman state played a more prominent role than the Dutch.[36]

Historians today agree that it is not possible to understand either European or world history without factoring in the Ottoman experience. But serious study of Ottoman economic and material history is just gathering strength. The story of tulips begins to furnish the empty spaces.

If the tulip has received so much attention, it is because of its star role as the enduring symbol of Ottoman culture and society, their achievements and failings. Along with coffee shops, tulips feature prominently in stories about rise and de-cline in Ottoman history. One such story centers on Istanbul's own supposed tulip craze, during the so-called Tulip Period, *Lāle Devri* (1700–1730). It was an early twentieth-century historian, Ahmed Refik, who first coined the term, which has now entered the official history syllabus and the Turkish heritage industry.

For Refik and other young Turkish republican intellectuals of the early twen-tieth century the Lāle Devri functioned as a morality play, just as the Dutch bubble served European moralists. The reign of Sultan Ahmed III (1703–1730) was a period of modernization and Westernization, a herald, albeit unsuccessful, of the changes Refik and his friends hoped for. After the war between the Ottoman Empire, on the one side, and the Republic of Venice and the Habsburg monarchy of Austria, on the other, came to an end with the Passarowitz peace treaty in 1718, the sultan appointed Ibrahim Pasha, a reformer and a passionate tulip lover, as his grand vizier. The vizier sent a mission to France in 1720–1721 to observe the "means of civilization and education," including fortifications and industries, that could be applied at home. In 1722 work began on Saadabad, a palace supposedly modeled on Versailles, and the first printing press was established in Istanbul. In addition to their public popularity, tulips symbolized the Ottoman regime and its new policies. Myriad tulips were planted in royal gardens and flaunted at lavish court ceremonies where, for example, tortoises with candles on their backs illuminated evening feasts held in tulip gardens.[37] In Refik's tale, tulips punctuate a story of precocious imitation of Western modernity brought to an end by a violent popular uprising that cost Ibrahim Pasha his life, followed by a wave of Islamist reactionism that dragged the Ottoman Empire out of the modern world.

Refik's story reverses the place of tulips. The movement of tulips from East to West in the seventeenth century and its role in catalyzing modernity are now echoed by a matching movement of tulips from West to East in an Ottoman tulip craze a hundred years later. Not surprisingly, the experiment cannot prevail over Oriental traditionalism, and the project of modernization fails. Reflecting the secular, nationalist aspirations and fears of the Young Turks of the 1900s, this is a very Eurocentric representation of Istanbul as a place of tulips. More postmodern scholars have uncovered both the historiography of Refik's tulip history and the purposes it has served. They also provide alternative interpretations. Can Erimtan, for example, notes that tulip culture in Istanbul, including imports of Dutch and French varieties, flourished uninterrupted between 1600 and 1800, while he finds more regional than French inspiration in the plans of the destroyed Saadabad palace. Erimtan argues that both the palace and the period may say less about European influence than about how the Ottoman Empire was projecting a satisfactory conclusion to its rivalry with the Safavid (Persian) Empire to its east. Ariel Salzmann, for her part, reinterprets the outbreak of violence not as religious reactionism but as social conflict: the passions of ordinary people impoverished by years of war and official neglect were ignited by lavish court expenditure on frivolities like tulips.[38]

In these stories, we can see how the movement of tulips gains new meanings from the larger perspective of the cropscape. Cropscape teaches us that instead of the traditional movement from east to west, the tulip cropscape and its meanings can be seen to move from east to west and then back east again. Perhaps it is in Istanbul that we should look for important turning points in the history of global capitalism, which springs from surprising soils and contains sophisticated tastes, luxury, and refuge from the world as well as markets, finance, and trade relationships that signify supply and demand. Tulips tell us of new places to look as the cropscape provides new ways of looking.

Traditional global history treats capitalism as originating in the early modern West and then moving to the Americas. Specific mechanisms of capitalist enterprise are often traced along the same path.[39] Contracts for future delivery, for example, associated with the dormant period of tulip bulbs during the dreary winter of 1636–1637, eventually blossom into the story of the commodification of wheat in Chicago. Was Chicago the new Amsterdam? Was wheat the new tulip in the history of global capitalism?

WILD WESTS OF WHEAT
THE WESTERN WHEATSCAPE

D. W. Griffith filmed it better. In *A Corner in Wheat* (1909), a ruthless speculator storms the wheat-exchange pit and gains control over the whole world grain market, produces the ruin of farmers in their fields, makes bread prices unaffordable for poor urban dwellers, celebrates his immense profits with a lavish banquet, and drowns under a torrent of grain after inadvertently falling into a grain elevator.[40] Griffith's experimentation with the new media connected the disparate places that constituted the American wheatscape—fields, bakery, exchange, elevator, banquet table—while enabling the confrontation of people who would have never encountered one another in real life. The unprecedented use in film of parallel editing juxtaposed the hungry workers in the bakery line with bacchants making toasts to the wheat speculator.

Effective but not free of demagoguery. American wheat farmers on the Great Plains in the early twentieth century, organized in cooperatives that owned their grain elevators, bore little resemblance to the idealized passive peasant filmed by Griffith, who carried on his shoulders the injustices of the world.[41] Railways, while absent in the movie, transformed the plains of the American West into the hinterland of Chicago, with wheat flowing like torrents of gold from farms in the Dakotas or Oklahoma into the city's grain elevators and from there into major consuming markets of the world such as New York and London.[42] The standardization of wheat into main three types—white winter wheat, red winter wheat, and spring wheat—subdivided into four categories according to quality—club, No. 1, No. 2, and rejected—facilitated transportation by replacing sacks with bulk shipping in railway cars.

A Corner in Wheat. A high-society party was part of the wheatscape. Still from D. W. Griffith, *A Corner in Wheat* (1909), courtesy of Photofest, Inc.

Standardization (an element significantly missing from the Dutch but not from the Ottoman tulip stories) also crucially enabled the buying and selling of contracts for the future delivery of grain independent of its actual presence in Chicago elevators. In 1875, the size of the actual grain business in Chicago was some $200 million, while the trade in futures amounted to no less than $2 billion. The emergence of the futures market in Chicago turned wheat into the epitome of commodification, a process through which the material product of tilling the soil seems totally detached from the market value of wheat futures, object of the risky games of speculators. While in Griffith's film the commodification of wheat had a mysterious, elusive nature, with the different places of the cropscape connected by the director's innovative use of editing, historians following the path of William Cronon's *Nature's Metropolis* have revealed the materiality of such connections and their dependence on railways, telegraph lines, grain elevators, standards, and futures contracts.

MANY WHEATSCAPES

Nevertheless, oversimplification was one of Griffith's main virtues. If one embraces the abstract nature of the film, the wheat cropscape loses its American exclusiveness and might instead be perceived as a more global phenomenon. The viewer could not in fact tell if the story had to do with Chicago and the American West or if it referred instead to San Francisco and wheat cultivation in California, since wheat was the primary agricultural export of this state until late in the nineteenth century.[43] Or did it refer to Odessa, the main wheat port of the Black Sea, and that mythical peasant captured by the camera was tilling the southern steppes of the Russian Empire instead of the Great Plains? Or was it the Pampas and Buenos Aires? Sydney and Southeastern Australia? Karachi and the Punjab? At the turn of the century, there were many other wests and Chicagos connected through telegraphs and railways loaded with wheat.

In 1900 exports from the United States and Russia made up no less than 45 percent of the world wheat market, each exporting one to three million tons of grain every year.[44] Odessa is thus an obvious example to counter Chicago exceptionalism, with the steppes of the southern parts of the Russian Empire as

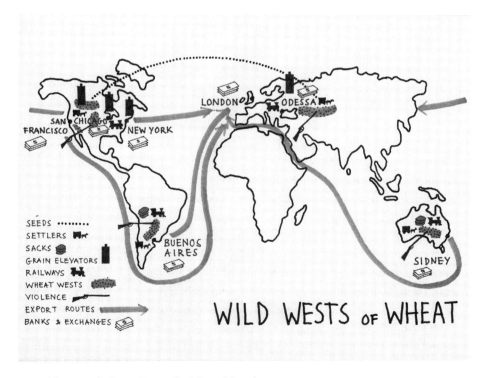

Wild wests of wheat. Drawn by Marta Macedo.

the eastern functional equivalent of the American West.[45] The Indian wars waged by the U.S. Army in the 1870s on the Northern plains, to replace Lakotas, Cheyennes, and Arapaho with white settlers, had their counterpart one hundred years earlier with the settlement on the northern shores of the Black and Caspian seas of peasant farmers from Russia, Ukraine, and Germany, at the expense of nomads and their pastoral economy.[46] While the peasant population of the region in 1719 was about fifty thousand, in 1897 there were almost five million peasants living on the steppes. Odessa's harbor became the central node of a network of commerce that connected the black-soil wheat steppes of southern Russia with urban consumers in Western Europe. By 1852 the city boasted no fewer than 564 grain warehouses, "built with the same elegance as the dwelling houses," owned not only by rich Russian landowners turned wealthy merchants but also by international traders of Greek, Italian, German, French, and English origin.[47] Griffith could easily have filmed his lavish banquet in one of Odessa's many luxurious French restaurants.

INTERCONNECTED WHEATSCAPES

Economic historians have urged us to look at wheat markets of the second half of the nineteenth century as more than parallel stories of fast-growing cities connected through technological infrastructures to some frontier settlement area. They have emphasized how convergence of wheat prices demonstrates the global nature of the commodity: while in the 1850s price shocks in London had major impacts in the United States and in continental Europe, by the end of the century, with the increased presence of American wheat in the global market, the ups and downs of wheat prices in New York determined not only the affordability of bread in London but also the fortune of thousands of peasants in the Ukraine. It's not just that the different wests shared common elements of the cropscape, they were also interconnected.[48]

Interconnectedness goes a long way in accounting for the specificities of each wheat frontier. The Argentinian and Canadian wheat booms of the early twentieth century, for example, make for interesting connected comparisons.[49] Both have in common the combination of railways, settlers, and international capital operating in all other wheat frontiers, but while the wheatscape of Canada's western provinces depended on a large network of grain elevators, these were absent in the Argentinian case. The Canadian storage infrastructure allowed for wheats from Manitoba or Saskatchewan to arrive in Europe already classified according to the different standards, but Argentinian wheat from the Pampas was mostly shipped in bags and was priced only upon arrival by officials of the London Corn Trade Association, who established a monthly "medium quality."[50] The different roles of Canadian and Argentinian wheats in the European market might help explain such contrasts. Europe's domestic wheat production reached the market mostly from July to December. The main interest of Argentinian producers, who started to harvest in January, was to ship as much wheat as possible, as fast as possible across the Atlantic, so it would reach Europe in the periods when it had less domestic grain to rely on.

Canadian wheats, by contrast, were harvested in August and September, and they were sold in Europe in the fall, mostly as hard wheats that complemented European soft wheats to produce better quality flour. They were used for "tuning" flours suited to the increasingly mechanized bread production of the turn of the century. This specialized role of Canadian wheat justified its high market value but also required that it arrive in Europe already graded. Now, grading of grain demands its storage in elevators, and grading is virtually unattainable when grain is handled in bags. Argentinian producers whose challenge was to get as much volume of their soft wheats as fast as they could to the European market had no interest in investing in an expensive storage infrastructure and continued relying on bags. But Canadians depended on the standardization enabled by elevators to make their hard wheats such as Manitoba and Red Fife useful for European millers.

WHEAT VARIETIES AND THE VIOLENT WEST

This reference to the different wheats, soft and hard, circulating across the Atlantic suggests the importance of not taking wheat as a homogeneous entity. It is not just that markets demanded different grades of wheat to commodify it. To properly understand the interconnected development of the several wheat frontiers, it is crucial to unpack wheat and acknowledge its many different varieties. As eloquently demonstrated by Alan Olmstead and Paul Rhode, the invasion of Europe at the end of the nineteenth century by cheap grains imported from the Americas, Russia, and Australia depended on the introduction of wheat varieties able to reproduce and thrive under the harsher conditions of the new settlement regions.[51] In the United States, "all the transportation improvements imaginable could not have induced English wheats to thrive in North Dakota."[52] Railways, grain elevators, and futures exchanges depended on the introduction of varieties adapted to the different wests.

The expansion of the American wheat frontier moved the center of grain production some 1,260 kilometers northwest from West Virginia in 1839 to Nebraska by 1919.[53] Such movement was achieved not by continuing to cultivate the soft wheats previously used in Pennsylvania or Ohio but by substituting hard wheats entirely new to America, namely, Red Fife (hard red spring wheat), Turkey (hard red winter wheat), and Kubanka (durum wheat). These three varieties originated, significantly enough, in Russia and Ukraine. Red Fife, which spread to the northern U.S. plains (Montana and the Dakotas) in the 1860s and dominated production for forty years, was introduced by David Fife, a Scottish immigrant who on his Ontario farm inbred a wheat plant he had obtained in 1842 on the docks of Glasgow from a shipment received from Danzig.[54] (Before Odessa on the Black Sea became the primary export center of Russian wheat in the mid-nineteenth century, the Hanseatic ports of the Baltic such as Danzig dominated the shipping of Russian grain to Western Europe.) As for Turkey wheat, the dominant cultivar of the southern Great Plains (Nebraska, Kansas, Oklahoma, Texas), it arrived in Kansas with Mennonites in the 1870s. After leaving Prussia to settle southern Russia in the end of the eighteenth century, profiting from the privileges granted by Catherine the Great, Mennonites moved to the American plains, attracted by railway boosters.[55]

Looking at Red Fife and Turkey wheat brings overlooked humans into the global narrative of the wheat frontier.[56] Griffith had filmed peasants as passive elements trying to survive the ups and downs of elusive market forces. But human migrants played an active role in expanding commercial wheat cultivation areas. This is not to suggest favoring one class of historical elements—human migrants, wheat varieties—over others—futures, railways, elevators. The point is rather to embrace the complexity of the wheatscape in order to write more insightful stories of the global wheat frontier. Mentioning Mennonites is not simply a redemption tale of the hardworking farmer of German origin made invisible by the global market. The Mennonite story is one that involves individual migrants as well as state policies of settling new areas for commercial agriculture on the Black Sea steppes or on the American Great Plains. Russia's state bureaucracy or American transcontinental railways backed by the federal state shouldn't be neglected in any story of Mennonites cultivating Turkey wheat in Kansas. In fact, frontier settlement was brutal business, and the wests mentioned here were scenes of some of the most violent episodes of the respective national histories of the United States, Argentina, Canada, Russia, and Australia.

Moreover, the method of seriously considering the nonhuman wheat plant as deserving historians' attention also displaces the historical role of Mennonites as brave settlers of the frontier. The wheat varieties they cultivated in the Crimea and later in Kansas were the result of practices associated with Nogai Tatars expelled from the region by Russian eastward expansion. Consistently misrepresented as nomads who had to be removed to make place for civilizing European settlers, Tatars were the ones responsible for the existence of wheat varieties valued for their ability to resist the continental climate conditions of the steppes and later the American Great Plains.[57] Like our earlier story of dates, the story of the Turkey wheat cultivated by Tatars on the steppes of the Black Sea, taken by Mennonite settlers to America, and then triumphing in the global wheat market undermines the simplistic binaries of nomad/settler and West/East. The wheatscape filmed by Griffith, which made Chicago the fastest-growing metropolis of the Western world in the second half of the nineteenth century, was the result as much of Russian eastward expansion onto the steppes and Tartars' agricultural practices as of American expansion onto the Great Plains.

The traditional tale that associates wheat with standardization, Chicago, and capitalism is far too simple to truly understand the dynamics of global history. Examining wheat as a crop on the move reveals a more complex geography, and a deeper history, to that iconic cropscape.

TUBER TRAVELS

The grand narratives of agricultural history reserve the star roles for cereals. Today's global crops of wheat, maize, and rice dominate narratives of the rise and fall of civilizations and empires, the development and circulation of expertise and capital, and the shaping of terrain, technical practices, and social relations, from prehistory through to the present. Anthropologists have long been fascinated by the material, moral, and ontological intricacies of small and apparently isolated tubergrowing societies. The "Irish" potato's well-documented impact on industrializing Europe has ensured its recognition as a crop that "changed the world's history."[58] But otherwise historians have seldom incorporated tuber crops into their models of historical process, relegating them to the status of local, minor, or secondary crops despite their demonstrable contribution not only to human diets but also to colonial expansion and industrial development.

So, do tuber crops and their cropscapes constitute a distinctive category? And if so, what could this category contribute to our historiography of places, whether at the micro- or the macroscale?

Although they belong to different genera, all tuber crops share three key botanical and material characteristics that govern how they are grown, consumed, conserved and exchanged, and theorized by scholars. First, tuber crops are typically reproduced not from seed (sexual reproduction) but by planting eye sections of selected tubers (vegetative reproduction or cloning), which ensures the permanence of desirable characteristics but risks vulnerability to disease.[59] Second, tubers thrive on poor land and yield vastly more calories than other food crops, but they are typically lower in proteins than cereals are. Only if consumed with supplements like game, fish, vegetables, or milk do tubers provide a sustaining diet.[60]

76 Places

Finally, unlike cereals, many of which can be kept for years, unless intensively processed tubers soon germinate or rot. This means that reciprocities and exchanges of tubers are typically more local than those built around cereals, while power relations and value creation take very different forms.

These characteristics distinguish tubers from the cereals and other commodity crops around which various familiar historical theories and models have been constructed.[61] Tubers form distinctive cropscapes and travel differently from other major crops. They cross oceans as treasured staples or useful ballast but seldom travel as commodities in themselves. Sometimes they are the primary food crop shaping a society, as in the Trobriand Islands or the Andean Altiplano. Elsewhere, as subsistence crops, they sustain the production and export of commodities like wheat and flax (in nineteenth-century Ireland) or sugar (in colonial Brazil or late imperial Guangdong). Tubers prompt us to develop alternative ways of theorizing food, commodity production, and history. Colonial historians have recently proposed *anti-commodities* as a way to think about these fluctuating relations, though *para-commodities* might more accurately describe the symbiosis in the case of tubers; we return to this later.[62] Meanwhile, anthropological perspectives on tuber cropscapes raise significant extra-economic questions about plants and humans that historians of biopower and biopolitics cannot afford to ignore.[63] So here we consider the anthropology of tuberscapes and "small places, large issues."[64]

"ALWAYS HUNGRY, NEVER GREEDY"

The densely theoretical anthropological literature on small-scale tuber-dependent societies, notably the Trobriand Islanders, highlanders of New Guinea and small Amazonian tribes, focuses on kinship, meaning, value, and forms of exchange in worlds where humans, plants, animals, and spirits are all active and where identities often fuse.[65] "Manioc beer is the life of Runa people," and "Trobrianders regard yams as people and people as yams."[66]

While the numbers of people concerned are small, the literature on small-scale tuber cultivators and the theories elaborated around their lives are very complex. To simplify the picture, we begin with the Trobriands, then bring in some salient features from Highland New Guinea and Amazonia. Readers may suspect our use of the "ethnographic present" in the following accounts, yet—as we note in the final section of this riff—materially and socially these tuberscapes have shown remarkable resilience in the face of global transformations, raising some interesting questions about the historiography of the longue durée.

Bronisław Malinowski, the founder of fieldwork-based anthropology, first brought the Trobriand Islands to the intellectual attention of Europeans with

Filling a yam house (*bwaima*) in a Trobriand village. The yams are taken from the conical heaps and put into the storehouse by the owner's wife's brother. Bronisław Malinowski, *Argonauts of the Western Pacific,* Plate XXXIII, p. 160. Archives of the London School of Economics and Political Science.

Argonauts of the Western Pacific (1922). These flat coral islands off the east coast of New Guinea support yams as the main crop, supplemented by fish, taro, bananas, coconuts, and pork at feasts. The Trobrianders, Malinowski observed, are "splendid tillers of the soil and first-rate fishermen," and they use the rituals of their garden magicians to inaugurate every stage of cultivation. Every man has biological or adopted sisters for whom he grows plots of yams; in return, his family is fed by yams grown by his wife's brothers. A man is the father of the yams he grows in the plots he tends, his wife is their mother; the circulation of these yams, and of their daughters (planting yams) and sons (exchange yams), "enmeshes the whole community into a network of obligations and dues, one constant flow of gift and counter-gift." The chief gives out land and in return receives about a third of all the yams grown, which he displays in magnificent yam houses, *bwaima,* built and ceremonially filled by the villagers.[67]

Since yams don't keep, the sequence of growing, harvesting, presenting, and displaying them must be constantly repeated. Villagers describe how these collective tasks transform them morally: they begin as hungry, greedy people ready to devour yams without stopping; by the time the bwaima is filled, they have lost their hunger for yams and are content to see the community's wealth gathered in their chief's bwaima.[68] The lavish bwaima display confers prestige on the chief and honor on the village; the chief redistributes yams as food to provision public feasts, trading expeditions, war parties, and working groups or converts them into objects of permanent wealth and prestige by providing yams to craftsmen who make stone axe blades, necklaces, and armshells. These valuables the chief collects or bestows as ceremonial gifts within the village itself, or feeds into the archipelago-wide circuits of the famous *kula* ring. As the armshells and necklaces pass ceremonially between hereditary kula partners they accrue value—but they are not commodities, they cannot be sold for money or converted into the yams that constitute the subsistence sphere of Trobriand exchange.[69]

Yams, then, are the fundamental substance that circulates through Trobriand society like blood, nourishing, sustaining, and defining. Yams are food, wealth, and social responsibility, the children of farmers, the bond between brother and sister, the stuff of chiefly wealth and prestige. Yams circulate locally as goods in the subsistence sphere of exchange; converted upward into the shell necklaces of the kula sphere, the produce of the tiny yam plots binds together far-flung islands and knits together partnerships that endure for many generations.

Malinowski explained that the gift relations of the Trobriand exchange do not exist outside economics but represent an alternative form of rationality from the profit maximizing and "enlightened self-interest" that supposedly drive capitalism.[70] Marcel Mauss further developed this insight into a theory of the dynamics of gift exchange, the obligation to give, receive, and repay. Mauss contrasted the moral obligations and enduring social entanglements inherent in the ideal type of "pure" gift exchange with the impersonal, one-off interactions of another ideal type, "pure" commodity or contractual transactions, while noting that both rationalities coexist in varying degrees in any real act of exchange. Malinowski's Trobriand research also inspired the political economist Karl Polanyi's critique, in *The Great Transformation,* of modern capitalist markets, which, he argued, were a specific historical formation rather than the natural outcome of rational progress. Polanyi insisted that it was dangerous to treat markets as if they were disembedded from society, prompting a long-term debate between formalists, "who believe that the difference between Western-type market and primitive-subsistence economies is one of degree," and substantivists, "who believe it is one of kind."[71] These anthropological investigations of regimes of value resurface in the cultural analysis of capitalism offered by some of the most perceptive current global historians, including Arjun Appadurai.[72]

The sweet-potato cropscapes of Highland New Guinea prompted the elaboration of another influential social theory, cultural ecology, which addresses the role of culture in resource management.[73] Among the mosaic of small Highland groups, pigs play a crucial role in building prestige and maintaining social alliances and identity.[74] Pigs are paid in compensation to the families of allies killed in raids, they are sacrificed to the ancestors in cyclical rituals of tribal boundary marking, and they are the key valuable in the region's *moka* exchanges: escalating gifts and counter-gifts between clan groups in which "big-men" wield great influence. In a boundary ceremony, where hundreds of pigs are sacrificed, all but the immature pigs are slaughtered, the blood is dedicated to the ancestors, most of the meat is given to allied tribes, and some of the meat is consumed in a communal feast. In a moka the live pigs are given away to another tribe: the goal is to give more than has been received, ratcheting up the stakes continually. For one moka, in 1974, prepared over five years, Ongka, big-man of the Kawelka tribe, hoped to assemble six hundred pigs as well as sundry cows, cassowaries, a truck, and £5,500 in cash.[75]

How is it possible for small tribes of swidden horticulturalists to raise such huge numbers of pigs? In 1967 Roy Rappaport's classic of ecological anthropology, *Pigs for the Ancestors,* investigated the sustainability of the pig-based ritual cycle, conducting a quantitative, energetic, and environmental study of Highland villagers' garden yields, dietary requirements, labor resources, and the costs of pig raising.[76]

Ideally, boundary rituals were held every five years; moka likewise took several years to prepare. Noting that the size of the tribe's pig herd fluctuated wildly depending on the point reached in the cycle of ritual obligations, Rappaport concluded that there was a tipping point in pig raising. Big-men acquired most new pigs but kept only a few themselves, for their wives to raise, and "invested" the others with in-laws. Up to a certain number, pigs could conveniently be fed on imperfect sweet potatoes and household waste, while their manure and rootling improved the sweet-potato gardens. But too many pigs damaged gardens and competed with villagers for food. At that point holding the ritual became urgent. Wives, who tended the pigs and grew the sweet potatoes and manioc that fed them, were the first to agitate for pig-eliminating rituals to be held.

Despite the violent short-term fluctuations, research on the historical ecology of the New Guinea pig-potato cropscape argues for its long-term sustainability, prompting Jared Diamond to portray the highlanders as a society that "chose to succeed."[77] Cultural ecology's interest in human-environmental cycles and their durability intersects with the concerns of historians of both climate and world systems.[78] Meanwhile the methodological fusing of biological science and cultural analysis pioneered by cultural ecology in studies of environments such as the Highland pig-potato cropscape is currently finding new forms in historical ecology and the historiography of the Anthropocene.[79]

The jungles of Amazonia are the heartland both of manioc domestication and of structuralist anthropology, whose theories address the restless, fertile tensions and resolutions of raw and cooked, male and female, human and nonhuman. The Napo Runa of Ecuador are hunter-gatherers who also tend manioc gardens. Men fish and hunt for game; the meat they bring back is prepared and cooked by women and thus converted into food, human sustenance. Women grow, prepare, and cook manioc, the food staple; more important still, they brew it (in pots referred to as wombs) into *asua,* manioc beer. Men passionately desire asua, which women bestow upon them in erotically charged presentations when they return from the hunt. Women just as passionately desire meat. Thus every action, every meal becomes a celebration of gender complementarity. Asua itself is celebrated as the essence and breath of Runa being. Meat and asua circulate constantly between relations. In marriage feasts, they are exchanged among groups often living many kilometers apart, binding together the local community and the whole Runa people.[80]

Such expressions of Amazonian value and identity through local and long-distance exchanges of food and drink, substance, and spouses, can be traced back through ethnohistorical research to pre-Hispanic times.[81] Today's research brings together local people, botanical scientists, and anthropologists to recover the history of forests and of forest crops like manioc. Mirroring the indigenous Amerindian custom of recognizing the agency of animals and plants along with humans, this research unfolds a story where the desires and affordances of the manioc plant itself, as well as of humans, account for a domestication that is a dialogue between "wild" and "tame," adventitious and tended plants, gatherers and gardeners, evolving over millennia.[82]

The cropscapes of manioc and other tubers sustained areas of dense population— possibly states—for centuries before the arrival of the Spanish, while other forest-dweller groups tended "cultural forests" of palms, Brazil nuts, and other resources. We are thus dealing not with a definitive pre-Columbian transition from foraging to farming, followed by a postconquest collapse and reversion to primitive ways, but rather with a series of shifts in the equilibrium between alternative lifestyles. In the livelihood mosaic of Amazonia, argues Laura Rival, groups chose according to circumstance to move between "trekking," which relies on the semidomesticates of "cultural forests," and settled farming of intensively cultivated domesticates. Such choice making is still observed today.[83] These insights could usefully be extended to unpack the complex synchronicities and mobilities that underlie apparently linear crop histories or homogeneous cropscapes elsewhere. They also evoke the slippage between para-commodity and commodity discussed in the section on tubers in chapter 5, "Compositions."

In fact there are still more challenging lessons to be learned from the Amazonian cropscape, for it calls into question the very concept of domestication that plays such an important part in European representations of the stages of human civilization and mastery over the natural world. The boundaries between humans and other species that appeared so clear and insurmountable to European colonizers were meaningless to the peoples of lowland South America and the Caribbean. With regard to what we think of as human-animal relations, Amazonian thought, characterized by anthropologists as perspectivism, "supposes a constant epistemology and variable ontologies. . . . What changes when passing from one species of subject to another is the 'objective correlative,' the referent of these concepts: what jaguars see as 'manioc beer' (the proper drink of people, jaguar-type or otherwise), humans see as blood.' "[84] Less attention has been paid by anthropologists or historians to the place of plants in such interspecies intersubjectivities, although Philippe Descola observed that when planting manioc cuttings Achuar women water them lavishly with a red concoction of annatto: this is the blood that they hope will satisfy the vampiristic hunger of the infant manioc plants, who will otherwise suck the blood from village infants for the sustenance they need to burgeon.[85] Meanwhile, several instances of Amazonian cultures representing "manioc as a plant person animated by a 'spirit owner' " lead Laura Rival and Doyle McKey to propose that perspectivism might be an important element guiding indigenous plant domestication practices.[86]

While Rival and McKey still employ the term "domestication" in an Amerindian context, Marcy Norton argues for discarding the wild-domesticated binary altogether. "The fundamental dividing line was between wild and tame beings [which] bridged and superseded the human/non-human binary, grouping human kin and tamed animals on one side and human enemies and prey on the other." Animals killed on the hunt were wild and could therefore be eaten. When human enemies were taken in war, adult men were killed and often ritually cannibalized, a procedure that literally incorporated them into the community of their captors. Captive women and children, however, were deemed suitable for taming, feeding, and incorporation into the community either as adoptive kin or as slaves.[87] But when Amerindians caught and tamed a wild animal—whether a parrot, a fox, a deer, or a manatee—they did not seek to domesticate it, that is to say to confine its movements, control its reproduction, set it to work, or consume it. Once a human had started feeding the animal it became their *iegue,* the same term used for an adopted child. It was unthinkable to eat it or even its eggs (in the case of the chickens introduced by Europeans and valued by indigenes as companions and, surprisingly to us, for their song).

As with the slippages observed by Rival between gathering and gardening, trekking and settling, Norton argues convincingly for the longue durée of this distinctive categorization of self and other, human and nonhuman. While historians and anthropologists have already drawn lessons from Amerindian societies for understanding human-animal relations not only in the Amazon but also in human experience more generally, we do not know how well these perspectives on wild and tame might apply to human-plant relations. After all, Amerindians eat the manioc that they garden or gather. Nevertheless, we probably should think of the relationship in terms other than of domestication, or indeed of crop or cropscape. And we should also be ready to draw upon these qualifications of the boundaries between wild, tame, and domesticated to reflect more generally on how human-plant relations have been understood historically and in the present.

TUBERS AND HISTORY

Anthropological theories around tuberscapes have grown rhizomatically, shooting out roots and tendrils of debate from fertile eyes and nodes, and growing in tangles as thick, vigorous, and enduring as the tuber plants themselves.[88] The tuberscapes that the theories address might at first seem to be tiny, introverted backwaters cut off from the trading channels and great transformations of modern history and therefore without historical significance. Their spaces and temporalities are shaped around cycle and counter-cycle and the knitting together of small, isolated places, rather than straight lines of outward travel or evolutionary trees of progress and expansion.

Yet, as the anthropologists have also shown, these tuber places do not exist outside history: they have successfully ridden challenges from pre-Columbian states, conquistadores, and missionaries; rubber, mining, and timber companies; sugar and coffee plantations; and colonial officers, parliamentary representation, NGOs, and contemporary media to survive into the present day.[89] As historians we should ponder the implications of this resilience. We should also consider the part that such alternative, "anti-historical" patterns of scale, direction, and chronicity might play in the grand sweeps of global transformation that captivate the global-historical imagination.

Studies of small-scale tuberscapes emphasize the social, moral, and extra-economic efficacy of crops and cropscapes, and highlight alternative spatial and temporal scales. What if we extend such analysis beyond the ostensibly precapitalist cropscapes of Melanesia or Amazonia studied by anthropologists to consider analogous dimensions of value and potency in other, more clearly capitalist or longue durée cropscapes? Within the familiar frameworks and narratives of global history, as we shall see in "Compositions," a focus on tubers and their travels highlights how often the dynamics of "major" crops, their patterns of reproduction and expansion and the institutions within which they are produced, depend upon place making by "minor" crops (or para-commodities) like tubers.

TEA: LOCAL CROPSCAPES, GLOBAL MARKETS

Tea, on the other hand, has almost invariably been cultivated as a commodity. In 1840 the world's tea came from China; half a century later, India rivaled China as the preeminent "tea country." In "Sizes" we discuss the rise of the Indian tea industry from the perspective of unfolding tensions between ideologies and practical realities of scale. Here we trace the selective processes by which the British reassembled elements of the Chinese commercial teascape to build up their own rival tea industry in India. We ask what kinds of place were constructed to grow tea in India, and how China as a tea place was affected by the global competition with Indian tea plantations.[90]

THE CHINESE ROOTSTOCK

In the late 1830s the British began experimenting with tea growing in Assam to provide substitutes for expensive imports from China. They transplanted Chinese tea plants, Chinese tea workers, and many other forms of Chinese skill and expertise into Indian territory, adapting them to this alien natural and social environment through various processes of *naturalization,* which notably included scaling tea gardens up to plantation size and applying "the skill and science of the Europeans."[91]

Tea was already long established as a commercial crop in China. In the 1830s, as for most of the preceding millennium, it was grown in large quantities but on a small scale by independent peasant farmers.[92] The Chinese tea industry was a dispersed network of small cultivators, local processing enterprises, and tea merchants. It was upon this network that the British East India Company (EIC) depended for its purchases from the 1650s, when it began importing tea to Britain.[93]

By the eighteenth century the southeastern coastal province of Fujian was exporting huge amounts of tea to Britain from this small-scale system. The tea places that fed this global market were similar in their scale, flexibility, and decentralized networks to the Chinese ricescapes discussed in "Times." Farmers cultivated at most one or two acres of tea, typically as part of a more diverse portfolio of crops and activities. Some owned their land, others rented from landlords. Tea was grown either as one crop among several in the village or in gardens high up in the hills, far above the family rice and vegetable plots. Family labor sufficed for tending the tea bushes. When the plucking season came, farmers with more bushes than the family could manage hired extra tea workers from the neighborhood or even—as the export tea trade expanded—from neighboring districts or provinces. Plucking was limited to three two-week harvests, in late spring and early summer; it was common wisdom that over-plucking weakened the bush and spoiled the tea. Tea farmers had a small out-house containing a stove set with two iron woks. Before nightfall the freshly plucked leaves were toasted and tossed in the woks to stabilize them (preventing oxidation). The *maocha* (raw tea) could then be stored and transported without spoiling, and at the end of the harvest the farmer would take his maocha to one of the merchants who toured the tea districts, with whom he would typically have signed an advance contract. The merchant would arrange for further processing of the maocha in a local specialist workshop (again, woks and manual dexterity were the chief equipment) and would then ship all the tea he had acquired downriver to one of the ports.[94] The merchant was thus the person who controlled quality. This infuriated the tea purchasers of the EIC, who believed (not without grounds) that the merchants provided them with inferior teas, keeping the best teas for sale in China.

THE INDIAN GRAFT

The EIC decided to establish its own rival system of tea production in India, primarily because its monopoly on the Chinese tea trade was terminated in 1833. But the project was also in tune with a more general conviction that Britain could and had to use its colonial territories to produce all the useful tropical crops that were now part of British industry or the British diet.[95] With Britain's accumulated experience of colonial plantation agriculture, along with a mechanizing boosterism prompted by the Industrial Revolution which was unfolding at home, it is not surprising that when the EIC began growing tea in India, the cropscape that developed was radically different from the Chinese scenario. The cultivation of tea in India entailed the creation of completely new places. The plantations radically altered the forests they replaced. Unlike tubers in the Trobriands or tea in Fujian, the tea cropscape was not tied intimately to the local communities and their customs. Instead, tea in India tells a story of new places and new cropscapes, brought into being artificially, implanted in locations represented as virgin territory, far removed from existing communities and cropscapes.

The creation of such a place was no accident. Prior experience of colonial plantations had naturalized the plantation paradigm in British minds as the economically and scientifically rational way to produce commodity crops in its tropical colonies.[96] The commercial ambitions behind the creation of such places coincided with the cultural zeal to "civilize" India and Indians. The wild forests had to be "tamed" and brought to "fruitful" use by felling, clearing, and then assembling new elements in the cleared spaces. Through this work of civilizing the place, the jungles were transformed into (tea) "gardens."[97] The reconfigured cropscape involved civilizing not only the place but also a local variant of "wild tea." Even as the EIC made efforts to transfer tea plants and seeds from China to Assam, British plant hunters "discovered" a local forest tree, resembling tea, from which the Assamese gathered leaves to brew a medicinal drink.[98] With Amazonian concepts of taming in mind, we might refer to this relationship as companionate. Initially viewed with suspicion by British botanists as unsuitable for tea production, the wild Assam trees were eventually officially recognized as tea species, and meanwhile were gradually tamed by tea-plantation workers. This entailed domestication in the full Western sense, confining the trees spatially, controlling their reproduction, and exploiting their produce. Flourishing vigorously in the local climate, the Assam tea plants eventually completely displaced Chinese varieties in all but a few of India's tea gardens.[99]

PLACE, POWER, AND CONTROL

Moving tea meant not only physical, botanical, and ecological changes but also creating new social patterns and relationships in the new tea country. One located, renewed, and guaranteed a workforce, another built reliable markets for the tea leaves. We have seen similar far-flung circulations at work in making Amsterdam the place of tulips, and Chicago the place of wheat. As in the Trobriands, multiple circuits were needed to make and stabilize the Indian teascape. Unlike the tuber cropscapes, however, the network of relationships, exchanges, and dependencies that sustained the places where tea was grown in India were almost entirely artificial and took considerable work to devise and maintain. Land, crop plant, and workforce all required taming, civilizing, domesticating, and disciplining, but all threatened continually to revert to the wild state or to elude or resist control.[100]

Plantations require large labor forces. This introduced another element of mobility—bringing families of indentured workers from the plains or far-off provinces to the new tea habitats.[101] Thus the tea place was a new habitat both for the plant and for all the people around the plant—whether owners, managers, or laborers. The racial hierarchy of management, running from the white British manager down to the indigenous laborer, was reinforced by the spatial configuration of the tea estate—the luxurious bungalow of the white manager was perched high above the ramshackle huts of the "native coolie lines" in a characteristic colonial topography of power.

The new settlements were almost self-contained and closed entities as far as the human inhabitants were concerned. The entire family of the laborer was tied to some aspect of the tea estate—the husband doing the outdoor cutting work or indoor factory job, and the wife and children engaged in outdoor plucking of leaves or some factory work. The lives and destinies of the workers and the families were almost entirely left in the hands of the estate managers, to the point where each estate functioned like an autonomous territory, a state within a state (or "state within estate"), with the manager as its chief.[102] In addition to organizing work, managers disciplined workers, checked their health, distributed rations, led religious services, and sometimes set up schools or clinics. It was not just production that was managed but also the very lives of the inhabitants, precisely because of the nature of the estate as a place—its remoteness and its vastness. The Indian teascape incorporated social and political relationships as structural components of the place it made.

Orderly and well disciplined though the rows of tea bushes and the native lines might seem, the estates were embattled territory. Place making created risks. Local fauna resisted exclusion from what had been their realm: attacks by leopards, boars, and wild elephants were a regular threat to the workforce.[103] Worse still, waterlogging in the tea estates' drainage trenches introduced mosquitoes to the Assam cropscape. Malaria and its fatal consequences introduced a further element of ferment and cruel dynamic into the tea place, with labor forces perishing and constantly and with great difficulty being replenished. The later discovery of connections between mosquitoes and malaria brought further dimensions to the place making—it entailed the introduction of even newer elements, such as the cinchona grown to combat the malaria menace. The new place was thus rendered a constant war zone, through the very nature of the place making. The necessary digging of trenches set mosquitoes against men; cinchona against mosquitoes; animals and men against each other; and men against men.[104]

PROPAGATING THE MODEL

After tea's successful introduction into Assam as a plantation crop, the crop was trialed and successfully expanded to several other parts of India, like Darjeeling (also in the eastern part of India), Kangra (in the north), and the Nilgiris, Wayanad, and Munnar (in the south), with active aid from the state, botanical gardens, and researchers. Each of these regions had differences in terrain, elevation, climate, rainfall, and the like. In each location a different place resulted.

Places 87

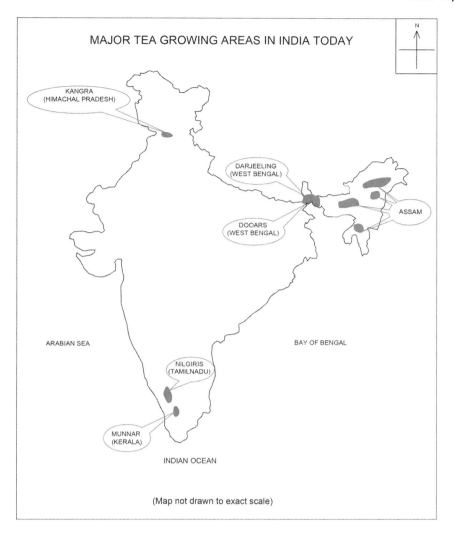

Tea map of India. Once tea's future had been credibly established in Assam, the plant and its new scales and modes could confidently be moved to other suitable areas in different corners of India. Illustration: Jeyakumar P and John Lourdusamy.

Not only did estates have different features, their linkages to surrounding areas, through labor recruitment, transport, provisioning, and so on, varied too. Mountain trains, for instance, formed an important part of the reconfigurations of the cropscape in hilly Darjeeling plantations. Hydroelectric power projects, quite unsuitable in the Assam tea cropscape, formed an important part of the new cropscape of mountainous Munnar. The creation of tea estates in hilly areas also coincided with another variant of place making: the establishment of hill stations (not seen in the Assam cropscape). The cool climes of the hill stations partially assuaged white planters' love and longing for the temperate homeland and its flora. On the sidelines of the tea plantations, within the managerial bungalows, they could recreate the floral beauties and hedges that they missed and longed for.[105]

The trenches that provided indispensable drainage on the Assam plantation had no place in the slopes of Darjeeling, Ootacamund, or Munnar. But the presence or absence of trenches impinged on the cropscape in larger ways. The search for solutions to the waterlogging problem led to the introduction of eucalyptus trees, known to suck up large quantities of water. From this point of view the plant was unnecessary in the hills of Ootacamund, but it was introduced there too—as a source of firewood for households and as fuel for machinery. This demonstrates again the changing nature of creation and re-creation of places, as different elements of the cropscape enter at different times and play different primary roles in different places. It also shows that the making and remaking of cropscapes do not constitute linear, irreversible processes. Deforestation marked the original creation of the Indian tea cropscape, yet planting new trees within the cleared spaces marked a reverse trend. As well as eucalyptus for fuel, silver oak was widely introduced as a shade tree. Some Kerala plantations became tea-and-pepper plantations, as silver oaks provided ideal support for pepper vines. Meanwhile fuel trees might be abandoned when coal or petroleum became available.

VALUE, PLACE, AND DISTANCE

While all these Indian places produced teas, the teas had different characters, distinctive flavors that influenced demand and decided the market. Regional teas' identities were continually evoked, reinforced, or reshaped by advertising, investment, and consumption across the globe, in chains stretching from Darjeeling estates, to Calcutta warehouses, to grocers' shops or travel agents in Britain.[106]

Such far-flung entanglements were and remain an important feature of India's tea cropscapes. It was due to an action in London—the British Parliament's abolition of the East India Company's monopoly of the tea trade with China—that the very creation of a teascape in remote Assam took shape. Add to this the growing commercial interests of the Court of Directors of the EIC, the role of the managing agents in Calcutta, the operations of the London Tea Auction, and classifications and breeding projects in the botanical garden in Calcutta and at Kew.

The value of tea is a product of the scale of these linkages. It changes as it travels. After the tea leaves the estate factory, and before it reaches its customers, it travels hundreds or thousands of kilometers: to auction centers that decide its grade and price, to blending houses where further meaning and value are added, and on to retailers who advertise their blends and brands. These distant places determine the fate of the tea as eventual commodity as much as the place of its growth and processing. As with the archipelagos of wheatscapes, events and changes acted across kilometers and oceans to shape and dynamically constitute teascapes across India.

And yet, despite its global reach, the Indian teascape was producing not a universal but a culturally specific beverage, a British brew that nourished British institutions and worldviews.[107] The plantation model, the technologies of processing and marketing large Assam-bush leaves into strong black teas to be drunk with milk and sugar, spread steadily throughout the spaces, races, and classes of the British Empire. Upwardly mobile young men from England and Scotland went out to manage tea estates established wherever the ecology was deemed suitable, even beyond India—first in Ceylon and then East Africa. This outward flow of aspirant white youth converged with the outward migratory flow of Indians from impoverished regions. Signing up as indentured laborers on tea plantations, they contributed to the plantation-crop Indian diaspora that shaped colonial and postcolonial racial politics (and cuisines) across the tropical zones of the empire. From a luxury for the rich, tea became the everyday beverage of the middle and then the working classes, first in the British Isles, then across the white-settler colonies, and eventually among "natives" in India and other British colonies.[108] The consumption model of Indian tea, like its production model, grew up within, and was confined to, the British Empire—in which places it largely remains.

Having identified the complex factors that shaped India's tea estates and the quintessentially British tea tastes that supported their rise, let us turn back for a moment to China, as we returned from Amsterdam to Istanbul in "Tulips."

For British tea-producers and legislators, China remained, at least until around 1900, the quintessential Other, the ever-looming competitor of British tea. But what was the view from China itself? If we step back to look not just at Fujian province, the chief source of British tea imports, but at the broader Chinese teascape sprawled across the mountains of the southern and southwestern provinces, we observe that tea served segmented markets: the internal market, mainly for green teas, for which the best teas came from the Lower Yangtze provinces; the overland trade to central and western Asia of dark, brick teas, produced in Sichuan and Yunnan; and the sea trade to the West, principally supplied by Fujian, which was actually just one factor in the shaping of China's complex and continuously shifting tea industry.[109] China has been producing huge volumes of tea, and tea exports have been crucial to the Chinese polity, at least since 700 C.E.[110] The crucial period of the China-India encounter, 1800–1900, is a small if significant slice of Chinese tea history. The growth of British tea drinking and of India's tea industry profoundly affected Fujian but left the broader geographies of the Chinese teascape relatively untouched.

In the 1700s, just as European demand for teas began to rocket, some monasteries in Fujian began serving a new style of tea. Semi-fermented, darker, and stronger than green teas and reputed for distinctive medicinal properties, it won some popularity among Chinese connoisseurs. Initially, Western tea merchants purchased for their European customers the bitter green teas judged finest by Chinese tea drinkers. But, at least in Britain, the new semi-fermented teas (Boheas or oolongs) found increasing favor. Between the 1750s and the 1820s Fujian tea makers expanded production of these teas and perfected new techniques of processing. The teas that they developed ("red" in Chinese, "black" in English) required less labor than green teas to process, spoiled less easily in transit, and eventually became the staple of the Fujian export tea industry and the favorite of the growing base of British consumers.[111] The strong "black" teas of Assam were the logical culmination of this trend in taste—and the Chinese industry was unable to compete once that taste was enthroned, for nothing as black and strong could ever be made from the drier, smaller leaves of the China tea bushes.

From around 1780 the contours and dynamics of the Fujian teascape were largely determined first by British markets, then by competition with the nascent Indian estate teascape.[112] Timber, tea, and paper, all produced on a small scale, were the main products of upland Fujian. With the strong growth in British demand for tea, smallholders and merchants shifted more land and capital into its production, and Fujian tea farmers switched to making the semi-fermented, darker teas that British drinkers preferred. Fujian's output of export teas, boosted after 1850 by the new clipper ships, rocketed from thirty-five to ninety-two million pounds in weight between 1856 and 1885.[113] At that point Fujian produced almost a third of total Chinese tea exports, almost all going to Britain. From 1895, as the Indian industry expanded, Fujian's exports of black teas dwindled rapidly. The province's ranking in total Chinese tea exports also fell dramatically: by the 1920s Fujian was producing only around 4 percent of the tea grown in China, and local livelihood choices had switched back to timber, paper, and other woodland products. Across the straits in Taiwan, however, the Fujian model of teascape, which had been introduced in about 1800, was flourishing under Japanese colonial rule. The Taiwanese tea gardens produced the lighter, traditional oolong teas for export principally to the United States.[114]

Although competition with India almost wiped out the Fujian tea gardens at the end of the nineteenth century, the most important spatial characteristic of the Chinese teascape remained unchanged. The main destination for most Chinese teas was still the huge, complex internal market. Most of the teas consumed inside China were green, and prices depended on origin, variety, rarity, and quality of processing. Although rare teas sold for great prices, the bulk of the tea was ordinary grade, consumed in every household as the basic everyday beverage. Population growth, therefore, supported the long-term expansion of the industry. Internal demand was affected primarily by national levels of prosperity and civil order; its volume plummeted in the years of strife following the fall of the Qing dynasty in 1911, revived somewhat as the Nationalist government gained control in the early 1930s, and then disintegrated when the Japanese invaded in 1937. It revived only slowly post-1949, not least because tea remained a luxury unaffordable by the masses during the first decades of socialism, but has rocketed again as China has become wealthy. Then there were the exports of brick teas from southwestern China that went overland to central and western Asia, Nepal and Kashmir, Persia, Russia, and Turkey.[115] This branch of China's tea industry increasingly had to compete with new tea regions that developed along the route, notably around the Black Sea, starting in the 1880s.[116] Finally, the exports to Western countries were not solely determined by British demand. Americans did not acquire the British taste for strong black teas, so Chinese exports to the United States continued after the 1880s, though increasingly displaced by Japanese teas (including, post-1895, the ex-Chinese teas of Taiwan). From the 1830s Calcutta and Glasgow played a crucial role in place making in the tea gardens of Fujian, but in other important tea regions of China the ancient commerce with Karakorum and Ferghana was still more significant, although now reformulated as trade with Tibet, Iran, Russia, and Turkey.

In highlighting place making, our story of tea takes materiality as the fulcrum of analysis. Weaving together the multiple material layers and interactions that structured and defined the Indian teascape on the spot helps ground the labor, gender, and economic histories of the industry that have added so much to our understanding of empires and nationalisms. Meanwhile the dynamics of connection between India and China as tea countries remind us not to discount the historical impact of sociotechnological and commercial systems stigmatized as backward by ambitious Western competitors.

The riffs in this set indicate the difficult, contingent, and sometimes unsuccessful work that went into rooting a particular crop in place or transposing it to a new setting. Each riff treats its crop as a cultural artifact, exploring it first as a

92 Places

product of place and then as a connector of places. Our microhistories highlight the refashioning entailed in moving crops and underline how fundamentally the choice of frame shapes the histories we tell of a place and of its connections.

Microhistories can engage readers with vibrant images of sites where the familiar becomes strange, where encounters or connections involve not only the adoption of new goods or practices but also negotiations over meaning.[117] Giovanni Levi, a founding figure of microhistory, argues for using microhistories both to illuminate and to connect places, in the process distinguishing the project of global history from the phenomenon of globalization.[118] Sanjay Subrahmanyam pioneered this approach two decades ago, arguing that the best alternative to the grand narrative of modernization is to study multifaceted interactions, beyond political boundaries and on multiple scales, as a means to question the "established facts" of national or global narratives.[119] To which we would add, questioning the established meanings and significance of modern things, a perennial pitfall in histories of technology, comparative history, and many of the most successful global histories of commodities.[120]

Locating a scientific practice, institution, moral principle, or taste in its place as well as time, then scrutinizing how—rather than simply observing that—it moves between certain places has become standard practice for historians of science, consumption, or global encounters.[121] In these histories of global exchange, sometimes the adventures of a thing rather than a person will identify the place and provide the drama. Marcy Norton describes tobacco and chocolate as "cultural artifacts" whose existence was predicated on "knowledge and techniques developed over millennia in the western hemisphere." Her analysis revisits the impact of the New World on the Old not only in the domain of material culture and its meanings but also in science and statecraft.[122] In hindsight it may seem logical and natural that the Spanish adopted chocolate as their breakfast drink or that a transplanted teascape flourished in British India. Flows of people, knowledge, capital, and things between places are the very stuff of globalization theory. But the concept of flow as natural is, as Augustine Sedgewick argues, a historical construct that has served disciplines like economics well, by obscuring contingency and depoliticizing processes that involve both effort and the exercise of power. The metaphor of flow "vanquished a rival conception of motion and change, 'work'—meaning both labor, and, in a technical sense, the energy required to move or transform matter in space."[123]

We show the crop plants themselves at work in these histories. Acknowledged as sentient beings with a capacity to shape their environments, to resist as well as comply with human intentions, and to create communities of codependent life-forms, some anthropologists are now urging us to consider plants as ethnographic subjects.[124] We have not attempted to offer full-fledged ethnographies of crop-plants here, nor to present our plants as the heroes of microhistories. But in each instance of place making we systematically emphasize our crops' species-being, their needs, preferences, and partnerships, as well as those of the humans who select them and use them.[125]

From the human perspective, rooting a new crop into the soil requires enormous and sustained amounts of work. It is an act of violence as often as a fact of nature; keeping a "traditional" cropscape going invariably involves the exercise of power. The trail of wheat dispossessed Tatars on the Russian steppes and drowned the native peoples, animals, and plants of the American prairies under "amber waves of grain." Tea plantations invaded India's forested mountains, inconvenienced the local elephants (see "Actants"), and legitimized an oppressive system of long-distance labor extraction through indenture. Tubers sustained tightly knit and relatively homogeneous societies in the Trobriands and New Guinea, but as well as affirming kinship they served political ambition and provisioned war.

Work of course can be material or symbolic, political or social. All our cases in this book, but perhaps particularly the riffs in this chapter, emphasize the interplay of material and other kinds of resources and work that were necessary, first, to produce and maintain a crop in a specific place and, second, to forge connections with other places. We don't take a connection as a foregone conclusion to an encounter. As Sebastian Conrad notes, "It is the analysis of a connection's strength, character and impact that distinguishes the global historian." Global history needs to explain the context in which things are brought together and connect—why here, why now? As befits an intellectual heir of world-systems theory, Conrad argues that it is "basic structural transformation that [makes] the exchange possible in the first place." But what, then, catalyzes the structural transformations of a connected world? We prefer to think of the influence as reciprocal.[126]

In both our tulip and our tea cropscapes, we integrate those places traditionally identified as origins into a long-term narrative, rather than abandoning them once a crop has moved. It was in Britain's interests to portray the Chinese competitor as backward and corrupt, and to emphasize the progressive nature of its own teascapes. But as Indian-grown teas morphed into a completely new type and taste, Chinese production continued unabated. The two great tea countries effectively divided the world between them, competition waning as their markets diverged. The markets for and competitors to Chinese teas populate maps less familiar than those centered on the British Empire, linking countries across the North Pacific and along the overland routes of Eurasia.

The American mid-West is conventionally identified as the quintessential capitalist wheatscape. Reframing wheat production as a transnational system shows how Chicago and the Dakotas were knit into a worldwide web of wheat farms and exchanges, a vast global wheatscape that operated as much by complementarity as by competition. Although a booster politician or a historian of finance or technology might be tempted to rank the wheatscapes, it would be pointless to identify American elevators as more advanced than Argentinian jute sacks: each local technology responded to the specific ways in which local wheat production was inserted into global markets.

We proposed tulips east and west as a way to think about different ways in which capitalism works, and also about the complexities underlying connections. A different counter to European capitalist development appears in the tuber gardens of Oceania and Amazonia. Their connection to what we acknowledge as global history is powerful precisely because it is construed as a nonconnection. Easily dismissed or romanticized as places outside history, primitive worlds untouched by money and calculation where humans live in direct contact with nature, these "small-scale" societies have been mined by social theorists for alternative interpretations of the logics of capitalism, prompting us to see the Other in the making of our modern selves, and to reconsider the rationalities and moralities underpinning our everyday social dealings. We return to the theme of size and virtue in the next chapter.

Chapter 3 Sizes

Undoubtedly, philosophers are in the right when they tell us that nothing is great or little otherwise than by comparison.
—Jonathan Swift, *Gulliver's Travels*

Size is relative, and "greater" is meaningless unless a "less" also is forthcoming. For the largest beetle (*Scaraboeus*) is a thousand times smaller than the smallest goat (*Capra*). Hence any degree of comparative size is erroneous, whether it has regard to the plant as a whole, or to a part of it, its leaves or flowers or fruit: it is not scientific to make one plant a standard for one's study of another.
—Linnaeus, *Critica Botanica*

Glumdalclitch, the little girl who befriended Gulliver on Brobdingnag, stood "not above forty feet tall, being small for her age." Gulliver was equally astonished to find himself a midget on Brobdingnag and a giant in Lilliput, being of perfectly average size at home. The scales of farming, along with norms and ideals of size, vary just as dramatically, and may cause equal surprise to travelers from another scale zone.

The ideal size of farm in the rich rice-and-silk cropscapes of late imperial Jiangnan (Southeast China) was not much more than one hectare; anyone owning more land was advised by experts to rent out the rest to tenants.[1] By contrast, in England in around 1800 experts reckoned that an ideal modern farm, combining crops with livestock and selling its produce at competitive rates, should cover at least three hundred acres (120 hectares).[2] In the United States, the homestead or family farm grew steadily in size as machines and other industrial inputs allowed fewer workers to manage more land. In 1935 the average farm size in the United States was 155 acres; in 2017 it was 444 acres.[3] In 2018 almost half the U.S. cropland was occupied by farms of more than 1,450 acres, family-run but often working under contract to agribusiness corporations and specializing in one crop or animal. Yet, while big farms in America are getting bigger and more numerous, farms of under fifty acres have also increased in number since 2000, currently making up almost half the total.[4]

Business experts say increased farm size is the way of the future: farming at industrial scale is essential to feed the world's growing population. This position reflects a wider orthodoxy, supported through the twentieth century by influential historians as well as agricultural experts and policy makers, that larger farms enable innovation and raise productivity, while smaller farms are less productive, less efficient, and resistant to improvement. Yet populists and peasant movements, and historians too, have argued passionately against this orthodoxy for many years, while environmentalists and some economists now add their voices to the debate. In organizations like the FAO and the World Bank, which used to promote larger farms as models for raising output and enhancing efficiency, the new orthodoxy is to bet on smallholder productivity, community welfare, and stewardship of the environment.[5]

So is bigger better, or is small beautiful? This chapter seeks to transcend the dualisms and teleologies inherent in such debates, while highlighting the politics and historical constitution of any specific orthodoxy of size. As Linnaeus states, size is relative: our construction of difference, our judgment that a field, a farm, an apple, or a harvest is large or small depends on our frame of reference, as well as the scale of analysis that we decide is appropriate.

The scales of observation, analysis, and interpretation that we choose to apply in evaluating farm size, and the outcomes of that choice, are the products of historical circumstance, politically charged. Unconsciously or deliberately, the choice of scale and the values implicit in using that scale reflect broader goals and ideologies.[6] Shifting the scale of observation of a farming system from markets to ecosystems means that profit gives way to sustainability as the primary criterion for efficiency. A policy of food security will promote a very different size of farm and scale of farming from a policy of food sovereignty. What counts as productivity, sustainability, or efficiency changes depending on whether we are concerned with gross domestic product (GDP) or farmer livelihood. Is our time horizon one crop cycle, a Five-Year Plan, the rise and fall of dynasties, or a program to save the planet? Are we focusing on farms as producers of calories or lifeways, as components of a local ecology, links in a commodity chain, recipients of government subsidies, business managers, or anchors of community life? How we perceive and evaluate norms or trends also depends on the timescale we choose. If we select the period between 1000 and 1750 c.e. to evaluate Chinese small-scale farming, we find ourselves sharing the view of the many Enlightenment savants who saw in China a prosperous and productive society worthy of emulation, in which small units of operation (farms and workshops) supported a prosperous economy and a successful state. If we take 1950 as our end point, extending our timescale to include the century of defeats, colonization, rebellions, civil war, and revolution that followed China's defeat in the first Opium War in 1842, then China's tiny farms are easily recoded as a recipe for disaster.

This chapter, "Sizes," experiments with the different scales at which the historian might choose to examine a particular cropscape, treating size and scale as historical categories. Our approach brings together dimensions of cropscapes usually ignored in mainstream global or agricultural history, to refine and develop existing arguments about the trajectories and transitions of farming. Taking the farm, the unit of operation, as our frame of reference and our viewpoint for examining norms and ideologies of size, we explore the moral and material values attributed to different sizes and scales by the historical actors, the circumstances that shaped the corresponding cultures or ideologies of size, and the physical or structural violence necessary to achieve those goals. Our cases of tobacco in Virginia and North Carolina, coffee in Ethiopia, tea in India, and water in North and South China have been selected to test some common mythologies of size and scale and their relations, whether at work in the building of cropscapes or in their historical representation. They illustrate different dialectics, linearities, and linkages between size of operation and scale of cropscape. In other words, size is crucial, but it is also contingent. We begin with a riff that asks where the idea that "bigger is better" originated, and why it became so powerful.

ORTHODOXIES OF SIZE: BIGGER IS BETTER VERSUS SMALL IS BEAUTIFUL

It is widely accepted in the worlds of science, business, and policy—and in public understanding—that the most advanced and productive form of farming is on an industrial scale, and that within that scale, large farms typically perform better than small. For more than a century the Fordist industrial ideal of bigger is better, with its assumptions about the direction of historical progress from small to big units, and about the benefits of specialization and economies of scale, has profoundly structured national agricultural and food policies, international models for agricultural development, technical education, and agriculture-related research. It has also often influenced how the history of agriculture is written, for instance where the size of farms in a specific context serves as a yardstick for assessing historical progress or for comparing the world-historical significance of different agrarian regimes.[7] How did this idea become so powerful? And in what terms are objections raised?

The ideal of big is better in farming has deep roots in European agronomy. The slave-labor *latifundia* of Spain, Gaul, Libya, and Egypt were praised by ancient Roman agricultural writers like Columella (greatly revered among Renaissance agricultural experimentalists) because they were so profitable and productive, supplying Roman cities with wheat, oil, and wine. Research suggests that the dense population of the central regions around Rome was in fact largely supported by technically advanced and highly productive smallholdings, but the take-home message of Roman agronomic writers, who were themselves estate owners, not peasants, was that scale mattered and latifundia were the model to follow.[8] Centuries later, the model of huge specialized farms run with enslaved labor spread from the Mediterranean into the "plantation kingdoms" of the Atlantic world, where it flourished well into the modern era as reputedly the most effective way to produce commodity crops.[9] Historians note the enduring potency of the plantation paradigm in channeling the logic of colonial, and indeed postcolonial, crop science.[10]

ENGLAND'S AGRICULTURAL REVOLUTION

While plantations were spreading through the Atlantic world, England was starting its rise as the paragon of a different model of rational and profitable farming. Starting in the early 1600s and gathering momentum during the so-called Agricultural Revolution of the eighteenth and nineteenth centuries, peasant strips gave way to consolidated farms large enough to reward capital investment in improvements such as marling, draining, and crop rotation.[11] As early as 1600 the ambitious authors of books with titles like *A Way to Get Wealth* maintained that only large farms could afford to improve.[12] The association of size with efficiency was further consolidated once reliable farm machinery and other industrial inputs became available in the mid-nineteenth century, assimilating the agricultural sector into industrial logic.[13] Well before mechanization or the adoption of other industrial inputs, however, the association of size, performance, and quality both reflected and fed into a broader theoretical and practical consensus taking shape among British political economists, industrialists, and agricultural improvers that scaling up production promoted efficiency. This orthodoxy of size was by no means politically neutral: its calculus was rooted in mechanisms of extraction made possible by hierarchies of class and, in the case of the plantations, of race.

Historians trace the tenurial and legal changes that launched the transformation of English farming to as early as 1500, when the old system of common lands and open fields was first seriously challenged by private ownership.[14] Fifteenth- and sixteenth-century Acts of Enclosure allowed investors to purchase and consolidate large areas of land, often establishing commercial farms to specialize in wool or cereals for an expanding urban market. Successive acts of Parliament allowing enclosures of common fields as private property steadily concentrated land ownership in the hands of the wealthy and politically powerful. Dispossessed peasants either left to seek jobs in towns or looked for local work as hired laborers, a rural proletariat. Landowners rented out parcels to tenant farmers, men with some education and enough capital to take out a lease and to invest in the farm. The farmers hired laborers to work the fields and sold their produce on the growing urban or, latterly, global markets.

By 1600 there was a flourishing industry of publications on how to get rich by applying ingenious new methods or machines in farming; soon thereafter polymaths like Samuel Hartlib began to argue that the principles of natural philosophy could and should be applied in agriculture.[15] A flow of exciting new theories, practices, and inventions continued through the seventeenth and eighteenth centuries, generating enthusiasm at home and abroad and providing a general sensation that things were astir in the farming world. Figures like Jethro Tull (1674–1741), inventor of ingenious machines including a seed drill and a horse-drawn hoe and author of *The New Horse Hoeing Husbandry* (1731); "Turnip" Townshend (1674–1738), who popularized new crop rotations; and the animal breeders Robert Bakewell (1725–1795) and Coke of Norfolk (1754–1842) won England's "New Husbandry" a reputation as the most advanced agricultural system in Europe, famous for its high crop yields and improved animal breeds, its profitable farms, its prosperous and educated tenant farmers, and its scientific crop rotations.[16] By the early 1800s, English farming was also becoming famous, or infamous, as the vanguard of farm mechanization.[17]

But how well do these claims match the facts?

> From England the New Husbandry conquered the world by means of books and writings . . . [yet seldom has there] been a wider gap between theory and practice than in the agriculture of the eighteenth and to some extent the nineteenth century. In the books and pamphlets, in the dissertations of learned societies, there are all sorts of luminous ideas for improvements and innovations. If we judged by these, we

should get a very distorted view of the situation. . . . Some of the new agricultural methods were really put into practice, and gradually came into more general use. Even so, there was a great distance between the "New Husbandry" of the adepts of the modern school and the ways of the ordinary farmer.[18]

The gap between what excited and impressed improvers and their public and real change on the ground was particularly evident in the case of mechanical inventions. Most historians of the Agricultural Revolution agree that "the 'wave of gadgets' that is said to have swept over England passed it by until well into the nineteenth century," and that the flood of ingenious inventions that were published or submitted for patent typically "got no further than the drawing-board or the experimental model."[19]

Agricultural historians today call for a much more nuanced interpretation of the long-term evolution of English farming. The revised history downplays the role of gentleman improvers, private property, prize bulls, and ingenious machines. It emphasizes how much British "improvements" owed to the intensive, highly productive methods and crops developed by smallholders in Brabant and Flanders—an integral element of that region's "industrious revolution."[20] It also shows how often innovative practices deemed incompatible with common holdings or strip fields were in fact pioneered in Britain by surviving smallholder communities.[21] As in the case of ancient Rome, some historians argue that the real gains in farm productivity were accomplished on smallholdings, through a "yeoman's agricultural revolution" in the seventeenth century; the "landlords' revolution" of the eighteenth century simply redistributed income from farmers and laborers to landowners.[22]

In other words, agricultural historians disagree profoundly about the dates, the key characteristics, and the broader impact of the English agricultural revolution.[23] Did it begin under the Tudors, in 1600, or not until the nineteenth century? How much improvement was actually the fruit of smallholder and commoner initiatives, ignored in the booster literature because it would send out the wrong message? Was the chief vector of progress the transformation of rural institutions and legislation that favored accumulation of land and control of labor by the rural gentry and their tenant farmers? Or was it the improvement of agricultural methods, bringing gains in factor productivity? Did it generate urban markets for food and raw materials or was it a response to new demands? Was improved farming the trigger or the beneficiary of industrialization?

Agricultural historians have shown that the concept of the English Agricultural Revolution is flawed, and its role in England's industrialization was far from simple. Nevertheless, the basic narrative remains both appealing and powerful. Economic historians still use it in analyzing England's supposedly Promethean rise to scientific and industrial eminence, as do comparative historians asking why the industrializing West surged ahead of India, China, and Japan. Their evaluations of agricultural systems closely reflect the views of such noted improvers as Arthur Young.[24]

Arthur Young (1741–1820) played an important part in propagating the orthodox account of the dynamics of improvement. A gentleman farmer who experimented on his own land and made repeated tours of England, Wales, Ireland, and France to observe farming practice, Young became a renowned agricultural expert, historian, and political economist. He founded *Annals of Agriculture* in 1784 and was appointed secretary of the Board of Agriculture in 1793. Young's writings on farming history and practice emphasized the progressive role of the great estates, the advantages of private enclosure, and the importance of scientific rationality and mechanical innovation in improving farming. This was a welcome message to the propertied classes at the time of revolution in France and widespread worker unrest in Britain.[25] To these positive arguments in favor of bigger farms owned by a better class of people we may add the constant denigration of smallholders by many "improvers." Ignorant, lazy, disorganized, and wasteful: such epithets justified the transfer of resources from one class to another in the name of progress and the public good. Garrett Hardin's influential "tragedy of the commons" is but the modern, technical formulation of a well-worn argument: peasants are losers.[26]

Young's opinions, which exerted enormous power at the time, still influence our world today. They celebrate a scale dynamics that first took shape in England around 1600, was consolidated through the eighteenth century, was thoroughly reinforced by the mechanization of agriculture, and has continued to define technical goals and choices, and to shape legislation and policy, in capitalist and socialist nations alike, right up to the present. While small farms and commons management also played their part in developing English farming to the point where it could feed an urban industrial workforce, it was the landlord-centered view of how land, labor, and capital should be exploited for maximum advantage that became the unchallenged orthodoxy, shaping how contemporary commentators and later savants understood the role of agriculture in history, molding the values of agronomic science, determining rural aid and development policies through the twentieth century, and—as already noted—shaping historians' narratives and explanations.

A key element in the enduring and universal appeal of the Agricultural Revolution story is its entanglement with the birth of industrial society. It was the political economist and radical Arnold Toynbee who first argued, in his lectures at Oxford in the 1880s, that England had experienced an agrarian revolution that laid the foundations of its industrial revolution.[27] The concept of the Agricultural

Revolution was further developed and popularized by the agricultural expert and Conservative politician R. E. Prothero (later Baron Ernle) in *The Pioneers and Progress of British Farming*, published in 1888 and reissued many times. Ernle's accounts of heroic men and ingenious devices "captured the popular imagination"; men like Jethro Tull, "Turnip" Townshend, and Arthur Young were "seen to have triumphed over a conservative mass of country bumpkins and single-handedly transformed English agriculture within a few years from a peasant subsistence economy into a thriving capitalist agricultural system capable of feeding the teeming millions in the new industrial cities." In addition, Toynbee and Ernle pointed out, by displacing agricultural workers, the Agricultural Revolution helped create England's industrial workforce.[28]

MODERN AND POST-MODERN ORTHODOXIES

The linking of agricultural with industrial revolution gave the big is better logic of the English model immense appeal wherever modernization was the goal. Once the English experience was translated into the technical terminology of economics as an example of scale economies and increased returns to factors of production, once it was presented as the logical outcome of applying science and technology to farm as well as factory production, the class politics of its history were erased, translating it into a set of neutral, universal principles, a model equally available to a society that valued thrusting entrepreneurs or to an aspiring dictatorship of the proletariat. In the socialist world, including the Soviet Union and the People's Republic of China (PRC), the agricultural-industrial model of bigger is better took the form of collective farms or people's communes. The practices of collective farming were expected not only to raise output but to transform backward peasants into modern, technologically competent socialist citizens. In the USSR in the 1930s and the PRC in the 1950s, colorful posters of women driving tractors symbolized the revolutionary new society in which women were fully integrated into modern production.[29]

Scaling up was an ideal that transcended politics. In the 1920s Soviet agronomists appealed to American colleagues and corporations for help in planning huge wheat farms and setting up tractor factories. Paradoxically, "for many of these [American] agriculturalists, searching for a new and better way to organize agriculture in America, the most interesting thing about Soviet agriculture was that the Soviets seemed to be doing what the Americans were only talking about—industrializing agriculture."[30] In fact the Soviets did not succeed in industrializing their agriculture.[31] But in the "Free World," for instance in the United States or Argentina, or under the European Union's Common Agricultural Policy, the orthodoxy of scale was propelled by policies that effectively promoted ever-larger farms, and by a rhetoric of technological determinism that presented the trend toward industrial farming and agribusiness as "the product of an inescapable history."[32]

Colonial agricultural policies and post–World War II development and aid programs exported the bigger is better doctrine of agricultural improvement to the rest of the world, mandating plans and programs premised on scale economies that favored the consolidation of smallholdings into larger units, the pursuit of comparative advantage by specialization in monocultures, the integration of local cropscapes into global markets, and the displacement of local food systems by cheap imports—a local and global flattening of the cropscape.

In Asia's rice regions in the 1970s, the technologies of the Green Revolution were presented as a peasant-friendly counterpart to this trend, a program for increasing food production that would be equally accessible to poor and rich, small and large farmers. The egalitarian effect was judged important because one key goal of the Green Revolution was to prevent Red Revolution.[33] But outside the experimental plots, the ostensibly scale-neutral technological packages (seed plus chemical fertilizer plus pesticides plus irrigation and/or mechanization) proved almost invariably to favor bigger farmers with better access to credit and more capacity to take risks. Small farmers only benefited equally if the local government invested heavily in support programs.[34] To some, such outcomes simply add weight to the argument that small farming is doomed by history and should not be kept alive artificially. To others, it signifies bad design or bad faith, a failure of technocracy where Green Revolution planners prioritized urban over rural needs or promoted increased commercial production of cereals over the livelihood of small farmers.[35] Certainly, history and current experience show that it is not impossible to breed seeds or develop inputs suitable for smallholders, once the orthodoxy of bigger is better is set aside.

In recent years, with growing concern about environmental degradation, biodiversity, climate change, food sovereignty, and social justice, the creed of "small is beautiful" (famously formulated by E. F. Schumacher in the 1970s) has begun to rival the ideology of bigger is better even among institutions that unquestioningly used to support that position.[36] There were significant precursors to this change. Although they struggled for recognition in the shadow of projects organized around economies of scale, peasant-friendly crop-breeding programs had roots stretching back to Germany in the 1880s.[37] In the 1970s Farming Systems Research (FSR) emerged as a counterpoint to the bigger is better formulations of rural development paradigms. The FSR scale of observation and evaluation was smallholder and rural community centered rather than focused on the national economy or global markets; virtuous cycles, diversity, and flexibility were envisioned rather than efficiency through specialization or backing winners.[38]

This shift in scale is now gaining support as a new orthodoxy even in such bastions of power as the Rockefeller Foundation and the FAO. They are among leading transnational funding organizations that have lately come not only to accept but even to celebrate smallholders as legitimate "stakeholders" and partners, devising new forms of support for small-scale farms, taking "local knowledge" seriously, investigating labor-intensive techniques for raising output, and emphasizing sustainability and livelihood ahead of output and profits. A Second Green Revolution is promised, that will develop small-scale, locally tuned high-tech applications to benefit small farmers while minimizing environmental damage.[39] The celebration of family farms as entrepreneurial engines of growth has become muted, in tune with environmentalist sensitivities: small farmers are now celebrated as natural conservationists, knowledgeable husbanders of increasingly scarce resources (water, for example). There is new interest in how a national economy can integrate and mobilize small- or medium-scale production regimes to achieve food self-sufficiency, maintain or increase GDP, or meet the challenges sparked by urbanization and population growth. Small is now beautiful even in the corridors of the World Bank, and repeasantization has become a word to conjure with. The United Nations has designated 2019–2028 its "Decade of Family Farming."[40]

Switches from large- to small-scale farming are in fact historically quite common. The disbanding of plantations in the postbellum United States and elsewhere in the Atlantic world is one case that has attracted sustained attention from historians; it features in the section "Tobacco" below. Paradoxically, in USDA reckoning the farm lots worked by Southern sharecroppers or tenants would not count as family farms, although they were family operated, because the farmers did not own the land. At exactly the same period, along the advancing Western frontier, we find a parallel switch from big to small. Gigantic capitalist bonanza farms played a crucial role in the homesteading movement. Homestead lots were 160 acres; the minimum for bonanza lots was three thousand acres and the average size was seven thousand.[41] Purchasing huge swathes of "virgin" land dirt cheap at the latest railhead, a bonanza corporation brought in an army of managers and laborers, along with the latest machinery, to break in and work the land. The biggest gains for these companies were not in selling wheat as such but in selling off the land in homestead parcels to family farmers once the new zone had established a reputation as being viable for farming. The huge-scale bonanza farms helped anchor medium-scale family farming across the Midwest and West.[42]

One of the most dramatic switches from large-scale back to small-scale farming, however, came recently, in the socialist nations. The rationales were ideological, the processes abrupt—although never as violent as those that had accompanied

Kulak crushed. Debates about the size of the cropscape make tragic history. The stubborn petty-minded kulak with his smallholding was eliminated to cultivate a new man in the expanding and mechanized collective farms of Stalin's Great Break. Courtesy of Swarthmore College Peace Collection.

land reform, collectivization, and the dispossession of those classified as kulaks in the Soviet Union or as rich peasants in the PRC. Under Mao it was politically unacceptable to mention the widespread evidence that under collective ownership commune members often worked less and consumed more than was consistent with raising productivity for the common good. After Mao's death in 1976 the Chinese government switched from mass-line politics to a strategy of modernization that displayed "socialism with Chinese characteristics." To raise rural productivity as rapidly as possible, the communes were dismantled and land redistributed to family units under the "household responsibility system." The family farms did indeed increase and diversify agricultural production and raise farmer incomes, as well as meeting state goals of increasing supplies of staple grains and consumer products for increasingly prosperous urban households. In 1986 Vietnam followed suit.[43] With the disintegration of the Soviet Union in 1991, collective farms were disbanded across the former socialist bloc. Western observers had long criticized the excesses of socialist zeal that collective farming represented, along with its dampening effect on productivity, so it is not surprising that they welcomed the shift to a system intended to unshackle productivity by mobilizing self-interested entrepreneurial energies.

So, whether as a sign that communism had been vanquished or as a promise of a kinder mode of living off the land, from the 1980s small is beautiful became increasingly acceptable to the great and the good. This rather dramatic reversal of creed among the powerful has not yet led to any noticeable dwindling of the power of capitalist agribusiness or the volume of global trade, nor have nations or corporations around the world abandoned projects for expanding the frontiers of the oil palm industry or soy production. Yet such turnarounds remind us that beneath a trend or an ideal lie much more complex realities: growth is not historical destiny, the trend can be reversed, and often what looks superficially like a linear progress, a logic of growth, on closer inspection turns out to be a shifting equilibrium of multiple coexisting sizes and scales (as discussed in "Coffee Mosaics" below), a series of oscillations in size within a steadily expanding scale of market ("Tobacco Oscillations"), or a system that took many decades to fulfill its ambitions of scale ("Tea and Ideology").

TOBACCO OSCILLATIONS: CHANGING
SIZE ON THE SPOT

The idea of the cropscape provides new ways to think about how scales of interpretation affect perspectives on history. In this riff we return to tobacco, which made an earlier appearance in terms of the flexibility of its life cycle—a perennial grown commercially in colonial Virginia as an annual.[44] On the Virginia–North Carolina border tobacco has been produced consistently from at least the 1600s to the 2000s. By staying in place, we can trace oscillations in the size of the farm, or cultivation unit, that spooled out across three centuries. These size oscillations show how non-plant elements in the cropscape (legal and technological changes) reconfigured both farm acreage and labor organization. Changes in the size of tobacco farms in this single location demonstrate a non-linear history. The size of tobacco cultivation units typical in the region moved from small to large, to small, and to large again over four centuries. The oscillation in the size of tobacco farms shows that cropscapes need not move to change: farm scales changed as legal and technological frameworks changed, linking in turn to other changes in the contours of the cropscape.

The founding mythology of Virginia tobacco is that of a crop on the move, when John Rolfe imported the tiny seeds from the West Indies and started Virginia's English settlers on their path to history. Cultivated and shipped to England, tobacco leaves fetched a high price in 1617, and colonial settlers were so excited by the profit possibilities that they planted the streets of their settlement with tobacco.[45] The price did not determine the size of cultivation unit—for the next century, English colonists cultivated tobacco everywhere they could, on small farms as well as large plantations.

Small plantations predominated along the tobacco coast through most of the seventeenth century.[46] But as new settlers and indentured servants sought their own farms, policies and culture tended toward larger cropscapes. The Virginia Company, for example, granted "headrights" after 1618—land grants to those who paid the Atlantic passage of bound laborers. This gave land to those rich enough to supply labor, usually indentured or enslaved.[47] Profligate with land, planters cultivated tobacco year upon year rather than fallowing fields or planting regenerative but unprofitable crops. As a result, British colonists tended to move the crop onto new lands and enlarge their settlement to new places. "Tobacco growing and land-clearing went hand in hand."[48]

In addition, the burgesses regularly meddled in markets to try to raise the value of the colony's exports—and of their currency, for that matter (colonial officials were paid in tobacco). They first tried to limit how much tobacco would reach market, figuring that less supply would raise the price, so they set "stint laws" to limit growers to a certain number of plants per "headd" [sic]. For example, "two hundred pound[s] for a Master of a family and one hundred and a quarter for every servant." Another effort allowed three thousand plants per tithable person "workeing the ground" or "where the familie consisteth of children and woemen which doe not worke in the ground . . . not above 1000 plants per pol." Any attempt to assign quantity sown or sold per person raised the question of who was a legal person—as women, children, servants, and slaves were not. While headrights had early engrossed land in the hands of planters with the money to import labor, these provisions gave them the right to plant more tobacco per head. Conflict over reduced opportunities led to violence, including an uprising on the western frontier in 1676, known as Bacon's Rebellion. Cultivation units of different sizes represented different settler groups with different access to resources, but conflicts between them were eventually softened by their mutual hatred of natives.[49]

TOBACCO GOES LARGE

In the 1720s, rather than simply limiting the quantity of tobacco raised, the burgesses enacted new regulations intended to improve the quality of tobacco exported. These "inspection laws," as they became known, approved for export only high-quality tobacco, outlawing export of the plant's second growths. So the inspection laws dictated that only the first-growth leaves could be legally sold—and thus did away with agricultural routines that cultivated suckers and ratoons.[50] The inspection system created incentives to grow those first-growth leaves as big and heavy as they could be made.[51] The laws therefore made profitable a particular cultivation routine. The eighteenth-century Virginia agricultural system involved regular labor removing suckers as trash, and—most important of all—one big single harvest at the end of the summer, with a rapid curing to preserve the leaves for later grading, packing, inspection, sale, and transport.

The harvest demands of tobacco, themselves shaped by the inspection laws that made first-growth leaves the only marketable thing produced by the plant, created the second phase of the oscillation in size of tobacco farms in Virginia. It is in the 1720s, the same decade in which the inspection laws began to take hold, that quantitative economic historians can discern a "steady upward drift" in the size of tobacco farms and of enslaved labor forces. The tendency was there already: expansion into the west had troubled the territory in the seventeenth century, and laws after 1660 demonstrated emerging distinctions between slaves and servants, patriarchs and laborers, people who were taxable property versus wives and heirs.[52] But the changing legal landscape of the 1720s decisively favored planters who could command large numbers of workers at crucial harvest points, disadvantaging smallholders. After Bacon's Rebellion, Africans had been only 7 percent of Virginia's non–Native American population and 13 percent by 1700—but in 1730 Africans numbered 27 percent of that population, and 40 percent by 1750.[53] The second-phase cropscape of large cultivation units employed and facilitated a patriarchal ideology characteristic of the plantation system. As production units, these plantations mirrored the manors of medieval Europe, with planters viewing the entire household as familial, organized in webs of mutual responsibility and obligation. "Thirty of my family are down with the smallpox," a planter wrote to a merchant in 1846, as if his workforce were his children.[54] The colonial inspection laws combined with provisions granting land to planters who had labor, along with the laws governing and taxonomizing those laborers, all contributed to the changing size of the tobacco cropscape. While seventeenth-century Virginia had been settled in a mosaic of small farms and large, the tobacco cropscape became the traditional large-scale plantations of the British American South in the eighteenth century.

EMANCIPATION AND SCALED-DOWN CULTIVATION

Federal law, in the form of the Emancipation Proclamation of 1863, initiated a third phase of oscillation as the size of tobacco farms shrank after the Civil War—they scaled down into smallholdings for sharecropping. Of course, land-ownership mostly remained concentrated in the hands of the former slave masters and other large-scale capital entities—it is the historians' choice to focus on the Delta and Pine Land Plantation (at nine thousand acres) or on the operations of an individual sharecropping family or community. Here we emphasize the size of the cultivation unit itself, which dropped as formerly enslaved farmers pushed to control their own work and their own lives and households on individual farms. Planters generally preferred to centralize control of agricultural operations but lacked the cash to provide agricultural inputs and pay wages all year long. Both landlord and farmer had to wait for harvest for a payout, and so did the storekeeper who kept their crops growing with credit. While planters wanted to control the work, workers sought to maximize their freedom. Without wider opportunities, freed people at least achieved their own farms—the small cultivation units associated with sharecropping.[55]

Emancipation changed not only the size of production units but also the nature of cultivation practices. Sharecropping relied on annual credit: farm families waited for harvest for their pay but owed landlords and storekeepers for rent and food and seeds and fertilizer. Each group provided credit to the others, with all bills due at the end of the year. To keep all parties afloat, harvest and curing methods emerged after emancipation that allowed a new annual production cycle of several harvests. Instead of chopping down the whole plant, as had been done for centuries, a new system emerged, organized around plucking individual leaves. Harvesting individual leaves, then going through the fields

Tobacco family. After the U.S. Civil War, tiny cultivation units were carved out of large antebellum plantations for sharecropping. But tobacco growers harvested and cured the leaf in rotation throughout the farms of their extended families, which facilitated plucking and curing similar leaves, which graded the crop for sale before curing. This sped up the marketing process, which suited the annual credit calendar of sharecropping. Black and White Photographic Print 0019: Wilson County: Wilson: Tobacco Production, circa 1926: Scan 4, in the Commercial Museum (Philadelphia, PA) Collection of North Carolina Photographs (P0072), North Carolina Collection Photographic Archives, the Wilson Library, University of North Carolina at Chapel Hill.

again to pluck another set of leaves, meant barns could be filled for curing and then cleared out for another round. Barns filled with leaves from the same place on many plants were often of similar size and quality; grading was done as part of the harvest. Extended-family labor systems fit the new techniques.[56] "We barned Uncle Montgomery on Monday. Saturday was Uncle Dewey's day. All of us worked together. No one would barn Wednesday or Thursday . . . because that would mean adjusting the fire on Sundays and, well, this is the South."[57] Thus the nuclear family on the small farm was one part of a larger web of labor arrangements and technical strategies needed to make the whole cropscape work in its new configuration.

Sharecropping on small farms involved other changes in the cropscape. For example, Virginia farmers after emancipation adopted chemical fertilizer in ways that large-scale antebellum planters had not, even though it had been available to them. Fertilizers allowed small postbellum farmers to plant on poor, sandy soils, and this cropscape produced a brighter, milder tobacco than the old colonial crop. Here too the state aided the adoption of new technology, adding new elements to the cropscape, not through legislation, but by providing chemists to test fertilizer brands and to adjudicate disputes over quality. These chemists worked at the new North Carolina Agricultural and Mechanical College, one of the land-grant colleges established after the passage of the Morrill Act in 1862. State chemists also provided instruction in the harvest and curing methods that reliably made tobacco bright, yellow, and mild enough to inhale. Bright tobaccos turned tobacco manufacturing into Big Business in the last decades of the nineteenth century as cigarettes became monopolists' premier product. Small firms that had previously produced mostly chewing tobacco were absorbed by a large-scale consolidated producer of cigarettes, the infamous combination (some, imprecisely, call it a monopoly) known as the American Tobacco Company. Big Tobacco bought bright tobacco from small farmers in warehouses, with auctioneers to help farmers sell and manufacturers or middlemen buy a small pile of leaf in a basket—just a hundred pounds or so at a time.[58]

Thus large-scale tobacco plantations from the colonial and antebellum periods became small farms under new postbellum regulatory and labor systems. In the 1930s, New Deal policies locked farm size into its small space for a few decades more. Federal support for agricultural prices limited how much tobacco each farmer could sell and therefore capped farm sizes. In the last three decades of the twentieth century, however, the size of cultivation units grew once again, this time to justify investment in new harvesting machines. The postbellum method of harvest, the plucking of individual leaves, became embodied in a machine patented in 1971. Purchasing and operating such a machine was viable only for farmers who had larger plots to work than the New Deal allotments permitted. Earlier legal changes had paved the way for this mechanization: in 1961 and 1962, new laws permitted farmers to sell or lease their tobacco allotments to other farmers within their county, which allowed farms to grow large once again.[59]

FARMS GROW AGAIN

The new larger farms were the fourth phase of size oscillation in the tobacco farms of the Virginia-Carolina region. Once again this transformation was catalyzed by interlocking changes in law and technology: the softening of the limits on farm size inherited from the postbellum South, the hardening of these limits by New Deal policies in the 1930s, and the harvesting machine that made only larger farms profitable. Other sociotechnological changes accompanied the mechanization of the harvest: the move to bulk curing eliminated the labor of women who had looped individual leaves onto sticks for men to hang in the curing barns. As the cultivation routine shifted along with the increasing farm size, the labor arrangements of nuclear and extended families also changed, yet the mechanization of harvest and curing was sold to farmers as a return to family farming—a way to be rid of sharecroppers and wageworkers.[60] But the larger context played a role in making the tobacco harvesting machines operate profitably: the Civil Rights movement and the loss of cheap farm labor as farmers fled to Northern cities, the decline in family farming nationwide, and even the spread of suburbs into the countryside made small-scale farming less effective than it had been. The expertise of the USDA and the North Carolina State University contributed to the development and marketing of the machines, and the harvesting machine patent was assigned immediately to R. J. Reynolds Tobacco Company, indicating the likely support of the biggest buyer of the region's tobacco for the mechanization of cultivation and its associated growth in farm size.

The size of the tobacco cropscape changed repeatedly on the Virginia–North Carolina border as a result of larger trends in U.S. history, embodied in laws that influenced technological choices. From a crop that suited small and large farmers alike, in the eighteenth century tobacco became a plantation crop that rewarded only large-scale producers using enslaved labor. After the Civil War, emancipation of enslaved workers and changing credit arrangements shrank the scale of tobacco production to small sharecropped farms, and in the 1930s the small scale of production became law, as allotments limited how much each farm could sell. This scale of production expanded once again when government permitted the allotments to be sold or leased, creating consolidated farms that repaid mechanization in ways that smaller units could not. While the location of production stayed the same, the cropscape's inputs changed dramatically with each oscillation phase. Fertilizer helped make farms small postbellum; in the 1970s farms grew to accommodate the harvesting machine, which required regular infusions of gasoline to do its labor-saving work. Through the demand for gasoline, mechanizing the tobacco harvest linked tobacco farms to new markets. It also solidified cultivators' relationships to older ones—the corporations that bought their produce.

Tobacco's oscillations are a simple history that unveils how many different elements play a role in size, and they complicate the perceived causative relations among them. The plant itself did not dictate the farm size, but the cropscape in its entirety incorporated, caused, and was caused by changing farm sizes.

COFFEE MOSAICS: MULTI-SIZE
ON THE SPOT

Size is likewise an important element of the history of coffee—whether in the traditional story that supports the commodity-chain mythologies of global history or in the cropscape-focused version we present here.

COFFEE PLACES: A HISTORY

A native plant of the mountain forests of Abyssinia, *Coffea arabica* was taken sometime in the mid-sixteenth century by Muslim merchants to Yemen, where it was cultivated in terraces by local farmers in small garden plots amid subsistence crops.[61] Exported from the Yemeni port of Mocha, coffee consumption spread first to Arabia, then to North Africa and India, and in the middle of the seventeenth century to Eastern and Western Europe. From there, coffee history entered its imperial phase. Merchants from Cairo had at first dominated this long-distance coffee trade, but in the 1690s Dutch merchants took seedlings from Yemen and started to produce *arabica* in Java. The Dutch forced Javanese peasants to tend and harvest several hundred trees each and sell the cherries at fixed prices to the VOC. This was typical of the shift to colonialism: extending national territories allowed self-sufficiency instead of imports, so crop plants rather than crop fruits had to be captured and domesticated.

Taste shaped the cropscape and the movement of the crop. Coffee from Java initially supplied consumption centers in the Indian Ocean, but by the early eighteenth century Amsterdam had taken over from Cairo as the world's chief coffee entrepôt. Amsterdam warehouses were supplied with coffee beans not only from Yemen and Java but increasingly from the Americas as well. Building on previous experience with sugar cultivation, French and Dutch merchants had brought *Coffea arabica* to Saint-Domingue (Haiti), Martinique, and Dutch Guiana. The large American slave plantations dominated world coffee production in the eighteenth and nineteenth centuries, first in the Caribbean and later in Brazil. The São Paulo region, sustained by a dense railway network and cheaply available land, would become the world's top producer of coffee—a position that it maintains to date.[62] Its large monocrop plantations were cultivated first by slaves then, after Abolition in 1888, by indentured and wage laborers. Brazilian plantations supplied sophisticated cafés in France and Germany, but from the end of the nineteenth century American households became their main consumers and New York the world's main coffee exchange.

The traditional history seems inescapable: coffee moves from a Muslim-controlled commodity market in the Mediterranean and the Indian Ocean in the fifteenth to seventeenth centuries, to a Europe-centered world trade in the eighteenth and nineteenth centuries, leading to American supremacy in the twentieth century. Parallel to the increasing size of the market in the Global North, the size of the production site in the Global South also seems to grow. Collection from the wild in Abyssinia, cultivation of multicrop small gardens in Yemen, forced cultivation in Java, large plantations in the Caribbean and in Brazil: coffee seems the dream object for commodity-chain-based world history and its obsessions with global circulation. Second only to oil in global commerce, easy to transport over long distances, produced mostly in the Global South to be consumed in the Global North, coffee has been instrumental in reproducing teleological tales of globalization.

Historians who challenge the reductionism of such tales have paid a great deal of attention to coffee as a result. After all, coffee is now "produced in over a hundred countries, on five continents and many islands."[63] The linear trajectories described above were always more complicated. Unearthing the role played in the coffee cropscape by Banya agents of Gujarati firms who controlled allocation of credit in Yemen, and the commercial circuits that reached India and Iran, destabilizes the usual story of the shift of markets from the Middle East to Europe (Cairo to Amsterdam).[64] Adding complexity to coffee's global history are species of coffee other than *Coffea arabica,* namely, *Coffea robusta.* Recognizing this Congo native brings sub-Saharan Africa to the forefront and challenges a historiography that has largely ignored the region.[65] More and different geographies, people, and nonhuman actors can also be considered, added, foregrounded, or backgrounded, in one or another cropscape.

But no other element challenges the usual coffee narratives as vividly as does size. While the large Brazilian monocrop coffee plantations were considered by both enthusiasts and critics of globalization as the end of the story, we now have myriad Latin American, African, and Asian smallholders challenging the orthodoxy around big size.[66] Foregrounding small farmers, sharecroppers, women, children, or commercial intermediaries sheds light on alternative ways of integrating global markets in Nicaragua, Colombia, Angola, Cameroon, the Philippines, or Vietnam.

ETHIOPIA: HISTORICAL INTERLOCKINGS

Here we would like to add an alternative way of thinking about size. Slightly changing tack from the tobacco case, which explored the historical dynamics that led from one size to another, we further challenge the binary of big and small by positing the existence of different sizes *simultaneously*. The Ethiopian story of coffee is illuminating in this respect. In most global histories of coffee Ethiopia just shows up as mythical point of origin. *Coffea arabica* was a native species of the mountains of the Ethiopian southwest, where indigenous people collected it. Although Ethiopia is currently the fifth-largest producer of coffee in the world, and the largest on the African continent, historians enticed by a global history of flows—the transoceanic travels, financial markets, and cafes— are quick to leave Ethiopia behind and follow the *arabica* trail to Mocha, Cairo, Amsterdam, Haiti, Java, or Brazil. The only justification for historians to keep looking at coffee's primordial forest seems to be its position as source of genetic diversity—saving plantations worldwide that are always at risk of being destroyed by pathogens, such as the infamous rust *Hemileia vastratix*.[67]

This was also why following the brutal invasion of Ethiopia of 1936 by Benito Mussolini's Fascist regime, Italian scientists concentrated their attention on these high-altitude forests of the southwest, hoping to tap into their diversity as the source of genetic material for future Italian settlements in the region.[68] They considered coffee the only reliable source of income for the newly conquered country. Coffee would sustain so-called Italian East Africa, Mussolini's most cherished imperial conquest. Its brave settlers from overpopulated regions of Italy would survive if their newly planned communities were organized around coffee cultivation.

But scientists were quick to understand that generic references to "coffee in Ethiopia" did not account for the mosaic of reality. In the eastern parts of the country in the valley of the Errer there were a few large coffee plantations owned by Europeans (some as large as fifteen hundred hectares), surrounded by no fewer than ten thousand small Muslim producers. In the southwest highlands, west of the Great Rift Valley, in Sidamo, Gafo Goma, and Kefa, Italian scientists found very different conditions: "an immense region in which coffee inhabits the slopes and the bottom of the valleys between 1,500 and 2,500 m above sea-level. . . . [It] constitutes the most beautiful coffee park in the entire world."[69] Descriptions of coffee in this region seem less like agriculture and more like a form of gathering by Omotic and Sudanic indigenous people who took advantage of coffee shrubs growing wild under the forest canopy. Wild coffee in mountain forests in the southwest, small plots of coffee cultivation and scattered large plantations in the east: the coexistence of different systems of production that Italian scientists found, the synchrony of the Ethiopian coffee cropscape, also suggests its diachrony, as a cropscape that has conserved layers from different epochs. But rather than thinking of time here as an ordered accumulation of static, tidily superposed layers, like the timeline of geological strata, it might be more instructive to envision this Ethiopian coffeescape as the materialization of interactions between different historical layers.

Islamized peoples from southeastern Ethiopia had consumed coffee picked wild in the moist southwest mountain forest by Omotic and Sudanic natives since at least the fourteenth century.[70] It was from here that coffee consumption habits reached the Yemeni ports of Aden, Mocha, and Zabid in the first half of the fifteenth century, gaining favor among Sufi brotherhoods for keeping the mystic awake during demanding rituals.[71] Archaeologists have found evidence of increasing numbers of smaller cups in Yemen from the second half of the fifteenth century onwards, pointing at coffee's transition from a ritual communal drink into mundane beverage.[72] From Yemen, it spread to the Holy Places of Islam and the coffeehouses of Mecca and Medina, and by the end of the fifteenth century it was being drunk by university students in Cairo. In 1554 Suleiman the Magnificent introduced a tax on coffee to limit its consumption in Istanbul. Until the mid-sixteenth century coffee beans from southwest Ethiopia's forests, transported by caravan to the port of Zayla (south of Djibouti), were the single source of the café craze in the Muslim world. Only afterward did Yemeni farmers start cultivating coffee in the terraces overlooking the coastal plains and the ports of Aden, Mocha, and Zabid.

The Muslim coffee smallholders of eastern Ethiopia near Harar, described by Italian scientists in the 1930s, in fact grew varieties that came not from the southwestern Ethiopian forests but from these Yemeni terraces of the sixteenth century. This kind of Ethiopian coffee was sold in Mediterranean, European, and Indian markets together with coffee from Yemen; distinguished from the latter by its larger bean, it was eventually being called "longberry Mocha," likewise taking its name from the Yemeni port. Although coffee from Java and the Americas would progressively conquer the market, Mocha coffee (including the one cultivated in Ethiopia), would keep a niche market as a luxury product among connoisseurs. Dutch, English, and American merchants would ship coffee from Mocha until Aden took supremacy the moment British made it a free port in 1850. British and American houses moved from Mocha to Aden, followed soon after by Muslim, Jewish, and Banya traders. Most of this coffee was produced in Yemen, and only small quantities originated from Ethiopia.[73]

In Ethiopia, coffee consumption had been limited to the zones of Muslim presence (namely, around Harar), Christians from the northern high plateaus of Shewa considering it "savouring too strongly of the abhorred Mahomedan."[74]

What is today considered a symbol of Ethiopian identity, the coffee ritual, was first performed by Muslim communities mimicking the Christian Eucharist with the intention of being accepted by dominant Christian rule, and it was only adopted among the whole population in the twentieth century.[75] Indeed, only by the late nineteenth century would the expanding empire of Menelik II take an interest in coffee and promote its cultivation. The conquest of the southwest by the Shewan-dominated empire in the 1880s possibly halved the population of the region, namely, the Oromo: the devastating effects of the war were multiplied by a rinderpest epidemic. Much of the forest observed by Italian scientists in the 1930s, "the most beautiful coffee park in the entire world," was not wilderness but a secondary-growth forest from previously cleared and farmed land produced by the ravages of war and epidemics.[76]

The Christian conquerors alienated the southwestern lands in favor of northern landlords who perceived coffee as a potential major source of income, now that the Suez Canal had been opened and Red Sea commerce was once more flourishing. Also, the inauguration of the French-funded Ethio-Djibouti railway in 1917, connecting Addis Ababa with the port of Djibouti on the Red Sea, considerably lowered transportation costs from the landlocked Ethiopian plateaus. Southwestern forests where coffee grew in the wild were now owned mostly by absentee landlords who depended on tenants and sharecroppers to make a profit out of them. In lieu of rent for farmland to cultivate food crops, tenants "cleared the forest floor around existing wild trees, thinned them, and replanted young bushes. The forest itself provided the required shade and soil moisture. No fertilizer was needed, only labor to pick berries, prune back old growth, transport seedlings, and slash weeds."[77] This was accomplished through sharecropping agreements with local laborers, who were entitled to half the coffee they harvested. Coffee was sufficiently profitable for sharecroppers to make enough capital to buy their own land in the forest and establish their own smallholdings mixing coffee and food crops.[78] By 1925 coffee production in the southwest was already greater than in the east, around Harar, the traditional area of Muslim smallholders. Previously snubbed as an identifier of infidels, coffee had become the principal export of the Christian kingdom and its principal source of revenue.

The potential for increased profits grew during the brief period of Italian colonial rule (1936–1941), when the old 350-kilometer mule trail was replaced by a new road linking Jimma in the southwest to Addis Ababa with its rail connection to the sea. High prices of coffee on the international market after World War II further increased the expansion of coffee cultivation in the southwest of Ethiopia. In addition to local tenancy and sharecropping agreements, landlords increasingly contracted labor from outside the region. Building on their kinship relations in the north, they brought in migrants to clear new forest areas in exchange for permission to farm the land for two years, after which they were evicted and their farmland was turned over to coffee cultivation.

These new coffee farms were weeded and harvested with seasonal wage labor, also from outside the region. By the 1970s the seasonal workforce arriving in the southwest from neighboring regions numbered no less than fifty thousand people, who stayed in the area from October to December, the peak of coffee season. Many stayed on permanently and invested their salaries in buying small plots to cultivate their own coffee, increasing the population of the area. Working seasonally as pickers of wild coffee on some large landlord estates was an additional option for the new smallholders to make enough cash to buy oxen to farm their own land. They mostly cultivated maize as their food crop instead of the traditional grains of Ethiopia's northern regions, teff, eleusine, and wheat.[79] While the annual labor demands of these grains conflicted with the demands of coffee cultivation, the short maturation cycle of maize, its high yield, low labor cost for sowing and processing, and, more important, the flexibility of its harvesting schedule, made it the perfect companion species to coffee cultivation.[80] The arrival of maize in the Ethiopian southwest around the end of the nineteenth century through Muslim merchants of whom we know little was in fact an essential element enabling the existence of coffee smallholders, forming what James C. McCann calls the coffee-maize complex. Maize was what saved so many of the smallholders from bankruptcy in the ups and downs of the international markets, so characteristic of the dark stories of monocrop areas. Maize points at another historical trail that further complicates the multisized Ethiopian coffeescape of the southwest in which coffee is simultaneously picked from the wild, cultivated on large coffee estates, and grown next to maize fields in smallholders' plots. All these significantly challenge the dominant narratives that explain coffee histories or advocate coffee policy and practice from a perspective valorizing large-size holdings and operations.

If coffee and tobacco complicate the role of size in models of historical change, then the case of tea in India underscores that ideals of scale are not always simply or easily achieved on the ground.

TEA AND IDEOLOGY: STRIVING FOR SIZE

As already discussed in chapter 2, "Places," the implantation of a tea cropscape in India in the 1840s required not simply the adaptation of the original Chinese crop plant but also the creation of new tea-centered assemblages and styles of

Nine scenes on a tea estate. Produced for a British audience and supposedly showing work on an Indian tea plantation, only two scenes from this series are actually set in India (Assam). The others, directly copied from the popular export art albums painted by Chinese artists for European markets, depict Chinese processes of tea cultivation and production, which at that time British planters were trying, with only partial success, to establish in India. Engraving by T. Brown, c. 1850, after J. L. Williams. Courtesy of the Wellcome Collection.

place making. Here we focus on four aspects of size that crucially shaped the development of the Indian teascape.

The first two were intertwined ideologies. First was the British ideal, still taking shape but soon to become the liberal norm, of large-scale, capital-intensive enterprise as the most efficient and profitable form of production. Here was the imagination, the ambition that set the ball of Indian tea production rolling. Economies of scale were currently demonstrating their advantages in the colonial sugar industry and the home textile factories, and in the systems of "scientific farming" taking shape in East Anglia and Lowland Scotland. Together with scale economies and capital concentration went ambitions to replace human labor by machines: the ideal of mechanization. True, there were no machines suited to tea production available at the time, but this daunted nobody: the promoters of tea cultivation in India were confident that "the activity, the energy, the inventive genius of the Anglo-Saxon race" would quickly transform traditional, "crude" Chinese techniques.[81]

A third size-related factor at play in Indian teascapes was botanical: the native Assamese tea plant was larger and more vigorous than its Chinese counterpart, and better suited to local conditions. Once Indian planters acknowledged its potential and accommodated their techniques accordingly, discarding the Chinese plants, which largely failed to thrive in India, the stage was set for expanding the tea industry to new locations in India, and for developing year-round harvesting regimes that raised both output and profits, outcompeting China and establishing India as the world's primary black-tea exporter. But India's success in shouldering out Chinese teas was not a simple matter of competitive pricing: Indian teas tasted quite different. The last expression of gigantism that we discuss in this section is the drive for ever-expanding sales, and the efforts that went into creating and expanding first export and then local markets for strong, dark Indian teas.

When investors rushed to buy shares in the newly chartered Assam Company in 1839, it seemed inevitable that the industrial ideals of scale economies and technological innovation would translate into steady growth, improvement, and shareholder profits. In fact, for several decades progress in the Assam Company, as in the myriad other Indian tea enterprises into which British investors greedily poured capital, was unsteady and uncertain. Despite unequivocal and generous support from the British state, more than once the Indian tea industry found itself on the brink of collapse. Just as local estate managers or engineers complained that their London- or Glasgow-based Board of Directors lacked all understanding of the facts on the ground, so too metropolitan ideals of industrial rationality, innovation, and progress proved a difficult fit for the grounded skills inherent in local work processes—and more so in the face of unexpected pests and diseases challenging both the plants and the human settlers.

SCALING UP THE CHINESE MODEL:
TECHNOLOGICAL RESISTANCE

As mentioned in "Places," the Chinese tea industry was based on small-scale production. The experimental tea gardens established in India in the 1830s by the colonial government were small too. But although in principle the British could have attempted to set up a Chinese-scale smallholder-based tea system in India, this would have been unattractive to the British men the government wanted to attract as owners and managers, and—as the East India Company's experience in China had shown—such a decentralized mode of production would have been difficult to manage in ways that would generate reliable profits for British shareholders. Directly managed plantations, on the other hand, had amply proven their worth across the empire; they tamed "the wild" and rendered the alien landscape legible.[82] And in the process generated lavish profits. Furthermore, the Dutch had already begun running tea plantations on Java, providing a model of a working capitalist teascape.[83]

It was the scale of tea cultivation envisaged by the British rulers that determined the very location of the Indian teascapes. Because huge stretches of land, often five hundred to a thousand acres, were considered necessary for a viable enterprise, Indian tea plantations were located in isolated, usually forest regions where large tracts of land could more easily be alienated to British planters.

One scalar characteristic of the Indian tea industry, then, is the size of operations. From that perspective, the typical teascape stretched across many hundreds of acres of remote areas and hillsides. As a cropscape this production mode was further extended in space by its link to a labor source, often many hundreds of kilometers away, in one or more impoverished rural communities in what the government considered the overpopulated plains. For the tea industry was not only large scale but also labor intensive. Workers were needed to clear land, plant and tend the bushes, pluck leaves, process them, and pack them—fifteen hundred workers for a thousand-acre estate was reckoned average in the 1930s.[84]

The tiny Chinese tea farms were run with family labor and some seasonal hiring from nearby villages. The Dutch plantation managers on Java could draw on dense local populations. But in the isolated regions of the Indian tea gardens populations were sparse, and most locals were reluctant to work for the British. Securing adequate, regular, and docile labor was a huge challenge from the start, and it has remained a challenge even in the post-Independence era.[85] The British colonial government did all it could to support tea growers' steadily increasing labor needs. In the 1860s Indian tea gardens began to make reliable profits in large part thanks to the passage in 1863 of the first Transport of Native Labourers Act, formalizing a notoriously exploitative system in which brokers signed up whole communities of impoverished peasants from the crowded plains as indentured workers. Because they had to be housed and fed on the estate, about a third of the land was occupied by workers' houses, food plots or grazing, and service buildings.

Although the scale of even the earliest tea enterprises cried out for mechanization, the processes of tea production proved stubbornly resistant.[86] Despite many ingenious engineering experiments through the first half century of the Indian tea industry, it was only in the 1880s that reliable machines were developed for a limited number of tea-processing steps. Then, as the scale of tea-processing operations inside the factory expanded, it did not reduce but actually increased the need for manual labor outside the factory, for field-workers to produce and deliver sufficient leaves to feed the hungry machines. The indenture system persisted. A sequence of Labour Acts was passed from 1863 right up to World War II, generating the wrath of anticolonial activists for whom tea, like salt and indigo, became a symbol of British oppression.[87]

From the outset the big enterprises like the Assam Company employed a professional engineer, and these engineers were typically enthusiastic and dogged in their efforts to develop suitable machines. But the history of the Indian tea industry reminds us how many failures typically precede successful innovation. Delicate processes involving both dexterity and judgment, such as rolling or drying, long proved resistant to mechanization. But design failures were not the only obstacle; so too was the physical and psychological distance between staff grappling first-hand with complicated material problems on remote estates, on the one hand, and managers comfortably ensconced in their metropolitan headquarters, on the other. The Assam Company for one had a long history of the London Board falling out with local engineers and managers. In 1842 Assistant Strong devised a machine for rolling leaves but was instructed to desist. In 1859 Superintendent Henry de Mornay was experimenting with mechanical fans for grading the leaves when he was implicated in "irregularities" and fired; also in 1859, Company Engineer James Gibbon was developing a rolling machine but was "dismissed for intemperance and violence." Finally, in 1868 Company Engineer James C. Kinmond built the first successful and officially approved rolling machine. Initially powered by specially trained ponies and later by three-horsepower engines, Kinmond's sturdy rolling machine proved a lasting success and was widely adopted on larger estates. But the machines could not provide "the nice final twist" that brought a higher price, hence many estates returned to hand rolling or used the machine only when labor was scarce.[88]

The tide really changed in the 1880s. Tastes in Britain were finally shifting away from Chinese whole-leaf teas, so fine rolling became less of a priority. Heavy-duty rollers and then effective drying and sorting machines were becoming standard. At last machines were starting to earn their keep, so that mechanization within the factory significantly lowered production costs, opening an era of more profitable trading and industry expansion. By the 1890s most estates had a steam engine to run their other machines; if anything went wrong an engineer would have to be called in, often from a great distance. Yet, as mentioned earlier, although mechanization gradually displaced human workers from at least some of the processing tasks inside the factory, most outside work resisted mechanization. Ambitious plans for mechanical plowing or plucking fell by the wayside. Hoes, pruning knives, sickles, axes, elephants' trunks, and above all skilled human fingers continued their work; the overall need for estate labor never dwindled, and the expertise of the labor-gang organizers remained just as essential to the success of the enterprise as that of engineers, estate managers, botanists, and chemists.

BOTANICAL AFFORDANCES

The size of production units was a significant spur to the mechanization of the Indian tea industry, but mechanization might never have succeeded if the Indian estates had stuck with the original Chinese tea varieties. The Chinese tea plants were delicate, and so too were their leaves, both requiring highly skilled treatment. Native Assam teas, larger, more vigorous plants with bigger, more sapid leaves, had been domesticated on the experimental stations of the 1830s, but their leaves produced a much stronger, darker brew than appealed to British tea drinkers accustomed to light, perfumed Chinese teas. Initially companies forbade planters to grow the sturdy Assam varieties, which they could not sell at home. But the Assam bushes produced more leaves and more flushes than the Chinese bushes. The Assam teas were clearly more suitable for large-scale production, and by the 1860s Chinese bushes were dismissed by planters as "the curse of Assam." Yet Indian teas still struggled against Chinese imports on the British market. The long campaign to transform public taste and shift preferences to strong, dark teas was uncertain for several decades but finally triumphant in the 1880s. By 1890 Indian teas had soundly thrashed their Chinese competitors on British markets.[89] The profitability of large-scale, mechanized tea estates, and the resilience and productivity of the Assam bush, led to multiple reproductions of the characteristic teascape across the empire, as big colonial companies like Finlays of Glasgow rushed to buy up tracts of land across India, Ceylon and other subtropical colonies, like Kenya.

Finally, in the context of size and scale, it is important to note that whereas the China leaves were easily damaged by mechanical treatment, the tougher Assam leaves not only withstood machine treatment but if they were damaged during processing their special characteristic, the strength of the liquor, was enhanced. Once consumers were won over to strong Indian teas, mechanized treatments were devised to make them stronger still, culminating in the CTC (crush-tear-curl) machine of the 1930s, which enormously increased the volume and speed of processing and significantly lowered prices. A key outcome of the switch to Assam-style teas was the subalternization of tea drinking, which meant a continually expanding market. Even in the mid-nineteenth century tea was still an expensive purchase, restricted largely to well-off households. But the price of the strong Assam-style teas fell steadily from the 1880s. Even poor people, first in Britain and its white colonies and then in India itself, began to consume tea regularly, the stronger the better. Factories no longer discarded broken leaves or even tea dust: they had become profitable commodities. In the 1930s the CTC machines began churning out large amounts of really cheap, strong tea. A hundred or even fifty years earlier this would have been unsalable anywhere. But in the 1930s, to counter the impact of the Great Depression on their metropolitan markets, British tea companies seized the opportunity to market tea to working-class Indians.[90] As average prices at London auctions tumbled, the lure of "350 million throats only awaiting initiation" became irresistible, and the Indian Tea Market Expansion Board was established in 1935 to pursue "what was undoubtedly the largest marketing campaign in Indian history."[91] The board's intensive advertising campaigns contained an interesting paradox of size. In what could be seen as one of the earliest instances of "tapping the bottom of the pyramid," tea vans distributed free cups of tea and sold satisfied customers small-size individual sachets ("pice packets") at prices that psychologically appeared affordable. The small size of the packaging proved an effective way to grow the (local) clientele.

The large-scale teascape of British India was anything but a natural construct, and yet from the very beginning it seemed to its prime movers a natural goal. The mechanized tea plantation represented a shared ideal toward which all the white human actors strove, a dream that epitomized the translation of manufacturing industry into the vegetable world. Together the British government, its imperial legislature in India, its commercial companies, greedy investors, ambitious young men, and dogged engineers labored to realize their shared dream: tea bushes stretching in rows over thousands of acres, which they hoped would one day be cultivated and harvested by machines, then processed almost entirely mechanically on the estate factory into a reliable, uniform tea that the whole civilized world would drink with gusto. In spite of the mismatch between the dream and the pace at which it could be realized, the underlying ideology and the teleology adamantly persisted.

MUDDY WATERS

While the productivist logic of increasing size, capital, and mechanization in the Indian tea industry went unquestioned by the British government or by most planters, the cases of coffee in Ethiopia and of tobacco in Virginia and North Carolina suggest that the logics of size are much more complex. What new perspectives open up if we focus at a microscale, seldom considered by global historians, the realm of the all-essential nematodes and water capillaries without which no cropscape would exist? Here we propose analyzing water as a crop that humans cultivate just as carefully, and with as many variations, as they do plants. Furthermore, instead of starting with the giant dams that have generated so much social theory, we scale down to the worm's-eye view, or rather to the farmer's-eye view, as reflected in almost all farming treatises, ancient or modern. This riff focuses on a matter of vital importance to anyone trying to grow plants: namely, how a cultivator brings about the marriage of a drop of water and a crumb of soil.

WATER, POWER, LIFE

Curiously, when it comes to water, the best-known theories hold that "big is bad." In 1957, at the height of the Cold War, Karl Wittfogel, a historian of China and a disenchanted Marxist, published *Oriental Despotism,* in which he propounded his influential theory of *hydraulic society:* hydraulic civilizations, including Egypt, Mesopotamia, imperial China, and preconquest Mexico, were founded on large-scale irrigation and flood-control works whose construction, maintenance, and control required bureaucratic management by a centralized, absolutist state. Such states were inherently inimical, Wittfogel argued, to democratic debate, personal freedom or the spirit of innovation: their historical trajectories and fundamental values were therefore quite distinct from those of the Western nations.[92] An elaboration of Marx's concept of the Asiatic Mode of Production, the imprint of Wittfogel's hydraulic theory remains potent today, for instance in debates about why eighteenth-century China failed to "develop" while Japan succeeded, or refracted in contemporary assessments of the authoritarianism inherent in big dam schemes. Whether they accept or contest Wittfogel's hypothesis, all explanations of the relations between water control and social organization have to take size and scale into account.

We usually think of water management and the associated political power and physical control as cascading downwards, from the top to the bottom, the large to the small, the central to the local. Yet (as the water bureaucrats of imperial China were ruefully aware), if local farmers refused to dredge the village ditches enough silt could quickly build up to cause floods all along the giant Yangtze River; if markets shifted and peasants upstream switched from cotton to irrigated sugarcane, rice harvests downstream might be ruined. In other words, small-scale actions are decisive too. Disasters and crises capture our attention as historians: what caused this drought, that flooding? We have perhaps paid less attention to the laborious and ingenious techniques that went into building and maintaining the everyday routines of water use. So, what insights do we gain if we start, not at the top, with the Colorado River dams or the Imperial Bureau of Public Works (*gongbu*), but at the base, focusing at ground level on how farmers domesticate, plant, cultivate, and harvest water? What can we learn if we analyze water itself as a crop—which is, in essence, how farmers must treat it?

Water is an essential component of every cropscape, slaking the thirst of all its life-forms and activities: crop plants need water, but so too do humans, animals, and micro-organisms. Human populations also use water for keeping clean, and for almost every kind of processing and manufacture, from cooking and pot making to nuclear cooling towers. Technologies for managing water range from grandiose hydraulic systems like Angkor Wat and the Hoover Dam to barrels collecting rain from the roof, from rituals in rain temples to phone apps for meteorological reports, from pre-germinating rice seed to rolling frost into the soil. Granted, many farmers past and present depend on public works of various sizes for some of their water supply. Granted, too, that water systems almost invariably operate at multiple levels or scales: field and farm, perhaps also village, watershed, river valley, county, or even state. But whether it comes from rain, a local stream, a community-built tank, or a state-built reservoir, farmers have to work with the available water as a raw material, carefully planting, tending, and harvesting it and processing it into manageable and useful forms. Their water-cultivation techniques are a fundamental component shaping the local cropscape and its linkages. This working with water is what we consider here, exploring the water-cultivation techniques characteristic of two distinctive cropscapes: wet-rice cultivation and dryland farming.

WET-RICE FARMING

Many crops are grown in swampy or wet fields, including taros, sugarcane, ginger, and wet rice, whether rain fed or irrigated.[93] Wet rice is the most widely grown and offers the most numerous variations in habitat and cultivation techniques: self-sown floating rices keeping pace with the floodwaters in the Mekong marshes, rice double-cropped or alternated with winter wheat, rice grown in bunded fields on gentle slopes, in dizzying terraces, or on diked islands reclaimed from the river. Rice farmers worked with stone, soil, bamboo, and wood to build their fields; they used simple but sophisticated techniques and tools to carry water across the landscape and distribute it between plots and people: hoes, wooden or iron pumps, flumes made from tree trunks or bamboo, wooden sluices, incense coils or temple bells to time water shares.[94]

Whereas dryland farmers typically rate individual fields by the fertility of the soil, wet-rice farmers grade them by the quality of the water supply, which they put great effort into managing and improving. To thrive, rice requires several inches of water through the growth period, which should then be drained or dried away a few days before the harvest. Sometimes the monsoon rains suffice to grow wet rice: rainwater is retained in the fields by building low earth walls (bunds); sometimes the rain is collected in individual or collective tanks and released gradually into the fields; often water is diverted from a stream into a gravity-fed system that allows the water to trickle down from one field to another; or water may be pumped up from a nearby ditch or river.

In a farm handbook written in 1149 by Chen Fu, an inhabitant of Jiangnan (the Lower Yangtze region), which at that point was China's chief rice bowl, we find the following advice on how to create a sustainable and effective waterscape:

> On high land identify the places where water accumulates and dig out tanks. Out of 10 *mu* [0.66 ha, reckoned to be the amount needed to support an average household] you must be prepared to set aside 2 or 3 for water storage. At the end of the spring when the rainy season begins, heighten the banks and deepen and widen the interior [of the tank] to give it the best capacity. Strengthen the banks with mulberries or silkworm-oaks to which water-buffalo may be tethered in the shade, as their nature requires. The buffalo's trampling will strengthen the banks, the mulberries, being well-watered, will grow into fine trees, and even in the dry season there will be sufficient water for irrigation, yet in heavy rains the tank will not overflow and harm the crops.[95]

Chen emphasizes the importance of storing water to support the typical Jiangnan rice-sericulture assemblage. The tank waters the rice fields and sustains the mulberry trees and oaks, whose leaves not only feed silkworms but also

128 Sizes

protect the precious water from evaporation and the buffalo (a surprisingly delicate animal) from heatstroke. Letting water from the tank into the paddies in carefully regulated quantities assures healthy growth of the crop and buffers the farmlands (and the farmers) against both dearth and excess of water. In the paddies, the water supports a dense population of algae, fish, and ducks. The fish and ducks feed on the algae and on insect larvae, keeping malaria at bay. (In China, as elsewhere, malaria became a scourge when new rice lands were opened up or where stagnant water went unattended.)[96] When the fields are drained for harvest, the fish too are harvested. This is just one of many Asian variants of water cultivation that support productive rice-based multicropping.[97]

Let us now consider another crucial product of water in the rice systems: namely, mud. Rice seed germinates, and rice seedlings thrive, in a layer of silky mud. Over years of use the soil in wet-rice fields separates into two layers: a top layer of mud, with an impermeable hardpan underneath (which usefully prevents the essential standing water from seeping into the subsoil). Again, there are various ways to produce the right consistency of mud after the rains fall and soften the soil of the harvested field. In eighteenth-century Java farmers drove their cattle down into the paddies. More typically, farmers let water into the field and left it for a few days to stand before harnessing the buffalo to plow, cross-plow, then use a harrow with ferociously sharp tines to puddle the clay into mud. Rice seed is usually soaked in water and pre-germinated before sowing in the field; often it is sown not in the main field but in a carefully tended and manured seedbed, then transplanted once it has grown about twenty centimeters tall. This reduces the time needed for the rice to be ready to harvest and increases the yield. The success of these operations all depends on mud.

Mud and water are good, however, only in their place and time. Draining water from the soil is as crucial as adding it: the water must not drown the plants, and as they near ripening, they like to have dry feet. The shallow earthen bunds keep water in while the rice is growing, but a few strokes of the heavy iron hoe that all rice farmers use opens a gap that allows water to flow into the next field, or out into the drain. The famous Chinese wooden chain pump, where so many farmers spent so many hours pedaling, was essential both for raising water into the field from the surrounding ditches, and for pumping water out. In many regions paddy-fields grew several crops in a year. In Jiangnan summer rice was frequently followed by winter wheat or barley. After the rice-harvest these "twice-ripe" fields had to be deep-plowed, down to but not through the hardpan, so the soil could dry out thoroughly before the next sowing, and then plowed again into ridges and furrows, so that the spring rains would drain off and not damage the roots of the barley.

Chain pump in the rice fields. As the chain pump was considered a labor-saving technology compared to other common devices for raising water, such as buckets or sweeps, late imperial Chinese artists liked to depict the workers chatting, singing, or even—as here—reading. 1639 (1st) edition of Xu Guangqi's *Nongzheng quanshu* (Complete treatise on agricultural administration).

A final, crucial point to be emphasized in our mud-centered perspective is that wet-rice farming depends upon a carefully leveled field: the water must be the same depth for all the plants. In the days before laser leveling and Green Revolution land-consolidation programs, this meant that all paddy fields were very small. Their edges no more than a few meters long, they clung to the contours of the land, and the steeper the topography, the smaller the fields. Wooden plows or hoes sufficed to work these tiny surfaces effectively, and yet because rice gives such high yields, a farm of under an acre could feed a family and support a vigorous economy of commercial cropping and rural manufactures. Such tiny rice farms underpinned Ming China's role as the world's leading exporter of manufactured goods; in Tokugawa Japan the dynamism of these small farms prompted a scale of national development that Japanese historians refer to as the "industrious revolution."[98]

DRYLAND FARMING

Here again we take a Chinese example to show how water was manipulated to generate a cropscape. North China is not an easy place to farm productively. It has intensely cold winters and burning summers; the low rainfall is concentrated in a couple of months in spring or summer and often falls as violent thunderstorms. The loess soils of the inland regions are fertile but fragile; the soils of the Yellow River plains are often heavy, stiff, and prone to waterlogging. Hardy and drought-resistant millets (setaria and panicum), sown immediately after the spring rains, were the main cereal crops from Neolithic times, as they still are in many northern villages today.[99]

One of the classics of Chinese agronomy, the *Qimin yaoshu* (Essential techniques for the common people), completed by an official called Jia Sixie in about 540 C.E., describes a cropscape organized around setaria millet as the staple, and premised on sophisticated and precise techniques for bringing together seed, soil, and water. "Grain is always best sown just after rain. If the rainfall is slight you should sow immediately while the soil is still damp; if it is heavy wait for the weeds to sprout first. (If the rainfall is slight and you do not sow immediately there will be no moisture to make the seed sprout, but if you do not wait for the soil to turn pale after heavy rain then the dampness will be trapped in the soil and will make the roots sickly.)"[100]

The cultivation techniques that Jia advocates for field crops build upon principles first set down in a political treatise of 239 B.C.E., quoting a work now lost, *Houji shu* (Book of Prince Millet):

> Are you able to make low, wet land fruitful? Are you able to conserve dry soils and temper them with damp? . . . Can you ensure that your millet heads will be rounded

and the husks thin, that the grains will be numerous and plump so that food is plentiful? How may you do all this? By these fundamental principles of tillage: The strong [soils] must be weakened, the weak strengthened. The rested must be set to work, the hard-worked rested. The lean must be fattened, the fatter made leaner. The compact must be loosened, the loose compacted. The damp must be dried out, and the dry dampened. . . . Till five times and use the weeding-hoe five times. Observe all these rules closely.[101]

The *Qimin yaoshu* elaborates an intensive system of tillage designed to ensure that, from the moment of sowing until the harvest, whatever the type of soil it was kept moist but not wet, its surface finely crumbed into what modern agronomists call a dust mulch in order to reduce the evaporation of moisture and the erosion of soil. In autumn, after the harvest, deep plowing followed by the use of a tined harrow broke up the clods before the winter frosts, which crumbled the soil and killed insects. At the end of winter cartloads of manure from the stables were emptied onto the fields and turned in. Any snowfall was rolled into the fields. From the first lunar month onward (late January or February in modern reckoning) a series of shallow plowings with narrow furrows took place, each followed by several cross-harrowings, where a bush harrow was dragged across the field first along the rows and then at right angles to them. Then, in a tillage system anticipating Tull's horse-hoeing husbandry (mentioned in "England's Agricultural Revolution" above), the field was plowed into ridges, and the seed was not broadcast but sown in rows using a drill. The drill saved seed and economized on soil moisture and fertilizer; it also facilitated hoeing, either by hand or using a multiblade device drawn by an ox or mule. This eliminated weeds that competed with the millet for moisture and fertilizer, thus producing a much better crop.

The *Qimin yaoshu* described large-scale operations. For several centuries between about 200 and 700 C.E. most land in North China was concentrated in large estates owned by powerful families. Client families provided labor. There were draught animals to pull the plows, flocks to manure the fields, and sufficient land to rotate crops or set aside land for orchards or timber. This was the scale at which the dryland tillage regime was most productive. Through most of the rest of the imperial period, however, North China was divided into smallholdings, and the tillage regime was still effective even at a much smaller scale of operations (although a northern family typically needed six hectares rather than the 0.6 hectares considered sufficient in Jiangnan). This dryland cropscape, with its characteristic techniques of soil and water management, survived in North China into the modern era. Despite its apparently low-tech machinery compared to the technology now common on Western farms, in the early twentieth century it garnered praise from various foreign visitors, some of whom admired it as a horticultural alternative to bonanza-style farming, others as a system of arid-land cultivation that could advantageously be imported to semidesert colonial territories like Algeria.[102]

We have looked here at how water is husbanded so that it travels through the veins of a cropscape, connecting and nourishing different spaces and actors, knitting together seed and soil. Although we have noted historical and geographical variants in how the two tillage regimes link to modes of production at the very general level, there is no space here to discuss the intermediate scales in the politics of water as crop, the knitting of groups, the confrontations and strife, or the identities, positive or negative, formed by or attributed to working with water.[103] Treating water as an object of nurturing viewed at the level of the field or farm rather than at the big-dam or infrastructural scale brings to the fore the techniques and experience, the everyday care, decisions, and planning that farmers employ to keep soil and plants in good heart as they grow. This densely material perspective highlights vital aspects of work and maintenance, both material and social, that do not always appear clearly in histories that focus predominantly on the larger scale.

While the technical challenges of mud making and mulching may seem trivial in relation to the grand sweeps of world history, microhistories of these farming principles and practices illuminate the concerns and resources of farmers, the articulations between different scales of hydrology and of management, and the mechanisms enabling the chronological oscillations (changing size on the spot) characteristic of so many "hydraulic societies," from Mexico to Sri Lanka, where we see alternation between state-level coordination and reversion to self-contained local water-control projects.[104] We hope that this experiment with size, starting at the level of the marriage between a drop of water and a crumb of soil, suggests a novel and fruitful way to think about water, scale, and human history.

In this set we took the farm, the unit of operation, as our frame for examining norms and ideologies of size. We paid special attention not only to the conditions under which different sizes or ideals of size take shape and evolve but also to the ways they are represented and morally coded, institutionalized by historical actors, or retrospectively organized into histories that justify the present and predict the future. As deterministic accounts of history so often justify policy choices, and as historical analyses of agrarian systems are so often driven by political assumptions, in this chapter history writing and policy intermingle more than in any other chapter.[105]

Despite the deep lineages of the big is better ideal in Western thought, it is nevertheless a local value that was not shared in many other parts of the world. Furthermore, establishing a trend depends on the scale of observation, including when you cut time. Between collectivization and at least the 1970s, the USSR could claim that its eradication of small farms in favor of large had brought success; by contrast Poland was deemed a failure because it maintained its small farms through the period of Communist rule. Post-1989, however, Russia's huge collective farms were deemed to have failed, while Poland, with its thousands of small farms now thought of as enterprises producing for the market, had become a success.[106] The tensions that underlie a prevailing ideology of size are often intense, and transition from one scale to another can seldom be effected without what often proves to be extreme class violence, whether in Soviet anti-kulak campaigns, land reform in China or Mexico, or the enclosure movement of early modern England.

In selecting multiple scales to examine cropscapes, including reframing them to ask how smaller units—farms, fields, factories, families, or even small crumbs of soil and their meeting with water—are embedded within them, we have invited further reflection not only on the dynamics of size but also on alternative periodizations, chronologies, or temporalities. In exploring the coexistence of sizes, the persistence or ephemerality of sizes, oscillations or displacements, and small-scale operations at grassroots level supporting large-scale economic systems, we have challenged a range of dualist models and some of the strong mythologies or assumptions about size deeply lodged in policy, social theory, and history. Equally important, our riffs highlight erasures in historiography consequent upon these assumptions and suggest ways in which we might recoup these hidden movements or moments within larger histories, and evaluate their impact and relevance. Each of our four cases confirms that there is no natural or optimal size for a cropscape, no universal logic of growth. The riffs also underline the importance of recognizing the persistence and the necessity of the small within the big—and vice versa. How do our questions and explanations change as we zoom in from a complete tea commodity chain, encompassing headquarters in London and plantations in India, to the engineer's shed on a remote tea estate? The cropscape allows us to encompass both, or make other choices. What do we learn about the wider cropscape, in particular about social forms, technological cultures, and the relations between locality and state, if we start not with dams and despotisms but with moisture conservation, harrows, and the daily round of a farming household?

Chapter 4 Actants

What makes a yam crop flourish? In a conversation on this all-important topic Kayla'i, a Trobriand chief's son who "wielded the magic of the garden" in his village, observed to the anthropologist Bronisław Malinowski: "The missionaries state: 'We make divine service and because of this the gardens grow.' This is a lie." "The natives," Malinowski explains, "do not accuse the missionaries of deception, but rather of a certain feeble-mindedness or, as Professor Lévy-Bruhl would put it, of a prelogical mentality when it comes to gardening magic. . . . To the native, magic is as indispensable to the success of gardening as competent and effective husbandry": the magician presides over each important step of yam growing, and with each spell uttered, "magical virtue enters the soil." "Garden magic is in the Trobriands a public and official service"; similarly, in the missionaries' home churches back in Britain vicars led their congregations in prayers to speed the plow or swell the grain. Both Trobriand and Christian theories of plant growth framed the yamscape to include ritual experts as actors and the supernatural as an integral dimension of the plant's growth cycle.[1]

Agronomists would dismiss both missionary and Trobriand theories of plant growth as feeble-minded. In their secular ontology of the cropscape, fertilizers, not magic or church services, stimulate healthy plant development; research chemists and agrochemical companies, not priests or garden wizards, are the farmer's trusty allies in the struggle for a good harvest. Agronomists recognize earthworms as playing beneficial roles in soil health, including "enhancing soil porosity" and "providing channels for root growth."[2] In the yam gardens of Nyamikum village, in Papua New Guinea, earthworms are also seen as beneficent, acting "as the facilitators of tuber development, both by softening the ground in which the tubers will grow (the actual agronomical role of earthworms), but also as observers of the gardener's behaviour." The worms perceive any failure to work quietly and respectfully in the garden; they can also smell in his tainted sweat any failure by a worker to observe the sequence of yam-garden rites that take place at the village altars.[3] In the yamscape of Nyamikum a worm is not only a biological but also a social and spiritual actor.

We have defined cropscapes, drawing on concepts developed in STS, as assemblages of humans and nonhumans, within which a particular crop in a particular place and time flourishes or fails (see our introductory chapter, "Orientations"). This chapter applies the associated concept of actants to explore the power of things in history, including plants, animals, concepts, and institutions. Bruno Latour defines an actant as "something that acts or to which activity is granted by others. It implies *no* special motivation of *human individual* actors, nor of humans in general. An actant can be literally anything provided it is granted to be the source of an action."[4] The criterion is that an actant changes things: "Remember that if an actor doesn't make a difference, it's not an actor."[5] Paraphrasing, as historians we can take actors or actants as people or things that produce a difference in history. But unlike our actor-network theory (ANT) colleagues, as historians we must not only reassemble or dismantle our actors and their assemblages but also historicize them.

In taking nonhuman actants seriously, iconoclastically sidelining Great Men and scientific societies to push a microbe, a mussel, or a computer printer center stage, STS has radically recast how we frame and interpret the *processes* by which types of knowledge, things, and institutions come into being. Cropscapes, as assemblages, allow us, in the spirit of STS, to identify commonly ignored or invisible actors and to bring obscure connections to the surface. But in our recasting of historical scenes and stories we aim to integrate two approaches: first, the anti-humanist or post-humanist lens of ANT and the new materialists, which gives no analytical or moral preference to humans; and, second, the emic, anthropological, or ontological approach, richly mined in recent cultural histories of science and technology, which seeks to recapture worlds coming into being on their own terms. Nothing in those worlds is predetermined: their quests and questions are not to be understood as prefiguring the modern, their actors and actions are often radically strange, and their spatial and historical scales disrupt conventional geographies and chronologies. STS studies typically avoid deep engagement "with general historians about the historical significance of their things."[6] In contrast, recent "new materialist" works by Pablo Gómez, Kathryn de Luna, and others insert these processes of coming-into-being into historical debates about race, power, ontologies, and matter.[7]

Paraphrasing Marx, men make their own cropscapes, but they do not make them as they please. The cropscape perspective both requires and permits us to reject nature-human dichotomies. The concept of actant eases the incorporation of nonhuman actors into history by allowing for agency without intentionality. Another important aspect of actants, human or nonhuman, is their instability. It is through their associations with other elements in the assemblage that their identity and composition are constituted at any particular point, meaning that neither is necessarily permanent: in the process of acting, an actant is continuously being unmade or reconfigured, even when its name (tea, pig, market, or laboratory, for instance) remains unchanged. Similarly, agency is distributed between actants. The degree and the nature of the power of an individual actant to effect change depend on its associations, and therefore they alter over time, as does the environment, the web of associations, which has fashioned its power, and which it has fashioned around itself. It is this ecological interplay between mutability and world building that we seek to highlight and explore in the following riffs, by framing each cropscape around an unexpected actor or set of associations. The riffs mark a crescendo from human to nonhuman actants, from reassessing the powers of apparently powerful and powerless humans in the section "Rubber and Violence," to tracking the ruthless territorial expansion of a tree in "Anthropocene and Eucalyptus."

RUBBER AND VIOLENCE

Violence holds together the rubber cropscapes that we know best: laborers are kept in place by brutal foremen; incisions are made on trees tapped until exhaustion; forests are cut down to make space for plantations. Engaging with the violent history of rubber calls into question the neutrality of narratives concerning the agency of humans, plants, or soils. Taking violence seriously forces us, we hope, into the core of agency and power discussions: violence coerces people and things to perform unwanted acts. It is also an acknowledgment of the power limitations of those performing it. Rubber stories unveil horrendous human actors whose violent practices in the Amazon or Southeast Asia kept European bicycles and American cars rolling smoothly. They weave deep connections between modern mobility and utter exploitation of colonized peoples. But they also urge us to go beyond pure horror, to acknowledge actants only apparently voided of agency by violent perpetrators.

RUBBER IN THE FOREST

Here is an exemplary violent tale of the rubber cropscape of the early twentieth century, as told by the British consul at Iquitos, the major Peruvian river port in the Amazon basin: "The entire Indian population is enslaved in the *montaña* and whereon the devil plant, the rubber tree grows and can be tapped. The wilder the Indian, the wickeder the slavery."[8] The crop, the Castilloa rubber tree, is empowered with agency, as suggested by its characterization as the devil. Also, helpless Amerindians enslaved as rubber tappers are blamed for their own miserable condition, guilty of being wild. This said, most narratives dealing with this well-known episode point at Julio César Arana as *the* evil actant.[9] A prominent member of the local Creole elite, Arana had already been elected mayor of Iquitos and president of the city's Chamber of Commerce when in 1905 he made good by acquiring some thirty thousand square kilometers of Amazonian jungle. He envisioned tapping the latex from the many Castilloa rubber trees along the Putumayo River (a tributary of the Amazon) to supply the expanding European and American tire industry. He also secured the monopoly of rubber transportation along the Putumayo with his steamboat, the *Liberal*, ensuring that no one extracted latex from the area without his consent. Arana headed the respectable Peruvian Amazon Rubber Company, with offices not only in Iquitos but also in Manaus (Brazil), the major trade post of the Amazon basin, and London, one of the centers of the rubber global trade.

The business model of extracting a commodity from a tropical jungle and placing it on the international market was sound enough to attract British investors, who gladly purchased shares in the company. Only the issue of the labor force was vexing. It was not obvious how to find the right incentives to convince people to establish themselves in small huts at the head of rainforest paths they were supposed to tend. In addition to extracting latex from some 150 trees in the middle of the forest, the rubber tapper was also responsible for curing it, smoking it in his hut by burning ucururi nuts, which produced fumes of toxic carbonic acid. Twirling sticks coated in latex, the tapper would redip and rotate the growing lump of hardened rubber three hours a day, producing fifty-pound balls of solidified rubber, ready to be shipped downriver into Iquitos and from there to one of the transoceanic ports of the Amazon basin.[10]

Initially Arana had relied on the masses of Brazilian *flagelados*, workers expelled from the cotton and sugar fields of Brazil's northeast by the El Niño droughts of the late 1890s.[11] Estimates point to some 190,000 of these migrants extracting rubber in the Amazon basin by 1912. Attracted by the rubber boom, they were indebted to their contractors from the moment they embarked on the trip to the Amazon. To the price of the river passage one had to add the cost of the tapper's knife, hammocks, cups, buckets, and foodstuff, all acquired on credit at the company store. This typical debt-bondage scheme was not enough for Arana.[12] Allegedly after being assaulted by drunken Brazilian tappers, he started to think of ways of producing more compliant workers. He turned to the local Amerindian population, whom he terrorized using a private force of two hundred West Indians imported from Barbados, British subjects under two-year contracts not bound by Peruvian laws. Roger Casement, the British consul general in Rio de Janeiro, connected the dots between the profits of apparently respectable British companies and violent extraction methods: The £966,000 made by the Peruvian Amazon Rubber Company on the London market between 1904 and 1910 from selling some four thousand tons of rubber meant the killing of at least thirty thousand indigenous people out of a total population of fifty thousand. Commissioned by the British government to investigate the company's practices, Casement denounced the "deliberate murder by bullet, fire, beheading, or flogging to death . . . accompanied by a variety of atrocious tortures" of those failing to deliver their rubber quotas. And he didn't shy away from describing "broad weals and lashes" on children's bodies and how "little boys, some of them 5 and 6 years old . . . with soft, gentle eyes and long eyelashes" often carried through the forests loads of rubber "30 lbs or more on their tiny backs."[13]

Casement has deservedly been celebrated as an early champion of what later would be called human rights, deploring how the combination of capitalism, colonialism, and modern technology was promoting new forms of slavery in the first decades of the twentieth century: "The steamboat and steam engine and modern armaments & the whole scheme of the modern government [are] all aiding it [the spread of slavery]—with the stock gambling and share markets the pillars of the scheme."[14] This generalization was not derived only from the horrors Casement saw in the Amazon. Before his Brazilian and Peruvian experience, he had already produced a report on the Congo Free State, the private colony of the king of the Belgians, Leopold II, and the epitome of Europe's scramble for Africa in the nineteenth century.[15] The atrocities Casement described included the routine practice by European overseers of cutting off the hands of Congolese natives to punish those who didn't meet quotas of produce collected from the rain forest, namely, rubber from *Landolphia* vines. The extreme violence unleashed by the *Force publique*—the armed colonial police— in the rubber regions of the Congo led to a catastrophic decrease in population, from some twenty million in 1880 to 8.5 million in 1911.[16] Casement's reports were not the most gruesome. While Protestant missionaries told of canoes loaded with smoked human hands fed to anthropophagic dogs, Joseph Conrad in one of his most celebrated novels took his readers up the Congo River, show- ing them the flowerbed of a Belgian fort decorated with human skulls: Europeans had found in the Congo their "heart of darkness."[17]

Casement pointed at concrete individuals such as Arana and Leopold II as guilty, but he pointed as well at European colonialism as the main cause of the spread of new forms of slavery. He didn't ascribe violence to individualized acts alone, identifying a modern imperial logic of profit and extraction as the prime motives for violence. Nevertheless, the anthropologist Michael Taussig, one of the most provocative scholars to engage Casement, questions his assumptions about the violent dynamics of the rubber cropscape of the Amazon.[18] Reading Casement's reports closely, Taussig quotes a reference to the brutal foremen hired by Arana who "had lost all sight or sense of rubber gathering—they were simply beasts of prey who lived upon the Indians and delighted in shedding their blood." This passage suggests that profit and greed alone could not explain the brutality of the acts Casement described. Or, as Taussig puts it, "terror and torture do not derive only from market pressure but also from the process of cultural construction of evil as well."[19] To understand such a construction Taussig replaces the figure of the wicked powerful foreman extracting maxi- mum work from enslaved Indians with less confident actants: the foremen from the West Indies employed by Arana were themselves under debt peonage, call- ing into question the free will of their acts. More important, foremen obsessed over their own vulnerability and possible attacks by allegedly wild Indians. While Casement's rhetoric exaggerated the docile and peaceful character of Amerindians, describing them as childlike creatures with no proper agency and under the total control of authoritative foremen, Taussig calls attention instead to how Arana and his foremen were haunted by images of being devoured by violent cannibals. Their evil derived in large measure from their distorted im- ages of indigenous people as savage cannibals. Or, as mentioned by the British consul in Iquitos quoted above, "The wilder the Indian, the wickeder the slav- ery." The rampant violence unleashed in the Amazon and the Congo didn't so much derive from a sense of uncontrolled power over inferior people as grow out of a sense of fragility of supposedly civilized men in the middle of a sup- posed wilderness.

140   Actants

PLANTATION RUBBER

Human rights scandals around Amazon and Congo rubber production were considerable embarrassments for European-controlled ventures, but nonhuman actants were behind Southeast Asia's supplanting of those two regions, from 1913, as the undisputed global leader of natural rubber production. Brazil had a long, violent history of slave plantations, namely, the seventeenth-century sugar plantations of the northeast around Bahia and the nineteenth-century coffee plantations of the Paraíba Valley. As the twentieth century began, it seemed the country was now on the path to developing a new major rubber-plantation economy in the Amazon. This didn't happen, first and foremost because of endemic leaf blight. For millennia the fungus *Microcyclus ulei* and *Hevea braziliensis,* the rubber tree producing better quality latex, had coevolved. The low density of hevea among a host of other trees in the forest constituted the best defense of the tree against the fungus (the latex produced by the tree being an evolutionary adaptation to repel insect pests). But when cultivated in a plantation system, the monocrop of hevea trees proved to be an ideal ground for the catastrophic spread of the fungus, condemning the endeavor to failure. Despite many attempts, among them the famous scheme envisioned by Henry Ford and the founding of Fordlandia in the Brazilian state of Pará, rubber plantations in the Amazon were never successful, and latex would still be collected mainly from hevea trees scattered through the forest.[20]

Not so in Southeast Asia, where the fungus *Microcyclus ulei* was not present. Hevea seeds, famously smuggled in the 1870s from the Amazon via London's Kew Gardens, found their way into Malaya, Ceylon, Indonesia, Siam, and Vietnam, where they were cultivated according to the plantation system already in place for sugar and coffee. Another fungus, the no less famous *Hemileia vastratix,* or coffee rust, which had been devastating *Coffea arabica* plantations in the region, spurred interest in investing in a new commodity and crucially opened the way for the expansion of the rubber cropscape.[21] Building on well-developed commercial and wage-labor circuits, the cultivation area of *Hevea brasiliensis* expanded rapidly, from 1.1 million acres in 1910 to four million acres in 1920 and ten million acres in 1940.[22] Most narratives point to the role of European plant hunters and botanists in the transfer of rubber production from South America to Southeast Asia, but although recognizing the obvious human agency in this story, it would be ludicrous to ignore the role of *Microcyclus ulei* and of *Hemileia vastratix* in enabling the transoceanic travels of the rubber tree.[23]

New large estates in European and Chinese hands brought rubber trees into remote areas such as the red soils of Cambodia, the jungles of Sumatra and

Malaya, and the interior of New Guinea.[24] The characteristically ordered plantation space, cultivated in rows, with low density of trees and clean weeding, depended on a constant supply of indentured laborers from faraway places.[25] Local populations always refused to live under such disciplinary regimes. By 1911 there were already some 180,000 "coolies" working in Malayan rubber plantations, 100,000 from India, 18,000 from Java, and some 46,000 from China. Before the Japanese invaded Malaya in World War II the total number had reached some 350,000 people, of whom 220,000 came from India and 86,000 from China. French-owned plantations also relied heavily on imported labor, and by 1940 there were some one hundred thousand Tonkinese workers on Vietnam's rubber estates. Human workers had been the main cargo of ships bound for Malaya since the nineteenth century, but this scale of operations was unprecedented. The region had its equivalents of Casement: there was no scarcity of reports denouncing the appalling conditions endured by the masses of migrant laborers. Malaria, dysentery, and diarrhea were rampant among the Tamils employed on Malayan rubber plantations, their mortality in 1910 reaching no fewer than fifty deaths per thousand workers. Reports also referred to overcrowded barracks for accommodations, poor nutrition, hard work regimes, and common beatings of workers treated as "human livestock, terrorized by the overseers."[26]

While Taussig's revisiting of the Tupumayo questioned the agency of the different characters involved in the violent story of rubber extraction in the Amazon, Ann Laura Stoler has offered a no less compelling and sophisticated interpretation of Deli, the plantation belt of Dutch Sumatra.[27] Here, some one million hectares of jungle in the northern part of the island were converted from the second half of the nineteenth century into large estates, under European control, for the cultivation of tobacco, tea, oil palm, and, of course, rubber. The area was (in)famous for labor violence and racial and social discrimination, contrasting with the softer regime of Java and its higher presence of Creoles. Beyond delving into the reasons for such contrasts, Stoler is interested in showing how unstable the cleavages based on European/ non-European classifications were. Instead of accepting the divisions imposed by the colonial regime, Stoler inquires how such divisions were produced, unveiling the daily practices of producing white and nonwhite identities, of policing racial barriers. The proliferation of prostitutes in Deli, Stoler maintains, should be understood as contributing to the maintenance of whiteness of European employees in the plantations. Considering the difficulties of maintaining a family on a plantation-employee salary, it was preferable to accept the social blight of prostitution rather than accept the formation of poor-white families whose living standards would be indistinguishable from those of nonwhites, thus blurring racial

142 Actants

boundaries. To these fears of white destitution was added the fear of the archetypal Asian coolie running amok, killing every white he encountered in his way. As in the Amazon, in Deli we see violence being exerted not by brave, confident white colonizers but by humans always fearful of their surroundings and over-conscious of their fragile white status.

SMALLHOLDERS' AGENCY

The work of scholars such as Taussig and Stoler made the rubber cropscapes of the Putumayo forest and the Deli plantations significant sites for questioning oversimplified diagnoses of agency and colonial violence. But looking at the prosaic figures for rubber production, we see that in fact neither site was able to compete in the long run with other forms of extraction of natural rubber. In Southeast Asia, after an initial period of exclusive production by large plantations, native smallholders contributed an increasing share. In Malaysia the acreage of rubber trees in smallholdings overtook that of large estates in the 1960s; statistics for the Dutch East Indies indicate that by the 1930s smallholdings were already responsible for more than half of the total rubber output.[28] This is the kind of historical trajectory from large to small we explored in chapter 3, "Sizes." Here we are more interested in underlining how such figures point to the presence of underappreciated actants in rubber's history.

In contrast to the monocrop system of the large estates dedicated exclusively to the production of rubber trees, in Southeast Asia local swidden (*ladang*) farmers added rubber trees to their multicrop cultivation systems: *Hevea brasiliensis* seeds were densely cultivated along with the first rice crop in fresh forest clearings. While the plantation is constantly fighting pests, soil erosion, or coolie rebellion, no intensive maintenance was needed here: after three to five years, cultivators needed only to get rid of low-lying undergrowth to access rubber trees. As eloquently stated by a sensitive observer, "To add rubber to this system costs nothing in effort, cash or displaced alternatives."[29] The triumph of smallholder rubber in Southeast Asia thus dissociates rubber trees from the reputation they had earned in the Putumayo as devil trees.[30] It also suggests a less deterministic notion of agency: Asian smallholders not only had more agency than plantation coolies employed by colonial companies, they were also less heavy-handed in creating the conditions for the proliferation of the Brazilian rubber tree. In other words, they acknowledged the power of nonhuman actants, preferring to work with the elements already present in their small plots to compose a new cropscape (see chapter 5, "Compositions").

The story of rubber in the Amazon was not too different. While Brazilian rubber lost prominence in international markets in the early twentieth century due to a sharp increase in production by Southeast Asian plantations, the commodity maintained its position in the national market due to protectionist measures. The conditions of rubber tappers in the Brazilian part of the Amazon were never easy, but they were not as harsh as those described by Casement in the Putumayo. Rubber tappers migrating from impoverished areas of the Brazilian Northeast, although bonded by a debt system based on credit dispensed by the warehouses located at river junctions, always had more agency than the natives enslaved by Arana on the banks of the Putumayo.[31] It is good to remember that Arana had turned to the local indigenous population because he had found Brazilian tappers too recalcitrant. Also, the failed attempts of dedicated rubber plantations in the Amazon, exemplified by Fordlandia, were due both to the ravages of fungus and to the difficulty of converting rubber tappers in control of their working rhythms in the forest into wageworkers performing tasks according to American scientific management techniques. This combination of human and nonhuman actants is a good example of the possibilities opened up for historical writing when agency is problematized.

There was no author more skilled at revealing the historical importance of unexpected intersections between humans and nonhumans than Euclides da Cunha.[32] The Brazilian engineer and writer, who surveyed the disputed Amazon frontier between Brazil, Bolivia, and Peru in the early twentieth century, insisted that the region should be understood in terms of its rich human presence instead of being characterized as empty wilderness. Like Casement, Cunha had extremely harsh words for the depredatory rubber extraction practiced on Peruvian territory, which involved "ransacking the surroundings, killing or enslaving in a radius of several leagues. The caucheiros would stay only until the last caucho tree fell."[33] Cunha contrasted this grim picture with the accomplishments of the drought refugees (flagelados) of Brazil's Northeast, who had been capable, with no official support, of carving a dwelling from the tropical forest in the area that corresponds today to the Brazilian state of Acre. His nationalist description delights in the details of small communities thriving in forest clearings, tapping rubber trees while growing crops like maize, beans, potatoes, or manioc, displaying "well-tended orchards and prudent husbandry."[34] Cunha's account is certainly too rosy, but his narrative did transform rubber tappers from subjects of the many atrocities of Brazilian history—expelled by droughts, impoverished by failed cotton and sugar plantations, exploited by local merchants and contractors—into active participants in national history, who claimed the state of Acre for the country while dwelling in the rubber cropscape of the Amazon.

The case for recognizing the value of the practices of these communities of Brazilian rubber tappers in the Amazon came to world attention in the 1980s.[35]

Chico Mendes, son of drought refugees from the Northeast and a rubber tapper in Acre, was able to connect local labor demands with rising environmentalism in the United States and Europe concerned with the burning of tropical rainforests and associated loss of biodiversity. Mendes and his union of rubber tappers made a convincing argument that their rubber-extraction practices had promoted forest conservation while enabling the economic sustenance of local communities, a case to be emulated worldwide and one that gained official recognition in the "extractive reservations" first delineated by the Brazilian government in 1990 to prevent the clearing of the tropical forest by the menacing expansion of the ranching frontier. The awkward notion of extractive reservations recognized that making strict divisions between natural and man-made areas was actually damaging the Amazon rain forest, and that the rubber cropscape had contributed to its conservation. To think of Amazonia as wilderness or jungle is in fact a failure of imagination that doesn't acknowledge how much tree distribution patterns have been historically determined by slash-and-burn cultivation practices of Amerindian communities promoting certain associations of plants while preventing the proliferation of others.[36] This doesn't turn the Amazon into a human-made plantation: clearings in the forest have a short life span. But it does point to how Mendes and the union of rubber tappers were building on a longue durée practice of refusing to divide the world into passive nature and active humankind, recognizing instead mutual dependencies of the elements that constitute the cropscape (see "Places" on manioc). The rubber tree certainly had agency in guaranteeing the livelihoods of Acre inhabitants, who in turn were crucial to guaranteeing the tree's survival and reproduction. Tragically, in 1988, Chico Mendes was murdered by a rancher dedicated to the destruction of the forest and its living beings. In the twenty-first century such brutal episodes have only become more common, confirming that the Brazilian rubber cropscape is still a very violent place. But while we started with violence sustaining the rubber cropscape, we end with violence threatening its survival.

CINCHONA: AGENCY AND THE HISTORY OF KNOWLEDGE

Rubber stories make us suspicious of any laudatory imperial tales of intrepid British and Dutch explorers collecting specimens of cinchona trees in Andean forests and bringing them (via Kew Gardens) to India and Java in the mid-nineteenth century. Braving the dangers of tropical nature, corrupt South American governments, and recalcitrant Amerindians, white male Western scientists, those tales taught us, were responsible for the long-distance transfer of the cinchona tree to Southeast Asian plantations where huge amounts of quinine would be produced, saving humanity from the ravages of malaria.[37] Critical historians didn't have to dig deep. It suffices to recover stories located in the British Raj—the main importer of cinchona bark at the end of the nineteenth century—to deconstruct the imperial civilizing mission rhetoric built around quinine. Antimalaria campaigns undertaken on tea plantations, in prisons, and in schools made obvious the role of quinine in expanding the reach of the colonial state among the Indian population, identifying locals with passive sick bodies waiting to be saved by Western medicine.[38] In addition, quinine became a powerful military technology for opening up vast parts of the globe to predatory European colonialism.[39] While enacting multiple genocides in Algeria, Congo, or Angola, European armies were kept safe from the ravages of malaria by quinine. In both the heroic and the critical narratives, the agency of quinine as a crucial tool of empire manufactured by European scientists seems undisputed.[40]

For those who accept the language of contemporary science without questioning it historically, there is no doubt that the role of cinchona tree in history derives from the therapeutic properties of quinine even when humans were unaware of the existence of chemical things such as alkaloids. Quinine, the alkaloid discovered by French pharmacists in 1820, seems to hold the key to cinchona agency in history. Its chemical properties make it toxic to *Plasmodium falciparum,* the unicellular protozoan identified as the causal agent of malaria, by interfering with the parasite's ability to dissolve and metabolize hemoglobin. But what happens when we situate knowledge about cinchona in its historical context and explore the historical implications of understanding cinchona alternatively as tree, bark, or alkaloid? To place a crop in history, to understand its historical significance, also involves studying how people thought about the agency of the crop they were dealing with. Let us, then, complicate the cinchona story by referring back to a period before quinine had been identified in European laboratories, to a period in which quinine didn't exist.

BARK AND ANDEAN KNOWLEDGE

For Andean healers of the Loja region situated in southern Ecuador, the bark of the cinchona tree came from a cold plant and could thus be effectively used to counter the hot effects of many fevers, including those we today identify as malaria, brought into the region by Spanish conquistadores in the early sixteenth century.[41] The hot or cold identity of a plant was determined by the character of the region in an inverse relationship: plants growing in hot regions such as the mountain passes near Loja, among the lowest altitudes along the Andes, were cold plants and were thus appropriate for use against hot fevers.

146 Actants

Andean healers understood health as a state of equilibrium between cold and hot, as well as between human and nonhuman forces, their task being to restore broken equilibriums such as those caused by the ravages of malarial fevers menacing individual bodies and the social order as a whole.

More than stressing the parallels between Andean and European medical practices based on humoral theories, it is important for our argument about agency to call attention to the fact that Amerindian populations were not just passive historical subjects of the Columbian Exchange, passive bodies infected with pathological agents brought in by European conquest.[42] The coastal areas and lowlands of Ecuador were certainly fertile breeding ground for Anopheles mosquitoes, the main malaria vector brought into the Americas by the slave trade from Africa, making them part of the epidemiological frontier that decimated local populations, which were reduced by no less than 85 percent in the sixteenth century.[43] But healers from the Loja region, or "ministers of idolatry" as some Spanish Jesuits preferred to call them, belonged to what ethnobotanists have characterized as "the healing center of the old Central Andean cultural area that stretched from Ecuador to Bolivia."[44] Tapping into the biodiversity produced by the "rapid transition between humid mountain forests of the northern Andes to the dry, deciduous forests and deserts of the northern Peruvian lowlands," or, in other words, taking advantage of a transition area located between the Amazon basin and the Pacific lowlands, Andean healers had access to a vast array of medicinal plants, cinchona trees among them.[45] When cinchona bark was first imported to Europe in the 1630s by Jesuit missionaries and Spanish officials returning from Peru, Andean healers had been experimenting with its use for more than a century; they had been actively engaged with the tree and its bark as response to the environmental disruptions produced by colonial conquest. And although imperial archives do reveal the common presence of the bark in pharmacopoeias of Jesuit colleges across the Americas, it is also apparent that we have overlooked how it also increasingly became part of the "healing material culture" of non-sanctioned practitioners, namely, those in the Caribbean region. Among these were what were called "brujas, sorcerers, witches, witch doctors, warlocks, or shamans," all terms used to denigrate Caribbean practitioners of knowledge mostly of African descent, who had added cinchona bark to their repertoire of things through which they intervened in the world.[46]

QUINA AS SILVER

Cinchona, the "Jesuit bark," became an object of great interest in Europe. In the 1750s the port of Cadiz, which had held the monopoly of Spanish colonial trade since the early eighteenth century, imported some 242,000 pounds of it annually.[47] It was this sustained increase in commerce that finally caught the attention of Spanish imperial officials who had previously supported initiatives for the import of other American medicinal plants to Europe but who until then had been oblivious to cinchona. A 1751 royal order declared *quina,* as the cinchona bark was known in Spain, an "object worthy of curiosity, interest, and attention," whose production and distribution had to be controlled by the Crown. Crucially, the bark was dealt with on the same basis as the Crown's most profitable business in South America, the mining of silver in Potosí. As with silver, the Crown intended to acquire the whole of quina production, putting in place a monopoly to guarantee purity and prevent smuggling. The hills around Loja, where the best quinas were extracted, were made into a royal reserve, and local bark collectors suggested they would give the Crown a fifth of their annual production, reproducing the existing arrangement with silver miners in Potosí.[48] The very methods of producing quina for an expanding market, by uprooting the tree and removing its bark, suggest a purely extractive activity, confirming the silver parallel.

This quina as silver was a scientific commodity, its quality evaluated by the myriad experts serving the Spanish imperial administration. Physicians, pharmacists, chemists, and botanists (these different professional roles were of course not well established) were all involved in establishing the commercial value of the bark.[49] Scientific debates like the ones around quina were an important and revealing feature of Spanish imperial practice. But until recently they were largely invisible in narratives of early modern Spain, dominated as they were by a "Black Legend" that saw the country as fanatical and resistant to the scientific mindset consolidating elsewhere in Europe.[50] One should also bear in mind that the Spanish Empire was a complex structure and that the experts just mentioned served different agendas. More than a king imposing his will on vast territories covering large parts of the globe, this was an empire built on constant debate, with different historical actors writing to the court to have their reasons heard.[51] This was also the case with quina. While royal pharmacists in Madrid focused on the visual characteristics of the product, fundamental for asserting the high value of bark gifts by the king, local experts in the service of the viceroy of New Granada (to which Loja belonged) preferred to call attention instead to taste, odor, and texture. When the royal pharmacists pointed to the low brightness of the bark arriving in Madrid to justify complaints about its low quality, the local experts in New Granada countered that its healing strength was confirmed by its extreme bitterness. Local agents could claim familiarity with production processes unknown to experts located in Madrid; accordingly, bitterness was guaranteed by judicious collectors drying the bark immediately after stripping it from the tree.

148 Actants

THE BOTANY OF CINCHONA AND
IMPERIAL POLITICS

It was not only that those in the outskirts of the empire used local knowledge to counter perceptions produced at the court in Europe. This was more than a question of tensions between center and periphery. Quina disputes also sustained different local ambitions. Botanists in search of a new green Eldorado, promising to turn plants into the new bullion that would restore the Spanish Empire in the late eighteenth century to its alleged previous glories, tried to expand the areas of quina production beyond the Loja region.[52] Some reports confirmed that planting trees from Loja in new locations diminished the bark's healing capacities, but there was other evidence of trees whose bark yielded good-quality quina, which would allow the expansion of the production of a vanishing resource into new areas of the empire. Botanists did make the case that a new reserve should be established in the hills surrounding Santa Fe (present-day Colombia), confirming that the healing properties of local barks deserved the demarcation of a new quina reserve that would constitute a new bounty for the viceroyalty of New Granada. But botanists under the patronage of Lima elites in the viceroyalty of Peru, from where most of the Loja bark was shipped, were quick to refute such pretensions, asserting that the cinchona trees from the new area did not belong to the same botanical species. They boldly argued that only Loja quina was true quina. In this version, quina was defined by the species of plant it originated from, not by *materia medica* and its healing effects, as had been advanced by experts in New Granada. Historians like to point to the failure of the Spanish project when compared to other empires that put botany at the service of the imperial economy.[53] They tend to overlook the fact that the triumph of botanists in the Spanish Empire served different local imperial projects. In this case, instead of expanding areas of quina production, which would have served one version of the Spanish Empire put forward from New Granada, botanists sustained another definition of what quina was that contributed to maintaining Loja's monopoly, serving the imperial ambitions of the viceroyalty of Peru.

The generic characterization of the failure of eighteenth-century Spanish botanists in serving the economy of the empire is thus based on simplistic assumptions about the agency of knowledge in history. Using Britain's Kew Gardens as the point of comparison tends to make the narrative still more naive. The "cinchona scheme" of the 1860s for collecting seeds in South America and transferring them, via Kew, to British colonies in Asia has been used as an exemplary case of science as a tool of empire. Building on scientists' own propaganda, Kew Gardens is described as an authentic global seed exchange organizing collecting expeditions to the Andes, growing seeds in greenhouses in London, and transplanting saplings into satellite botanic gardens in Ceylon and Madras. The new India Office, established after the Indian Mutiny of 1857 that spread panic among British imperialists, was eager to support the whole endeavor, hoping that cinchona plantations would enable increased military British presence throughout the empire without fear of ravaging fevers. The historical irony is that British botanists of the nineteenth century were neither more nor less successful than their Spanish counterparts of the eighteenth century. They proved very efficient in turning the new cinchona cropscape in India into a public relations operation demonstrating the importance of Kew Gardens for the British Empire, but they failed spectacularly at making India into a major producer of cinchona bark.[54]

DUTCH IMPERIAL MONOPOLY ON ALKALOIDS

It was instead the Dutch colony of Java that became the world's leading producer of quinine, and British India the leading importer. Cinchona trees did acclimatize well in India's Nilgiri Hills, as had happened previously with coffee and tea, promising to enable the further expansion of plantations in India by saving laborers from malaria. But the bark of the transplanted trees produced low quantities of quinine, the alkaloid that chemists had identified earlier in the century as the substance responsible for curing malaria. The Dutch, following the British example, had tried their own transplantation operation in West Java, with similar results. More than one million cinchona trees were planted, generating a minor scandal in the Dutch colonial administration. In 1875 it sent a chemist to the island to salvage the expensive endeavor. Developing chemical methods to identify the quinine content of bark samples, he offered an expeditious way to select among different trees planted at the Government Cinchona Estate. Chemistry, not botany, had now become the crucial source of knowledge in producing a valuable cinchona cropscape, yielding increases in quinine of more than 10 percent.[55]

It was this Dutch success that by the end of the nineteenth century put British cinchona plantations in India out of business. High quinine content cinchona bark from Java supplied the European pharmaceutical industry, and Amsterdam became the dominant market for cinchona. To guarantee that Java plantation owners would be able to reap the benefits of the quinine bounty and avoid the effects of overproduction the Dutch state organized the Quinine Bureau in Amsterdam, which forced the main pharmaceutical companies to pay a minimum price for the bark. In other words, under the patronage of the Dutch state, Java planters formed a monopoly that controlled the price of the bark now

Harvesting and drying cinchona bark, Cinyiruan government plantation, circa 1880. Dutch colonial plantations of cinchona trees from South America in West Java were organized around identifying quinine as actant. While chemical methods allowed for selecting trees with higher quinine content, the Dutch government controlled the world supply of quinine, thus guaranteeing the livelihoods of plantation owners in Batavia. J. C. Bernelot Moens, *De kinacultuur in Azië*, 1854 (Batavia: Ernst, 1882).

defined in chemical terms by its quinine content.[56] This scheme was in place during the entire interwar period, the Dutch Empire boosting its humanitarian role in saving world populations from malaria, while international health organizations denounced high prices of quinine as a major obstacle to organize campaigns reaching whole populations. In 1942, Japanese troops invaded Java and took control of the cinchona plantations, rushing chemists in the United States into synthetically producing quinine only two years later. After it had been reduced to an alkaloid in the nineteenth century, it was only appropriate that cinchona bark was now replaced by chemically synthesized drugs.[57]

More than disputing that quinine was the real basis for the historical agency of cinchona bark, we are interested in underlining the historical significance of knowledge about cinchona.[58] It mattered historically how cinchona was understood, as materia medica, plant species, or alkaloid, enabling different arrangements of the cropscape. In this narrative, cinchona trees were initially elements of the Andean forest collected by Amerindian healers responding to the new diseases brought into the Americas by European colonizers; this cropscape was then imagined as a silver mine, a monopoly of Jesuit bark, or quina, controlled by the Spanish Crown and sustained by the work of botanists and pharmacists; the transfer in the nineteenth century of the cinchona tree into British India and Dutch Java made it into a plantation crop whose survival depended on chemists tending quinine yields and on the colonial state guaranteeing benefits for planters. The agency in history of the different elements that constitute a cropscape is inseparable from the historical forms of knowledge about such elements.

SEEING LIKE AN ELEPHANT

More than plants, animals have driven radical proposals for writing history from a nonhuman perspective.[59] Historians have apparently found it easier to produce narratives that challenge cherished notions of human agency by invoking worlds as seen from the eyes of mosquitoes, sheep, pigs, bison, dogs, horses, or elephants. It is not just that humans acknowledge the agency of nonhumans, as when tappers speak of rubber trees as devils, or that knowledge about nonhuman agency is itself historically contingent, as underlined through cinchona's stories. Here we take one step further, daring to ask what we see if we try to look at a cropscape as an *elephant* would, considering its elements of desire and its ability to shape its surroundings and dwell in its own world. Asian elephants and their contested status as domesticated or wild animals constitute a fascinating point of entry to experiment with historical agency beyond humans molding nature to their needs.

WARRIORS

The history of the war elephant already suggests the high stakes of an elephant-centered history. Elephants were first used in wars in North India between 1000 and 500 B.C.E.; the elephant corps had the same status as infantry, cavalry, and chariots. This technological innovation in warfare traveled first into South India, then to Sri Lanka, showing up around the first century C.E. in the emerging kingdoms of Southeast Asia.[60] The war elephant's travels to the West were no less significant, adopted by Persian, Greek, Carthaginian, Roman, and Turkish armies. Here elephants themselves were transported from east to west,

Wild elephants bathing. Elephants were exiled or summoned according to the varied demands of the plantation enterprise, but they also had their own desires, pleasures, memory, and power, which could not be easily ignored. *Wilde Elefantenherde mit Bad in Bergsee, Albumblatt (Einzelblatt),* Mughal India, circa 1600. Album page, gouache. Inv. I. 4596 fol. 16. Credit: bpk Bildagenture / Museum fuer Islamische Kunst, Staatliche Museen, Berlin, Germany / Johannes Kramer / Art Resource, NY.

but rulers in Southeast Asia tapped into the local wild populations of elephants in the forest. The formation of Southeast Asian kingdoms coincided with the increased presence of war elephants in the region, pointing to the deep connection between these nonhuman actors and kingship, between war elephants and state power. Elephants became part of diplomatic offerings and tributes, and protagonists in royal processions, not only as "visible signs of military potential," but also as signifiers "of the superlative character of kingship."[61]

But war elephants did not travel to China. We must invoke human agency to explain this sharp contrast between India and China, namely, the clearing of forests in China and the extension of cultivated areas, destroying the natural habitats of elephants who had once been present in almost every region of the country. Protecting millet fields and rice paddies from the ravages of these huge mammals also entailed getting rid of the elephants.[62] In India, rulers promoted conservation practices that guaranteed elephants would find forests and pastures to forage in. While peasants might have wished to extend their cultivable land or keep elephants at bay by harming or scaring them, state power punished humans who endangered elephants' livelihoods. Mughal rulers made significant allocations to elephants, demarcating pasture in forests and reserving cropland for growing fodder.[63]

The challenge of maintaining a population of elephants ready for use in war questions human agency as the single key to this story. War elephants can hardly be considered fully domesticated animals. They were not bred in captivity, and it was reckoned too costly and laborious to feed young elephants; instead, adults considered mature enough for battle were captured in the wild. Even in captivity, in the evening mahouts let their animals forage in the forest: protecting forests was a necessary condition for the subsistence of these massive animals. In demanding access to forests, elephants resisted delegating to humans total control of their reproduction and feeding, unlike most other domesticated animals and plants. The mutual dependence of kingship and elephants found in South and Southeast Asia ensured not only that nonhumans served the political intentions of humans but also that humans served nonhumans by guaranteeing their livelihoods through forest conservation. In the provocative language of animal studies, we could affirm that in India elephants engineered the state to protect their reproducing and foraging grounds, while in China rice engineered the state to expand its growing fields and eliminate its enemies.

SERVANTS

Elephants were historically successful in their conservation endeavors. Their population in India did not diminish drastically until the early nineteenth century, due first and foremost to British colonial fondness for hunting.[64] But if hunting large mammals has been identified as part of the colonial strategy to assert male dominant status over tropical nature, it must also be acknowledged that the British colonial state in India built its presence on preexisting human-elephant interactions. British military were certainly well versed in the habits of war elephants in India.[65] More important for our argument is the fundamental role of elephants in the expansion of plantations in British India, notably in the formation of the Assam teascape discussed in "Places." Charles Bruce, the East India Company superintendent of the first tea gardens in Assam, explicitly acknowledged the importance of the animals for his endeavor. When trying to locate tracts of wild tea plants in Muttack country in the northeastern part of India, Bruce had to cover vast areas, and in that "region of fever-ridden jungle, the only way to get about from one place to another was, over the shorter distances, on foot or on the back of an elephant at three miles an hour, which was far safer considering the place was stiff with tigers."[66] Riding an elephant, the colonial surveyor was offered both a privileged view of the terrain from above and protection from wild animals. Indeed, much of the survey work in the hilly region of Assam and other frontier areas of India was undertaken by following paths in the forest first opened by elephants in their foraging meanderings. The dense patterns of such paths speak to elephants' capacity for changing the landscape for their own purposes. Basically, the surveyor's work of translating the territory into data useful for the colonial enterprise was directly built on elephants' capacities of perception and transformation of that same territory.[67] Thus the colonial enterprise entered into a contradictory relationship with elephants: it wanted to retain the benefits that elephants conferred while simultaneously undercutting their pasture space and penetrating aggressively into their wi(l)der forest space.

The elephant's view from on high was co-opted for the colonialist project of seeing like a state. Planters were disabled without their elephants, as a visiting partner of the Assam Company made plain when thanking the senior manager in charge for "the inconvenience he suffered" by sparing his elephant, without which "it would have been impossible" for the visitor to "go around the Company's property with despatch and comfort."[68] The plantation had been carved from the forest through elephant labor used in surveying and clearing, to which the planter now added the function of overseeing that made the tea gardens a fully controlled space. Planters depended on elephants' bodily capacities to reach every corner of their estates. In 1935, another tea planter from Assam recalled in his memoirs how "the changing courses, which prohibited the building of permanent bridges, the deepness of the water and its swiftness . . . compelled us to use an elephant as the only method of negotiating those parts of the district lying between the river beds." Crossing the river courses, the elephant would walk with her head at an angle upstream, "moving inch by inch sideways . . . the root of her trunk cutting across the water like the prow of a ship," while feeling "the bottom with her trunk for a secure place to plant her feet."[69]

Elephants were mobilized by British plantation owners for the destruction of their own habitats, set to clearing forests for tea gardens, and intensively employed in exploring forests for timber, responding to "a sharp rise in the local and international demand for tropical hardwoods," especially for railroad and steamship construction.[70] While precolonial rulers in India had preserved large tracts of land supporting elephants' livelihoods, under colonial rule elephants experienced the disappearance of their habitats, now reduced to islands of forest surrounded by expanding plantations. Wild elephants who followed foraging paths established by their ancestors now found themselves crossing cultivated fields of tea or sugarcane, earning the status of dangerous pests that should be eliminated to keep the profitability of colonial commodity production. As their habitats receded, their disruption of plantation operations increased, including the ever more frequent death of coolies, making elephant raids on Assam tea gardens as dangerous to colonial order as raids by mountain peoples unwilling to submit to British rule. British colonial officers were expected to shoot unruly elephants in the same way as they shot human rebels.[71]

ENTANGLED AGENCIES

So far we have discussed the agency of elephants in colonial India with respect to the foreign white elite of administrators and planters. But it was "native" agency that made the elephant available to planters. Elephants' and mahouts' agencies met in the process of taming and training, which entailed both local expertise and knowledge systems, and the formation of a close and lasting relationship. "Handlers' skills, the mutual attunement of elephant and human bodies, and the shared social and ecological worlds in which they are both embedded" built empathy.[72] The literature celebrates what it presents as a relationship of affection and loyalty. In war, it was said, "many elephants loved their drivers dearly" and "sometimes carried their dead riders from the battlefield or rushed to defend them."[73] In the forest, continuous everyday interaction between them turned humans and animals into intimate companions.[74] Co-opted in the colonial plantation enterprise, the mahout may appear bereft of agency, a mere tool fulfilling the goals of the planter. Yet the planter did not create the relationship between mahout and elephant: he summoned and redeployed an existing communion built over long periods of time and shared ecologies.

As for the native mahout's entente with the elephant, a recent study confirms that it is "an ambivalent intimacy." Even when trained, elephants retain "their inherently 'wild' nature: they remain unpredictable, and the mahouts know that their non-human companions could kill them at any time."[75] They remain fundamentally "unpredictable" creatures that may attack their drivers without any obvious provocation.[76] We must recognize that elephants have their own worldview, exercising their freedom to decide on actions that in the human worldview may have no apparent reason.

The ideas of multiple, layered agency and interspecies agency can easily be appreciated in this context. The planter, in devolving the responsibility to the trainer, is manifesting the limitations of his own agency and power. Similarly, the trainer in his relationship with the elephant—whether in "captivity" or while "taming" or "training"—cannot be absolutely sure that the elephant will always oblige and cooperate, and thus admits to the limitation of his own agency, contingent on the agency of the elephant.

Elephants' particular ways of understanding their surroundings proved important weapons in the resistance to colonial rule. The adventurous escapes, during the monsoon season and through muddy terrain, of rebellious leaders of the 1857 mutiny, arguably the biggest challenge to British rule in the subcontinent in the nineteenth century, often took advantage of elephants' ability to negotiate otherwise inaccessible environments. Mounted high on elephants, the rebels could cross large bodies of water and unstable terrain. Elephants expand and contract their feet as a function of ground consistency, making them more mobile in muddy soils than other cargo animals; with their trunks they can detect slippery boulders or remove logs from the way. By their allowing rebellious humans to see and move like an elephant, what at first sight might seem merely anecdotal zoological features actually made elephants actors in global history.

Understandably, scholars detailing human-elephant alliances have focused most attention on formal state structures, such as Mughal or British imperial rule. But more recently they have started to unveil the importance of such alliances for sustaining alternative forms of sociability across so-called Zomia: the uplands of the Southeast Asian Massif stretching from northern Indochina to northeast India (Assam), including the Shan Hills of northern Myanmar and the mountains of southwestern China, which have resisted the encroachment of state structures—either precolonial, colonial, or postcolonial—originating in the lowlands.[77] From colonial mutinies to more contemporary guerrilla warfare, elephants have been essential allies for navigating remote regions, areas out of sight of state control.[78] James C. Scott, probably the main person responsible for the fame of Zomia in academia, has praised upland alternative communities by contrasting them with the regimented order of the lowlands, the much criticized paddy states.[79] If we acknowledge how much human livelihood in the uplands depends on elephants' senses for reading their environment, and on their trailblazing work of opening paths through the forest, we add a nonhuman dimension to the dichotomy.

COTTON MARKETS AND THE CROPSCAPE CONCEPT: THE FUTURE ACTS!

In November 1903, a Dallas convention about the boll weevil heard the following analysis of the weevil as an actant in the American cotton cropscape:

> There are some good points about this insect. He is a first class bull in the cotton market, and we will never see any more six cent cotton as long as he is abroad in the land. His partner in price raising, Mr. Brown, takes profits and quits; but in the vocabulary of this little fellow there is no such word as "quit." We farmers have had convention after convention to curtail cotton acreage and reduce the crop, and each farmer rushed home and planted more cotton, thinking the other fellows would obey instructions and thereby raise the price. The boll weevil is doing for us exactly what we tried to do for ourselves and could not.[80]

The judge who spoke these words understood that actants in the cropscape were interchangeable—fungible, in economic terms. He spoke of cotton in terms of its price, which he described as the result of certain actants and their actions. The boll weevil, a cotton broker named Mr. Brown, an individual farmer among other farmers, curtailing the acreage: any of these could play a role in raising cotton's price. We adopt this speaker's approach to understanding the cropscape. By examining the elements that go into making a price for cotton, price helps us uncover the actants in the cropscape. In this riff, we use the cotton market to enlarge our understanding of these actants and their roles in the cropscape.

Traditionally, economic historians have seen that market forces drive historical actors.[81] But people contributed to those forces with their individual actions. Transactions make prices, but prices also signal people to buy or to sell. This back-and-forth relation between market forces and individual agency is an invitation to the historian of technology, a conceptual moment that invites the field to employ its approaches to understanding complex, nonlinear causation.[82] In the fashionable field of history of capitalism, only big men have agency: brokers in Liverpool strike deals that influence the price a farmer receives for his year's cotton harvest.[83] According to the critiques offered by more quantitative, positivistic economic historians, these popular explanations ascribe too much power to the individual master's whip (as we did in our riff on rubber), while they see

Memphis Cotton Exchange Chalkboard. Chalkboards in cotton exchanges displayed changes in future prices, drawn from and also affecting brokers' perceptions of supply and demand. Future prices also could influence farmers to grow more or less of the staple, while the quantity they grew also had an impact on the price. Photo: Marion Post Wolcott, 1939. Library of Congress, Digital Collections, LC-USF34-052568-D [P&P] LOT 1479.

seeds (the introduction of new cotton varietals) as playing the crucial role in expanding cotton production and productivity across the American South in the nineteenth century.[84] Meanwhile, evolutionary environmental historians tell us that long-span Amerindian selection resulted in longer fibers from New World species, and that these fibers permitted the inventions of the British Industrial Revolution in textile production.[85]

We turn to the cotton cropscape after the U.S. civil war and take a less linear view of the agency that makes it happen, that acts within it. We find that the price of cotton and the market mechanism are devices to which historical actors delegate what they know and guess and predict about the cotton cropscape. Where economics sees the interaction of supply and demand making a price, acting practically as laws of nature, we see supply and demand, and the price they create, and the image of the future, and weevils, farmers, plants, and others all as actants. This riff reassembles some of the relationships among the individual actants. First we take price as the lens for identifying actants and their roles in the cotton cropscape, their part in making that price. Then we turn the tables and see the price acting upon the other actants. This makes it possible to redistribute agency to many actants, which allows us to begin to reassemble the forces at work.

We begin with price, which is determined by something called the market. But "market" has two meanings. The first is an abstraction: the interaction of supply and demand, which creates a price for cotton. The second is more material, more physical. A cotton market was also a specific place at a certain time—an institution where buyers and sellers met and conducted transactions at particular prices. This market could be at a Mississippi crossroads store where a sharecropper sold his harvest to the storekeeper to pay off his year's supplies, or it could be on the exchange flags in Liverpool where a pair of cotton brokers met outdoors to buy and sell imported bales. The more abstract version of the market is often referred to as a mechanism in the way it establishes a price based on the transactions of these actants in their specific markets. This interaction between specific and abstract markets reminds us of the way that people delegate goals to technological mechanisms so that the technology produces a script for our desired behavior—a stoplight to embody our rules and expectations about traffic, or a cotton price that rose when weevils ate most of the supply.

So too with the market mechanism, to which actants delegate their doings. The spread of weevils will diminish cotton yields and raise the price. A cotton corner run by brokers raised the price by cornering the market in New Orleans in 1903.[86] A dry spell that limits how fast the plants grow would likewise raise the price. By organizing all the actants in the cropscape into establishing a price, markets express their equivalence. As the American agricultural economist Henry Wallace wrote in 1920, farmers know that "foot-and-mouth disease, interrupted railroad service, and falling foreign exchange may influence prices without changing either potential supply or potential demand."[87]

In other words, as economists know, price movements convey information: a rising price indicates a smaller crop than expected, or an infestation by weevils, or an acreage reduction that is limiting supply, or a large buyer, a bull broker whose purchases raise the price. Conversely: imperial expansion to new cotton lands (which increases supply), or labor unrest in Lancashire or Massachusetts (which lowers demand), or a bear broker's bet that the price will go down, his purchase at a lower price in the future—each contributes to a lower price. By summarizing and condensing all this information, the price veils the agency and even the identity of actants. Price makes the hand of the market invisible, when in fact its most abstract iteration is created by its most specific transactions—by a wide range of actants.

TRADITIONAL ACTANTS: THE PLANT, THE SOIL, AND THE FARMER

Cotton is cultivated from some species of *Gossypium*. This plant produces seeds in a boll and beds them in a fluffy cellulose fiber that can catch the wind to carry the seeds away to propagate the plant. Humans usually cultivate the plant to produce this fiber, and that process requires at least 175 days without frost, in sunshine and heavy soil, moistened by twenty-four to forty-seven inches of rainfall a year. The plant thrives between 30° and 37° latitude, lines that border the U.S. South from the top of Virginia to the Gulf of Mexico. After American independence from Britain, the slaves of American planters grew the cotton that fed the industrializing textile mills of England. Antebellum Southern society grew up with cotton. The cotton cropscape included not only plants and soil but also planters and slaves and the entire legal and political system that supported bound labor. After the Civil War ended in 1865, emancipated workers turned sharecroppers grew cotton on other people's land, and the entire system of production relied on credit provided to farmers by local storekeepers on an annual basis. These are the features of the U.S. cotton cropscape, well known in folklore and also to historians. Within this traditional cropscape of plant, land, and farmer, including the structures that support their relations, we remember more actants.

INTRODUCING OTHER ACTANTS: WEEVILS ON THE MOVE

Long before humans cultivated *Gossypium* cotton, it hosted weevil pests that had migrated from other wild plant hosts in Mesoamerica. This prehistoric host migration foreshadowed later movements; the cultivation of cotton was a means by which the pest adapted and expanded into cooler climates. As the commercial cultivation of cotton spread across the Gulf of Mexico in the late nineteenth and early twentieth centuries, weevils infested new fields. They flourished especially in wet warm summers. When weevil populations became denser and more established on particular cotton cropscapes, some bugs would catch the late summer winds and ride them to new homes, fresher fields. Adults overwintered in weeds, haystacks, or Spanish moss near the cotton fields. Weevils therefore benefited when cropscapes assembled in new territories, a process that created not only monocrop cottonscapes but also marginal lands, around the edges of the cotton fields, where the mature weevils wintered. In 1894, pioneer weevils (an isolated population with distinct characteristics) made their first appearance in the U.S. cotton cropscape, moving from northeastern Mexico into Texas. Eventually boll weevils would spread across the southeastern United States in the early twentieth century. As the weevil advanced across the American cotton cropscape, the threat of its arrival often inspired sharecroppers to make their last big crop and then abandon the field, sometimes leaving agriculture altogether and heading north to factory jobs in a phenomenon known to American historians as the Great Migration. This socially segmentary pest had different effects on agricultural extension agents (who found work and purpose in the weevil), on sharecroppers (those who left and those who stayed and learned new methods of cultivation), and on landowners (many of whom lost some laborers). The weevil acted in ways that had different results for each group.[88]

ACTANTS: THE FUTURE ACTS, AND FUTURES ACT

A farmer's decision to abandon cotton cultivation in advance of the weevil's arrival was shaped by his perception of the future. In other words, the future also acts on the cropscape. Now, treating the future as an actant allows us to once again deconstruct and redistribute agency in the cropscape. The future is an idea, it is an image of the world. But when it is made a practical actant, we find that the future operates in several different ways upon the cropscape, on several different historical scales.

We know that the fear of weevil infestation acted upon farmers' decisions and therefore on the acreage planted with cotton—and therefore it affected supply and therefore price. But the future price of cotton had already shaped the farmer's decisions about how much cotton to cultivate, as the judge described at the 1903 boll weevil convention in Dallas. The predicted price also made possible the farmer's credit at the local store and therefore his family's well-being as they grew the crop. So prices as well as weevils were agents of the future as it acted on the cotton cropscape. There were more ways the future acted: opening new regions—of the American South and of the world—to cotton cultivation made the future increase in supply act upon the price and therefore on the cropscape. In this way, the actions of imperial expansion had long-term effects through the idea of the future.[89] Finally, too, the future acted on a more individual scale, as an individual farmer shaped his cultivation strategies to meet the demands of an annual credit calendar. The farmer's bills at the local store came due at the end of the year, creating an end to the production cycle, based on the need to pay up. But as we noted above, the storekeeper's credit itself relied on price predictions, and it determined the farmer's welfare. Meanwhile, the annual production calendar shaped the decisions of brokers who guessed pretty carefully when the year's cotton would be harvested and sold, predicting when the annual cycle of harvest would drop the price.[90] Price is a prediction of the future—which means it is just another actant.

So the future acts not only upon the individual farm but also on other, more distant parts of the cropscape—on the brokers transacting on the exchanges. Each broker is a transactor who participates in the market mechanism. Every contract to buy or sell cotton sets a price, which is a guess about the future—for example, a prediction of the price when the broker intends to deliver the bales. The broker's prediction of the future acts upon the world through the market because his buying from and selling to other transactors results in the price, which sends a signal to other actants (though probably not to weevils, except indirectly through other actants). More: the market as an institution developed financial devices to make the future act more visibly and transparently. The futures market established and regulated by some cotton exchanges reified the idea of the future into prices. Contracting now to buy or sell cotton at a particular price at some specified date in the future is a prediction of what the price will be in the future. In this way individual brokers act, and their predictions gain traction in the world: each one has a guess and—when combined with all the other guesses that have become transactions in the market—his guess shapes what the price will be. These guesses become real transactions, contracts for future delivery—and the transactions result in a price, which acts upon the other actants in the cropscape.

The work of cotton exchanges and futures markets is an opaque reality for the public in general and for farmers in particular. The farmers see prices paid for their crops going up and down for no apparent reason, and while speculators in Chicago or London amass immense fortunes, the farmers find themselves in chronic debt to banks and creditors. This generic criticism had strong political purchase in the late nineteenth- and early twentieth-century United States fueling a populist movement led by farmers, mainly from the West and the South, that shook the country's political system. In the following decades, every reformist politician, either Republican or Democrat, would try answer farmers' complaints of unregulated markets working only for a privileged few. Political and economic historians have rightly obsessed over the consequent increased role of the federal state in fighting monopolies and promoting market efficiency, but we also need to pay attention to how the same federal state envisioned turning the future into a knowable and manageable entity in order to guarantee a fair market for farmers. In 1923, agricultural statisticians working at the U.S. Department of Agriculture started to publish annual outlook reports intended to offer farmers price information they could use when taking decisions about how much cotton to grow or bring to market in a given year.[91] In other words, federal experts tried to offer control of the future to American farmers to avoid overproduction, lowering of prices, and recurrent rural crisis. Statisticians identified the key variables (the actants, we would say) determining prices of the main farm commodities, cotton among them, turning price formation into a political issue crucial to the survival of American democracy. As secretary of agriculture during the New Deal years, Henry A. Wallace, the statistician quoted at the beginning of this riff, would indeed use statistics as the basis for the Agricultural Adjustment Act of 1933 to save American farmers from the overproduction crisis of the Great Depression. In what has been called one of the largest experiments in participatory democracy in the United States, farmers were mobilized through town hall meetings with USDA experts and financial compensation to lower production and stabilize commodity prices.[92] Compensation often went to white landlords and removed African American sharecroppers from their farms.[93] In simpler terms, the Agricultural Adjustment Act reduced cotton acreage, making Wallace into the functional equivalent of the boll weevil.

We have now circled back to the beginning—the price summarizes the contribution of each actant in the cropscape, and as a result the actants become interchangeable at a certain level. But price also acts. A prediction of a higher price in future will cause brokers to buy more now, which will shape the farmer's ability to pay his bills and his decision about how much to plant in the future. Because the price summarizes all the actants and their actions in the cropscape, it changes when any action occurs: an infestation of weevils will damage the crop and the supply, and thereby raise the price—but so will the opening of a new mill that increases demand. We delegate the morality of our individual decisions to the future by means of price predictions, and we also undelegate it—resolve it back into its parts, into the actants.

REDISTRIBUTING AGENCY

The interchangeability of actants in the cotton cropscape can be traced to the original interpretations of cotton when the fiber first entered European consciousness, viewed as the product of a vegetable lamb, the sheep that grew on trees—the *Baumwolle*, or tree wool, that meant cotton was available for mixing into existing cloth types, exoticism made familiar. To this we add the scholarship from science and technology studies that views financial models not as cameras—images of some real market where plant, humans, insects, institutions, and prices interact—but instead as engines that set these actants into a single cropscape, acting together to result in a product with a price that is also acting on the others.[94]

Distributing agency this way in the cotton cropscape epitomizes for other cases the way that interrelated, oddly equal actants operate on multiple scales. The cropscape concept helps us to understand how farmers, plants, pests, regions, brokers, prices, and the future are related to one another. Even as each actant acts in its own specific spatial and historical context, the weevil that catches a wind to new territories acts upon the brokers and the deals they strike on Liverpool's exchange flags. On a smaller scale, a weevil's imminent arrival shapes the farmer's decision to leave the field. The weevil's urges could also make Spanish moss an actant in the cotton field, as a cropscape margin to which an adult weevil would prefer to repair for the winter. Thus the interrelated actants reveal the way scale acts on historical analysis.

ANTHROPOCENE AND EUCALYPTUS

In an inspired early experiment in writing narratives of the Anthropocene—the present geologic age in which humans have become global-scale actants changing Earth's climate—the historian of sciences Michel Serres turned his attention to the skies and seas painted by J. M. W. Turner.[95] In a first approach, Serres connected the "burning colors" in Turner's canvases of the early nineteenth century to the Industrial Revolution occurring in Britain in the same period. Dramatic depictions of fire, smoke, and fog emanated from the new world of coal, steel, and steam, suggesting the intertwinement of art, machinery, and climate, and forcing cultural historians to become historians of technology, who in turn became environmental historians. Turner announced no less than a new atmosphere produced by humans and their technological endeavors, and he might thus be considered an early herald of the Anthropocene.

But when Serres turned to data gathered in the geological record, he found unexpected traces of nonhuman agency trumping the linear causality of humans as the main actants in Earth's history, changing its climate. Samples of ice drilled from Greenland glaciers revealed the presence in northern latitudes of particles from the 1815 volcanic eruption of Mount Tambora in the Lesser Sunda Islands of Indonesia. The aftermath of the eruption was catastrophic, with thousands of deaths caused through failure of crops destroyed by acidic rains and low temperatures due to reflective ashes in the atmosphere. Turner's canvases were no simple reflection of the power of the new humans of the Industrial Revolution, they also spoke of the power of volcanoes from the southern seas whose ashes offered the British painter "lacquered shadows at noon, with winy dawns and carnelian dusks."[96] While too many scholars understand the Anthropocene as a moral tale denouncing the excesses of human powers disturbing the planetary system—a Prometheus myth for the present day—Serres's nuanced take on Turner points instead to historical narratives of the Anthropocene in which nonhumans proliferate and weave unfamiliar spatial and temporal connections: the moving of tectonic plates, atmospheric currents, volcanic particles, steamships, railways, and romantic sensibility are all necessary to make sense of Turner's paintings.

In the summer of 2017, British skies were pleading for new Turners. Early afternoon skies produced the orange tones typical of sunsets, as strong southern winds transported dust from the Sahara and debris from forest fires ravaging southern Europe through the upper layers of the atmosphere. The particles scattered short-wavelength blue light, allowing more red light through, just as the Tambora ashes had done two hundred years before. The ashes from burning forests in the interior of Portugal were carried northward to Britain because rising temperatures in the Atlantic Ocean had sent hurricane Ophelia on an uncommon track toward Ireland instead of following the usual hurricane trajectory toward the Caribbean and the East Coast of the United States. The connection seems anecdotal, no more than Anthropocene trivia. After explaining the effects of ashes in the atmosphere on light, the British Met Office phlegmatically noted: "An interesting phenomenon that is the result of the movement of Ophelia is the colour of the sky this morning, and dust on cars."[97]

For those who identify the beginning of the Anthropocene with the Industrial Revolution, the connection is of more consequence. By 1850, Britain alone was responsible for no less than 60 percent of all CO_2 emissions into the atmosphere from burning fossil fuels.[98] British coal reserves produced "a quantity of energy equivalent to the cumulative oil production of Saudi Arabia, allowing the motive power used in British industry to expand by about 50 per cent every decade" of the nineteenth century.[99] The historical causality seems inescapable: northern industrialized nations have been largely responsible for emissions causing climate change, which has turned forest fires in southern latitudes increasingly catastrophic. Temperatures in Portugal in those dramatic days of 2017 were some 10°C above the average for the same period in the previous three decades.[100] The death of 114 Portuguese people in the 2017 fires, a scale of mortality previously unknown in the country, makes those orange British skies into more than "an interesting phenomenon," evoking instead the ruins and disgrace produced by expanding capitalism through fossil-fuel consumption. In this reasoning, historians should focus their attention on the coal mines and textile factories powered by steam engines of the British Industrial Revolution to investigate the genealogy of our current condition, which according to some scholars should be known as the Capitalocene.[101] Replacing Anthropocene with Capitalocene is an important reminder that the entire human species should not be blamed for the ravages of climate change, tracing these instead to very concrete historical options for building a socioeconomic system based on harnessing coal and later oil. This is the equivalent of Serres's initial hint that connected Turner's skies to British furnaces and chimneys.

THE ARSON TREE

But as suggested by Serres, actants from less investigated geographies and periods also deserve the attention of historians willing to make sense of those ashes in the atmosphere. Here, it is particularly important to acknowledge the relevance of eucalyptus, the Tasmanian blue gum (*Eucalyptus globulus*), and to understand how the tree became the prevalent species in Portuguese forests, where it currently occupies some eight hundred thousand hectares, an area surpassed only in China, Brazil, Australia, and India, countries with considerably larger landmasses than the small European country. No other country in the world has such large proportion of its territory planted with eucalyptus. The ashes producing the "interesting phenomenon" in Britain originated mainly from Portuguese forests of eucalyptus trees and pine trees. A native of Tasmania, eucalyptus's evolutionary history is tightly connected to fire regimes in Australia. Although the tree is highly flammable, thus contributing to the proliferation of uncontainable forest fires registered in Portugal and elsewhere, it is not easily killed by fire. Eucalyptus loses its external bark during the fire, but afterward new dormant branch buds sprout vigorously; seed capsules remain intact when fire reaches the crown of the tree, then accelerated seed shedding occurs, giving birth to new trees. And it is not only that eucalyptus trees regenerate quickly after a major fire but also that the trees exacerbate the fire effects: "The bark catches fire readily, and deciduous bark streamers and lichen epiphytes tend to carry fire into the canopy and to disseminate fire ahead of the main front," and the fallen leaves do not rot but form dense, readily combustible carpets.[102] All this, together with the flammable oils produced by the foliage and the open crowns with hanging branches, suggests that rather than talking of a tree that resists fire, one should describe eucalyptus as an arson tree molding the landscape for its own reproduction.[103]

Eucalyptus first reached Portugal in the mid-1850s, introduced as an ornamental tree in urban-reform projects. In the following decades, its rapid growth would make it a valuable tree for railway construction, its timber used for sleepers, in a country that had cut down most of its forested areas in the previous centuries. Dedicated plantations also commercialized the much-publicized medicinal properties of its leaves. Areas of cultivation expanded, though over lesser areas than pine trees (*Pinus pinaster*), the local favorite for projects stabilizing sand dunes on the seashores or fighting soil erosion in mountainous areas.[104] The Portuguese eucalyptus chronology and the motives for its propagation were similar to other famous travels of the tree out of Australia.[105] In South Africa, the tree would be used on railways and would become a crucial building material for cladding the galleries of the Transvaal gold mines. In California and Palestine, eucalyptus formed borders around orange orchards, protecting the fruit trees from winds. In Brazil, the coffee boom of the São Paulo region led to massive clearing of the Atlantic Forest, and eucalyptus would be cultivated by railway companies to supply the growing infrastructure transporting the commodity (see chapter 5, "Compositions"). In colonial India, eucalyptus was cultivated to reclaim swampy areas and thus increase commercial plantations, also becoming an important ally in antimalarial efforts (see chapter 2, "Places"). In all these stories of the late nineteenth and early twentieth centuries, eucalyptus was a remediation tree cultivated to cope with environmental change caused by the expansion of plantations, mines, or railways. In other words, eucalyptus was a technological fix of the Capitalocene.

PLANTATION POLITICS

But to understand the dramatic expansion of eucalyptus in Portugal, the global dynamics of capitalism are not sufficient, and the historian must also consider fascism. Like many other fascist regimes across Europe, the Portuguese New State, institutionalized in 1933 and lasting until 1974, had a romance with the idea of a national forest.[106] Authoritarian rule overcame the resistance of local populations from the interior of the country to a dramatic expansion of forested areas that eliminated communal uses of the land in the name of rooting the national economy in the national soil.[107] State forestation services planted pine trees on a massive scale in mountainous regions, supporting an expanding timber and resin industry while turning shepherds into social pariahs, denounced as enemies of the trees and the nation for burning the forest to open paths for their sheep.[108] After World War II, development visions of import substitution and energy self-sufficiency, building on the regime's nationalist obsessions, promoted the construction of large dams, again forcing rural populations to move from the interior of the country after losing their best lands, drowned beneath artificial lakes surrounded by newly forested areas. The depopulated region, dominated by dams and forests sustaining a national industry while ignoring local livelihoods, would become the major site for the large wildfires of the 2000s.

Hydroelectric power made viable dreams of new industries, namely, paper-pulp plants that demanded the further expansion of the Portuguese forest with fast-growing trees such as eucalyptus. When engineers working for Portuguese companies in the late 1950s devised an innovative way of producing pulp for high-quality paper from eucalyptus trees, overcoming the notion that only the long fibers of conifers from northern latitudes could be used for such purposes, they opened the possibility of displacing the highly polluting paper-pulp industry from Scandinavian countries to Portugal.[109] While growing environmental concerns made paper-pulp production increasingly problematic in northern Europe, in Portugal the authoritarian regime guaranteed that no one would dispute that expanding paper-pulp companies strengthened the nation. As in countries like Chile and South Korea, authoritarianism paved the way for rapid industrialization of the country. More than four decades after the fall of the dictatorship in Portugal, it is still hard to find critical voices in Portugal against these companies and the immense eucalyptus forests that sustain them. From the point of view of eucalyptus, there was no democratic revolution in Portugal.

The unbroken monocrop eucalyptus forests that dominate so much of the Portuguese landscape may suggest a major success story, of foresters engineering the territory for industry's purposes. Catastrophic fires, such as the 2017 one, point to the foolishness of such hubris. Yet counting only the risks associated with industrial development offers a weak explanation for this multidimensional phenomenon. Inspired by Serres, we see how historically productive it can be in narrating the Anthropocene to take the point of view of the eucalyptus, producing an account in which the Tasmanian native, through fire, fascism, and capitalism, colonized a Western European country.

As our riffs show, introducing nonhuman actants in no sense erases or denies human agency or power. On the contrary, it offers a method to delve more deeply into the affordances and barriers that shape or channel human agency, and to reveal unexpected but significant ways in which power is exercised. The term "actant" offers a historically helpful alternative to the position that agency depends on intentionality, prompting us not only to pay more attention to how nonhumans contribute to shaping human projects and histories but also to recognize that, on the spot, much human action has little to do with intentionality, however much planning or logic historians may write into their narratives with hindsight. Plants, animals, and things bite back, they have their own temporalities and preferences, their own reproductive imperatives. On the other hand, the assemblage perspective restores contingency and historicity to all our actants, rubber trees or elephants, plantation owners, prices, or fire.

But how do we identify our actants? On what basis do we claim to know who or what mattered to other actors at the time, or judge what made a historical difference? One angle for approaching the problem is *etic,* the view of an outsider—namely, our modern selves—looking in. When looking at assemblages in etic mode, bringing in knowledge and concepts from contemporary natural or material sciences can add significantly to our understanding of historical actants. To this end, Edmund Russell proposes a coevolutionary history, looking at cases where "populations of people and other species repeatedly shaped each other's traits over time." For example, Russell applies ecological and evolutionary concepts to track centuries of shifting relations between Englishmen and their beloved greyhounds, in the process revealing fresh insights into the histories of capitalism and industrialization.[110] Timothy LeCain deploys material and biological sciences to trace the distinctive agencies and ontologies of silkworms, cattle, and copper in the evolution of Japanese or Texan landscapes.[111] Russell and LeCain do more than give us lineages of physiological or material entanglement: the emic mode, which seeks to recapture the insider view, is also essential to their experiments in the new materialism. They show not only how their material or nonhuman actants bite back but also that their historical agency is embedded in the human culture that accretes around them, from the power of metaphor to class distinctions enacted through sport.

If we are talking about what makes a difference in history, particularly as historians of science or technology, the temptation is strong to treat the past as a path to our present. Histories that do not prefigure our present, whose outcomes were not inevitable, and whose boundaries do not correspond to our expected periodizations or geographies, require a more radical reimagining of the past and its inhabitants. Here—as proposed in the "Cinchona" section—applying today's science and its categories may appear an obfuscation, an exercise in retrospective colonialism in which "any assumptions we make about what makes these things operate in the world, based on our own western perspective, are fundamentally flawed."[112]

Pablo Gómez's experiment in recapturing Caribbean ontologies in *The Experiential Caribbean* argues that in the seventeenth century the future of knowledge creation was not yet foreclosed. Gomez's account of how and where epistemic authority was made and negotiated, and what kinds of power it mobilized, aims to show us a transitory world on its own terms, one in which "black ritual practitioners" made themselves "the intellectual leaders of a region saturated with ideas from all over the globe." For this, Gómez was able to draw on a wide range of contemporary sources, including an exceptionally rich and varied holding amassed in the Inquisition's office in Cartagena, Colombia.[113] In contrast, in the absence of written records, Kathryn de Luna, building on a method pioneered by the anthropologist Jan Vansina, retrieves some of the "hard-to-reach" history of technological thinking in Africa and its significant objects by combining ethnographic research with historical linguistics. "The processes of language change . . . illuminate such understanding [of how different technologies work] on very large social, chronological and geographical scales," while ethnographic experience, living with communities in the field, sensitizes the historian to the small-scale intimacies and proximities, with other humans and the environment, "that sustained daily life among [our] historical subjects and among the communities with whom [we live] in the field."[114]

Whatever its scope, the ontological turn in historiography requires a type of source and level of meticulous close reading to which, in our riff format, we can only occasionally aspire. Rather, we strive to bring an open mind to the cast of characters in each cropscape, juggling between etic and emic approaches to illuminate not only their historical roles and associations but also the tales historians use them to tell. We also keep an open mind about chronology and causes: the tactic of "follow the actor" often prompts stories that spill over familiar boundaries. What, then, do our riffs achieve?

"Rubber" focuses principally on relations between human actors but qualifies their agency by emphasizing the materialities of the plants from which rubber is extracted, illuminating, in Zsuzsa Gille's terms, "a dance of agency between the material and the social."[115] In "Cinchona" we consider the history of knowledge: how different historical human actors knew cinchona. By looking at the Dutch, British, Spanish, and Andean stories with the same eyes, we retell cinchona's history not as a linear path toward modern pharmaceutical science but as a sequence of epistemic disjunctures and discardings—as so many other histories of science could be told.

The riffs on elephants, cotton markets, and eucalyptus shift the primary focus toward nonhuman actors, experimenting with taking these actants seriously on their own terms. We deliberately move away from ontological approaches that focus primarily on how humans think about other beings or things, or even (as in the Amazonian-inspired perspectivism that itself inspires so many to take the ontological turn) how humans think nonhumans think. Instead, here we reframe cropscapes to incorporate the outcomes of nonhumans following their own predispositions or pursuing their own goals.

Donna Haraway's interspecies approach presumes mutuality between species: humans and dogs are "other," but they "matter" to each other.[116] The "Eucalyptus" section offers an eloquent example of another take on interspecies relations, one of radical difference illustrated by Hugh Raffles, writing of locusts ravaging the fields of a village in Niger that "they are so busy, so indifferent, and so powerful."[117] The locusts matter to humans and make a difference in their lives, but their indifference to humans, their Otherness, is total. Still, we can object that locusts enjoy the fruits of human labor even if swarms do not deliberately set out to find crops; the eucalyptus flourishes and reproduces in a new way in the plantations that humans create. Those are forms of mutuality, of profitable association for nonhuman actors, that are among the relations between species, and things, that we explore in the next chapter, "Compositions."

Chapter 5 Compositions

Locusts ravaged not only the fields of Niger but the fields of imperial China too, relentlessly devouring the precious crops while farmers "wept and cursed helplessly."[1] In the 1590s a talented young official, Xu Guangqi (1562–1633), later to become a leading statesman, combed the imperial archives to compile a systematic study of all the available historical and contemporary records of locust swarms.[2] This enabled Xu to locate their origins (in marshy areas), the climatic conditions under which they were most likely to swarm, and their behavior during a swarm—from which he was able to suggest methods for locating and killing locusts early in the cycle, thus averting much of the damage. From unknowable, uncontrollable disaster, locust attacks were to be rendered a predictable, manageable risk. To this end, marshes—conventionally categorized as wild places for wild plants, beasts, and people, the antithesis of carefully tended and controlled farmland and its orderly denizens—were patched into the composition of the Chinese cropscape as an object of state observation and management.[3] Although Xu believed locusts metamorphosed from frogs, his locust science was otherwise sound, and his methods were widely adopted. His locust study reflected his guiding philosophy for dealing with disaster on any scale: "Prevention is the best strategy, preparation is second-best, and relief should be a last resort."[4]

Xu was personally familiar with hardship and risk, whether from hailstorms or floods, a fall in the price of cotton, or an outbreak of silkworm disease. He grew up in Shanghai in the heart of China's rice-and-cotton zone, a wealthy, highly commercialized but vulnerable region regularly ransacked by pirates. Fallen on hard times, Xu's father made a precarious living working a vegetable garden, and his mother wove to bring in cash. Once Xu's official salary enabled him to acquire some land of his own, he experimented with various crops that he believed could help prevent food shortages from developing. With the risk of bad years always in mind, he hoped to encourage farmers and officials alike to diversify local cropscapes to increase what some today would call their resilience. He advocated an integrated form of mixed farming that harnessed commercial cropping to counter the threat of famine: the farmer would plant the normal mixture of staple grains and cash crops but would use hedges, borders, plantations, and marginal land for multipurpose plants. Sweet potatoes, for instance, grew well on poor ground, they would feed pigs in good years, humans in bad, and, growing underground, were immune to locusts.[5] The abundant fruits of the tallow tree (*Sapium sebiferum*) produced excellent wax and oil for lighting: here was a reliable source of income that, unlike the alternative oil crops hemp and rape, did not compete with food grains for precious arable land. Barnyard grass (*Echinochloa crusgalli*), a common weed of grain fields, was usually ruthlessly eradicated. Xu, however, advocated sowing it on poor land after spring barley for a second crop of grain that though low yielding was resistant to flood and drought.

Xu's vision of a composite, multipurpose cropscape organized around the expectation of shortage or adversity blurred categorical distinctions made by earlier agronomists and official policies between cultivated land and wild land; field crops, weeds, and famine foods; and staple cereals and supplementary or commercial crops. The ostensible changes were small: more care given to hedgerow trees, marginal lands integrated into the farm, wild plants or weeds coaxed into yielding food or commodities. But the broadened gaze, the advocacy of care for plants not officially categorized as crops, the attention to new associations and potentialities, marked a shift from an official agronomy of fixed priorities (with staple cereals and textile fibers as the indispensable constants), to an agronomy of flexibility and contingency that Xu believed essential to survive the hazards and meet the challenges of the time.[6]

Reconfiguring the local cropscape was, for Xu, the grounding of a national strategy to strengthen the dynasty. He envisaged a multilevel strategy of coordination and diversification enacted simultaneously on different administrative scales, from the level of the imperial court and its ministries, through regional and local officials, to grassroots workers disseminating technical skills.[7] Although

174 Compositions

Xu's proposals came too late to save the Ming dynasty (1368–1644), the legacy of his insights was reflected in the risk-management institutions of the Qing state (1644–1911) and its efforts to incorporate marginal zones into national regimes of agrarian care.[8]

Xu's multiple-scale attention to the composition of the cropscape nicely sets the scene for this chapter. On any scale a cropscape is composed of many elements, from seeds and soil through laws and markets to the cultures and meanings of a particular combination of the products of the land. In order to function and survive, to provide both human and what Anna Lowenhaupt Tsing and her colleagues call "more-than-human livability," cropscapes must sustain complex, interdependent webs of lives, institutions, and meanings.[9] This remains true even in today's world economy, dominated by capitalist, industrial-scale farming and global commodity chains that delink consumption from production. Highlighting compositions enables us to look more closely at different ways in which, depending on their propensities or agendas, human and nonhuman actors and elements interact to sustain or disrupt a cropscape.

The previous chapter, "Actants," focused on change, on things that made a difference. "Compositions" addresses cropscapes as ecologies or collectives, exploring the dynamics of stability or disruption. This requires acknowledging any crop as just one member of a community or collective. The approach through compositions also sensitizes us to the "patchiness" of cropscapes: even the most apparently homogeneous plantation or industrial monocrop landscape, when viewed up close, disaggregates into a complex mosaic of terrains and practices, "an uneven landscape . . . made and remade."[10] Continuing in ecological (or posthumanist) vein, our case studies of citrus, tubers, polycultures, weeds, and marigolds investigate how crop plants worked with other organisms to build a world around themselves, as well as how the humans concerned understood and sought to foster or impede those partnerships or antagonisms. We ask how a specific crop's propensities and associations might have changed as it moved and consider how the composition of cropscapes affected their mobility. Key themes include synergies and care, interferences and incompatibilities, control and spontaneity (or "domestication" and "ferality"), simplification and heterogeneity, and defined categories and blurred boundaries.

CITRUS IN THE RUINS

In 1848 Hercule Florence painted a watercolor of the Caxoeira plantation in the hinterland of São Paulo in Brazil.[11] The composition seems straightforward: blue skies with high clouds, vertical tall trees, horizontal cultivated rolling fields, small human figures at the forefront. The different elements that constitute the plantation cropscape are faithfully represented by an artist committed to scientific objectivity: Florence had acquired experience representing Brazilian landscapes while working as a geographer in one of the many early nineteenth-century expeditions exploring the interior of the country, before marrying the daughter of a wealthy plantation owner and thus becoming a full member of the local plantation elite. Brazil was of course the place where the plantation system first landed in the Americas, brought in by Portuguese colonizers who transformed the Northeast in the seventeenth century into a major sugar producer for European markets, soon to be followed by Caribbean islands under Dutch, British, French, and Spanish control.[12] And with sugar came slaves of African origin, making Brazil the first destination of the infamous transatlantic commerce in humans. Although there is no apparent violence in Florence's watercolor, he confessed how disturbed he felt after realizing that a foreman had used his whip on a slave just to demonstrate his diligence to the distinguished observer registering the whole scene.

The dynamics of slavery were indeed at the heart of the cropscape portrayed by Florence. The Haitian slave revolution started in 1794, leading to the country's independence from France in 1804. This meant a new boom for Brazilian plantations and the opening of new areas for cash-crop production. Sugar cane started to be cultivated on a large scale in the early nineteenth century in the São Paulo hinterland, previously—from the imperial point of view—a mere zone of passage between the sea and the gold mines of Minas Gerais. The first row of slaves diligently working the fields in the painting are in fact cutting cane, bundles of which are being carried to the mule wagon on the right.

Disturbingly, the slaves are undertaking their work among tall dead trees, the remains of the Atlantic Forest burnt to make space for sugar. Far away on the horizon the observer can discern areas of pristine forest, waiting to be conquered by the unstoppable "go west" dynamics of the plantation, pushing into the interior of Brazil. The cropscape of the plantation is constituted not only by sugar cane and slaves; it includes as well the ruins of the forest on which it grows. In other words, the history of the sugar cropscape in Brazil also demands a history of the burning and cutting of the Atlantic Forest, one of the most drastic events in the environmental history of the Americas.[13]

Other elements of Florence's composition suggest additional temporal dimensions of the cropscape. To the left, well-ordered rows of shrubs show that crops other than sugar were being cultivated on the property. These were coffee shrubs, which after having been successfully introduced into the Paraíba Valley, south of Rio de Janeiro, via French Guiana, were now being tried in the São

Caxoeira plantation, 1920 (after Florence, 1848). This rendition of Hercule Florence's "true to nature" depiction reveals the transformation of the São Paulo hinterland by a succession of commodities' cropscapes—sugar, coffee, oranges—grown by burning the Atlantic Forest. Florence shows the destructive effects of the Plantationocene. Artist: Alfredo Norfini (1868–1944). Title: *Fazenda Cachoeira, Canavial, 1840*. Oil on canvas from an original watercolor by Hercule Florence. Date: 1920. Museu Paulista Collection of the University of São Paulo (CC-BY-4.0). Photographed by José Rosael/Hélio Nobre/Museu Paulista (USP).

Paulo region too. In the 1830s the two hundred slaves of the Caxoeira plantation produced some 140 tons of sugar and thirty tons of coffee yearly: while sugar was cultivated in the lower, more humid parts of the property, coffee was cultivated in its hilly areas, indicating that the history of the two cash crops should be told in conjunction.[14]

What was still a minor element depicted in the composition in the first half of the nineteenth century would dominate the painting a few decades later. Building on the commercial networks and road infrastructure first assembled around sugar, and on increased imports of slaves, the São Paulo region would become the world's top supplier of coffee, a position it still holds today. In fact, during the nineteenth century the area became one of the major slave economies of the Americas.[15] Just before the abolition of slavery in 1888, some 285,000 slaves were responsible for Brazil's output of 350,000 tons of coffee. By then the coffee frontier had moved farther into the interior of the São Paulo region, following the expansion of a dense railway network of some seven thousand kilometers developed to transport the profitable commodity.[16] A few hundred families owning vast plantations with a hundred thousand to a million coffee shrubs dominated this immensely profitable business. These families would constitute both the political and the cultural elites that remained in control of the country until the 1930s.

Keeping in mind Florence's composition and its attention to the Atlantic Forest ruins, one should not forget the environmental degradation involved in the capitalist expansion of the São Paulo coffee cropscape. In the early twentieth century, the area portrayed by Florence, where he had his own farm, would be known as the "old west," losing prominence to the new frontier farther west, or the "new west." Coffee cultivation as practiced in São Paulo demanded relentless grabbing of new land, to replace the soils fast eroded by a particularly voracious plantation system "driven forward through consuming what it feeds on."[17] São Paulo's coffeescape is an exemplary case of capitalism's constant production of ruins.

This was made only more evident by the Great Depression. International market fluctuations had always been a constant cause for anxiety among São Paulo coffee growers, but the plummeting in 1929 of coffee prices in New York—the United States being the major importer of Brazilian coffee—meant catastrophic losses on a scale previously unknown. Public authorities burned tons of coffee beans in impressive sacrificial bonfires to prevent further devaluation of the commodity. While the coffee world seemed to have come to an end, one last element of Florence's composition promised the redemption of the cropscape: the citrus trees on the right-hand side of the watercolor.[18]

It is nevertheless hard to identify which fruit trees were represented in the painting. Florence mentions Brazilian grape trees (*jabuticaba*), pomegranates, jackfruits, avocados, and fruit trees in general with reference to his own coffee farm. But interestingly enough, a new version of the painting commissioned in 1920 by the Paulista Museum to celebrate the cultural heritage of the region overpaints the original undifferentiated fruit trees with citrus. The first orange orchards in São Paulo had been no more than a complement to the cash crops of the area, first sugar, then coffee. But today Brazil is the largest exporter of citrus in the world. Expanding from the fruit and vegetable gardens surrounding

178 Compositions

the main house, citrus would progressively take over the poorer outskirts of the property, namely, sandy soils deemed unfavorable for coffee.[19]

Citrus cultivation was initially meant for home consumption on the plantation, but in the last decades of the nineteenth century it piggybacked onto the transport networks developed for coffee to reach the growing urban population of São Paulo.[20] By the first decades of the twentieth century, still exploiting the routes opened by coffee, São Paulo oranges shipped through the port of Santos could be found on the docks of London and Hamburg. Significantly, the main centers of citrus cultivation were Limeira and Araras, located in the "old west," where the rapacious coffee plantations had left soils exhausted and unproductive. Among the first owners of orange orchards were European laborers who had saved enough to buy the small and medium holdings produced by the division of the large coffee farms, sold by their previous owners to realize capital for buying new lands farther west. Redeeming the land for orange orchards also portended a new social order, overcoming the hegemony of large coffee farmers.[21]

"A WEAPON READY FORGED": TUBERS IN THE LONG HISTORY OF GLOBAL CAPITALISM

We have unfolded a historical palimpsest of successive crops in the composition of the São Paulo citrus orchards. We now turn to the sustenance of the labor forces who produced commercial crops on plantations or their equivalents. In "Places" we considered how local tuber circuits shaped indigenous materialities and ontologies of social cohesion in regions cast by Western theorists as primitive and "outside history." Here we turn to tubers as *engines* of world history, focusing on the travels of three New World domesticates (the sweet potato, manioc, and the Irish potato) and on the cropscapes and commodity chains that they sustained.

It is now seventy years since R. N. Salaman proposed a grand historical role for the humble potato. A pioneer of today's wildly popular genre of histories of foodstuffs and food crops, from cod to coffee, Salaman's botanical-social study traced the path of the Irish, or white, potato (*Solanum tuberosum* L.) from the preconquest civilizations of the Andes to the aftermath of the Irish famine of the mid-1840s.[22] Salaman traced the steps by which an alien and initially unappreciated crop came to transform the farming system and labor relations of Britain and the diets of its rural and urban poor, ousting bread as their main staple and fueling the urban migration and cheap-food policies that powered England's Industrial Revolution while bringing Ireland's cottiers to ruin.

Prolific on marginal land and requiring little labor, the potato, Salaman observed, "can, and generally does, play a twofold part: that of a nutritious food, and that of *a weapon ready forged for the exploitation of a weaker group in a mixed society.*"[23] Fifty years later the eminent world historian William McNeill elaborated Salaman's argument on a global scale, arguing that the potato twice "changed the world's history." The Inca government had used *chuño,* potatoes grown and freeze-dried in the Andean altiplano, to provision its armies and workers. The Spanish conquistadores adopted chuño to feed the enslaved mine workers whose labors flooded the Old World with New World silver, triggering a dramatic rise in world commerce. This, says McNeill, was the first occasion on which potatoes changed the world. The second was in Europe between 1750 and 1950, when rapidly expanding potato cultivation sustained a pace of population growth, mass migration, and industrialization that "permitted a handful of European nations to assert dominion over most of the world."[24]

The transformative powers of the potato continue to fascinate historians. The current focus is less on the dynamics of class formation than on biopower, on food as an instrument of governance and embodiment of values. The consensus remains that the potato played a key role in shaping the sciences and ideologies as well as the diets and global reach of Enlightenment and modern Europe.[25] But the story of the potato in Europe's history is just one strand in a more complex story about tubers in the formation of the modern world. There is a parallel story to be told about sweet potatoes as engines of growth in China's thriving early modern cropscapes, which arguably contributed as much as their European counterparts to the formation of a modern world economy. The Chinese pattern of growth was quite different from that in Europe's dominions, however, sustaining what Japanese historians call an industrious, not industrial, revolution (see "Times" and "Sizes"). Manioc (cassava), meanwhile, was "as significant to the historical evolution of tropical countries" as the potato was in Europe.[26]

FEEDING AND BREEDING THE WORKFORCE

In the colonial world, tubers typically traveled in the shadow of "major crops" like sugarcane, rice, and rubber. If the potato, sweet potato, and manioc changed the world, it is because of their remarkable fecundity, and the ease with which they can be grown. Garden plots of tubers were a humble, barely visible feature in the vast landscapes of colonial plantations and factories, yet from Brazil to Ireland they were a vital cropscape within a cropscape in the colonial topography. Tubers, crops that stayed put, were a growth promoter for the commercial crops, or the workforce, that traveled. Provision gardens and laborers' smallholdings provided the cheap calories, fed the families, and sustained the ruthless

180 Compositions

systems of labor extraction that powered the ever-expanding early modern flows of silver, wheat and molasses, raw cotton and nankeens, navvies and coolies.

Tubers articulate labor to the world economy in distinctive ways. Cereals, the other principal source of starch in human diets, keep for years and are naturally suited to commoditization. They can be stored in bulk, transported long distances, kept or released according to demand. Regional and long-distance markets for cereals like wheat and rice developed early, disconnecting production and consumption, and frequently setting the interests of producers (peasants or farmers) against those of less affluent consumers (artisans or wage laborers). But because tubers are heavy, lumpy, and don't keep well, they have typically been garden crops. It is only lately, thanks to developments in plant pathology, processing and transport technologies, and culinary techniques, that they have been produced on a commercial scale and been transported over medium or long distances as commodities.[27]

Locally grown sources of cheap subsistence for the subaltern workforces producing the commercial export crops or goods of the emerging world economy, tuber crops functioned as *para-commodities* (see "Places"), essential to, but not entering, global commodity chains. The commodification of tubers came late and has never fully displaced their cultivation as para-commodities. Using tuberscapes to reflect upon the interplay between commodity and para-commodity illuminates alternative geographies, periodizations, and dynamics in global history. Let us begin with the story of the sweet-potato cropscape in late imperial China, and the alternative geographies and trajectories of modernity that it suggests.

In her study of South China's sugar industry, Sucheta Mazumdar has demonstrated the crucial role of sweet potatoes in intensifying Chinese regimes of production and trade from around 1600.[28] Other tubers, taro and yam, had been consumed in China since prehistoric times, but not as staples. The "foreign yam," as the South American sweet potato (*Ipomoea batatas*) was called, had arrived in China's southeastern coastal provinces, via Luzon, by the 1580s.[29] Its cultivation spread quickly, presumably passing from peasant to peasant like the potato in Europe. Official encouragement for planting sweet potatoes as famine food also helped their spread.[30] For comfortable Chinese, sweet potatoes were a "coarse food" (*culiao*), fit only for pigs and destitute humans; eating them was said to cause flatulence and dull the mind. Even during famines, urban populations refused distributions of sweet potatoes as a substitute for rice.[31] The rural poor of China's southern provinces, however, came to depend upon sweet potatoes as a reliable staple, a para-commodity, grown at little cost and effort on marginal lands, that enabled them to participate in an increasingly competitive commercial economy under the growing extortions of landlordism.

A ready supply of potatoes, whether sweet or white, allowed families to raise numerous children. In Ireland (see below), some of those children inherited the family potato patch, allowing them to stay put and work as laborers on the nearby farms producing wheat for export or flax for the sails of the Royal Navy. But with ever-dwindling access to land many had to leave home, for work as indentured laborers in the Caribbean, or as navvies, factory hands, or prostitutes in England. South China too sent many of its sons abroad as coolies. But the capacity of China's countryside to absorb labor was much greater. Unlike the almost cashless Irish communities, the Chinese villages were hubs of commercial activity, producing export commodities like tea, sugar, silk, and cottons, at smallholder scale but in volumes that continued to influence the growth, shape, and fluctuations of world markets, often well into the twentieth century.[32] If we think of China in isolation, it is perhaps understandable that one school of historians labels its long-term trajectory as involutionary. If we consider the countryside of Ireland in isolation from its contributions to England's empire building and industrialization, it too appears involutionary. A shift in scale of time or space can transform our understanding of historical process. So too can a shift of focus.

While some of China's exports went to Europe, the bulk of its exchanges involved other routes, marine and overland. Between 1750 and 1840, for instance, the raw cotton for nankeens woven in Jiangnan and exported to Europe was mostly imported from Bengal by Canton and Amoy merchants, who traded it for locally grown sugar.[33] As Mazumdar argues, where historians locate the main engines of history often depends on which sites they decide are central. If we focus on Canton, the only port where Europeans were allowed to dock, we are inevitably tempted to put China's trade with Europe center stage. China's defeat in the Opium War of 1839–1842 then looms like the end of an era. But if we shift our focus to ports like Amoy and Ningbo, and to the Chinese-junk trade across the China Sea, the Indian Ocean, and the Pacific, we learn that it continued to rival British and American trade well into the era of the steamship.

In its role as an engine of historical growth of the type characterized by Japanese historians as an industrious revolution, the Chinese tuberscape challenges several Europe-centered assumptions about scales, temporalities, geographies, and dominance. Manioc (cassava) in Africa is another good example of tubers complicating the periods and categories of global history.

Tropical tubers like manioc and yams, the staples for slaves working the colonial plantations of Brazil and the Caribbean, remained key para-commodities in the globalizing assemblages of European industrialization long after the formal abolition of slavery.[34] New World crops reached slaving ports in West Africa as early as 1500. Though the histories of their diffusion are patchy and often contradictory, it seems that many of them, including maize, peanuts, and chili, spread to new regions relatively early.[35] Cassava was particularly crucial in the Portuguese slave trade between Africa and Brazil, because it could be processed into flour (*farinha*) that was as easy to store or transport as a cereal. In the immediate hinterland of the African slaving ports, cassava typically became a common crop soon after its introduction.[36] Yet it appears that cassava cultivation hardly spread beyond the vicinity of the ports until the late nineteenth century—with the curious exception of the Lunda Empire (ca. 1600–1887) in "the remote interior of central Africa," where cassava became an important crop and staple in the early seventeenth century.[37] The crop's subsequent diffusion was triggered by the carving up of Africa's inland territories into European colonies. In the ensuing explosion of extractive enterprises—mining industries worked by migrant labor, along with large-scale production of export crops like rubber, cotton, and coffee—manioc, along with equally calorific and low-maintenance maize and plantains, rapidly replaced traditional sorghums, millets, or yams as the staples for rural hinterlands and industrial and/or urban workforces.[38]

The cotton-manioc complex of Mozambique is a typical example of how colonial governments operated post-emancipation to control and reproduce cheap labor.[39] To bolster its metropolitan textile industries, in 1915 the Portuguese government made cotton cultivation compulsory for African smallholder households in most of Mozambique's territories. Each household was to clear, cultivate, pick, and deliver a minimum of one hectare of cotton per adult member. The lint was purchased for shipment to the metropolis at derisory prices by the concession-holding companies. Cotton is a demanding crop; security forces (*sipai*) and overseers working for the companies, the state, or local chiefs imposed such a frenetic rhythm of work that the African farmer-laborers had no time to grow their traditional crops. A dormant resource in Portuguese Africa for four centuries, manioc proved to be the only crop sufficiently low-care, low-risk, and quick-ripening to be compatible with the new labor regime of cotton farming. It replaced millets and sorghum as "food" in just a few years.

ROOT OF MISERY OR ROOT OF HAPPINESS?
POLITICAL ECONOMY AND THE MORALITY OF
CHEAP STARCH

To Amazonians tubers signified cosmic belonging. In Oceania they were the root of wealth and prestige. But when the Spanish encountered the potato in Peru, "they immediately realized its economic importance and at once relegated it as a food for slaves."[40] In class societies, from Inca Peru to Caribbean planta-

A Sketch of the Great Agi-Tater. Daniel O'Connell, the Irish campaigner for Catholic emancipation, is shown as a huge potato supported on the ground by four sprouts called "Roots of Evil: Popery" (twice), "Intolerance," and "Bigitory." Hand-colored etching. Print made by Henry Heath, published by Thomas McLean, London, 1829. © The Trustees of the British Museum.

tions and the shores of Connaught and Galicia, tubers were despised as the poor foods of inferior, uncivilized people. Provision gardens in Brazil or potato plots in Ireland were patches of alterity that seemed to exist in another world entirely from the sophisticated forms of capitalism they sustained. Elites disparaged tuber eaters at home and abroad as savages. Even critics of capitalist accumulation concurred. In 1844, the year before Ireland's Great Hunger struck, Friedrich Engels wrote that competition from impoverished potato-eating Irish workers "gradually forc[ed] the rate of wages, and with it the Englishman's *level of civilization,* down to the Irishman's level."[41]

The misery generated by colonial systems of cheap-labor reproduction is uncontested today. Yet historians suggest that under some circumstances the provision grounds constituted a small patch of "freedom," offering customary or even hereditary entitlement to use a particular plot, or allowing unfree, unwaged workers the economic agency to produce goods that they could sell on their own account—sometimes even allowing them to save enough to purchase their freedom.[42] It has also been suggested that the organization of work in household gardens, in bringing together the whole family to plant, weed, or harvest, provided a rehumanizing alternative to the ferocious segregation and discipline of the plantation gangs, "an arena of socialization in which childhood and parenting took on what are, for us, familiar meanings."[43] From this perspective, tubers grown as para-commodities take on the role of *anti-commodities:* vehicles for emancipatory practices of everyday resistance to exploitative commodification.[44] But if this was happiness, it was happiness under the radar.

What are we to make, then, of Enlightenment rhapsodizing on potatoes as a source of public happiness? From the late eighteenth century, monarchs, agricultural societies, political economists, and philanthropists across Europe joined to praise and promote the potato as a superior food whose consumption would bring comfort to the poor and happiness to the nation.[45] In Britain, mulling over the roots of the wealth of nations, Adam Smith pointed to the strength and beauty of the Irish poor, fed on potatoes and flooding to England for work. Arthur Young argued that if the Irish cottiers were so strong and comely despite the oppression they suffered, the potato must indeed be a wholesome food.[46]

Several factors combined to produce the sea change in the potato's fame and fortune.[47] Across much of northern Europe this was a period of widespread enclosure of common fields, accompanied by an intense interest in scientific or "improved" farming. New crop rotations comfortably incorporated "roots" like potatoes and turnips in a cycle that reduced fallows while raising yields of wheat and livestock.[48] In the calculus of the political economists of the time, wheat exports were a significant source of national wealth. As promoters of wheat production and substitutes for bread, potatoes became valued as catalysts of national prosperity. Produced as commodities, they would provide cheap and reliable food for the growing masses of urban laborers needed to advance the national economy. Savants now declared potatoes not only filling but also nutritious and tasty—a source of comfort and pleasure for the working poor. Here was another source of happiness and public good.

Elite nudging did not always succeed in converting populations to the potato cult. In industrializing Britain many workers who poured from the countryside into the factories and cities were already eaters of potatoes, and glad to get them. But France was a different story. Antoine-Auguste Parmentier (1737–1813) was the most famous of the potato evangelists, and given the precarity of wheat supplies in ancien régime and revolutionary France he had many influential supporters. For a couple of heady years, between 1794 and 1796, the Directoire government proclaimed that the potato manifested all the qualities of a true republican patriot: modest, self-reliant, healthy, vigorous, and resistant to hoarding, it was a gift of Providence, a revolutionary staple for revolutionary citizens. But the French public proved immune to such arguments, remaining faithful to bread. Once state food policy changed in 1796, potatoes faded from the scene except in parts of northern and eastern France where they had already been grown for some time.[49] Enclosures and rapid industrialization propelled the rise of the potato in Britain. Revolution, the survival of peasant agriculture, and slower industrialization obstructed the potato's progress in France.

The Enlightenment discourse of potato happiness conveniently collapsed differing class interests into a common "public good." The poor were to eat potatoes so that the collectivity might thrive. As Rebecca Earle notes, for the first time European governments were not simply concerned with the quantity of food available but sought to direct the dietary choices of their subjects, and to legitimize their advice with experimental evidence and scientific theory.[50]

Returning to our arguments about the persistent linkages between commodity and para-commodity, in nineteenth-century England, the epitome of a progressive modern economy, the potatoes sold in towns were grown by farm laborers who typically lived on homegrown potatoes.[51] Potatoes from kitchen gardens or allotments remained an essential staple for British agricultural workers right through to World War II, permitting farmers to pay wages far below those of urban laborers.[52] But homegrown potatoes were also essential to the reproduction of Britain's industrial working class. Despite the cost, both urban and village families eagerly sought to rent allotments. Like the provision lots of the Caribbean, allotments constituted patches of freedom where a man could chat and smoke and grow flowers as well as necessities like potatoes and vegetables.

186 Compositions

Paternalist organizations like the Labourer's Friend Society argued that allotments fostered Victorian values: responsibility, independence, industry, and sobriety. "When [laboring men] can talk of '*my* potatoes,' and '*my* peas,' and '*my* beans,'—it gives a new current to their thoughts, and is often the commencement of that self-respect which one likes to see in their character."[53] Social critics from Marx to Salaman continued to emphasize the degrading results of potato dependence. But from 1750 this motif interweaves with a new vision of potato-bred civic virtues. Albeit for very different reasons, French revolutionary ministers, Victorian Liberals, and Nazi autarkists all agreed on the potato's morally and socially uplifting potential.

In much modern writing of history, tuber crops (except for the Irish potato) are nearly invisible, but here we have treated them as engines of history. Refocusing on sugar plantations or Lancashire cotton mills to view them as tuberscapes, placing tubers and their circulation at the center of emerging and changing world systems of commodity production, throws new light on the genealogies of world capitalism. This takes us to another form of overlap and intersection usually invisible in a modernist perspective: the workers' cooperative.

WORKER COOPERATIVES

In the section "A weapon ready forged" we explored linkages between the reproduction of human labor and the production of commodities. Here we emphasize not linkages but collaborations, natural or human-induced forms of cooperation between the nonhuman denizens of cropscapes that pool energy and resources to mutual benefit, allowing the collectivity to flourish. Looking at the varieties of interspecies synergy that have helped cropscapes prosper also draws attention to contrary processes and trends, to the human sortings and separations of species and processes that have been part of agriculture from its very beginning.[54]

Deciding that one type of plant is more useful than others, selecting similar ears for seed grain, weeding a plot, planting only one crop in a field, breeding white cattle with white and black with black: these are all simple and obvious human techniques of cropscape purification that date back to the origins of farming.[55] Yet cereals needed manuring, animals needed fodder, delicate plants needed the protection of shade trees, crop rotation and polyculture enhanced yields and variety: interspecies exchanges and cooperation remained essential to successful farming until quite recently.

With the rise of industrialization, commercial and scientific crop breeding and chemical inputs, however, modern agronomy has reduced interspecies interaction to a minimum, naturalizing the disconnection of many long-standing, deep-rooted interdependencies. The rise of first the guano industry, then the chemical fertilizer industry, followed by the adoption of the tractor, effectively decoupled livestock raising from crop cultivation, transforming local and global patterns of land use and specialization. For productive and profitable farming today, a single variety of a single crop plant is grown on a large scale, weeds and pests are eliminated with chemicals, and nutrients are likewise added in chemical form. Once manure and draft animals are no longer needed, livestock disappear from the cropscape. With chemical pesticides, so too do insects. Many of today's major crops, including wheat, rice, maize, and soybean, are self-pollinated; but for those that depend on pollinators, like California's huge almond orchards or Maine's cranberry and blueberry fields, billions of bees are trucked in at flowering time by industrial beekeepers.[56] Meanwhile, "the function of livestock-farming [has come] to be regarded as the provision of standing room, preferably covered, on which eating machines may consume imported feeding stuffs and convert themselves into eggs, oven-ready chickens, or beefsteaks as quickly as possible."[57]

As assemblages of mostly external inputs combining commercial seeds, machinery, fuels, chemicals, and pollinators, today's specialized cropscapes and their products move easily across the globe. Yet the uniformity and scale of monocultures and of industrial livestock farming make them vulnerable, while their heavy dependence on chemicals and fossil fuels is proving environmentally damaging and unsustainable.

The simplification and standardization of cropscapes was intrinsic to the spectacular advances in farming productivity achieved over the past two centuries, to the philosophies that legitimized them, and to their global success.[58] But the damage they cause to soils, biodiversity, and environment are now causing serious alarm. Agronomists and governments are urgently reconsidering fundamental agronomic principles, studying surviving small-scale, locally specific, mixed cropscapes for their potential to balance human and environmental needs.[59]

CARING AND SHARING

"To grow melons," we read in a Chinese farming treatise of about 540 C.E.

the best land to use is fertile soil that was previously sown with pulses;[60] next comes land previously used for glutinous panicled millet.[61] . . . Dig pits as wide as a large dish, and sow four melon seeds and three soybeans on the slope of the pit that faces the sun. Once the melons have sprouted a few leaves, pinch off the beans. Melons have weak shoots and cannot sprout for themselves, so you need the soybeans to lift the soil for them. If you don't pinch off the beans once the melons have sprouted, then they will overshadow the melons so that they cannot grow vigorously. But from the bean stumps sap will flow, fertilizing and moistening the soil, so do not pull them up. If you do, the soil will become crumbly and dry.[62]

This passage provides a good illustration of polyculture, or companion planting, a widespread system of interplant care typically labeled "horticultural" by modern observers.[63] The scarce resources of water, fertilizer. and tillage are concentrated in pits, mounds, or beds in which several crop species of different habit help each other to thrive, carefully observed, tended, and directed by the human farmworker.

Such a nexus of observation and understanding, action and adaptation, is central to what feminist STS theorists conceptualize as *care*.[64] Carers must be patient, resourceful, attentive to small signs and reactions, able to combine different skills and resources as they strive to sustain, mend, or grow the living, vulnerable, reactive beings who are the recipients of their care. Reciprocity is an essential dimension of care: as a moral agent, the carer is connected to the person cared for, open to receiving as well as giving. Caring creates interdependence and coevolution (as Donna Haraway points out, domestication is a two-way process). And it can involve tough love and violence: we prune vines, thin lettuces, kill slugs to protect strawberries, and destroy bacteria to heal a wound.[65]

Care is more easily exercised at the intimate scale. In *Cuban Counterpoint,* his manifesto for breaking out of the American imperialist orbit to achieve true independence, Fernando Ortíz contrasts the two predominant Cuban cropscapes of the 1930s, sugar plantations and tobacco farms, in terms of scale, care, and moral and political economy: "Tobacco requires *delicate care,* sugar can *look after itself;* the one requires continual attention, the other involves seasonal work; intensive versus extensive cultivation; steady work on the part of a few, intermittent jobs for many; . . . liberty and slavery; skilled and unskilled labor; hands versus arms; men versus machines; *delicacy* versus *brute force.* The cultivation of tobacco gave rise to the *small holding;* that of sugar brought about the *great land grants.*"[66]

The tobacco and sugar cropscapes serve Ortíz as metaphors for the qualities of contrasting moral and cultural landscapes. He envisages the relation between the two as a *contrapunteo,* a sung duet, typically a humorous dispute or battle of the sexes. Ortíz spells out an elaborate argument for tobacco as an essentially male substance, sugar as female (his theory of *cubanidad* is untinged by feminist sensibilities). Yet Ortíz is not making an argument about crop determinism, for at every stage he contrasts tobacco cultivation in Cuba, its ethnic, social, and historical evolution and the political and moral economy it sustained, with the tobacco industry of Virginia, which he represents as having quickly developed into, and persisted as, "a large-scale capitalistic slave enterprise"—not choosing to address its multiple pre- and postbellum transformations (discussed in "Sizes").[67]

Ortíz suggests that the scale and quality of farmers' care for crops translates into the scale and quality of relations between humans. Today the scope of care as a concept has broadened to include environmental health and interspecies coalitions. Theorists propose the logic of care as the antithesis of the abstract instrumentalism of modernist rationality, including its application in productivist agriculture.[68] The remorseless pace and rhythms imposed by the practices of intensive agriculture, says María Puig de la Bellacasa, outstrip the capacity of plants to absorb the nutrients lavished on them, and of the soil to renew its structures. The whole system is designed to "increas[e] the soil's efficiency to produce for humans at the expense of all other relations." If we are to change course to a more sustainable agriculture, in which soils are repaired so that they continue to produce, we must abandon selfish and ultimately destructive anthropocentrism, seriously "investigat[e] biodiversity as a factor of soil fertility and system stability," and acknowledge that humans are just one of many species with a stake in the survival of what she calls "soil communities."[69]

As farming is a human activity carried out for human benefit, it is inevitably anthropocentric. Yet, although we have only recently discovered the existence of such important members of the soil community as mycorrhizal fungi and bacteria, or realized the full importance of insect and other pollinators, historically humans have been far more aware of the necessity, and benefits, of interspecies coalitions than today's agribusiness operators. They have devised innumerable systems of interspecies symbiosis that multiply the fruits of a given plot of land and extend its seasons.

We have already focused on such interspecies synergies in two historical cropscapes. The first was the networks of date palm oases of West Asia and North Africa, where fruit trees, cereals, and other crops thrived under the canopy of the palms, and camels played a vital role in transporting palm shoots for replanting between oases. The second was the rice paddies of South China, where algae and silkworm droppings fertilized the water, fish and ducks ate the larvae of insect pests, and barley or vegetables were planted after the paddies were drained and the rice harvested.[70] It would be impossible to list all the ingenious cooperative combinations devised over the centuries, but here we introduce three *principles* for mobilizing interspecies synergies, each of which translates into multiple local cropping practices across the world.

POLYCULTURE

The first principle, illustrated by the medieval Chinese melon pits, is polyculture, or companion planting. The melon pits are a very simple case, involving just two annual plant species. The palm groves discussed in "Times" are more

Milpa forest garden, Chiapas, 1977. The crops grown on this milpa include tobacco produced for trade (foreground). Photo: © James D. Nations.

complex: tall trees, small trees, shrubs, and annuals each occupy different levels of the soil and of the air above it.

The milpa gardens of Mesoamerica are a particularly intricate form of swidden (slash-and-burn) polyculture that combines garden cropping with long-term forest management.[71] Garden plots are fired each year by specialist "wind tenders," who engineer even, low-temperature burns that do not damage trees or valued shrubs. The soil, fertilized with ash, is hoed into mounds or beds where maize is planted; beans and squash are sown later between the maize seedlings. In this combination, known as "the three sisters," maize provides a stem for the beans to climb, the roots of the beans fertilize the soil by fixing nitrogen, and the leaves of the squash shade the soil, trapping moisture; as food the three sisters together provide starches, protein, and vitamins.[72] Avocado, guava, chili, cacao, cotton, and tobacco are among the other crops typically grown in milpa gardens. After three or four years gardening stops, the soil is left to recover, and a carefully tended and harvested forest regenerates, yielding fruits, fibers, medicines, and construction materials, and providing shelter to game as well as to the bats and insects that pollinate crops and trees. Eventually the site is cleared of low growth, and gardening begins again, in a cycle that may last between sixteen and thirty years.

Today the milpa in Mesoamerica is the poor cousin of mechanized modern farming, practiced by poor indigenous peasants and restricted to marshes, forests, and mountains unsuitable for tractors or plantations. Shifting cultivation is viewed by modern agronomists as an extensive form of land use with low productivity. But in fact milpas, like most other swidden systems, can be highly productive, of food and other goods. Depending on the region, milpa maize yields today range between 850 and 2,800 kilograms per hectare, not counting the output of all the other plants in the milpa community; archaeologists calculate that in the classic period (ca. 250–900 C.E.) milpa farming in the zones around Maya cities supported densities of population ranging from 140 to 390 people per square kilometer.[73] Inputs, meanwhile, are minimal: fertilization comes from mulching, burning, and companion planting; hand tools are the norm; labor inputs are the crucial factor determining output. Like wet-rice farming, milpa farming is a skill-intensive small-scale system, diverse, resilient, and flexible. It has been practiced for at least three thousand years, from sea level to two thousand meters, across Mesoamerica. While today milpa farming provides modest subsistence for isolated villagers, preconquest it provided much of the labor, food, and materials that raised and maintained the great cities and monuments of Maya civilization and sustained their trading networks.

There was little place in mainstream modernist agronomy, with its preference for tidy boundaries and narrow measures of efficacy, for the millennial milpas of Mesoamerica. Yet today, along with other locally specific systems of polyculture, such as Chinese traditions of pit cultivation or the ancient raised fields of the Lake Titicaca basin, the milpas have become a practical and philosophical resource for alternative agricultural movements with global ambitions, such as permaculture, while providing both material and symbolic sustenance to anticapitalist and *indigenista* movements like the Zapatistas.[74]

CROP ROTATION

The Chinese text on growing melons also mentions another powerful synergy in crop communities: rotations. Some crops, like wheat or cotton, are greedy and deplete the soil. Others, like beans, nourish it, reducing the need for manure. Rotating between greedy and nourishing crops allows farmers to dispense with fallowing, cropping the same field each year or even multicropping. This system multiplies the output from a field while typically reducing the need for manures and, through more frequent turning, hoeing and weeding, keeping the land in good tilth.

Chinese farm treatises from the Han dynasty (206 B.C.E.–220 C.E.) already documented sophisticated systems of rotation and multicropping that allowed farmers near cities or in fertile regions to crop their fields continuously.[75] Between 150 and 700 C.E. North China was often war-torn, but in periods of peace larger farms produced surpluses for market, of cereals, seasonal vegetables, timber, meat, or cloth, the choice often depending on their distance from the city.[76] During roughly the same period, the Roman Empire experienced a more sustained trend toward intensive commercial cropping.

The Roman agricultural treatises of the second and first centuries B.C.E. by Cato, Varro, and Virgil suggest that a two-course rotation between cereals and fallow was then typical for farms in Italy. Manure shortages severely limited yields, but cropping combinations could help. In Pliny's and Columella's treatises (first century C.E.), rotations alternating legumes with cereals are frequently mentioned, along with profitable combination cropping of cereals in olive groves, vineyards, and orchards.[77] Roman agriculture really took off, however, with the acquisition of an empire.

Roman conquests in Iberia, Gaul, and North Africa led to "an impressive boom in intensive mixed agriculture" producing grain, olive oil, and wine for export to the metropolis.[78] Bread was famously the price of urban order in Rome. Thanks to huge surpluses grown on villa estates in Andalusia, Egypt, and Sicily, the Roman state could afford to distribute free or subsidized bread and other comestibles to the plebs in Rome, Constantinople, and other large cities. A new system of *mixed farming* or *convertible husbandry* developed that fully integrated livestock into arable farming. Fields were continuously cropped for several years, alternating cereals and legumes (including fodder crops like lucerne), then left fallow for several years as pasture. Farms could raise more and healthier livestock, providing more manure for crops; yields were often tenfold or fifteenfold those of medieval and early modern Europe. Such productivity was not seen again in Europe until the first stirrings of the New Husbandry in Brabant and Flanders around 1600.[79]

THE COW'S IN THE CORN

Like the Romans, farmers in Brabant and Flanders raised output by successfully integrating intensive rotations with livestock rearing. They replaced the fallow year of the traditional three-field rotation (two fields of cereals, one field left fallow to graze flocks) with a planting of turnips or clover that improved the soil and provided feed for animals. By the 1650s English enthusiasts were urging the adoption of the rotations and forage crops of the Brabant system; by 1750 the New Husbandry was firmly established in Britain as the way of the future.

Through medieval times livestock had been a "necessary evil" for most European arable farmers.[80] Shortage of feed meant that many animals had to be slaughtered toward the end of the year; in spring the chosen few would be taken out to pasture, some so weak that they had to be carried. But fields had to be plowed, and the more manure, the more corn. Farmers devised ingenious ways to feed stock and to divert dung onto their lands. Manorial lords obliged serfs to graze the common herds on demesne fields. Rights to graze in woodlands were often fiercely contested.[81] Shepherds led large flocks from village to village, exchanging grazing for manure, in annual circuits covering hundreds of kilometers.[82] Transhumance, the leading of animals up into the mountains to graze on lush pastures through the summer, remains common today, producing some of Europe's most famous cheeses.[83]

The burden of maintaining livestock extended medieval cornscapes, often far beyond the village bounds.[84] The New Husbandry methods gathered back the vital, complementary components of food and feed, field and meadow, crop and manure into a "self-sufficient productive unit whose production cycle is a closed circuit."[85] On model farms, cereal yields could be doubled or tripled.[86] Nor were the animals the meager kine of earlier times. Livestock were bred by experimentalists like Robert Bakewell according to new criteria; cattle breeders, for instance, no longer sought the strong shoulders needed by draft oxen but instead selected for a well-fleshed rump and loins in beef cattle. Milk yields in selected herds were up to triple those from ordinary cows, and prize bulls could reach double the weight of ordinary specimens.[87]

The New Husbandry allowed British farming to keep pace with the urbanization and growth of manufacturing catalyzed by the Industrial Revolution, although typical practice tended to lag far behind the model (see "Sizes").[88] By 1800 "each farm worker produced enough to support two workers in manufacturing and services."[89] The New Husbandry embodied an ideal of integrated mixed farming that has huge appeal today: a collaboration between humans, plants, and animals in which a largely self-sufficient cropscape generates significant surpluses of cereals, meat, dairy, or wool.[90]

Alas for this idyll, by the 1850s Britain's advanced farms had broken out of the closed-circuit cropscape and transformed their operations into a manufacturing model. Purchased inputs, notably fertilizers (guano and nitrates) and feed, did away with the interdependencies of mixed farms.[91] They permitted new, more competitive levels of specialization, and extended the catchment area of the cropscape once again. As Britain cornered imports first of animal bones from Europe, then of guano from Chile and Peru (extracted by imported Chinese contract laborers under hellish conditions that observers declared "worse than slave labor"), and finally of nitrates from Eastern Europe, Justus von Liebig deplored how British farming "looted the soil of its nutrients and then sought to compensate for this by robbing other countries of the means needed to replenish their own soil." Karl Marx observed in *Capital* that this new form of agriculture "industrially divided [and degraded] nature at the same time that it industrially divided [and degraded] labor."[92]

In these imperialist cropscapes there was little room for complex networks of care and interdependence, whether between species, races, or classes. Rather, in each field care was narrowly targeted on the specific crop being grown, often year after year now that chemical fertilizers had rendered crop rotation unnecessary. Continuous cropping encouraged pests and weeds, but here too chemicals offered immediate solutions. Perhaps the acme of this narrowing of care was the chemical corporation Monsanto's marketing, starting in 1996, of varieties of soy, maize, canola, cotton, and sugar beet genetically engineered to withstand large dosages of glyphosate, a broad-spectrum weed killer, also manufactured by Monsanto, under the trade name Roundup. The genetically modified (GM) seed and herbicide package reduced both water requirements and the need for tillage, reducing soil erosion and farming costs. It was immediately attractive to commercial farmers haunted by narrow profit margins, and also to many environmentalists impressed by the benefits of no-tillage farming. On the other hand, the herbicide damaged the health of farmworkers and pollinator insects, and over time its use generated "superweeds." Roundup Ready and other GM crops were protected by stringent utility patents: farmers were prohibited from replanting the seeds harvested from a licensed plant even for their own use—and with crops like canola, whose pollen flies freely, the contamination of neighboring fields meant that farmers who had not planted GM varieties might be prosecuted for supposed infringement of patents or might have to give up marketing their crops or honey as organic.[93]

Roundup cared extremely effectively for Roundup Ready varieties but threatened the health and diversity not only of competing weeds but also of the surrounding cropscape. The case is extreme, but all weeding is an act of selective care achieved through violence, a choice between what survives and what is eliminated. The significance of weeding in creating and tending the cropscape deserves further reflection.

WEEDS

Implicit in cropscape is not only assemblage but also the exclusion of "plants out of place"—weeds. Cropscape maintenance depends on policing a dichotomy between cultivated and wild plants, sown and self-seeded species, and removing weeds requires the regular care of cultivation. But distinguishing weeds from crops is obviously complicated, historically contingent, and culturally specific. While "scientists . . . tend to agree that 'weeds,' 'invaders,' 'pests' can be measured in relatively objective ways," the cropscape concept complicates the picture. There is no such thing as an absolute weed. Weeds in one place may be crops in another location or at a different time.[94] So let us conceptualize a little more broadly.

A weed is a product of the imagination, of a particular conception of the boundaries between the orderly and the feral. As Michael Dove notes, in order to establish their desired cropscape of commercial plantations, Dutch settlers in the East Indies had to "imagine something that is not there and that does not resemble anything that is there. This is the central conceptual project of settler colonialism, inimical to which is the existence of alternatives."[95] To prepare a tabula rasa for plantations, and to impose the mindset and topography of what Corey Ross calls the plantation paradigm (see "The Social Life of Cocoa" in "Times"), native crops needed to be weeded out to make way for sugar or rubber. So too did native land-use practices. Indigenous smallholder farmers tending their apparently weedy and disorganized fields or gardens were imagined as primitive and underproductive, impeding progress—a view that has persisted in the postcolonial world—while groups dwelling deep in the forests were imagined as feral species, "wild men" to be domesticated or destroyed. Yet, as Dove shows (and as we mentioned in "Rubber and Violence" in "Actants"), seldom have either colonial or postindependence states succeeded in eliminating these human weeds or in suppressing their imagination of alternative realities. In the rubber sector alone, in Indonesia native smallholders "wrested the dominant market share away from the colonial plantations" within a single generation; in Amazonia small-scale rubber tapping survived, while the plantations perished.[96] It turns out that *Hevea brasiliensis* needs cherishing at a level of human care that plantation-scale cultivation cannot provide.

What the settler farmer sees as weeds, historians or altermundialistas may see as indigenous species reclaiming lost ground. Wild elephants forage in the tea plantations that have intruded into their territory. Valuable native medicinals like purple coneflower (elk's weed, *Echinacea* spp.) crept back in amid the rows of introduced wheat on the nineteenth-century American prairies. White American herbalists like Uri Lloyd bought up the coneflower harvest and marketed the medicinals in the cities. But as large-scale monocropping and its imagined order gained ground, the wheatfields that had earlier eliminated Plains Indians, buffalo, and prairie grasses now weeded out the coneflower and its cousins, along with the small subsistence farms of early white settlers, from the Wheat Belt cropscape.[97]

Clearly one cropscape's treasure is another one's trash. Among Dove's examples is a sword grass of Southeast Asia, *Imperata cylindrica,* of ancient cultural significance: there is a traditional Javanese saying that "God lies in the tip of a stalk of *Imperata,*" as the leaves were used to sprinkle holy water in Hindu rituals; *Imperata* stalks also lie under the mat on which a bride and groom kneel to be wed. Ambiguity lies at the heart of weediness. In the upland cropscapes of Indonesia and the Philippines, though *Imperata* was treated as a pest in rice patches, on the hillsides where animals were grazed it was valued as fodder and as ground cover that promoted reafforestation.[98] But plantations on Java and Borneo intent on producing sugar or rubber as export commodities relegated *Imperata* unambiguously to the category of a weed that created an "unproductive wasteland" or even an "environmental hazard," a "never-ending object of government efforts at suppression and reclamation." Western scientists have followed the plantation perspective, classifying the native plant as a "major menace" and "one of the most troublesome and problematic weedy species throughout the tropic and subtropic regions of the world."[99] A wild man indeed! The flatter a cropscape is rendered by being clarified, controlled, and made legible and transferable, the more a weed becomes a weed, banished from the well-ordered plot and demonized.

Indigenes out of place in introduced cropscapes are one type of weed that particularly alarms modern agronomists. Another is the weed that travels as a feral stowaway in immigrants' baggage—the dreaded "invasive species," deemed to threaten biodiversity. But defining an invader is a political project. According to the Invasive Species Advisory Committee (ISAC) of the U.S. Department of the Interior, invaders are nonnatives who cross multiple barriers. To qualify, the immigrant plants must not only cross geographical boundaries, they must survive, establish themselves, and spread vigorously—a species is defined as an invader only "if it causes negative environmental, economic, or human health effects, which outweigh any beneficial effects."[100] We have little difficulty categorizing the rats that stowed away on Pacific outriggers as an invasive species, but how does Eucalyptus weigh in the balance?[101]

A cropscape like the Mayan milpa blurs the boundaries between garden and forest, crop, companion, and weed, cultivating and foraging. Interweaving multiple layerings of interspecies care, in the Western imagination of the good cropscape the milpa appears a disorderly mess. In the milpa imagination, however, almost nothing is feral, nothing is categorically a weed. In the Toluca Valley of Mexico, social scientists found that farmers harvested seventy-four varieties of "weed" from their maize fields, to use or sell as greens, medicinals, or forage. The self-seeded plants contributed as much as 55 percent of the net value of the field's harvest; they did not reduce maize yields, as they were harvested before its critical growth period; they increased field biomass, improved farmers' diets and incomes, and helped them raise the large livestock that were introduced to the region during the Spanish conquest and that contribute so much to the farm's production and the family's survival. Learning all this, the scientists decided to call them "spontaneous plants" instead of weeds.[102]

Even where a weed species demonstrably interferes with the main crop, many farmers like to give a weed a chance to prove itself. In Europe, oats and rye were developed from weeds in wheat and barley fields. Japan has records of farmers using weedy wild rices to develop new varieties. In Thailand what is called "weedy rice" has recently become a problem for farmers growing approved IRRI varieties along the tidy Green Revolution model, but farmers growing floating rice in marginal environments inspect the weedy rices for potential to mix into their habitual tinkering with varieties, an intensive process of observation, experiment, and care impossible—and pointless—under the strictures of mainstream farming.[103]

In modern monocropping, where efficiency is calculated based on the output of a single variety, plants are allowed no agency to choose when or where they grow. This system has no hesitation in identifying weeds and ruthlessly eliminating them. It is tempting to argue that meaning too is drained from these capitalist cropscapes. Money and meaning are often presented, in our own age, as antithetical. So when crops become commodities do they lose their aura as plants, or foods, or symbols? Clearly what people want from a plant, or what they see in it, changes as time goes by, or when a plant is moved to a new environment. The historical wanderings of marigolds highlight meaning-making in the composition of a cropscape.

MARIGOLDS AND MEANINGS ON THE MOVE

The Spanish first encountered the brilliant gold and scarlet flowers of *Tagetes* marigolds growing around tombs in Aztec cemeteries. The bold beauty of the flowers guaranteed them early passage, along with cacao and other exotics, across the Atlantic and through the Old World. Aztec marigold, French marigold, African marigold, *maravilla mexicana, cravo-da-índia, clavel de moro*, or *clavel chino:* as with other American species, including the turkey and maize, the names given these bright, highly aromatic flowers hint at glamorous travels from uncertain but exotic origins.[104]

Tagetes marigolds are most commonly valued for their flowers, but they have also been cultivated for their strong smell, their ritual efficacy, and the yellow

198 Compositions

pigment in their petals.[105] On their travels marigolds sometimes transported, sometimes shed meanings. Here we look at how marigolds wove together new associations and fit into differently composed cropscapes as they traveled the world over five centuries.

In Mexico, where they originated, *Tagetes* marigolds grew in house gardens and milpa gardens. Like so many other plants in the milpa cropscape, marigolds were at once crop and weed. They grew self-seeded among the maize and other plants; smaller seedlings were thinned out, the bigger ones were left; their flowers were harvested for ornamental, incense, or medicinal purposes. *Tagetes* is one of the most widely used herbs in Central America: the tea is a mild stimulant, and in other preparations the plants are used to treat afflictions from snakebite to ague.[106] But their most vital potency was religious—they were considered mediators between worlds. The Aztecs regarded the marigold as the flower of the dead. In Mexico and across Latin America the *flor de muerto,* as it is known, is still used in Day of the Dead celebrations, a late autumn festival that coincides with the plants' most abundant blooming. Families visit graves to pray for deceased relatives and friends, offering them foods, gifts, and flowers, especially marigolds. The dead awake to share the celebrations, and the strong odor of the marigolds guides the dead souls toward the living. Mexican burial sites are adorned with marigolds, as are the private altars constructed for the dead.[107]

Tagetes marigolds arrived in Europe in the early 1500s. The exact routes by which they made their way across the Atlantic are unclear. Phytogeographic observations and pre-Linnean nomenclature point to several simultaneous paths: direct to Iberia from New Spain (Mexico) or Brazil; via the Atlantic islands and the African coast; and perhaps even via the Iberian outposts in the East Indies. Like other New World introductions, *Tagetes* attracted the attention of European herbalists and plant scholars; the various Latin names they gave *Tagetes,* ending in *africanus* or *indica,* suggest they did not realize that the plants were originally American. *Tagetes* was also shorn of what had made it most precious in its homeland: its spiritual powers and healing virtues. Leonhart Fuchs in his *De historia stirpium* of 1542 classified *Tagetes* under pungent plants, other herbalists included them among noxious or poisonous plants; but nobody noted them as medicinals, which suggests that "the rapid diffusion of marigolds throughout Europe and South Asia can only be explained by their having been well-developed ornamentals prior to their introduction to the Old World."[108]

The history of the *Tagetes* marigold in Europe is not easy to trace before the nineteenth century, partly because it was easily confused, by contemporaries and by later botanists and historians, with various natives that had bright-gold flowers. A further level of confusion arises because the *Tagetes* was often rendered in

English as marigold or in Spanish as *maravilla,* both long-established names for *Calendula,* the Eurasian marigold, a flower known across Europe from antiquity. Through the linguistic fog, we glimpse *Tagetes* as a plant favored by designers of formal gardens in the Renaissance and later, though sometimes their descriptions of the plant's habit suggest that they were in fact referring to sunflowers.[109] Otherwise, it is difficult to say how widely known and used *Tagetes* was in Europe before its rise to prominence as a border plant in the late nineteenth century.

Although the English name marigold is loosely tied to the Virgin Mary, there seems to be no evidence that either *Calendula* or *Tagetes* was ever used in Christian ceremonies in Europe. But in New Spain, as a symbol of devotion *Tagetes* offered a symbolic bridge between the old religions and the new beliefs propounded by the Catholic Church. *Tagetes* became closely associated not only with All Souls' Day ceremonies, when cemeteries were strewn with marigold flowers in imitation of the Aztec custom of the Day of the Dead, but also with the Feast of the Annunciation, when banks of marigolds were heaped at the feet of the statue of the Virgin.

This religious use of marigolds seems to have skipped Europe, but it quickly took root in India. By 1600 the missionary endeavors of the Spanish and Portuguese Catholic orders encompassed the globe, from Japan to Peru. The church was as effective a conduit for transmitting material culture between East and West as the great trading companies. It is supposed that the Catholic fathers took *Tagetes* with them to India, where they soon brightened the churches of Christian converts. Indians had used *Calendula* marigolds for food, decoration, and ritual for many centuries. Heavy, scented garlands of marigolds and jasmine were hung around the necks of statues of deities, and of participants in rituals. The *Tagetes* flower, brighter still than the *Calendula,* was rapidly incorporated into the Indian culture of flowers, and the aromatic garlands of gold and flame soon decorated both Christian and Hindu ceremonies, in churches, temples, homes, and streets.[110] The *Tagetes* quickly found a place not only in the religious culture of India but also in its art, its medical practices, and its everyday material culture. *Tagetes* joined roses, pinks, and tulips in Mughal portraits and as a motif for fabrics, Ayurvedic medicine readily incorporated the aromatic, oil-bearing plant into its remedies, and artisans used the flowers as a cheap source of yellow or green dye.[111]

In Mexico the *Tagetes* marigold slipped smoothly from the Aztec cemetery into the Catholic chapel; as well as a lure for the souls of the dead, it became a token of veneration of the Virgin. In India, the Mexican marigolds soon moved beyond the church into the Hindu temple and the Indian street, assimilating the symbolic associations of *Calendula* as it went. In Mexico the marigold bundled together religious significance, visual pleasure, and healing properties. In India artistic resource and dye plant were added to the bundle of attributes. Futhermore, in India and in the Ottoman Empire, farmers grew *Tagetes* for the market.

Until recently the Indian marigold market was almost exclusively for marigold flowers, not plants. But in late nineteenth-century Europe and North America, *Tagetes* became a favorite with the plant breeders, seed companies, and nurseries who supplied amateur gardeners and public parks with the annual bedding plants that were now highly fashionable and increasingly affordable. According to Burpee's, one of the leading breeders of *Tagetes,* in the United States the marigold began to rival popular favorites like asters and sweet peas around 1900; in 1915 David Burpee, the new director of the company, decided to include marigolds in the catalogue and to fund research.[112] Since then hundreds if not thousands of new varieties have been developed. The irony here is that the Central American *Tagetes* took four centuries to reach North America, while it took only a few years to reach the Indian Ocean.

Tagetes cultivation expanded rapidly in scale and in geography with the rise of middle-class gardening culture, starting in the nineteenth century. Today the value of the *Tagetes* industry, as well as the area under cultivation, is exploding again: processes for extracting the food dye, lutein, and vermifuge compounds have turned *Tagetes* into a valuable resource for the processed-food industry and for agricultural chemicals. Mexico and India, China and Peru are all exporters; for these markets the flowers are grown on a large scale, often by contract farming.[113]

In these latter phases of *Tagetes'* travels, the flowers have been shorn of symbolic content. For gardeners they are colorful, easy to grow, and inexpensive; for makers of margarine they are a convenient source of approved "natural" additives.[114] The disenchanted culture of *Tagetes* as bedding plants in Pennsylvania or Manchester bears no resemblance to the symbolically charged culture that still attaches to *Tagetes* in Chiapas or Varanasi, yet Mexico and India are both among the world's leading commercial producers of the plant; Mexico in particular exports huge volumes of marigold colorant. The history of *Tagetes* illustrates how a single plant contains the germs of multiple meanings, multiple circuits of exchange or markets, and multiple scales of production. The place and significance of the same plant in the composition of these different cropscapes is quite distinct. As global historians, as we trace the trajectories of plants we ignore this malleability and multiplicity at our peril.

Xu Guangqi's vision of how to compose a cropscape at multiple scales was intended to build a resilient agrarian regime that could weather shocks and sustain

Thanking the Gods: from the *Gengzhi tu* (Pictures of farming and weaving), 1742 imperial edition. To members of China's official class such as Xu Guangqi, this image of a peasant family celebrating the harvest represented the ultimate goal of successful government: rural households were the building blocks of the state, and ensuring their welfare was the moral and material foundation of imperial rule. Reproduced as Plate LIV in Otto Franke, *Keng Tschi T'u: Ackerbau und Seidengewinnung in China*, Hamburg, L. Friederichsen & Co., 1913.

prosperity. It was a plan organized around the central principle of Chinese statecraft, that promoting the livelihood of peasant households was both the duty of the state and the foundation of its strength. Although Xu's vision was not realized in his lifetime, as mentioned earlier, many aspects were reflected in Qing-dynasty policies. At the grassroots level, Xu's approach to multipurpose farming displayed the caring, horticultural attention to individual plants characteristic of the Chinese peasant farm, supplemented by the boundary blurring more typical of Central American milpa farming. At the administrative level too, rather than seeking to realize an ideal of uniformity and regularity, as various earlier agrarian policies sought to do, Xu's overarching principle was coordinating complexity and mobilizing variety and complementarity. His ideal was a composition of patched cropscapes nested like boxes, from the scale of the empire, through the scale of cross-regional trade and comparative advantage, down to the scale of the individual smallholding and the composition of its hedgerows. Though complex, this cropscape was still transparent and thoroughly integrated into the state—Xu was not advocating that China's villages escape into Zomia. Rather, its envisaged composition was, in almost every way, the opposite of the simplifications favored by the plantation imagination in its colonial and later manifestations.

Plantation owners never sought to promote the welfare of peasants—on the contrary, they needed to sweep smallholders out of the way to establish their enterprise. Yet many basic principles of the plantation paradigm became agronomic orthodoxy and were thus built into the design of post–World War II agricultural development programs, including the Green Revolution, aimed at improving the livelihoods and performance of peasant farmers. It quickly became apparent that the consequent drive to simplify and homogenize complex local cropscapes incurred both social and environmental damage. We have already mentioned various critiques developed in response to the failings of such modernist programs, including Farming Systems Research and agroecology (see "Orientations," "Times," and "Sizes"). All insist that development strategies should acknowledge, investigate, and promote social, agronomic, and environmental diversity. While it is tempting to see these projects as responses to specifically Anthropocene dilemmas, the cases we have presented in "Compositions" invite us to evaluate today's arguments for care and complexity in the light of their historical antecedents, comparing their framings with other models through which humans have evaluated cropscapes and activated their denizens, and providing long-term perspectives on the synergies or interferences between what we have conveniently contrasted as the plantation and the milpa imagination.

In recent decades the opposing ideals of cropscape simplification and complexity have thrived through difference, in a contrapunteo or unfurling argument pitting large against small; discipline against care; planning against spontaneity; efficiency, output, and profit against sustainability, diversity, and livability. It was ever so.[115] We might imagine that the extreme simplifications of contemporary industrial-scale monoculture or livestock farming are unprecedented. Certainly, as most Anthropocene theorists agree, they represent the culmination of a historical trend that entwines the logics of technological innovation and capital accumulation.[116] This chapter has identified some of the key innovations, material and conceptual, that facilitated the decomposition of modern cropscapes into separate, independent sectors. Yet, as James C. Scott argues in *Against the*

Grain, there are ancient historical precedents for the implacable pursuit of "amber waves of wheat."[117] Where one cereal is the staple, farmers and governments alike will give precedence to the all-important source of sustenance; if sugar is the mainstay of the economy, other crops will have to fit in around its needs.

Anthropocene accelerations and capitalist ruins notwithstanding, we don't wish to imply that simplicity is invariably founded on violence whereas complexity fosters harmony. The provision gardens at the edge of colonial plantations may or may not have been refuges where enslaved workers could enjoy the pleasures of family life; nevertheless, the food they produced was an essential component of a world economy enriched by ruthless exploitation. The palimpsest of oranges, coffee, and sugar in the Saõ Paulo cropscapes reorganized the botanical actors but left the oppressive human relations of production essentially unchanged. Farming Systems researchers recognized that quite savage social inequalities within and between households and communities were often part and parcel of diverse rural livelihoods: poor villagers gleaned the fields not as a gesture against waste but because otherwise they would go hungry. Ecological sustainability means life for some and death for others.

So diversity is not necessarily benign. Conversely, apparent simplification is often underpinned by complication and care. In some imaginations of the cropscape this is denied or obscured, in others acknowledged. A similar degree of skill and care went into tobacco production in Cuba and Virginia, but while Cuba's small tobacco farmers glorified their skills as an art, a matter of national pride, in Virginia (see "Sizes") the quality of the product, not the quality of the labor, was a matter of public pride. The recognition that coalitions reduce the risks of simplification, that to thrive and produce maximum yields a main crop often needs help, was certainly not restricted to small-scale farming. Rotations, for instance, could be practiced at the scale of the allotment garden or the landed estate. In Europe, rotations and mixed farming flourished under the Roman Empire, then disappeared, to reappear many centuries later with the New Husbandry: in both cases it was the consolidation of operations into large centrally managed estates that enabled the system. Managers of large estates in medieval China, meanwhile, thought at one scale about how crops should be allocated in rotations to different fields, and at another about how to grow melons using soybeans to break the soil.

Perhaps we might recast these dialectics of scale and sensibility in terms of another concept—transculturation—imagined by Ortíz to explain Cuba's entangled histories. Cuba's history had thrown together indigenes and immigrants: native Tainos, enslaved Africans, Spanish of many classes and origins, then migrants from all over Europe and eventually incomers from the United States. Under such unequal power relationships, oppressed and oppressors were locked together in a "painful process" of unequal but unavoidable exchange that brought about "the consequent creation of new cultural phenomena."[118] Ortiz identified as the core case of transculturation in Cuba the historical transformation of tobacco, "whereby one *religion-based* social phenomenon goes on to become an *economic* phenomenon."[119] Tobacco, marigolds, and cacao all held sacred meaning in their native America. Borne eastward across the Atlantic to Spain, tobacco and cacao found favor only when they were repurposed as medicinals. This secular trajectory took them from expensive drugs to popular consumer goods, and thence plantation crops; they had to shed their sacred aura to travel successfully.[120] But the marigold initially traveled precisely because of its sacred aura, which propelled it from Aztec graves to missionary churches and Hindu temples. The aura has ensured its survival as a picked flower while not impeding a complete meaning makeover in other contexts, into bedding plants or petals for food dye. The meaning and the parts of the marigold traveled different routes and entered into new cropscape compositions as different elements.

What is true of the marigold is true of cropscapes: as they travel they shed some elements and acquire others. While it is true that simplified cropscapes have moved with relative ease, both historically and in the modern era, seldom have they been successfully transposed in their entirety. To function in any new setting, complex new coalitions (whether of the willing or the unwilling) have to be built, stable compositions built up.

The plantation paradigm has straddled the modern globe and transformed landscapes around the world into vast stretches of large-scale commercial monoculture. Yet, despite the powerful political, economic, and social interests and the scientific weight that have helped propel it through the colonial era and into the age of international development and global agribusiness, even the plantation model does not travel unchanged, nor does it provide a turnkey project on arrival.

The technical rationality of the plantation or industrial farm was, for example, easily appropriated for ideological ends quite different to those of commercial capitalism—although not necessarily with more benign outcomes. In "Sizes" we noted that in the 1920s it was not Americans but the Soviets who most enthusiastically pursued the industrialization of farming, uninhibitedly applying a capitalist system of production to socialist ends. The outcomes were sometimes appalling, often disappointing, sometimes surprisingly successful, and with the help of semilegal smallholdings the system limped on until the dissolution of the Soviet Union.[121] In a different twist, in the 1960s and 1970s the governments of Malaysia and Indonesia subverted the extractive principles of the settler plantations of their colonial past, establishing vast acreages of state-owned oil palm plantations as projects for poverty-reduction and national growth. Landless families were brought in from poor regions of the nation, not as wage laborers but as landholders, each allocated a designated plot or a notional acreage of the plantation, as well as a houseplot. The state settlement schemes are still key players today, holding their own with agribusinesses and independent smallholders.[122]

The appropriations of the plantation paradigm by Soviet state farms and Southeast Asian state oil palm plantations are good illustrations of transculturation, here of a capitalist fetish. But the patchiness of the resulting cropscapes, and their continuous dependence upon apparently marginal, antagonistic forms of production, are not distortions of the original "pure" model but inherent in its conditions of existence. Far from being a homogeneous cropscape or a smooth topography, even the most uniform plantation or monocropping region depends upon a mosaic or patchwork of interdependent, complementary, or antagonistic cropscapes, niched within its interstices, around its margins, or providing inputs from afar. As a working assemblage, the plantation or industrial farm exploits the resources of those other cropscapes that are typically contrasted as primitive, inefficient, and doomed to disappear. As dependency theorists argued long ago, however, these alternative patches are not in fact pockets of backwardness, marginal to the supposedly advanced cropscape, but *symbiotic* and essential to its function.[123]

"Patchiness" is a term recently borrowed from ecology by social scientists to counter the unilinearity and homogenizing of much Anthropocene theory. Scholars like Anna Lowenhaupt Tsing and Nils Bubandt argue that finergrained spatial as well as temporal analysis is fundamental to understanding the changes, trends, or tipping points attributed to the Anthropocene, and the differential nature of its purchase on the territories it is presumed to be transforming. They propose patchiness as a conceptual tool to recognize the variations, unevenness, and unexpected players (ghosts, cosmologies, imaginaries, or snails as well as shale-extracting sites, pesticides, or financial instruments) that inhabit these patches and enact their mutual entanglements.[124] Indeed, many critiques complicate the chronologies and processes of the Anthropocene, recounting deep histories of contrapunteo between exploitation and care of nature.[125] Rather than the historical ruptures or transitions around which simpler Anthropocene models are built, such critiques reveal layerings and braidings, entanglements and confrontations, while not denying the accelerating momentum and extension of impact of Anthropocene processes. The similarities to our cropscape approach are striking.

Our ecological emphasis in "Compositions" on collectivities, layerings, and patchiness points up the loopings, fadings, and resurgences, the counterpoints and transculturations that underlie the apparently broad, smooth, and inevitable path to the present, whether we define it as global modernity or Anthropocene ruin. Longue durée patterns in local cases, meanwhile, allow us to trace alternative lineages, for instance how basic principles and practices of care have spanned farming systems at different scales and times; how cropscapes or their components shed or carry meaning as they travel; and even how cropscapes we might have thought on the brink of extinction have flowered anew. In the 1980s the triumph of industrial farming seemed inevitable. Today we see a revitalized contrapunteo between large and small, agribusiness and milpa, Monsanto and Via Campesina, a disputation about farming in the world and in history that we revisit in the next chapter, "Reproductions."

Chapter 6 Reproductions

Noble palm-tree, you are also an exile to this soil.
Mild winds of the West lovingly fondle your leaves;
Your roots strike firm and deep into a fertile earth;
And yet, like me, you grieve,
If, like me, you remember!
I have dewed with tears the palms
Which bathe in the flood of Euphrates.[1]

Driven into exile in faraway Andalusia, Abd al-Rahman (r. 756–788) sought to recreate his beloved Damascus home by planting a date palm in his new palace gardens in Cordoba (see "Times"). The graceful tree with its bountiful fruits evoked for the emir lost friendships and affections, cherished sights and sounds. It was just one of many plants, familiar in Syria but as yet untried in the Western Mediterranean, that were being acclimatized in the Rusafa palace gardens in the hope of reproducing a lost civilization on new territory. Following the initial Muslim conquest in 711, new crops, including sugar, rice, and oranges, brought vitality to the Spanish countryside and stitched Muslim Spain securely into the flows of Mediterranean commerce and civilization. Seeds and slips were vital in rooting these new cropscapes, but so too was water.[2]

Under Muslim rule, neglected Roman aqueducts and irrigation systems were revived and extended and new irrigation technologies introduced. The qanat, probably introduced directly from the Middle East, was particularly useful in opening up arid zones to farming.[3] From this perspective, the history of the Rusafa date palm tree demands attention both to transportation of plants across the Mediterranean and to another longue durée perspective, on Roman engineering. The cropscape includes both the plant and the irrigation infrastructure that nurtures it, challenging the historian to tell connected histories of seeds and slips that move from one place to another, and of technologies that build upon previous reproduction practices.

This chapter completes the circle of our structure and returns to consider what many scholars consider the beginning of the cropscape—a plant's reproduction and how it shapes the cropscape associated with that plant. It emphasizes the element of production inherent in all processes of reproduction, thus bringing to the fore the different technologies and knowledge-making practices involved in re-producing a cropscape in place and extending its reach in space and time. We consider three successive phases: the selection and recombination of seeds, the processing through blending of crops to allow them to travel, and the making or recuperation of a cropscape's waste products (waste, like weeds, being a point of view or effect of practice, not a stable category). This set is where our sensibilities as historians of technology and science are most obvious.[4]

In the riff entitled "Breeding," we take the germplasm as the cropscape component that best reveals the sociomaterial entanglements of the cropscape. For example, the Svalbard Global Seed Vault has selected seeds for comprehensive coverage of crop diversity, but its genealogy of Soviet and Nazi imperial ventures reveals the importance of national histories to make sense of global infrastructures. Its technologies of seed preservation embody the work (by humans, by concrete, by temperature control) required to maintain the "natural," even in its seed forms. The "Blendings" section then shifts the focus from field to harvest, offering two unconventional accounts of the deep lineages of commodity production and how they wove into modern global markets. It examines how admixtures and fermentation, eventually extending to modern food processing, increase the usable life span of a crop product and extend a cropscape's reach by shifting markets and creating new ones. The last section problematizes "waste" as a fluid category that is constantly constructed and reconstructed in different places through different regimes, requirements, and viewpoints. "Reclaiming Waste" uses historical cases of the sorting of valuable from nonvaluable to ask how technologies and taste (cashew), the politics and science of racial justice (Carver), and the talismanic power of heritage as postindustrial redemption

(Globally Important Agricultural Heritage Systems) have served to reverse established categorizations of waste, and how such loopings and recuperations again and again over the history of cropscapes have disrupted linear trends, in material change, in models for the future, and in the telling of histories. This final riff in "Reproductions," on a milletscape in North China, brings us back full circle to the riff on ancient millet histories in "Times," just as the first riff in "Times," on dates, shows how historical nostalgia has recreated datescapes over the millennia along pathways from ancient Arabia to Islamic Cordoba to contemporary California.

BREEDING

Inside an Arctic mountain in the Norwegian archipelago of Svalbard, the Global Seed Vault opened in 2008, successfully concluding a thirty-year campaign for a world seed bank.[5] The precarious resource of crop diversity now seems to be safely conserved inside this technologically updated green version of Noah's Ark. Following the disaster rhetoric familiar to the current Anthropocene Age, the vault promises to conserve agricultural biological diversity for the benefit of humankind in case of major catastrophes ranging from tsunamis to terrorist attacks, from nuclear wars to dysfunctional states.[6] With the capacity to store some 4.5 million seed samples, it works as a safety deposit bank for the multiple collections of crops scattered around the world. The promoters justify their undertaking by stating that without access to the crop diversity necessary for adapting cultivated plants to changing environments, humanity's food supplies would be in jeopardy.[7]

Repeated references to endangered humanity's common heritage—echoed in the rhetoric of agricultural heritage programs (see "Reclaiming Waste")—evoke images of the conservation of a premodern world in need of protection from the overwhelming forces of industrialization and globalization.[8] The infrastructure at Svalbard was designed to resist major disasters, but its main function is to preserve and guarantee access to crop diversity endangered by the standardization of agriculture on a global scale.[9] There is now a general lament for the loss of the diverse world of local varieties produced through seed exchanges among farmers—a gift economy sustaining traditional commons—which gave place to the monotonous operations of industrialized agriculture.[10] The lament is based on convincing data: in the 1980s one single variety of rye accounted for half the acreage planted in Germany; Dutch farmers in the 1990s were devoting close to 90 percent of their acreage to no more than three high-yielding varieties of the main cereal crops (wheat, barley, and oats).[11] This section argues that the history

Svalbard Global Seed Vault. Deep in the remote Arctic, on an ice-capped Norwegian island, the Global Crop Diversity Trust preserves Earth's biodiversity in seeds collected from around the world. Svalbard's origins can be traced to the nationalist autarkic efforts of the Soviet Union and the German Third Reich. Photo: Crop Trust.

of conservation of global crop diversity materialized in the Svalbard facility is more than a mere simple enclosure of the commons by industrialization processes. As the technological sophistication of the Svalbard vault insinuates, crop diversity is much more than a "common heritage of humankind": meter-thick walls of reinforced concrete; heat-sealed, laminated, moisture-proof foil seed packages; standardized descriptors of the collection—all strongly suggest the technological foundations of global crop diversity.[12]

This approach to crop diversity through the history of technology also points to historical scales other than the global. As this section details, the seed collections that would lead to the Svalbard facility were first put together to sustain very national and imperial ambitions. The very notion of crop diversity as a global resource is deeply entangled with Soviet and Nazi dreams of empire.

CROP DIVERSITY AND PURE LINES

It is important to begin by establishing the importance of crop diversity in modern visions of plant reproduction and agriculture more generally. European plant breeders who in the second half of the nineteenth century launched the first seed companies based their business on the pedigree-selection technique first developed by the French plant breeder Louis de Vilmorin.[13] In contrast to the traditional farmer's mass selection in which seeds from the best plants are selected and sown together in the following year, in Vilmorin's pedigree selection all the descendants derived from a single individual through self-fertilization. Following the example provided by animal breeders and their stud books, plant breeders used detailed records to identify the genealogy of each individual plant cultivated in their plots. Much of the breeder's work entailed rambling around farmers' fields, identifying an interesting plant, reproducing it through self-fertilization, and carefully documenting the characteristics of the progeny. Through pedigree selection, breeders produced what geneticists would later call pure lines—stable homozygote varieties selected for some important feature such as pest resistance, early ripening, or milling properties—which constituted the basic unit of their work. They then combined different properties by crossing different pure lines to obtain the hybrids that made their name in the seed market.

Cropscapes cultivated with standardized pure lines coming out of the breeders' experimental plots promised to accomplish the dream of converting agriculture into an industrialized activity. The pure-line cropscape would allegedly put an end to the unpredictable cropscape made of unreliable traditional crop varieties, the so-called landraces, unstable heterozygous plants produced by farmers' mass selection over the course of centuries.[14] The irony lies in the fact that the first resource of the breeders' activity was none other than the populations of landraces from which pure lines were isolated by repeated inbreeding. No successful breeder could dispense with the genetic variability provided by traditional landraces. It is thus not surprising to learn that by 1911 the Vilmorin Company had amassed some twelve hundred varieties of wheat, making it one of the largest collections in all of Europe.[15] This diversity had been accumulated through voyages of exploration, participation in international fairs, and, more important, by a dense national and international network of correspondents who sent local landraces to the Vilmorin headquarters near Paris.

In order to sustain their operations the Vilmorins were tapping into a typical traditional local commons developed by farmers in the course of many generations, ruled by seed exchanges between neighbors characteristic of the gift economy identified by the traditional commons literature. Informal farmer-to-farmer exchange mechanisms allowed innovations to spread and be tested by others for adaptation and adoption, thus growing the commons.[16] What the plant breeders were doing was transforming this commons into a resource sustaining their private or state purposes. And by replacing the diversity of the landraces with new standardized forms of life they were simultaneously destroying the commons they relied on.

In 1914 Erwin Baur, one of the most distinguished German geneticists and future director of the Kaiser Wilhelm Institute of Plant Breeding, was already drawing attention to the need for collecting and preserving cultivated primitive races, especially of wheat and barley in the Orient, Asia, North Africa, and Ethiopia.[17] And considering the high costs involved in both collecting and preserving crop diversity, Baur didn't hesitate to plead for state intervention in the business of plant breeding. Correspondence and occasional visits between breeders were not enough to sustain the new scale of operations. Only the state had the means to promote systematic collection expeditions that would transform global crop diversity into a resource available to national plant breeders.[18]

The first institution built for the planned collection and preservation of landraces as well as their wild relatives was to be founded in the Soviet Union in 1924 as the All-Union Institute of Applied Botany and New Crops, later renamed the All-Union Institute of Plant Industry (VIR).[19] Its institutional ancestor, the St. Petersburg Bureau of Plant Botany, had already been carrying out surveys of Russian territory since the end of the nineteenth century, documenting local landraces. The bureau's director, Robert Regel, was responsible for a comprehensive treatment of Russian barleys from the different territories of the empire. But it would be Nikolai I. Vavilov, after assuming the direction of the bureau from 1920 onward, who would transform the institution into one of global reach in order to better serve the policies of rapid industrialization launched by the Bolshevik regime.

It is hard to overestimate the importance of the figure of Vavilov in discussions of crop diversity. Two theories made his name among the international community of geneticists, and the two were crucial in offering guidelines on how to deal with genetic diversity at the global scale. His "theory of the homologous series of hereditary changes" predicted how similar mutations appear in related species. Let us follow Vavilov's own words describing his work in 1920 to understand the significance of this theory for seed banks: "Vetch, lentil and pea cannot be crossed, but their series of variation, we may say, are almost the same. These days we have received new vetch samples from Kharkov, so all the gaps in the series are now filled. For 3 years we have been trying to do the same with other forms of cultivated plants. . . . We have not got enough examples. It is necessary to attract everything existing in the world. I shall do all I can to send somebody abroad in the autumn of 1921 to collect plant materials."[20]

The collecting of variability, in order to be systematic and avoid the "multitudinous chaos of innumerable forms" typical of commercial plant collections, had to fill up "all the gaps in the series," searching, if necessary, the "entire world" to collect plant materials. Instead of the networks of correspondents established by the Vilmorins, Vavilov suggested state-sponsored surveys to complete the series for every agricultural crop in the world. Through this cumulative method a world crop collection could be formed, bringing to St. Petersburg, then called Leningrad, the entire global resource of crop diversity.

And this was not all. The surveys were not to cover every territory of the planet in an arbitrary way. Following Vavilov's theory of the centers of origin of cultivated plants, the area of the greatest diversity of a domesticated plant is also its region of origin, where its wild varieties should still exist.[21] After missions to Iran and Mongolia in the early 1920s, he was proposing in 1926 five of such major areas of variability: "The areas of origin and type-formation of the most important cultivated plants which at the same time are the foci of a wealth of types, belong mainly to the mountain areas of Asia (Himalayas and its system), the mountain systems of northeastern Africa and the mountain areas of southern Europe (the Pyrenees, the Apennines and the Balkans), the Cordilleras and the Southern spurs of the Rocky Mountains."[22]

Although the number and extent of those centers was to be largely revised by later literature, Vavilov's insights would prove critical for every national plant-breeding program. After presenting his findings in 1927 both at the First International Wheat Congress held in Rome and at the Fifth International Genetics Congress in Berlin, Vavilov would become an inspirational figure for breeders all over the world. But let us set aside for now his international stature and focus on his relations with the Soviet regime.

According to Vavilov, his world collection would constitute the motor of the Soviet plant industry, providing peasants with improved seeds produced by VIR geneticists. In 1931 he urged the state to assume control of the replacement of farmers' landraces with the new varieties, instead of waiting for the "spontaneous processes that were relied upon in the past." He boasted that same year that one single newly introduced variety of maize was now grown on 1.5 million hectares, and that in a few years "all the seed material in the Soviet Union would be standardized."[23] Vavilov's promise was clear: genetic variability was a key resource for Stalin's Great Break of 1928–1930 combining collectivization of the peasantry, crash industrialization, and planned economy. VIR's seeds, whose name suitably reminded one of the industrial nature of the undertaking, would contribute to a new agriculture in which, following Stalin, "small, backward, and fragmented peasant farms [were to be replaced by] consolidated, big, public farms, provided with machines, equipped with the data of science, and capable of producing the greatest quantity of grain."

214   Reproductions

Due to Vavilov's later falling out of grace with the regime and the triumph of Lysenkoism, his proximity with the Soviet leadership in the 1920s and 1930s has been much neglected.[24] But it is only by placing Vavilov in the context of Stalin's Great Break that we can understand the amazing numbers that describe his scientific enterprise. In 1929 he was made president of the newly founded VASKhNIL, the Lenin Academy of Agricultural Science, created under the policy of "mobilizing science to the service of socialist construction." In 1932–1933 the research system controlled by the VASKhNIL included no fewer than thirteen hundred institutions, employing some twenty-six thousand specialists, and was without equal in the entire world.[25] Of those centers, 185 were engaged in plant breeding. The largest and most important of these institutions was the All-Union Institute of Plant Industry (VIR) located in Leningrad, directed, of course, by Vavilov himself. This concentration of power in one unique figure was characteristic of the Soviet organization of science, with a few chosen scientists having direct access to the Bolshevik leadership and thus being able to funnel funds from powerful state agencies to their research empires. In the case of Vavilov, this agency was Narkomzem, the People's Commissariat of Agriculture.

It was the Narkomzen that funded most of the work behind the assembling of the world collection of plants at Leningrad. No fewer than forty expeditions were organized by Vavilov and his aides around the globe to build up this first world seed bank. The two hundred and fifty thousand samples of cultivated plants and their wild relatives stored in metal cases in Leningrad by the end of the 1930s also included material from another 140 expeditions across the vast Soviet Empire. This appropriation of a "resource," as Vavilov liked to call it, by the Soviet state was intended not only to increase the output of Soviet agriculture but also to enable the colonization of new tracts of land previously deemed too harsh for sustaining human communities. The VIR seed bank was meant to supply genes for resistance to cold or for higher yields, thus putting flesh on the bones of Soviet dreams of settling northern Arctic regions and vast areas of Siberia.[26]

Vavilov's theories and institutions now offered a clear roadmap for any country willing to participate in the world scramble for plant genetic resources. Major world powers sent expeditions to the Himalayas, Ethiopia, Turkey, and Peru to harvest this new precious resource of genetic diversity. The expedition craze of the 1920s and 1930s immediately brings to mind the enlightened expeditions of the eighteenth century that made exotic animals and plants public patrimony by placing them in natural history museums and botanical gardens.[27] If by the end of the eighteenth century no European power could sustain imperial ambitions without a botanical garden, in the pre–World War II years to have a well-endowed seed bank became a crucial attribute of any country expressing continental ambitions. This was true not only for the Soviet Union but also for Nazi Germany.

PLANT BREEDING AND NAZI
IMPERIAL AMBITIONS

The Seed Law of 1934, passed only one year into Nazi rule, was to eliminate many of Germany's landraces by forcing commercial breeders to get rid of their less valuable varieties and replace them with the more productive and pest-resistant ones.[28] In the case of wheat, 438 varieties out of 454 were banished. For potatoes, of the previous some fifteen hundred varieties being cultivated by German farmers in the 1910s, in 1937 there were no more than seventy-four.[29]

As close followers of Vavilov's work, German plant breeders were well aware that this drastic replacement of traditional landraces by modern varieties demanded access to world crop diversity. It is therefore hardly surprising to find German expeditions being sent to the Vavilov centers of genetic diversity in Latin America, Turkey, Spain, and Ethiopia. While German plant breeders had been drawing attention to the importance of cultivated primitive plant races outside Europe since the 1910s, it was only in the Nazi years, following the Soviet example, that nationally acclaimed expeditions were staged.[30] In 1935 plant hunters were sent to India, Afghanistan, and Iran in the much-celebrated German Hindukush expedition. In 1938–1939 the Nazi SS (Schutzstaffel, or Protective Echelon) sponsored Ernst Schäfer's expedition to Tibet, where wheats and barleys were collected along with archaeological objects and anthropological data in search of remnants of Aryan people.[31] In the aftermath of these expeditions both the SS and the Kaiser Wilhelm Society were to found new plant-breeding institutes, whose first task was to store and manage the seed collections and explore their genetic diversity in order to contribute to what the influential Nazi minister of agriculture Herbert Backe called the "nutritional freedom" of the expanding Reich.

These new institutes were the Kaiser Wilhelm Institute for Research on Cultivated Plants in Vienna and the Ahnenerbe Institute of Plant Genetics near Graz.[32] The first, founded in 1943, was conceived as the center of a network of collection stations "from the polar sea to the Mediterranean area, from the Atlantic to the extreme continental region, from the sea coast to the Alps."[33] This network would guarantee German control of the plant genetic resources of the entire European continent. In addition to the finds of the mentioned expeditions, the institute profited from Nazi domination of southeastern Europe to tap the genetic resources of the Balkans, namely, of northern Greece and Albania.[34]

216　Reproductions

Ironically enough, it was the rhetoric of saving the endangered resource of crop diversity from possible destruction that was used by German scientists to justify their looting of the Vavilov institutes' network during the Nazi occupation of the Soviet Union, when several trainloads of seeds were sent back to Germany and Austria to augment the collections of the Kaiser Wilhelm Institutes of Plant Breeding and of Research on Cultivated Plants. The takeover made clear that the scientific commons of the breeders had been converted into a national resource. The accessions of the looted Soviet collection enabled German breeders to launch their ominous investigations into an ersatz rubber based on the kok-saghyz, a kind of dandelion first collected by a Vavilov-sponsored expedition to the Tian Shan Mountains. Because Germany lacked access to the world centers of rubber production, a potential shortage of this crucial raw material became a major concern for the Nazi war machine. In 1943 no less a luminary than Heinrich Himmler, the leader of the SS, was named "plenipotentiary for all issues related to plant rubber." And while it is true that no historian of the Holocaust ignores the importance of IG Farben's synthetic rubber plant for the expansion of Auschwitz, there is certainly less familiarity with the agricultural experiment station that was also part of the camp complex run by the SS. The main research task undertaken at the station was the breeding of kok-saghyz plants with higher rubber content.

In the years 1943 and 1944 kok-saghyz plantations managed by the SS occupied vast tracts of land in the east, namely, in Poland and in the Ukraine, where women and children were used as slave labor. The few historians of Nazi Germany who have dealt with this story have a tendency to downsize it by referring to the small amounts of rubber produced from kok-saghyz. They thus miss what this cultivation reveals about the place of Nazi imperial visions in global history: seeds from Auschwitz, originating from Soviet institutions, supplied SS rubber slave plantations in Eastern Europe. In other words, detailing the reproduction of kok-saghyz demands a connected history of the Third Reich that leads not only to the Soviet Union and its dreams of empire but also to European colonial history and its dark tales of global plundering in search for rubber (see "Actants").[35]

Most of the critical literature on the effects of the Green Revolution focuses on the seed essentialism of modern North American models of agriculture. In a simplified version of the story, the Cold War–era globalization of seeds produced in breeding programs financed by the Rockefeller Foundation and designed to take advantage of heavy doses of chemical fertilizers is identified as the primary cause of a worldwide loss of crop diversity.[36] Considering the prominent role American scientists also played in putting into place a global

Rubber plantations of the Ukraine. Areas in Nazi Eastern Europe cultivated with kok-saghyz. Dotted half-circles denote areas of cultivation abandoned after the Soviet counterattack; black half-circles indicate new areas under cultivation in 1944. The ersatz rubber plantations suggest the continuity between Nazi colonialism in Eastern Europe and other European imperial ventures in South America, Africa, and Asia. *Jahresbericht der Gruppe Anbau und Versuchswesen für die Zeit vom 1. Januar 1943 bis 31. Dezember 1943*, Bundesarchiv, NS19/391. Courtesy of Bundesarchiv Berlin.

technological infrastructure for the conservation of threatened varieties, it is no surprise that such narratives have produced a genealogy of globalization that traces its origins to American activities.[37] By calling attention to plant breeders' practices that led to earlier versions of the Green Revolution dating back at least to the early twentieth century, this section has emphasized what current forms of global governance owe to the national and imperial ambitions of European countries, notably the Soviet Union and Nazi Germany. Not only did collecting crop diversity on a global scale make Soviet and Nazi imperial imaginations seem plausible, the very understanding of crop diversity as a global phenomenon came into being through violent imperial projects. Meanwhile, in the aftermath of World War II, new forms of sharing crop diversity that standardized the cataloguing of collected seeds had to be developed among European breeders East and West to reestablish the breeders' commons.[38]

BLENDINGS

In "Worker Cooperatives" we looked beyond the seed at complex cropping systems, including polyculture, crop rotation, plant-animal collectives, and monocultures using chemical inputs, to explore how interspecies coalitions effectively expand or multiply the area of a local cropscape, extend its temporalities, and increase its total output. Here we take a similar approach not to crops in the field, but to the produce. The harvest becomes the point of departure rather than the destination. We focus here on different types of blending, processes that extend the life and reach of a cropscape product socially, temporally, or spatially. We begin with fermentation (soy sauce), where blending with yeast chemically transforms the main ingredient, and go on to titration (port), where different qualities or vintages of a processed comestible are blended to ensure consistency over time. As the raw material is physically or chemically transformed by the processing, it acquires new uses, scale, and scope, new meanings and powers. So blendings, like breeding and waste, offer a good opportunity for transhistorical reflection upon the dynamics and scales of cropscapes, as well as the ontologies of their crop products.

SOY SAUCE NATION

Fermentation transforms: turning boring barley into intoxicating ale is little short of miraculous. In brewing, pickling, or bread making, the enzymes in yeasts or bacteria break down the molecules of sugars contained in cereals, dairy products, or other foodstuffs, transforming dull and perishable basics like grapes, millet, milk, and cabbage into the delicious piquancy of wine, beer, cheese, and *kimchi*. The science of fermentation evolved slowly but steadily through the nineteenth century, but until then fermentation was widely regarded as a mystical or magical process, hedged about with rituals and prohibitions. Here are the instructions detailed in the Chinese treatise of about 540 C.E., *Qimin yaoshu* (Essential techniques for the common people) for preparing one of many types of what is known as ferment cake, made using different cereals. The process involves elaborate religious ritual intertwined with scrupulous procedures to keep the ferment isolated and free from contamination:

> *Preparing superior ferment from wheat:*[39] [One bushel each of steamed, stir-roasted and raw wheat are ground separately, then mixed.] Before sunrise on the 1st day of the 7th moon, a boy in dark clothing is sent to draw twenty bushels of water while facing west. No one else is allowed to touch this water. . . . The ground grain and water are mixed to a firm consistency by workers who face west. For the caking of the ferment, only young boys are employed and they too must work facing west. No dirty person is to be employed. . . . The raw ferment cakes are fabricated in a hut

roofed with thatch, not tiles. The earth must be clean and free from dirt. The floor is divided into squares with footpaths so that four alleys are formed. Figures are sculpted from the raw ferment mix, of which five are set up as "ferment kings." The ferment cakes are then placed on the floor in rows along the footpaths. . . . Offerings of wine and dried meat are made to the "ferment kings" in this way: the king's hands are moistened and used as bowls to receive gifts of wine, dried meat and pastry. The master of ceremonies reads the sacrificial incantation three times. Everyone kneels twice to the deities. The wooden door to the hut is then closed and sealed for seven days. [Over four seven-day cycles the ferment cakes are dried, turned, and redried; finally they are taken out, strung, sundried and stored.][40]

In early and medieval China ferment cakes were used to make beers, wines, vinegars, pickles, and soy pastes. Over time the range of fermented soy products expanded; they were particularly appreciated, in a society where salt was expensive, because they intensified salty flavors. Soy is also a good source of protein, although obviously this was not a recognized benefit at the time. By around 1000 soy sauce and bean curd, along with soy pastes of many kinds, were becoming regular items in the Chinese diet. But although China pioneered many soy products, it was Japan that eventually became the world leader in the production of fermented soy foods, renowned in particular for its many varieties of *miso* paste and soy sauce (*shoyu*). This riff explains how soy sauce helped nourish and define the modern Japanese nation.

It is said that the *tamari* variety of soy sauce was first discovered in Japan in the thirteenth century, as a dark, fragrant residue at the bottom of a pot that had been used to ferment miso paste. By the Tokugawa or Edo period (1600–1868) a host of different soy sauces had been perfected, some light, some dark, using ferments (*kōji*) made either from rice, barley, or soybeans.[41]

The Tokugawa period saw rapid and sustained economic growth. Thanks to innovations in engineering and hydraulics, and to improvements in rice varieties and farming equipment, irrigated rice production increased steadily. This enriched the daimyo class of feudal barons, whose income came from rents paid in rice. It also supported the growth of cities, manufacturing, and commerce and a general rise in prosperity.

In earlier times single-pot meals of barley or bean porridge were typical for all but the wealthy. By the mid-Tokugawa, however, in urban households, thanks to cheap and plentiful supplies of rice, what we now think of as typical Japanese cuisine and table manners (the *kaiseki* style) became routine. Steamed white rice was the main dish, accompanied by side dishes, sauces and relishes, and green tea.

As white rice became the regular urban diet, a rice-associated consumer culture grew up that shaped patterns of manufacturing development. Not only did the number of rice mills and rice shops burgeon, a host of associated industries also flourished, including ceramics and lacquer manufactures making dishes and chopsticks, and the soy sauce, sake, and pickle industries.[42] Specialist manufacturers of these fermented products expanded their scale of production and began exporting to cities along the network of canals and roads developed under Tokugawa rule. One important technological innovation here was the barrel. In the late sixteenth century the long saw was introduced from China, together with better planes. This allowed carpenters to make wooden barrels for sake and soya, to replace the smaller, heavier, and more fragile ceramic jars. Between 1724 and 1730 average annual shipments of goods between Osaka and the capital of Edo included 9.8 million liters of soy sauce and fifteen million liters of sake.[43] By the end of the Tokugawa era these brewing industries were Japan's most valuable manufacturing sector, "easily surpassing textile weaving and raw silk production."[44]

Soy sauce was a key ingredient of early modern Japan's famous urban culture: it not only enlivened white rice, it also went into the snacks that were served with sake in taverns and geisha houses or at drinking parties. Initially women had prepared miso and soy sauce domestically from locally grown soybeans, using recipes passed down from mother to daughter. Local flavors were very different, and local preferences very strong—at this point, soy sauce didn't travel far. But before long, small manufactures of soy sauce became a typical feature of the Tokugawa countryside. To meet the expanding and lucrative urban demand, daimyo in areas unsuitable for rice pressured farmers on their domains to grow soybeans commercially, often with damaging environmental consequences and at little gain to the peasant farmers themselves; the raw soybeans were transported out from the hinterlands, and soybean-processing zones grew up in regions along the major communications routes, or close to big cities.[45]

In 1868 the Meiji government (1868–1912) opened Japan to the world and began an ambitious program of militarization, industrialization, and nation building. Rural populations from remote regions were integrated into the national project. Young women were hired in textile factories far from their villages, sending money home and returning after a few years to marry. Young men were recruited into industries or the army. The food served in the canteens consisted of white rice served with pickles and soy sauce. As meat and fish were too expensive, cheap industrially produced soy sauce was an essential part of the canteen diet. Meager as this may seem, to young people who had grown up considering white rice a luxury, these foods were delicious, and emblematic of their incorporation into the nation as valued citizens. When they returned home many refused their mother's soy sauce and insisted on purchasing commercial brands.[46]

Meanwhile in the villages of Meiji Japan, although mixed-grain porridge remained the usual staple, the nation's opening to foreign trade had brought a sharp increase in demand for certain traditional rural products like raw silk. Women spent more time breeding silkworms or reeling thread domestically or in nearby filatures, adding significantly to family earnings. As the pressures on their time intensified, many village women gave up the time-consuming preparation of soy sauce, substituting commercial brands. And in Japan's modernizing, industrializing towns, the expansion of the urban proletariat provided a further clientele for industrially produced soy sauce, an essential supplement for those who could afford no side dishes to enrich a diet of over-milled rice.

Progressive homogenization of diet was a key process in the formation of the modern Japanese nation. Expanding rice production, first within Japan itself and then, from 1895 onward, in Japan's colonial territories of Korea and Taiwan, reshaped Japan's food cropscapes, replacing other grains with rice wherever possible. Expansion into Manchuria dramatically extended the acreage of soybean, the raw material for a range of essential supplements to a protein-poor but socially respectable diet of white rice. Consumer taste, cooking styles, citizen practices, and ideas about Japaneseness all cohered around this rice-soy pairing, a new habit represented as the "traditional" Japanese diet.[47]

With increased social mobility and modern aspirations, more and more Japanese lost the taste for the distinctive but unreliable soy sauces of home, different in every village. They came to prefer both the taste and the associations of big brands like Kikkoman. The period 1850–1900 saw the establishment of many famous food brands: Keiller's Dundee Marmalade went international in the 1850s, Heinz tomato ketchup first entered the market in 1876. The Kikkoman Company was founded in 1917, as an association of eight family-owned soy-sauce companies dating back to as early as 1603.[48] This deep company tradition and claim to local roots was, as with so many modern food companies around the world, an essential part of the brand image that allowed the product to travel far beyond its national boundaries.

A crucial factor in the scaling-up and branding of Japan's brewing industries was the separation of ferment making from the later stages of brewing, a division of expertise with deep historical roots. Ferment is easily tainted, as the elaborate procedures laid out in *Qimin yaoshu* suggest, and—as with seed grain—it is difficult to reproduce the same qualities in the product from year to year.[49] In medieval Japan a lucrative monopoly was held by firms that specialized in producing ferment cakes (kōji) to sell to brewers of soy sauce and sake. During the Tokugawa period specialized, licensed producers of the dried spores (*moyashi*) that seeded the ferment exercised a "private oligopoly," reinforced by frequent

Japanese soy barrels. Two huge old cedar vats guard the entrance to Yamamoto Yasuo's Yamaroku Soy Sauce Company, on Shodoshima Island, Japan. Here he is shown with a visiting food historian from Hong Kong. Photo: Izumi Nakayama, showing Yamamoto Yasuo (right) and Angela Ki Che Leung; with permission.

government bans on unlicensed kōji making. Increasingly brewers chose to devolve the difficult, costly, and risky production and reproduction of good-quality moyashi and kōji to specialists. During the Meiji period the scientific identification of the spores as microbes, *kin,* gave a new impulse and authority to this division of labor. From the 1890s government experimental stations, technical-school laboratories, and large brewing companies were all caught up in the effort to bring science into brewing. From around 1910 the development of techniques to identify, isolate, and reproduce good-quality microbes (*Aspergillus* in the case of soy) brought the rise of a new category of specialist companies purveying pure-culture microbes (*tanekōji*) to brewers.[50]

As Victoria Lee notes, reconceptualizing brewing agents and procedures in scientific terms dynamized but did not transform long-established trends and divisions of labor within the industry. The stabilization of pure-culture yeasts meant that companies like Kikkoman, which uses its own proprietary kōji, could rely on homogeneous quality in their product, which after several months of processing went straight into bottles.[51] This is the IR8 "miracle rice" approach to kōji, and naturally there is a counterculture of advocates for preserving the kōji equivalent of ancient landraces. Yamamoto Yasuo, a fifth-generation soy sauce brewer on the island of Shodoshima, welcomes the myriad spores that dwell in the wooden beams and barrels of his brewing sheds interacting with his homemade kōji; to smooth but not eliminate differences between annual batches, he blends and further matures the sauce.[52] In the past local soy sauces of unpredictable flavor seldom traveled beyond the village. Yamamoto's connoisseur sauces with their aura of terroir travel the globe just like Kikkoman, except in tiny quantities, like aged single-malt whiskies or rare vintage port.

PORT: BLENDING AND BRANDING

The blending of port is a good example of how processed comestibles in the modern world are stabilized, homogenized, standardized, and marketed. Cunningly varied manipulations of Douro-region grapes, spirits, wooden casks, and glass bottles, regulations and consumer markets, produce a spectrum of timeless wines that travel globally without spoiling. What interests us here is how the port cropscape and its procedures play with time and place in order to offer consumers the assurance of identical quality.

Food processing in general extends both the life and the reach of the raw product but arouses fears of spoilage, adulteration, or counterfeiting. Official regulation, of ingredients and production processes, is intended to protect consumers from unscrupulous producers. It can also be designed to maintain or guarantee quality and specific characteristics by designating and protecting certain groups of producers or regions of production, as in DOC labeling (controlled designation of origin). Certifying terroir cannot guarantee identical quality from different producers, or even identical taste from year to year, but it offers the knowing (and usually better-off) consumer the pleasures of connoisseurship. By definition, the output of a terroir is limited. We saw this in the "Cinchona" section, where the defenders of Loja argued for provenance, the small region where they claimed the best trees grew, as the guarantor of quality, whereas other agents of the Spanish Empire argued quality should be judged instead by the characteristics of the bark that was delivered to Madrid. The second approach, based on the quality of the finished product, invoked principles of authenticity similar to those that underpin blending.

The manufacture of the many types and grades of port wine involves different combinations along the spectrum from terroir to branding. But the stipulation that defines all port, of whatever quality or pretensions, has to do with the raw material: port must be made from grapes grown in the Douro Valley in the north of Portugal. This DOC designation dates back to a royal charter of 1756 that identified the boundaries of the terroir, limiting it to the schist slopes crossing a large stretch of the river Douro.[53] Restricting the area of port was a direct answer to a crisis of overproduction that menaced the profits of an otherwise very lucrative business. Landed aristocracy welcomed legislation that prevented small growers from other areas of the country from participating in the commerce established with England, and that also differentiated their product from that of unscrupulous external competitors who did not shy away from producing port from Turkish raisins.

While locality has thus defined port wine ever since, the very same name erased its Douro Valley provenance, identifying it instead with the city of Porto, from which the wine was shipped by British merchants. The port brands that dominated the market until the nineteenth century were all British: Kopke (1638), Warre (1670), Croft (1678), Taylor, Fladgate and Yeatman (1692), Offley (1737), Sandeman (1790), and the rest.[54] Emphasis on the merchants' role helps explain the first entry for port in the *Oxford English Dictionary*, which refers to wine, not from the Douro region, but brought from Bordeaux to England via Porto in 1692 in order to enter the ship's manifest as port and thus break the embargo on French produce.[55] This version of the story casts port as basically a British invention of the modern age: British merchants were the ones who made local Douro wine into global port wine by fortifying and blending practices in the warehouses of Porto and London. While the addition of some twenty liters of brandy per cask allowed Douro wine to travel unaltered across the ocean, blending techniques produced wines of different ages targeting various tastes and purses, enabling the formation of a hierarchized market.

Portuguese ruling elites, when describing the 1756 charter that rooted port in the Douro, praised it for restraining the "greed of the English traders which almost ruined the authenticity, the credit and the great reputation the Douro wines enjoyed, by adding green, weak, colorless, low-quality wines to them . . ., trying to make up for that low quality by adding elderberries, pepper, sugar and other mixtures and substances which, instead of improving them, turned them into insipid, weak, colorless, inferior wines when they reached the North."[56] Port quality is defined here in terms of purity through control of the provenance of the wines and prevention of mixtures. In this alternative version, the expansion of the Portuguese state's capacity for intervention is the essential factor in creating port by guaranteeing its purity. Maintaining high prices for port depended on a regulatory state that prevented farmers outside the demarcated area from smuggling in their grapes, forcing trespassers to uproot vineyards and convert them into maize fields. Considering that port constituted the main Portuguese export of the eighteenth and nineteenth centuries and one of the major revenue sources of the state until the twentieth century, a more radical interpretation might claim that port actually made the modern Portuguese state.[57]

The specific characteristics of the Douro region certainly played a role in determining the success of its wines in the English market. The shape of the Douro Valley, responsible for a Mediterranean microclimate in a region otherwise dominated by North Atlantic and Continental influences, guaranteed the high sugar content of grapes ripening at temperatures of 40° C in the summer months, the vines reaching deep through the schist soil for water. The most renowned British port merchant of the nineteenth century, James Forrester, explained the emergence of the now standard procedure of adding brandy to Douro wines during fermentation and not after (as in sherry), by invoking the exceptional quality of the 1820 harvest, "whose wines were all naturally rich, sweet, and tasty."[58] Forrester was probably exaggerating the effects of a mythical harvest in shaping the British taste for port, but his observations nevertheless accurately coincided with the spread of the practice among Douro winegrowers of stopping fermentation before all the sugar was consumed by adding alcohol and thus increasing the sweetness of the wine. The "new process of winemaking" contrasted with the "old process" of letting must ferment for about three days in the winery, resulting in "dry fine wines" to which alcohol had been added after. While some large landowners, like Dona Antónia Adelaide Ferreira, refused to adopt the new method and stuck to dry wines, the new sweet wines would become the dominant trend of the second half of the nineteenth century. The "new process" and its forceful ending of fermentation had frozen time in 1820.

Forrester would tragically die in a shipwreck in 1862, drowning in a Douro whirlpool from which Ferreira was saved by her skirts converting into floats. The drama of the scene did not soften the heart of Camillo Castello Branco, one of the most celebrated and polemical novelists of Portuguese romanticism, who exulted over "the terrible death" as "one of the most remarkable revenges wrought by the Douro river on the detractors of its wines."[59] For the romantic writer, Forrester and his repeated denunciation of the low-quality wine delivered by Douro farmers to British merchants deserved to be denounced as an "English bestiality." Castello Branco saw Forrester's criticism as just another expression of English hegemony over Portuguese national life, and not even his death made him worthy of sympathy. Indeed, because they exposed the country's manufactures to competition with British industry, many blamed the commercial treaties which guaranteed that port wine paid lower tariffs than its European competitors when entering English ports for Portugal's deindustrialization.[60] In other words, port had made Portugal into another British-controlled plantation.

226   Reproductions

As for Ferreira, she embodied alternative national development projects around wine. She was both a merchant and a landowner, who expanded wine production upriver farther east, establishing a model farm (plantation) in 1887. The upper Douro had traditionally been considered a poorly connected area, inhabited by barbarous people who barely qualified as Portuguese until the railway arrived, bringing civilization with it. Ferreira's new property in the area was carefully planned and "planted with grafted grape vines, olive trees and almond trees."[61] The train brought from Porto not only the food supplies—rice, salted cod, flour, and so on—for the wageworkers of the modern undertaking but also pesticides and fertilizers produced in a chemical factory in Porto located not far from the port warehouses. The drowning of Forrester and the survival of Ferreira meant that after being blamed for the country's dependence on England, port could now materialize dreams of modernity with trains and chemical plants, rooting Portuguese industrialization in the country's soil.

Neither Forrester nor Ferreira was willing to freeze taste in 1820: they were both fierce critics of sweet port, favoring dry fine wines instead. This said, their fortunes as port merchants also depended on other erasures of time achieved through elaborate blending techniques. The success of their businesses could be measured by their ability to ignore good and bad years, always making a profit independently of the conditions of a single year's harvest. Indeed, port merchants' warehouses stock casks dating from many harvests and many provenances, containing fortified wine of different styles. The goal is to produce a balanced blend that does not change from bottle to bottle or from year to year. Ruby ports, the cheapest version of port wines, are blends of ruby-style wines from different places and years, but all young. The blend is recasked into large barrels, to minimize the rate of oxidation, and left for two years. The ruby port is then bottled and marketed; the label carries the name of the shipper (the brand) and the term "ruby port," but no year and no provenance. The marketing image is young, lively, and fresh.

The tawny ports are likewise blends from several years and places, from wines selected to age well, developing nutty, oaky flavors. The blends are recasked in barrels, typically of a hundred gallons each. Throughout the maturation stage the tawnies are further blended in a system of fractional blending (the solera system) to ensure consistency.[62] The casks are racked in rows, the youngest at the top and the oldest at the bottom. Bottles are filled from the barrels in the lowest row; once these barrels are partly emptied, they are replenished with wine from the row above, and so on up to the top. This labor-intensive procedure may take place twice or as many as four times a year. Because the process is fractional, the port bottled from a five-rack solera will contain no wine younger than five years old; some of the older wines in the mix will be as old as the solera system itself. After the years in the solera racks, some port will be bottled and sold immediately as tawny port, some will be casked yet again into small barrels to mature further, and then bottled and sold as reserve ports, so-called ten-, twenty- or forty-year-old tawny ports. Here again the label gives the brand and an "age" if it is old.

In other words, ports blend time, mixing wines from multiple years.[63] Even those ports labeled as ten-year or twenty-year ports are a mix, although their average age approximates the age stated on the bottle. For the vast bulk of port consumed, from fine-quality ports to cheap mixers, the age on the bottle indicates an average, an expectation of a particular quality rather than a precise measure of time. Old tawnies call for elaborate and sensual description: a feast for the eyes in shades of topaz, gold, or green; tantalizing aromas of rockrose, tobacco, apricot, or aniseed; velvety flavors of cedar, caramel, or marmalade; elegance of balance, complexity of aftertaste—myriad elusive refinements for connoisseurs to roll over the tongue. But not all port was made to be passed clockwise around the table in the archaic male rituals of British clubs and colleges, Lübeck merchant families, or Portuguese elites. The sweet and easy ruby ports have over the centuries found big markets first in Brazil and later as an aperitif in France and as a cheap and cheerful drink for women (port and lemon) in post–World War I British pubs.

One fascinating characteristic of port blending is how it plays with time. Another is its thriftiness: the blending allows bad years to be redeemed and ameliorated, while the spirit added to fortify the wine is made from the pressings of grapes that in other circumstances might be treated as waste.

RECLAIMING WASTE

In the same years that Antónia Ferreira promised to civilize the "savage" populations of the northeast of Portugal by expanding vines upriver, African populations under Portuguese colonial rule were to be civilized by expanding their wine consumption. Keeping port profitable had always required identifying huge quantities of wine as waste. At the turn of the century, Douro farmers demanded a total liberalization of wine trading to Portuguese African imperial territories, to "open new markets" for products that could not be placed "in the old [European] markets."[64] To these lower-quality wines were added grape spirits, also produced in overabundance in the national territory. Colonization of Africa promised to transform European waste into profit. But selling Portuguese wine to Africans required suppressing competing local sources of alcohol, such as the cashew tree, branded by the governor of Mozambique the "vice and ruin tree."[65]

The contested fluidity of the status of grape and cashew wines suggests a historiographical point beyond the common assertion that "waste is in the eye of the beholder." Defining waste as "any material we have failed to use," Zsuzsa Gille argues that analyzing how a society at a particular moment construes, generates, and manages waste—its "waste regime"—and the metamorphoses of this waste regime over time, offers a powerful method for connecting macro- and microanalysis, materialities, expertise, and ideology. In a study of the history of waste in socialist and postsocialist Hungary, Gille shows how postwar industrial policy built around the material realities and expertise of steel production supported a culture of waste that valued reuse and recycling. When the chemical industry superseded steel production as the national mainstay, ideas about the nature of waste, its potential, and its temporalities changed radically, as did the class location of expertise.[66] The three cases we discuss here likewise address metamorphoses of regimes of waste and the shifts in technical expertise or political vision that fostered these changes. The riff on cashews shows how movement between cropscapes redefined which parts of the plant were considered waste or valuable, prompting technological innovations at every step. The riff on Washington Carver highlights the racial politics of waste by focusing on efforts to reconstruct underappreciated cropscapes. The riff on Globally Important Agricultural Heritage Systems shows how cropscapes once ignored or disparaged as useless are now put to use as potential seedlings of the future, sometimes to preserve and sometimes to contest the political order.

OF APPLES AND NUTS: THE (RE)PRODUCTIONS OF CASHEW

"The cashew tree is a vice and ruin tree," thundered the governor of Mozambique in 1893, adding that the trees should all be uprooted. "During the three months of the cashew season no force known to man can make the native work," another governor declared in 1910. The cashew was, in the eyes of the Portuguese colonial state, a potent anti-commodity that wasted national resources by nourishing subaltern resistance to economic progress. By 1952, however, the cashew had been recast as a valuable commodity, with economists predicting that it might surpass even cotton and sugar as Mozambique's most important product. In 1974 this prediction had come true, with cashews accounting for 21.3 percent of the country's total exports.[67] How did this metamorphosis of the Mozambican cashew from toxic waste to good investment come about?

One answer is that different parts of the cashew were involved. It was wine made from the cashew apple that aroused the ire and disgust of Mozambique's colonial rulers; it was the products of the nut that excited their ambitions. For the promise of the cashew nut to become apparent, however, an export market first had to open up. This market was created by technological innovations in India that transformed both the cashew kernel and the oil from its shell (cashew nut shell liquid, CNSL) into high-value export commodities. As demand rose after World War II, India's cashew industry began importing raw nuts for processing from East Africa; as the nut shell and kernel gained value, so the apple, previously the most valued part of the cashew fruit but for which no industrial uses had yet been found, was reduced to the status of waste.

Humans have found uses for every part of the cashew tree (*Anacardium occidentale* L.), including its bark, leaves, and timber. The tree is native to Brazil and its Atlantic neighbors, thriving in coastal zones with light, sandy soils. Its spectacular fruits consist of a sweet-smelling, astringent, bright red or yellow edible "apple" (the peduncle), from which hangs the true fruit, a kidney-shaped drupe or nut whose hard, acrid shell encases the seed or kernel (the part commonly known today as the "cashew nut"). In 1577 the Franciscan friar André Thevet published an account of the "land of cannibals" (the Tupi territories along the Brazilian coast) in which he noted how important the cashew was to local Amerindians: "The land . . . bears fruits in abundance, herbs and hearty roots, with a great quantity of trees which they call Acajou, which bear fruits as big as a fist, in the shape of a goose egg. Some make brews from it, as the fruit in itself is not good to eat, similar in flavor to a half-ripe crab-apple. At the end of the fruit is a kind of nut, as large as a chestnut and shaped like a hare's kidney. As for the kernel inside, it is very good to eat as long as it has been lightly roasted over the fire. The shell is all full of oil, very bitter to the taste, from which the Savages could make a greater quantity of oil than we do from our walnuts."[68]

Fr. Vicente Salvador, writing in 1672, says that in Bahia in the month of December the cashews fruited in such quantity that they afforded the local Tupi Indians all the sustenance they needed, apples, juice, and nuts providing the equivalent of the Portuguese staples of fruits, wine, and bread. Other writers suggested that Amerindian groups would fight over places where cashews grew, with the winners staying on the spot until they had consumed all the fruit.[69] Cashews are indeed ideal provender for nomadic groups, as processing the different parts on a small scale requires very little time or equipment. The apples bruise easily and soon spoil, but turning them into beer is quick and simple. An illustration in Thevet's account shows one man throwing down cashew fruits from a tree, while others detach the drupes (shown lying on the ground) and crush the apples between their hands, letting the plentiful juice run down into a large pot. It would then be left to ferment and would be ready to drink after a few hours or a couple of days. So all that was needed to turn cashew apples

Juicing the cashew apple. This illustration, from André Thevet's account of his travels in the Americas, shows Tupi Indians in Brazil harvesting cashew fruits and juicing the apples. The nuts of the harvested fruits can be seen strewn on the ground. André Thevet, *Les singularitez de la France antarctique* (1557), p. 319.

into "wine" were hands, a pot, and a little patience, while the cooking fire sufficed to roast the drupes and extract the tasty nuts.

It seems the Portuguese took cashew trees to their Indian Ocean outposts in Goa and Mozambique almost as soon as they had gained a foothold in Brazil. But why? The reason given in most papers published since the 1950s is that the trees were used to prevent soil erosion. But no supporting evidence is offered. Critics of this hypothesis note that it "smacks of a twentieth century concept being applied to a fifteenth century event."[70] A more plausible reason for the cashew's migration was the well-documented fact that in Brazil the Portuguese soon learned to value various medicinal and cosmetic properties of cashew bark, fruit, and leaves, which they had learned about from Amerindians. European settlers appreciated the astringent apples (dismissed by Thevet as unpleasant) as thirst quenching, breath sweetening, and good for the digestion as well as various common ailments.[71] Above all, they were a wonderful source of quick and easy alcohol. An abundance of evidence confirms that in India, Africa, and South America it was the apples, as fruit, juice, and alcohol, that were most valued.

For several centuries the easy delights of the cashew apple promoted the tree's steady spread through the tropical regions of the colonial world. Botanists suggest that bats, monkeys, and elephants as well as humans all played a role in seeding new trees, crunching the tasty apple and discarding the hard and acrid drupe as they moved along their trails.[72] The kernels, firmly encased in an unpleasant shell, were, at most, a by-product: in the Caribbean, for instance, an observer in the 1960s noted that it was quite common "to salvage the 'apple' and discard the nut."[73] But the apple flesh was highly perishable, and the wines did not keep unless they were fortified or distilled. Cashew-apple products were not easily commercialized, and generally the tree was cultivated on a small scale, or even cropped in the wild. Cashew kernels, on the other hand, were of high value and easily transportable. But they were difficult to extract, and like all nuts they were prone to spoil in transit, limiting their travels. The technical innovations that transformed cashew kernels into an accessible treat for northern nibblers created new circuits of trade and competition. One was between the tropical countries, notably India, Mozambique, and Brazil, that invested in growing and processing cashews, the other between the cashew producers of the Global South (increasing in number as they emulated the Indian example of processing as well as cultivating) and the consumer markets of the Global North. It was only now, as the culture of cashew consumption was internationalized, that the kernel ousted the apple as metonym for the cashew and its products.

The kernel's life as an export commodity began in the 1920s. India was the only exporter of shelled kernels at the time, with Brazil and Mozambique rising to prominence much later.[74] The main markets for cashews were in Europe and the United States, where demand was related to the fate of a popular commodity with a similar use—the filbert, or hazelnut.[75] When filbert supply fell, cashews filled the gap. But importing cashews raised concerns about quality and about insect infestation, especially in the United States. With strict inspections by the Food and Drug Administration (FDA), sometimes half the shipments were deemed unfit for human consumption. The specifications for export to the United States required that the kernels be "fully developed, ivory white in color, and free from insect damage and black and brown spots"; under the provisions of the United States Federal Food, Drug, and Cosmetic Act, the percentage of "deteriorated or unsound kernels" permitted was only 5 percent. Moreover, "all the other general provisions of the act as they pertain[ed] to sanitary conditions and fitness for human food" were strictly enforced.[76]

The strict controls and standards of the FDA rendered significant proportions of the cashew kernels exported from India "waste." The transition of India's cashew kernels from the category of waste to acceptable commodity was mediated by the new technology of "Vitapack"—a technique for packing food in inert gases perfected by the U.S. conglomerate General Foods Corporation. General Foods started an "India Nut Company" in the late 1920s in Quilon (Kollam, in the current southern Indian state of Kerala), bringing "Vitapack" technology to India, along with American technicians to inspect and approve the cashews packed using the new method.[77] Further innovations reinforced Quilon's position (which it still holds) as the center of cashew processing in India. An even greater technological challenge than hygienic packaging was the initial extraction of the kernel from the nut. In the early 1920s a Ceylonese, Roche Victoria, who had settled in Quilon developed advanced and convenient methods for removing the caustic, poisonous shell oil (CNSL). Meanwhile William Jefferies, working in the cashew branch of Peirce Leslie and Company, a British firm with multifarious commercial interests in India, not only developed a drum roaster, which revolutionized cashew processing by replacing the more primitive pan-roasting method, but also pioneered the "Hot Oil Plant," which broke down the CNSL and extracted the phenol component, "thereby converting the liquid from the position of *persona non grata* to the Taj Mahal of the world's paint, varnish, and resin industries."[78] The shell had been converted from noxious waste to treasure.

The phenomenal growth of India's cashew industry, centered in Quilon, was powered in part by the financial and technical inputs of foreign firms like Peirce Leslie, in part by an emerging and expanding class of local cashew entrepreneurs, the "cashew kings" whose families still rule much of India's cashew industry today.[79]

It was no coincidence that Quilon's nascent cashew industry attracted entrepreneurs and inventors. The city belonged to the princely state of Travancore, which lacked the labor regulations and protections (including maternity benefits) that had been introduced in some parts of British India. Cashew processing is extremely labor intensive, requiring roughly ten times as many workers per unit of capital as cotton or coir spinning and weaving.[80] But plenty of cheap labor was available in Travancore. As the company historian of Peirce Leslie put it, "Malabar [Travancore/ Kerala] has no monopoly of [the cashew], which is indigenous to Brazil and grows more extensively in East Africa; but what Malabar does possess above all others are the nimble fingers and unrivalled skill of its beautiful women, who alone make its benefits available to the markets of the world."[81] Then as now, in Quilon or in Lourenço Marques (today Maputo), this motor of the national export economy was powered by women paid a pittance, classed by virtue of their gender as unskilled dependents not needing a "breadwinner's wage," and rendered compliant, although fully aware of being exploited, by the overriding need to support children and kin. In both India and Mozambique, many women cashew workers became militant unionists when unions were available; in less auspicious circumstances they could voice their anger or bitterness only in whispers or songs.[82]

India's success in spinning the dross of raw cashew nuts into the gold of export income and company fortunes launched a global wave of interest in cashew production as a catalyst for national growth and regional poverty reduction. Slaves as ever to the plantation paradigm, the colonial government in Mozambique encouraged Europeans to establish cashew plantations, initially, from 1945, to export raw nuts to India and then, starting in the 1960s, to supply the processing factories proliferating in Lourenço Marques. The plantations generated abundant official statistics and scientific studies, yet, as Jeanne Marie Penvenne remarks with asperity, they amounted to only 3 percent of the total: 97 percent of Mozambique's cashews were grown or gathered by small farmers, most of them women who had to take over all farming responsibilities while their husbands worked as wage laborers in the mines or fields of South Africa.[83] On farm plots cashew trees provided shade for staple cereals, tubers, vegetables, and other crops growing among them. They grew happily on poor, semiarid land where livings were hard to make, they required little care, and they stayed healthier interspersed with other vegetation than on plantations. In fact this was, and remains, how most cashews are grown around the world, including India. Despite various state projects in the 1960s and 1970s to establish plantations with their own processing factories in poor rural regions like northeastern Brazil, the smallholder model was able to hold its own even in global circuits.[84]

In India women workers have been responsible for almost all the processing of cashew nuts; in Mozambique the cashew trees too fell to women's care. In another example of turning waste to treasure, meticulous studies by feminist scholars, visiting homes and farms as well as archives, collecting oral histories and songs as well as statistics, have rescued these neglected yet essential stories of modernization and globalization at the grassroots. Thanks to them we have some insight into the many reproductive roles of cashews in these societies.[85] Cash income from sales of nuts or from processing wages was vital to feeding, clothing, and educating children, to paying for medicine or helping out kin. We also see from these studies how work in the cashew sector reproduced and reconfigured local relations of class and caste, gender ideologies and discourses, agency and citizenship, as well as reinforcing the power relations and regimes of extraction embodied in global value chains. A focus on the waged workplace affirms the production of cashew kernels as a textbook case of the reproductive tensions and inequalities that support capitalist modes of extraction and competition. Shifting attention back to the cashew trees in the village, we see different reproductive registers at play. Here the cashew apple reappears, not as waste, but as a valuable resource: fruit or wine could be given in return for help in the fields, wine could be enjoyed with friends and kin or be bartered or sold for necessities or extras—it was a vital lubricant that kept the wheels of rural life and urban production turning, despite its negative official image.

As we saw, in around 1900, when Portugal was launching its project to develop its African colonies, zealous colonial authorities sought to civilize the population and integrate them as efficient contributors to economic modernization by persuading them to drink Portuguese wine made from metropolitan grapes instead of liquor domestically brewed from cashew fruit. Colonial officers pictured a stark cropscape counterpoint between the perceived present, an undisciplined terrain of small farms (*machamba* or *shamba*) worked by an African peasantry consuming liquor made from the cashew apples growing in their backyards and resisting demands to work on settler farms, and its hoped-for future, a regimented ("organized") territory of productive commercial plantations worked by African laborers who would purchase metropolitan wine with their wages. The cashew kernel, which later came to symbolize economic progress through disciplined native labor, was not yet visible as a significant component of the cashew fruit. The cashew apple, however, growing wild or lurking in the machamba, signified the inner Wild Man of the African, the drunken native reverting to savagery and disobedience. The apple's association with waste rather than value was already established in colonial discourse well before technological innovations and new circuits of trade established the supremacy of the cashew kernel.

GEORGE WASHINGTON CARVER AND THE
RECLAMATION OF WASTE

In 1896, when George Washington Carver arrived at the Tuskegee Institute in Alabama to start its agricultural experiment station, prospects were gloomy.[86] The land on which the Historically Black College stood had previously been a cotton plantation; its poor state epitomized the environmental degradation produced by intensive monocrop cultivation of the plant sustaining the industrialization of the West. Carver's first task was to restore a sandy soil so eroded that "one could throw an ox into a ditch and . . . have to look down to see it."[87] The challenge Carver faced with impoverished soils was common among the Black tenants of the South of the United States who characteristically rented the less fertile sections of properties owned by whites. The Civil War abolished slavery, but after the initial hopes of the Reconstruction Era (1863–1877) for a just society supporting Black ambitions, new forms of segregation followed that recreated the racial fault lines characteristic of American democracy. Instead of free people becoming independent farmers and getting "forty acres and a mule" to start their lives anew, Black people became sharecroppers bonded by constant debt to white landowners. Carver's attention to soil reconstruction held the promise of more productive fields yielding enough to free Black families from dependency from former slaveholders.

Carver was translating into agricultural practices the vision of Booker T. Washington, the director of the Tuskegee Institute, that Black self-reliance should be based on glorifying "common labor." As Washington (in)famously declared in his "Atlanta Compromise" speech of 1895, "It is at the bottom of life we must begin, and not at the top."[88] Washington owed much of his national reputation as a Black leader to reassuring anxious white audiences that it was morally right to keep racial hierarchy and segregation if Black people were given the chance to follow their own separate path of social improvement. As many of his critics have signaled, Washington was in fact trading Black civil and political rights for white philanthropic support for his Tuskegee Institute. In a more blunt formulation, W. E. B. Du Bois, always more radical than his rival Washington, blamed the latter for "mak[ing] the whites, North and South, shift the burden of the Negro problem to the Negro's shoulders."[89] Also invoking the soils of the South, Du Bois explained how white elites falsely blamed Black sharecroppers for the ruinous state of Southern agriculture at the turn of the century: "He [the former plantation owner] shows his Northern visitor the scarred and wretched land; the ruined mansions, the worn-out soil and mortgaged acres, and says, This is Negro freedom!"[90] In the racist interpretation of Jim Crow America, Black freedom was responsible for turning Southern soils into wasteland.

George Washington Carver holding soil. Frances Benjamin Johnston, *Portrait of George Washington Carver,* Library of Congress Prints and Photographs Division, LC-USZ62–114302 [P&P] LOT 13164-C, no. 104.

Carver's work fitted Washington's racial project by reconstructing poor soils and leaving uncontested the unequal property system of the South. Black people were not to question the structural racism that relegated them to tilling the poorer soils of the region; instead they had to find ways to uplift themselves. Making use of "pine tops, hay, bark, old cotton stalks, leaves, etc. in fact, rubbish of any kind that would ultimately make soil," Carver filled up the gullies and ditches of the ten acres of land of his Tuskegee experiment station and would proudly report a few years later that the "injurious washing has been almost completely overcome."[91] Dignifying lower pursuits, processing waste into topsoil, Carver allowed Washington to affirm, "The wisest among my race understand that the agitation of questions of social equality is the extremest folly."[92]

Transforming the leftovers of the cropscape into a resource, Carver showed how eroded soils tilled by black sharecroppers could be improved at low cost, leading to increasing yields and economic security. While most experimental stations across the country recommended increased use of chemical fertilizers to improve farmers' productivity, Carver, acknowledging Black sharecroppers' lack of capital, proposed viable alternatives to his constituency at Tuskegee.[93] One can understand Carver's work as a constant plea to Black farmers to learn how to imaginatively read the cropscape they lived in, identifying valuable elements in what was commonly seen as wasteland. The swamps and forests beyond the cotton fields should be understood as forming part of the cropscape, since swamp muck, tree leaves, and pine straw could all be used as manure to build up the missing humus of sharecroppers' plots. Woods, according to Carver, were no less than a "natural fertilizer factory," their decaying "trees, grasses, and debris of many kinds" producing "countless tons of the finest kind of manure, rich in potash, nitrogen and humus." The wooded and swampy areas beyond the plantation reaches, which in times of slavery had sustained dreams of escape and freedom, were transformed by Carver through soil science into spaces upholding visions of Black people's dignity.

Increasing the productivity of a cash crop—cotton—was certainly not Carver's only concern. He did experiment with cotton in the reconstructed soils of the experiment station but also turned his attention to other overlooked plants, making the case that the obsession with cotton was a double failure of imagination and knowledge, preventing the progress of Black people. Not surprisingly, he can be counted among the many fans of the boll weevil, the cotton pest that forced so many farmers to pay attention to alternative crops (see "Actants"). Cowpeas, sweet potatoes, and peanuts were unflaggingly promoted by Carver, since these neglected Southern crops not only fixed nitrogen in the soil and thus contributed to its reconstruction but were also edible, increasing the food security of poor sharecroppers. By developing new uses and recipes, he hoped to engage "the thoughtful housewife" in his relentless campaign against waste. Criticizing the relegation of so many edible plants to the lesser status of weeds, he sang the praises of "a good plate of dandelion greens . . . or . . . wild onions, seasoned and fried."

Carver's creative reading of the cropscape reached new audiences after World War I. The high demand for agricultural produce and high prices during the war years were followed by years of overproduction and thus of reduced incomes for farmers across the United States. Suddenly, major cash crops did not seem too different from the neglected crops Carver used to work with. Low prices for cotton, corn, or wheat rendered large quantities of these cash crops waste. Recognizing the value of Carver's efforts to explore new uses for plants neglected as waste, a self-christened chemurgy movement (from the Greek *chemeia* for chemistry and *ergon* for work) promised to put "chemistry at work on the farm," find new industrial value for American crops through chemistry, and thus solve the problem of overproduction.[94] Accordingly, Carver's identity as an agricultural scientist serving the poor Black farmers of Alabama shifted to that of a laboratory chemist finding new raw materials for American industry.

Henry Ford, always obsessed with making his gigantic River Rouge factory compatible with mythical visions of small-town America, became the most notorious supporter of chemurgy, putting together the National Farm Chemurgic Council in 1935. Building on American founding documents and stressing their radical nationalism, some three hundred industrialists, scientists, and farm leaders issued a "Declaration of Dependence upon the Soil and the Right of Self-Maintenance," which promised full employment, national economic independence, and the "preservation of America's destiny."[95] When one considers the efforts for autarky in Nazi Germany mentioned in our riff on breeding, it is not surprising to find many of the leaders of the chemurgy movement praising European fascist regimes. Ford invited Carver for a chemurgy conference two years later, and the two men apparently became close friends. By then, Ford's company used one bushel of soybeans for every car it manufactured. In 1941, Ford presented his soybean car, a prototype that, the *New York Times* assured its readers, used "a cellulose fiber consist[ing] of 50 per cent southern slash pine fiber, 30 per cent straw, 10 per cent hemp and 10 per cent ramie."[96] The new material had been developed by a team of twenty-nine Ford chemists commissioned to replace metal parts with plastics "from materials grown on the farm." The irony should not be lost that chemurgy, in its pursuit of new uses for wasted crops, incorporated these into the archetypical useless object: the car.

Although Carver was publicly lauded as "the first and greatest chemurgist," his chemistry laboratory at Tuskegee was on a very different scale to the industrial research undertaken at the Ford factory. His laboratory was characteristically underfunded when compared with major centers of American science, but he now enjoyed national fame, becoming a symbol of Black progress. He embodied the figure of the exemplary Black scientist, demonstrating the opportunities awaiting

Black people if only they followed the virtuous behaviors promoted at Tuskegee and refrained from "agitation of questions of social equality." If numbers of Black scientists and engineers were disproportionately low in American colleges, whites, such as the ones forming the leadership of the chemurgy movement, could always point to Carver's success to divert blame and put responsibility on Black shoulders for lack of achievement. Carver knew how to convert wasteland into a productive cropscape, but his exemplary story and work served American white supremacists invested in treating Black people permanently as waste.

In the 1930s, there was no louder voice in the U.S. Senate supporting the Jim Crow racist system of the American South than Theodore Bilbo from Mississippi. Making his case against anti-lynching legislation in 1938, he did not hesitate to quote Hitler's *Mein Kampf,* asserting that "one drop of Negro blood placed in the veins of the purest Caucasian destroys the inventive genius of his mind and strikes palsied his creative faculty."[97] Bilbo was the champion of poor rural whites, building his political career in Mississippi as a Southern populist attacking not only Northern capitalists but also the traditional planters' elite. In 1935, he proposed establishing a $250,000 chemurgy laboratory in Mississippi to research the industrial applications of cotton and cottonseed to increase the value of his constituents' main crop. Through chemurgy, Bilbo hoped to save his voters from the condition of "white trash." He apparently had no problem with the fact that the chemurgy movement he enthusiastically supported had seen in Carver an inspiring "inventive genius." As a critical Du Bois fiercely wrote in the same years, believing that assimilation and "accomplishment by Negroes [could] break down prejudice . . . is a fable."[98]

Bilbo was a key political ally of President Franklin Delano Roosevelt. He guaranteed the support of the bloc of Southern politicians that allowed Roosevelt's New Deal policies, designed to get the country out of the Great Depression, to pass through Congress. Among these policies was the Agricultural Adjustment Act of 1933, which compensated farmers for producing less in order to bring prices up for the country's major agricultural commodities.[99] After the act was found to be unconstitutional, New Deal policy makers transformed it into a soil-conservancy program, paying farmers generously to divert from production eroded parts of their properties, which then became the object of soil-recuperation procedures. Bilbo, always concerned that progressive policies of the New Deal risked undermining racial hierarchy in the South, made sure that federal aid would not reach the majority of the Black peasantry in the region: only landowners were entitled to participate in the soil-conservation program put in place by the U.S. Department of Agriculture (USDA), thus excluding from its benefits the masses of Black sharecroppers who did not own the land they tilled.

The USDA Soil Conservation Service famously salvaged large tracts of land from becoming permanent waste, and, as its proud leader stated, this had major social implications: "Soil Conservation means more than stopping erosion on hillsides. It means conservation of people as well as conservation of resources of the land."[100] In the 1930s the people conserved, those saved from becoming waste through state-supported soil conservation, were exclusively whites, deepening the racial fault line of American society. Carver, when arriving in Alabama some three decades earlier, had hoped instead that reconstruction of eroded soils through the use of neglected elements of the cropscape would free Blacks from dependency. By valuing Black crops and Black spaces, he was making the case that Black lives mattered.

AGRICULTURAL HERITAGE: FROM THE TRASH HEAP OF HISTORY TO ENGINES OF THE FUTURE

Echoing Carver's creative recuperation of waste lands, crops, and people, and as an expression on a different scale of the urge to conserve biodiversity that the Svalbard Global Seed Vault encapsulates, the past two decades have seen an accelerating global movement to recuperate farming systems and communities that modernist agronomics and national governments had discarded as doomed to extinction.

Through programs like the FAO's Globally Important Agricultural Heritage Systems (GIAHS), launched in 2002, the race is now on to conserve "the traditional knowledge and farming practices" of Maasai agro-pastoral systems, Chinese duck farming, or *chinampas* (floating fields) in Mexico.[101] Shifting cultivation, or swidden farming, once disparaged by agronomists as unproductive and environmentally damaging, is still treated by most governments as an illegitimate, primitive, and wasteful practice hindering the profitable extraction of national resources. But now the United Nations and the FAO praise swidden as "an important contribution to the conservation and sustainable use of biodiversity."[102] Not only does the practice provide relatively secure subsistence for small communities living in the mountainous margins of modern nations, the FAO argues, but, judiciously combined with cash cropping, it can integrate these isolated and disadvantaged social groups into the broader economy.[103] As we saw in our earlier riffs on rubber, coffee, and milpa polyculture, swidden cultivators have been supplying commercial networks for centuries, but only now is its potential gaining official recognition.

As well as inverting productivist agronomic principles, today's new small is beautiful ideals of farming also unsettle established epistemological hierarchies of expertise, and of gender, ethnicity, and class. It has often been noted, for instance, that colonial administrators and postindependence development experts alike worked to "masculinized" norms, taking it for granted that farming was primarily a male activity, and that farming expertise was a male preserve.[104] Hence, until surprisingly recently, women were typically excluded from the extension classes where local men would be instructed in modern farming techniques and offered loans, seeds, or tools. Now, in programs like GIAHS or participatory plant breeding, both the gendering and the flow of expertise are typically reversed. Local women have become—or are at any rate portrayed as—respected sources of local knowledge valuable in its own right and with potential for generalized application. In Chiredzi, Zimbabwe, a GIAHS crop reintroduction program

> relied on women's weather forecasting based on a set of environmental indicators [including] tree phenology, wild-animal behaviour and recent weather patterns, for instance the presence of migrant storks. . . . Women's forecasts are considered more accurate than the national weather forecasts, as the latter tend to cover wider areas and are therefore less specific. Taking women's particular knowledge about local environmental conditions, seed systems and crop-diversification strategies into account facilitated the farmer-to-farmer transfer of innovation and strengthened the capacity of (women) farmers to autonomously identify "new" coping mechanisms in traditional practices, knowledge and biodiversity for food and agriculture.[105]

Here a peculiarly female sensitivity to local complexes of social and natural ("biocultural") indicators is identified as an epistemological resource for promoting a new kind of farming: sustainable, empowering, and mobile. The Chiredzi example also suggests the highly complex compositions that researchers are willing to recognize in heritage cropscapes. The farming system is treated as both a social and a natural ecology in which environmental, livelihood, and cultural concerns are interwoven. In the 1970s agroecology and Farming Systems Research took shape as critiques of the flattened cropscapes of the Green Revolution.[106] Today both disciplines are integral to agricultural heritage system research.

China is one of the most active nations in promoting agricultural heritage programs, offering a good case for reflecting on their subtexts, contexts, and agendas.[107] In chapter 1, "Times," we saw how the millet regions of North China, once the productive heartlands of the ancient empire and the models for advanced agricultural practice, were relegated by late imperial governments and agronomists to the status of unproductive backwaters. We also saw how the post-1990s consolidation of China's self-image as a prosperous and productive consumer society has prompted a recoding of backwardness as authenticity:

supposedly unchanged villages such as Wangjinzhuang, wringing a scant living from harsh conditions, are now repackaged as heritage sites where tourists can absorb a taste of history while contributing to village livelihoods.

As noted in "Times," the supposed rustic simplicity of Wangjinzhuang is in fact a confection compounded from the legacies of long-term regional disadvantage; Maoist-era infrastructural transformation; post-1978 reversion from people's communes to household smallholdings; growing opportunities for market participation; and recent official rebranding as a heritage site. While poverty and isolation had previously limited Wangjinzhuang villagers' participation in national programs for agricultural improvement, now their "backward" practices have become ecologically praiseworthy money-spinners. Local farmers sell "peasant-grown and donkey-manured" millet online to middle-class urban families eager for organic foods. The most important new technologies for keeping this heritage cropscape functioning are not tractors, agrichemicals, or irrigation works, but the internet (where tourist boards advertise its attractions and farmers sell their produce) and the improved transportation networks that bring in busloads or carloads of visitors.[108]

In only a select few of China's myriad underdeveloped villages do donkeys outrank tractors as technological assets. Since 1949 a succession of campaigns to construct a New Socialist Countryside, while varying greatly in their political goals and modalities, have sought to build more modern and efficient cropscapes by encouraging or imposing the substitution of tractors for donkeys or buffalo, the consolidation of fields and other resources, the modernization of infrastructure, science-based schooling, and technical training for farmers.[109] But the rural population is aging, and the division of farmland (collectively owned under the constitution) into household smallholdings limits development. Policies designed to scale up production include allowing agribusinesses ("dragon heads") to contract for rentals of land, diverting farmers into intensive mass production of profitable but risky goods like pork or wine grapes.[110]

As agricultural modernization progressed, China's leaders, scientists, and public became increasingly concerned about the environmental consequences. Since the late 1990s the government has promoted genomics and other biotechnology research programs to develop more sustainable crop varieties, tailored to local ecosystems and the needs of smallholder farmers.[111] In summer 2005 China established its first Globally Important Agricultural Heritage Site pilot under the new FAO program. The site selected was Qingtian, a county in Jiangnan that still practices the rice-and-fish system we described in "Times." In 2007 the Chinese government officially nuanced its pursuit of industrial modernity by promoting the ideal of "ecological civilization" (*shengtai wenming*), of which agroecology is a key component.[112] A National Strategic Plan for Sustainable Agricultural Development (2015–2030) has initiated numerous conservation and restoration projects, including identifying more than a thousand villages "for development as model agroecological villages."[113] The Qingtian Fish-and-Rice System was just the first of many sites awarded GIAHS status; the millet-growing village of Wangjinzhuang, as mentioned in "Times," was awarded National IAHS status in 2014.

At one level, the goal of IAHS programs in China and elsewhere is to protect systems in place. To qualify, a cropscape must be evaluated as both environmentally and socially sustainable in local context.[114] In China interdisciplinary research teams comprising ecologists, economists, agronomists, historians, archaeologists, social scientists, and folklorists supposedly collaborate with locals to study the dynamics of local eco-social systems, assess threats (poverty, fragile environment, rural-urban migration), and work on solutions. In one sense these sites, like heritage sites elsewhere, represent pure terroir: the Wannian GIAHS in Guangxi Province has an area of only two hundred hectares; fed by a local spring and with a peculiar microclimate, its special rice varieties thrive nowhere else.[115] Nevertheless, these little niches are also carefully researched for their reproductive potential. Qingtian's Rice-and-Fish System, for instance, has apparently been adopted on two million hectares across South China, with plans to adapt it for implantation in other rice-growing zones in Asia, Africa, and Latin America.[116]

A loose-knit convergence around agricultural heritage and its redemptive potential for a planet in danger links the Chinese state, the FAO, environmentalists, altermundialistas, slow-food theorists, seed savers, food-sovereignty movements, and Indigenous rights groups. As in George Washington Carver's project, the received values of the dominant cropscape are turned upside down. The productivity of industrial agriculture is recoded as wasteful of resources, socially and environmentally destructive—a threat to planetary survival rather than a guarantor of peace and plenty. Backwater cropscapes neglected by progress are reconstrued as precious repositories of knowledge holding keys to a just and sustainable future. Their denizens (typically poor, often minority ethnic or Indigenous groups) are transformed from history's losers into stewards of the planet's future.

Although the concept of agricultural heritage contests or inverts many other modernist values, dynamism is at its heart. If these systems have survived, the argument goes, it is because they are resilient. The elements and systemic dynamics that make them resilient can be identified and bred into cropscapes elsewhere. But because they are complex assemblages of species, environments, and human practices and institutions, they cannot be reproduced identically in other settings: even in their home location they do not breed true, they are continually changing over time. Heritage farming systems are seen as a resource akin to landraces, valuable sources of cropscape genetic material surviving in the interstices of the modern global industrial cropscape that are unlikely to live for long frozen in foil packages.

These inversions of the scales and values of productivist agronomy are common ground across the spectrum of groups and institutions promoting agricultural heritage. But when it comes to the politics of heritage cropscapes, positions diverge dramatically. FAO programs, for instance, see them contributing to "a new vision for the planet," but doing so as "dynamic engines of rural development."[117] As befits an organization incorporating nations as politically diverse as China, Switzerland, and Saudi Arabia, we may infer that here ecological radicalism is not intended to disrupt the social order. Once again, the Chinese case highlights what is at stake.

A high proportion of China's agricultural heritage sites are inhabited by ethnic minorities. It is no accident that folklorists figure in the research teams: "traditional" songs, dances, crafts, costumes, and even rituals figure prominently in the attractions offered to visitors, and ecotourism is an important livelihood component of almost every IAHS, in China and elsewhere. As the anthropologist Stevan Harrell remarks, cultural performance for profit does not necessarily render it inauthentic: ritual experts and musicians were paid for their services in the past too, and the marketing of tradition sustains cultural survival as well as local development.[118] Nevertheless, the tradition presented in China's heritage sites is both ahistorical and apolitical. Minorities inhabit "unspoiled" niches of breathtaking beauty today because they were driven into marginal territories by the relentless expansion of the Chinese state and its Han population. These histories of dispossession are full of bloody battles and uprisings, quislings, rivalry between ethnic kingdoms, treaties honored and broken, intermarriage, trade, and smuggling—all erased from the sanitized lineages presented today as tradition. Minorities are encouraged by the state to celebrate a communal cultural identity, but only within the strictly policed limits of multiethnic national harmony.

At the other end of the spectrum, the Zapatistas' communal milpa gardens are intended to feed the revolution, sustaining active resistance to the incursions of the central Mexican state. The histories crafted by the Zapatistas in Chiapas, and by the many other agricultural heritage movements that have sprung up across the Americas, highlight anticolonial and anticapitalist struggle and ethnic claims to sovereignty: food sovereignty and seed sovereignty will enable political as well as economic autonomy; the maize, squash, and beans of the Central American milpas symbolize collective action and care; communal work in the gardens raises consciousness; the landrace seeds, carefully selected from year to year, embody the millennial rights of indigenous communities to control their own land and destiny—"es la hora de cosechar rebeldía" (the time is ripe for rebellion).[119]

The technologies of reproduction that guided our attention in this chapter are not glamorous: seed collection, fermentation, packaging and shelling nuts, manuring. These are not the focus of grand narratives in the history of technology obsessed with invention and innovation as keys to economic prosperity. Yet our choice of technologies has the advantage of identifying significant dynamics in history. Attention to practices of collecting global crop diversity connects the Nazi Empire in Eastern Europe not only to the Soviet Empire but also to previous European undertakings that colonized the tropics to tap their cropscapes. Studying fermentation processes reveals material and cultural registers of national reproduction in Japan and foundational debates about the place of Portugal in international capitalism. Technologies of packaging and processing alter both the scale and the scope of the cashew industry, and the ontology of the cashew. Manuring techniques reclaimed poor soils and Black people for history. The internet and the donkey plow resurrect neglected Chinese cropscapes as world heritage.

This is an invitation to explore technologies in history for their role in reproducing people, empires, and cultures, and less for their degree of novelty or sophistication.[120] We are certainly captivated by the complicated processes of blending port, but what justifies detailing the solera process is how it enables the extension of the cropscape by freezing time; how it produces a hierarchy of consumers by stabilizing the characteristics of differently aged ports. Discussions of the moment alcohol was added in port production fascinate the oenophile; to the historian they reveal how processing technologies evolve to replicate the successes of a particular year, how technology reproduces time.

Reproduction in agricultural history often refers simply to the life cycles of plants, where the first sets and riffs in *Moving Crops* began. Here the usual definition receives its due, in the consideration of breeding. And the promises of breeders that populate our first riff were, to be sure, formulated in terms of innovation: they created pure lines and hybrid varieties that sustained industrialized visions of the cropscape. But what the narrative also revealed is that from the first moment, such breeding practices demanded access to the variability encapsulated in landraces and wild varieties. The same scientists who produced new varieties occupying European fields were the ones devising forms of conserving crop diversity, namely, through seed banks. Breeding is as much about conserving global crop diversity as about producing new forms of life. Maybe unexpectedly, historians of the Global Seed Vault end up engaging the same literature as those narrating the FAO's Globally Important Agricultural Heritage Systems. When accounting for historical dynamics, more than insisting on opposing new and old or useful and waste, it might be productive to pause at the intersections and pay attention to the technologies that constantly make one category dependent on the other.

In taking technology as our red thread through this set of riffs on the reproduction of crops, rather than focusing exclusively on their biological reproduction, we have looked more broadly at the tools and knowledge that extended or redefined their reach, scope, meaning, and social impact. We have considered the import of the concrete and foil of the modern seed bank, of brewing methods and branding techniques, mulching soils or extracting oils—all technologies of an order different from the succession of "new reproductive technologies," from contraceptive pills to gene editing, that have captured the public imagination and radicalized scholarly critique in recent years.[121]

We do not discount the interest and importance of studies of crops that funnel analysis through the lens of biological reproduction. But the cropscape, as an arena for the reciprocal shaping of crops and humans through labor, sustenance, and struggle, provides a framework to temper genetic or procreative essentialism. Cropscapes are ideal sites for exploring the entanglements of multiple modalities of reproduction, social and symbolic as well as biological and material. In our previous works we engaged Huang Daopo, or Mistress Huang, "the first cotton cultivator," enshrined for introducing cotton cultivation and processing to the Yangtze Delta, to unveil forms of gender reproduction of the Yuan period; techniques of making tobacco bright that sustained the identity politics of the Populist movement in the South of the United States; the breeding of Ardito wheat in Fascist Italy that promised to transform Italian peasants into fierce Arditi (storm troopers).[122] Kathryn de Luna describes her longue durée study of bushcraft in south-central Africa as a "story about cultivation—the cultivation of food and the cultivation of forms of individual distinction and group association among the living and dead."[123]

Here we have seen Du Bois analyze the reproduction of race in the American South by weaving together landholding, plants, and labor, very deliberately omitting any reference to human biology.[124] Also important to our argument, he described the struggle for emancipation from slavery during the U.S. Civil War as "the General Strike," blurring the distinction between slaves and workers or plantation and factory, a move followed by other distinguished members of the radical historical tradition who rewrote the history of the Black Atlantic while decolonizing the very same act of historical writing.[125] In explaining the processes of race formation, these historians did not leave aside the sugarscape with its cane fields and boiling furnaces to focus on the biological reproduction of humans. In their narratives, the (re)production of white planters and Black slaves is inseparable from the (re)production of sugar, cotton, or tobacco.

Epilogue Beyond the Grain

In the spirit of jazz musicians, we have reworked standards from the global history songbook into new interpretations. Each of the chapters, "Time," "Place," "Size," "Actants," "Compositions," and "Reproductions," is a set of riffs on one key framework of historical analysis. The riffs, each exploring a particular historical cropscape in movement, play variations on the main theme at different scales and in different keys. Taken together, the riffs in each set point up the framing work that historians do. Riffing with crops on the move, in all the stubborn materiality of a cropscape at a particular historical moment, has made us face clearly and directly not only how our choice of scale determines the narrative we tell—its beginning, middle, and conclusion; its exposition, climax, and denouement—but also our role as authors in choosing what matters when we tell a story. We have presented a weevil's possible view of the cotton market or an elephant's perspective on a tea plantation not only to introduce unfamiliar narrators but also to challenge conventional global-history narratives about the emergence of the modern world: that history has moved from the local to the global, and from small to large units of scale; that the center of action and objects have moved from east to west and south to north, from peripheral to metropolitan; and that social structures have transformed from premodern to modern in characteristics described by Western social science theorists.

Undermining the linear narratives of global history has required a new method, one respectfully rooted in the local while at the same time revealing the global processes in which all history participates. To this end we settled on the cropscape: that ever-mutating assemblage of nonhumans and humans, material, social, and symbolic elements, within which a particular crop or set of crops in a particular place and time flourished or failed. By training, we are historians and historical anthropologists of crops and of technology, and scholars of science and technology studies, which means that we all study the physical, material worlds of the past. The way we examine the history of technology employs antimodern ways of seeing, in that the elements considered to be part of the story, their combinations and juxtapositions, undermine today's conventional linearities and categories. Instead our approaches and methods propose understanding historical layerings and patchworks, with multivalent objects and polyvalent frames of interpretation.[1] We layer objects, considerations, and scales in each set and invite historians—not just of agriculture but of all global and material processes—to do the same with their own stories. Cropscape analysis goes beyond crops to burst open the periodizations and geographies, the conventional scales, boundaries, and directionalities that usually structure global histories.

In *Moving Crops* we not only tell new histories of cropscapes but also confront and rearticulate the histories we tell about or with them. We do this not by delving into new archives but mostly by engaging with existing historiographies and exploring their potentialities. Global history, typically obsessed with the triumph of the West, the rise of China, seamless flows, and the planetary scale as seen from space, has rightly been criticized for reproducing in academia exactly the kinds of erasures it critiques in globalizing processes. More sensitive historians have produced important correctives by multiplying the archives they rely on beyond the West to reveal previously underappreciated connections and entanglements on multiple scales—regional, transnational, oceanic, and yes, global.[2] Nevertheless, this tendency has not only led to thick books with long lists of sources and archives from all different continents but also, and more problematically, has been leading to further disenfranchisement of historians writing from less privileged institutional settings.[3] Few scholars have the funds and cohorts of graduate students to put together the impressive bodies of endnotes that have become the standard of global history. By building our collection of cases from deep engagements with different historiographies—national, local, and environmental historiographies, historiographies of technology and science, historical anthropology—we gesture at the possibility of writing more inclusive histories that take seriously the places we write about not only as objects of historical knowledge but as sites of history production as well.

Healthy criticism of national and imperial historiographies has pointed to the problematic connections between the professionalization of history and the legitimation of nation-states and empires. It may be that the best alternative to the grand narrative of modernization is to study multifaceted interactions, beyond political boundaries and on multiple scales, as a means to question the "established facts" of national or global narratives.[4] But we should be careful not to do this by (re)producing the academic hierarchies that sustained such facts. Seeking to uncouple the project of global history from the phenomenon of globalization, in our riffs we use microhistories both to illuminate and to connect places, treating each crop as a cultural artifact explored first as a product and producer of place, and then as a connector of places. The collective nature of this book's authorship and the repeated reflexive signaling of the limits and potentialities of our historiographic perspectives point to alternative forms of producing history.

Reflexivity in historical writing led many to engage with metahistory and its taxonomy of forms of emplotment available to historians: romance, tragedy, comedy, and satire as exemplified by Hegel, Ranke, Michelet, Tocqueville, Marx, or Nietzsche.[5] Our method here has been less majestic, not relying on such well-ordered lineages of great European historical thinkers, preferring to build instead upon a diverse collection of cases and historiographies to offer readers entangled metahistories. The point of our thematic chapters, with the mosaics of cases they contain, is to take us up from the level of historiographical reflexivity within a case study to historiographical critique of concepts and metanarratives or metaframings. Our entangled metahistories join with and draw upon the work of many other scholars who study mobilities and thingness to rewrite the topographies of significance in global history.[6] We join these authors in complicating older notions of core and peripheries, market and taste, crops and weeds, and so on. But our approach, through the cropscape method and illustrated by our multiple riffs, presents multiple globals and locals, multiple circuits, multiple recuttings or extensions of periodization, surprising coalitions and assemblages, unexpected delineations of paths through space or time. We have not organized our research around a single artifact or region, and its boundaries of place, time, and actor are much more open. We are not offering another counternarrative, which would be a mistranslation of our intentions. Our mosaic (including its vaguenesses and missing pieces) is in some senses tantalizing rather than fulfilling. In some of the individual riffs—

for example, on marigolds—we can only suggest how to join all the dots. At the same time, this strategy is liberating—it ignores conventional boundaries and offers both new insights and new imaginative possibilities for historians.

We believe that the methods we have used to understand and present new histories through cropscapes are applicable beyond the realm of crops, and we look forward to learning how they might hack the archive of the global historian writing not only from wealthy institutions of the Global North but from locations in the Global South as well.[7] This is, we hope, a kind of global history that can be written from any place. Our collaborators in the Republic of Plants project and network demonstrate the feasibility of applying the method widely, around the world, across different fields of historical inquiry and beyond academia.[8] Many projects are working together and making new regional and global networks of academics and nonacademics that are agriculture based and reach out into broader material civilization from there, like the Subaltern Seed Stories project and its attention to Afro-descendant seed keepers in Jamaica, or India's Network of Rural and Agrarian Studies, or the "experiments in collaboration" of the Matsutake Worlds Research Group.[9] These are of course not limited to crops: Annapurna Mamidipudi and the Handloom Futures Trust use cropscape methods to advocate for weavers of textiles.[10]

As, however, we conclude this project and reflect on the cropscape method and the cropscape within which we cultivated this book—the elements that made our efforts possible—we must consider the funding and support from the Max Planck Institute for the History of Science that brought us and other scholars to Berlin to discuss these issues over several years, providing the rooms and cookies that were the seedbed and the fertilizer for our project, and the technologies of Skype and Google Docs and MSWord that allowed us to transplant our cropscape discussions into cyberspace and ripen them for harvest.

Notes

ORIENTATIONS

1. Harlan and de Wet, "Some Thoughts about Weeds"; on rootedness, see Bray et al., "Cropscapes and History"; on rhizomatic histories, see DeLanda, *A Thousand Years of Nonlinear History.*
2. E.g., Braudel, *Civilisation matérielle;* Diamond, *Guns, Germs and Steel.*
3. As we advanced in our discussions of cropscape as heuristic, we discovered that in 2011 the USDA had launched a CropScape website, "a geospatial service which offers advanced tools such as interactive visualization" of its comprehensive agricultural statistics; https://nassgeodata.gmu.edu/CropScape/ (accessed 9 December 2020). As a technical device and instrument of governance, the USDA CropScape would certainly reward analysis through our own cropscape approach.
4. Vidal de La Blache, "Les conditions géographiques des faits sociaux"; Bloch, *Les caractères originaux de l'histoire rurale française;* Braudel, *Civilisation matérielle.*
5. Bloch, *Les caractères originaux de l'histoire rurale française;* Braudel, *Civilisation matérielle;* Le Roy Ladurie, *Times of Feast, Times of Famine.* For evaluations of the long-term Annales influence in cropscape-related fields, see Willis, "The Contribution of the 'Annales' School to Agrarian History"; Watts, "Food and the Annales School."
6. Bloch, *Apologie pour l'histoire,* 76.
7. Burke, "The Annales in Global Context," 430.
8. Williams, *The Country and the City;* Scott, *The Art of Not Being Governed;* Scott, *Against the Grain.*

254 Notes to Pages 5–13

9. Bender, "Theorising Landscapes, and the Prehistoric Landscapes of Stonehenge"; Bender, "Landscapes on-the-Move"; Tilley, *A Phenomenology of Landscape*.

10. A sequence famously formulated by the cultural materialist Elman Service; Service, *Primitive Social Organization*.

11. Bender, "Theorising Landscapes, and the Prehistoric Landscapes of Stonehenge," 735, emphasis added.

12. Appadurai, *Modernity at Large*.

13. Li, "What Is Land?" 589.

14. On the ways of seeing produced by aerial photography, see for example Haffner, *The View from Above*.

15. Canet and Raisz, *Atlas de Cuba*, 3; Nuñez, "A Forgotten Atlas of Erwin Raisz."

16. Canet and Raisz, *Atlas de Cuba*, 42–43, 44–45, 48–49.

17. "Sugarcane occupies 52% of the total cultivated land. *No other country has dedicated so much of its best land to a single crop. This sugarcane economy is at present profitable but was and can again be dangerous'* "; Canet and Raisz, 43, emphases added.

18. Ortiz, *Cuban Counterpoint*, discussed further in chapter 5, "Compositions," in the section entitled "Caring and Sharing."

19. Ortiz, *Cuban Counterpoint*, 6–7.

20. Canet and Raisz, *Atlas de Cuba*, 49.

21. Canet initially supported the Cuban Revolution and in 1959 was appointed vice president of the Agricultural and Industrial Development Bank of Cuba. But disagreements soon arose, and in 1961 Canet and his family left for the United States. His *Atlas* disappeared from the Cuban record; a new national atlas of Cuba, published in 1970, was declared "the first"; Nuñez, "A Forgotten Atlas of Erwin Raisz."

22. Canet and Raisz, *Atlas de Cuba*, 35. See Curry-Machado, *Cuban Sugar Industry*, for more on the nature of this stimulus.

23. Coronil, "Introduction," xxvii. Studies that situate Ortiz in broader Latin American context include Cornejo-Polar, "Mestizaje, transculturación y heterogeneidad"; Jáuregui, *Canibalia*.

24. "We have already seen how sucrose, this 'favored child of capitalism'—Fernando Ortiz's lapidary phrase—epitomized the transition from one kind of society to another"; Mintz, *Sweetness and Power*, 214.

25. Drayton and Motadel, "Discussion."

26. Chatterjee, "Connected Histories and the Dream of Decolonial History"; Behm et al., "Decolonizing History"; Subrahmanyam, "Connected Histories"; Cañizares-Esguerra, *Entangled Empires: The Anglo-Iberian Atlantic, 1500–1830;* Smith, "Nodes of Convergence."

27. Other cosmologies categorize modalities of movement or mutation in terms that are equally interesting to apply both to plants and to human mobilizations of plants. Chinese cosmology, for instance, identifies five modes of mutation or movement characterizing natural transformations (water moistens and descends; fire burns and ascends; wood bends and straightens; metal yields and changes; earth receives and gives).

28. Attributing agency to nonhumans, from mussels or microbes to gazogenes, is an approach first formulated in actor-network theory (ANT) and more recently reformulated by post-humanists; see for example Callon, "Some Elements of a Sociology of

Notes to Pages 14–18   **255**

Translation"; Akrich, "A Gazogene in Costa Rica"; Bennett, *Vibrant Matter;* Tsing, "More-Than-Human Sociality." On ontologies that draw different boundaries, see for example Descola, *Beyond Nature and Culture;* Norton, "The Chicken or the Iegue"; Viveiros de Castro, "Exchanging Perspectives."

29. Cronon, *Nature's Metropolis;* Olmstead and Rhode, "The Red Queen and the Hard Reds"; Fullilove, *The Profit of the Earth.*

30. Crosby, *The Columbian Exchange;* Crosby, *Ecological Imperialism.* The idea of exploring the biological exchanges that followed the arrival of Europeans in the Americas, and their immediate and long-term ecological consequences, was so radical that Crosby had immense difficulty finding a publisher for *The Columbian Exchange.* Eventually the small publisher Greenwood brought it out in 1972. Considered a founding work in environmental history, it has been in print ever since (Gambino, "Alfred W. Crosby on the Columbian Exchange"). Today, however, in the light of post-human and interspecies approaches, Crosby's work can be seen as drawing a reductionist dichotomy between humans and nonhumans.

31. Sheller, "The New Mobilities Paradigm for a Live Sociology," 801, on subaltern (im) mobilities; crop histories of subaltern mobilities include Carney, *Black Rice;* Carney and Rosomoff, *In the Shadow of Slavery.*

32. On Champa rice see chapter 1, "Times." On Islamic agriculture see Decker, "Plants and Progress." On the Columbian Exchange see Crosby, *The Columbian Exchange;* Earle, "The Columbian Exchange." On the 1960s Green Revolution see Kumar et al., "Roundtable." On its earlier foundations, in Europe, Japan, Latin America, and the Southern United States, see Harwood, *Europe's Green Revolution and Others Since;* Harwood, "The Green Revolution as a Process."

33. On Farmer Systems Research, agroecology, and their antecedents see Harwood, *Europe's Green Revolution and Others Since,* 141–42. On the mindset of technological determinism inherent in breeding "seeds of change," key studies of how seeds veil relations of production, encapsulating political struggle, also include Kloppenburg, *First the Seed;* Richards, *Indigenous Agricultural Revolution;* Biggs, "Promiscuous Transmission and Encapsulated Knowledge"; Saraiva, *Fascist Pigs;* Fullilove, *The Profit of the Earth.*

34. See for example Crosby, *Ecological Imperialism,* on "neo-Europes"; Saraiva, *Cloning Democracy.*

35. Krige, *How Knowledge Moves;* Laveaga, "Largo Dislocare."

36. Gómez, *The Experiential Caribbean;* Chatterjee, "Connected Histories and the Dream of Decolonial History."

37. Smith, "Nodes of Convergence," 5.

38. Alder, "Thick Things: Introduction"; this approach, proposed in Latour, *We Have Never Been Modern,* was further developed by historians of science, including Rheinberger, *Toward a History of Epistemic Things;* Daston, *Things That Talk.* Modern crop and animal breeds are treated from this "thick thing" perspective in Saraiva, *Fascist Pigs.*

39. Akrich, "A Gazogene in Costa Rica."

40. Norton, *Sacred Gifts, Profane Pleasures;* Ko, *The Social Life of Inkstones.* For a contemporary case, see Hecht, *Being Nuclear.*

41. McNeill, *Mosquito Empires;* Cronon, *Nature's Metropolis;* Moon, *The Plough That Broke the Steppes;* Kreike, *Recreating Eden.*

256   Notes to Pages 19–33

42. This is a criticism that has frequently been leveled at actor-network theory with its call to treat human and nonhuman actants symmetrically.
43. Whatmore, "Materialist Returns"; Puig de la Bellacasa, " 'Nothing Comes without Its World' "; Tsing, "More-Than-Human Sociality."
44. Smith, "Amidst Things," 843, 848.
45. Bubandt and Tsing, "Feral Dynamics of Post-Industrial Ruin"; Chen et al., "Genetic Diversity and Population Structure of Feral Rapeseed."
46. Lemonnier, *Technological Choices.*
47. Haraway, *When Species Meet;* LeCain, *The Matter of History;* Russell, *Evolutionary History.*
48. Bonneuil and Fressoz, *The Shock of the Anthropocene;* Haraway, "Anthropocene, Capitalocene"; LeCain, "Against the Anthropocene."
49. Behm et al., "Decolonizing History," 170.
50. Raj, "Introduction."

CHAPTER 1. TIMES

1. Bergson, *Creative Evolution,* 21. See among many possible references Canales, *The Physicist and the Philosopher.*
2. Gros-Balthazard et al., "Origines et domestication du palmier dattier"; Tengberg, "Beginnings and Early History."
3. Méry, "The First Oases in Eastern Arabia."
4. Magee, *The Archaeology of Prehistoric Arabia.*
5. Lombard, "Du rhythme naturel au rhythme humain"; Charbonnier, "La maîtrise du temps."
6. Magee, *The Archaeology of Prehistoric Arabia.*
7. Flemming, "Date Honey Production."
8. Gauthier-Pilters and Dagg, *The Camel.*
9. Austen, *Trans-Saharan Africa in World History;* Lydon, *On Trans-Saharan Trails.*
10. Scheele, "Traders, Saints, and Irrigation."
11. Lightfoot and Miller, "Sijilmassa"; Dunn, "The Trade of Tafilalt."
12. Banaji, "Islam, the Mediterranean and the Rise of Capitalism." And see the discussion of the theft of capitalism by Western historiography, namely, by Braudel and the Annales school, in Goody, *The Theft of History,* 180–214.
13. Subrahmanyam, *The Portuguese Empire in Asia;* Chaudhuri, "O imperio na economia mundial"; Godinho, *Os descobrimentos.*
14. Dale, *The Orange Trees of Marrakesh: Ibn Khaldun and the Science of Man.*
15. Irwin, "Toynbee and Ibn Khaldun"; Davis, "Decentering History."
16. Irwin, *Ibn Khaldun.*
17. Abd al-Rahman, *The Palm Tree* (770 C.E.), translation after Poitou, *Spain and Its People,* 506.
18. Ruggles, *Gardens, Landscape, and Vision;* Menocal, *The Ornament of the World: How Muslims, Jews, and Christians Created a Culture of Tolerance in Medieval Spain.*
19. In 1934, two years before he was assassinated by fascists, Federico García Lorca composed *Diván del Tamarit,* his homage to the Arab tradition of poetry in Granada. *Diván* is Arabic for a collection of poems, and Tamarit, the name of Lorca's family orchard in the Valley of Granada, means "abundant with dates."

Notes to Pages 33–42   **257**

20. Critz, Olmstead, and Rhode, "Horn of Plenty."
21. Seekatz, "America's Arabia," 45.
22. Saraiva, "The Scientific Co-Op."
23. Popenoe, *Date Growing.*
24. Krueger, "Date Palm."
25. For another crop that proved unexpectedly resistant to mechanization, prompting growers to pressure government for favorable legislation to secure cheap labor, see "Sizes," "Tea."
26. Krueger, "Date Palm," 448; Seekatz, "America's Arabia." Saraiva, *Cloning Democracy,* analyses the class and race politics of cooperatives in the citrus industry.
27. Seekatz, "America's Arabia."
28. On the long history of the *braceros* in Californian agriculture, see Wells, *Strawberry Fields;* Molina, *How Race Is Made in America;* Cohen, *Braceros;* Mitchell, "Battle/ Fields."
29. Plevin, "Palmeros."
30. Krueger, "Date Palm," notes that in most date-importing countries dates are a cheap source of essential calories, not a treat.
31. Craven, *Soil Exhaustion;* Rhode in Hahn et al., "Does Crop Determine Culture?"
32. Hahn, *Making Tobacco Bright,* 35.
33. Brown, *Good Wives, Nasty Wenches.*
34. "Sizes," 'Tobacco Oscillations: Changing Size on the Spot."
35. Grist, *Rice,* 63. The rice grown as a crop in North America is a different species, *Zizania.*
36. Farmer, *Green Revolution? Technology and Change in Rice-Growing Areas of Tamil Nadu and Sri Lanka;* Saha and Schmalzer, "Green-Revolution Epistemologies"; Harwood, "Was the Green Revolution Intended to Maximise Food Production?"
37. See also "Actants."
38. Bray, *The Rice Economies,* 78.
39. Bray, *Agriculture,* 492.
40. Bray, "Science, Technique, Technology."
41. Elvin, *The Pattern of the Chinese Past.*
42. Ho, "Early-Ripening Rice," 173.
43. On the size of the imperial rice market within and beyond China see Shiba, *Commerce and Society;* Marks, "It Never Used to Snow." In the late eighteenth century, for instance, cotton farmers in several regions ate rice imported from Siam; Viraphol, *Tribute and Profit.*
44. Bray, "Instructive and Nourishing Landscapes." Most of imperial China's foundational institutions and cultural practices were first consolidated during the Han dynasty (206 B.C.E.—220 C.E.). By extension, the term Han was (and still is) used to refer to mainstream Chinese ethnicity and culture.
45. Bray, *Technology and Gender;* Hammers, *Pictures of Tilling and Weaving.*
46. Bray, *Technology, Gender and History,* 219–52.
47. Palat, *The Indian Ocean World-Economy.* Rice was the dominant crop of South India, wheat and millets were the staples of most of the north.
48. Flynn and Giráldez, "Born with a 'Silver Spoon' "; Marks, *Tigers, Rice, Silk, and Silt.*
49. E.g., Frank, *ReOrient;* Pomeranz, *The Great Divergence;* Arrighi, Hamashita, and

258 Notes to Pages 42–47

Selden, *The Resurgence of East Asia.* The arguments about this supposed Great Divergence harken back to the concept of "capitalist sprouts," developed by Japanese and Chinese Marxist historians in the 1950s to 1970s, which identified the commercial and manufacturing expansion of early modern China as an embryonic form of capitalist development; Brook, "Capitalism and the Writing of Modern History in China."

50. Blue, "China and Western Social Thought."

51. Wittfogel, *Oriental Despotism;* Geertz, *Agricultural Involution.*

52. The seminal work was Elvin, *The Pattern of the Chinese Past.* See also Huang, *The Peasant Family.*

53. Smith, *Agrarian Origins;* Francks, "Rice and the Path of Economic Development."

54. In earlier Japanese cropscapes rice was typically a prestige food crop rather than the dominant cereal; von Verschuer and Cobcroft, *Rice, Agriculture and Food.*

55. Smith, *Agrarian Origins.*

56. Francks, *Technology and Agricultural Development.*

57. The English term was first proposed by Hayami, "The Industrious Revolution." The concept has been further elaborated by economic historians, including Sugihara, "The East Asian Path"; Saito, "An Industrious Revolution"; Hayami, *Japan's Industrious Revolution.*

58. Bray, *The Rice Economies,* 113–39, 210–17.

59. Morris-Suzuki, *The Technological Transformation of Japan;* Francks, "Rice and the Path of Economic Development."

60. de Vries, *The Industrious Revolution;* de Vries, "Industrious Peasants"; Saito, "An Industrious Revolution."

61. Hayami, *Japan's Industrious Revolution,* 97.

62. Palat, *The Indian Ocean World-Economy,* iv.

63. Ohnuki-Tierney, *Rice as Self;* von Verschuer and Cobcroft, *Rice, Agriculture and Food;* Bray, "Health, Wealth, and Solidarity."

64. Lee, *Gourmets in the Land of Famine;* Biggs, "Promiscuous Transmission and Encapsulated Knowledge"; Schmalzer, *Red Revolution, Green Revolution.* Green Revolution wheats likewise built upon earlier breeding achievements, notably Japanese dwarf wheats; Harwood, "The Green Revolution as a Process."

65. Bray and Robertson, "Sharecropping"; Bray, "Feeding the Farmers."

66. E.g., Farmer, *Green Revolution? Technology and Change in Rice-Growing Areas of Tamil Nadu and Sri Lanka;* Lipton, *Why Poor People Stay Poor;* Pearse, *Seeds of Plenty, Seeds of Want.*

67. In recognition of both social and environmental concerns, in 1999 the president of the Rockefeller Foundation, Gordon Conway, called for a new "Doubly Green" revolution that would be small-farmer and environmentally friendly; Conway, *The Doubly Green Revolution.* M. S. Swaminathan, the crop geneticist known as the father of India's Green Revolution, had already started calling for a socially and ecologically more sustainable "Evergreen Revolution"; Swaminathan, *Sustainable Agriculture.* Many nations are currently investing in research for a "Second Green Revolution" to meet these twin goals, typically focused on genetic engineering for microenvironments.

68. Grist, *Rice,* 172–73.

69. The same applies to shifting cultivation, its history and its relationship to commercial production, discussed in later chapters. See Hill, "The Cultivation of Perennial Rice,"

Notes to Pages 47–52   **259**

on the historical invisibility of ratooning. Zomia, from the Tibeto-Burman term for highlanders, *zomi,* is a term coined by historian Willem van Schendel (van Schendel, "Geographies of Knowing, Geographies of Ignorance") to refer to supposedly peripheral societies inhabiting the mountainous zones of Southeast Asia and lying beyond the control of the lowland, wet-rice-dependent states. Scott, *The Art of Not Being Governed,* argues that these societies offer a counternarrative to long-term histories of modernization that stress progressive assimilation into state-building projects.

70. FAO, *Perennial Crops for Food Security;* Hill, "Back to the Future!"

71. Robertson, *The Dynamics of Productive Relationships,* 64.

72. Macedo, "Standard Cocoa."

73. Cooper, *Africa since 1940,* 21–23.

74. Hill, *Migrant Cocoa-Farmers.*

75. The cacao tree (*Theobroma cacao*) is native to Central America. For its place in the Columbian Exchange see Norton, *Sacred Gifts, Profane Pleasures.* For the rise of chocolate consumption in industrial Europe see Robertson, *Chocolate, Women and Empire.*

76. The origins of the Ghanaian cocoa industry are popularly attributed to Tetteh Quashie, a blacksmith, said to have established a cocoa nursery in Akwapim with pods he brought back from Fernando Po in 1879. Sir William Brandford Griffith also claimed to have introduced cocoa plants to the Gold Coast in the 1880s, when he was governor; Hill, *Migrant Cocoa-Farmers,* 172–73.

77. Ross, "The Plantation Paradigm," 63, citing Richards, *Indigenous Agriculture Revolution.* Ross analyzes why European agronomists continued to consider the plantation model superior, despite overwhelming evidence that in Africa cocoa plantations never matched the yields, profits, or efficiency of "native" farming.

78. Farmer interview 2015, Asante et al., "Farmers' Perspectives," 378.

79. Asante et al., 374. On diversifying local economies and sources of farm income, see Knudsen and Agergaard, "Ghana's Cocoa Frontier in Transition."

80. Ross, "The Plantation Paradigm."

81. This account, emphasizing the interdependent life cycles of cocoa trees, farms, contracts, and farming families, is based on Robertson, *The Dynamics of Productive Relationships,* 53–78. See also Ross, "The Plantation Paradigm"; Knudsen and Agergaard, "Ghana's Cocoa Frontier in Transition"; Asante et al., "Farmers' Perspectives."

82. Stigmatized by modernists from Lenin to development economists, sharecropping has a reputation as an archaic form incompatible with modernity. Studies by anthropologists, however, document how the flexible institution of sharecropping, far from being economically primitive, can efficiently match family time (with its waxing and waning resources of labor, land, and capital) with cropscape time and modern commercial cycles or the temporalities of state development projects; Robertson, *The Dynamics of Productive Relationships.*

83. Asante et al., "Farmers' Perspectives"; Knudsen and Agergaard, "Ghana's Cocoa Frontier in Transition."

84. Once cocoa yields began to decline, the owner's share reverted to half.

85. Knudsen and Agergaard, "Ghana's Cocoa Frontier in Transition," 335.

86. Berlan, "Child Labour and Cocoa," 3. On the relations in West African societies between apprenticeship and parenting, skill acquisition, and role delegation, see Goody, *Parenthood and Social Reproduction.*

260 Notes to Pages 52–63

87. Farmer in Brong Ahafo (Ghana's northwestern cocoa zone), interviewed in 2015; Asante et al., "Farmers' Perspectives," 379.
88. Ross, "The Plantation Paradigm," contrasts the environmental and economic efficacy of this system with the vulnerabilities of plantation cultivation of cocoa, in West Africa and in the Caribbean.
89. Knudsen and Agergaard, "Ghana's Cocoa Frontier in Transition."
90. Bray, "Instructive and Nourishing Landscapes."
91. *Lüshi chunqiu* (Spring and Autumn Annals of Master Lü), citing a lost work entitled *Houji shu* (Book of Lord Millet); Bray, *Agriculture,* 105 and 255.
92. Scott, *Seeing Like a State;* Scott, *Against the Grain.*
93. *Zhou li* (Ritual system of the Zhou), "Minister of Rites," quoted von Falkenhausen 1993, 2.
94. Needham, *Physics,* 201. The compilation of the *Hanshu* was undertaken by Ban Gu, a high official who was disgraced and died in prison in 92 C.E.. His sister Ban Zhao, a famous scholar and author in her own right, completed the work in 111.
95. For wheat and rice breeding programs under the Republic (1911–1949) see Lee, *Gourmets in the Land of Famine.* For the People's Republic of China (1949–) see Schmalzer, *Red Revolution, Green Revolution.*
96. Park, "Nongjiale Tourism."
97. Schmalzer, "Layer upon Layer."
98. Mintz, *Sweetness and Power,* 51. The classic paper on the industrial sense of time is by E. P. Thompson; Thompson, "Time, Work-Discipline, and Industrial Capitalism."
99. Scott, *Against the Grain.*
100. See "Places," "Tubers and History," and "Compositions," "Polyculture," on milpa gardens.
101. See "Compositions" and "Reproductions."

CHAPTER 2. PLACES

1. Raffles, "Local Theory," 323.
2. Urry, "The Sociology of Space and Place."
3. Schama, *The Embarrassment of Riches;* Neal and Weidenmier, "Crises in the Global Economy from Tulips to Today."
4. Goldgar, *Tulipmania,* 22, 286–87.
5. *Encyclopaedia Romana,* s.v. "Carolus Clusius," http://penelope.uchicago.edu/~grout/encyclopaedia_romana/aconite/clusius.html (accessed 20 May 2019).
6. Neal and Weidenmier, "Crises in the Global Economy from Tulips to Today," 476.
7. Garber, *Famous First Bubbles,* 46–47.
8. Garber, 34–35.
9. Goldgar, *Tulipmania,* 248–50.
10. Schama, *The Embarrassment of Riches,* 512; Garber, *Famous First Bubbles,* 30.
11. Gelderblom, de Jong, and Jonker, "The Formative Years of the Modern Corporation."
12. The new European presence helped reshape existing trade networks, including the long-established intra-Asian spice trade, but did not diminish their importance. See Chaudhuri, *Trade and Civilisation in the Indian Ocean;* Prange, " 'Measuring by the Bushel.' "
13. Schiebinger, *Plants and Empire,* 10.

Notes to Pages 63–72   **261**

14. For a general treatment of these matters, see Schama, *The Embarrassment of Riches.*
15. Another good illustration of such processes is cacao; see Norton, "Tasting Empire."
16. Harvey, "Turkey as a Source of Garden Plants."
17. This reinforces our point that the cropscape method applies well to other material things.
18. Goody, *The Culture of Flowers,* 102.
19. Salzmann, "The Age of Tulips," 84.
20. *Oxford English Dictionary,* s.v. tulip, the usage in J. Gerrard's 1597 *Herball* (accessed 2 May 2018).
21. Salzmann, "The Age of Tulips," 86.
22. Goody, *The Culture of Flowers,* 111 n. 41.
23. Demiriz, "Tulips in Ottoman Turkish Culture and Art"; Karababa, "Marketing and Consuming Flowers in the Ottoman Empire."
24. Karababa, "Marketing and Consuming Flowers in the Ottoman Empire," esp. 285.
25. Karababa, "Marketing and Consuming Flowers in the Ottoman Empire," 284–85.
26. Harvey, "Turkey as a Source of Garden Plants," 21.
27. Karababa, "Marketing and Consuming Flowers in the Ottoman Empire," 284.
28. Harvey, "Turkey as a Source of Garden Plants," 21.
29. Black, Hashimzade, and Myles, *A Dictionary of Economics,* 50.
30. Garber, *Famous First Bubbles,* 43.
31. Weber, *The Protestant Ethic and the Spirit of Capitalism;* Veblen, *The Theory of the Leisure Class.* Braudel set the pace for what we might call the "consumption turn" in world histories of capitalism and later global history when he chose consumption as the focus for the first volume of his three-volume study *Civilization and Capitalism,* with circulation for the second volume and production for the third; Braudel, *The Structures of Everyday Life;* Braudel, *The Wheels of Commerce;* Braudel, *The Perspective of the World.*
32. Goody, *The Theft of History.*
33. Goldgar, *Tulipmania,* 117; Lesnaw and Ghabrial, "Tulip Breaking: Past, Present, and Future."
34. Demiriz, "Tulips in Ottoman Turkish Culture and Art"; Karababa, "Marketing and Consuming Flowers in the Ottoman Empire."
35. Karababa, "Marketing and Consuming Flowers in the Ottoman Empire," 288.
36. Casale, *The Ottoman Age of Exploration.*
37. Erimtan, *Ottomans Looking West?* 23–58.
38. Erimtan, *Ottomans Looking West?;* Salzmann, "The Age of Tulips."
39. McCusker, "The Demise of Distance."
40. For a discussion of Griffith's film in the context of American capitalism see Henderson, *California and the Fictions of Capital;* Olsson, "Trading Places."
41. Postel, *The Populist Vision;* Sanders, *Roots of Reform.* On wheat as an example of industrializing agriculture in the United States see Fitzgerald, *Every Farm a Factory.*
42. Cronon, *Nature's Metropolis.*
43. Olmstead and Rhode, "The Evolution of California Agriculture"; Vaught, "Transformations in Late Nineteenth-Century Rural California."
44. Rothstein, "Centralizing Firms and Spreading Markets," 107–8. The other major wheat exporters of the early twentieth century were Romania, Canada, Argentina, Australia, and India; Topik and Wells, *Global Markets Transformed,* 130.
45. Siegelbaum, "The Odessa Grain Trade."

262 Notes to Pages 72–78

46. The full argument for connecting the history of the North American plains and the Russian steppes is developed in Moon, *The American Steppes.*

47. Siegelbaum, "The Odessa Grain Trade."

48. See, for example, O'Rourke, "The European Grain Invasion." For a critical overview of economic historians' arguments about wheat and global markets in the nineteenth century, see Bairoch, *Economics and World History.*

49. Zarrilli, "Capitalism, Ecology, and Agrarian Expansion in the Pampean Region"; Gallo, *La pampa gringa;* Friesen, *Canadian Prairies.*

50. Blain, "Le rôle de dépendance externe."

51. Olmstead and Rhode, "The Red Queen and the Hard Reds."

52. Olmstead and Rhode, "Biological Globalization."

53. Olmstead and Rhode, "Adapting North American Wheat Production."

54. Fullilove, *The Profit of the Earth,* 102.

55. On the peregrinations of the Mennonites in Europe and North America, see Fullilove, *The Profit of the Earth,* 99–135.

56. Another possible way of establishing the connection between the Russian steppes and American plains would be to focus on soil; Moon, *The American Steppes.* Attention to the early history of the McCormick reaper and the quality of different flours enabled Daniel Rood to connect, in significant and unexpected ways, the wheat fields of the Shenandoah Valley in Virginia with the coffee plantations of the Paraíba Valley in the Rio de Janeiro hinterland. Rood, *The Reinvention of Atlantic Slavery.*

57. Fullilove, *The Profit of the Earth,* 109–19.

58. McNeill, "How the Potato Changed the World's History"; see also "Compositions" on tubers in the worldwide reproduction of an industrial working class.

59. As in the case of the Irish potato blight; but see Rival and McKey, "Domestication and Diversity in Manioc" on combining sexual and vegetative reproduction.

60. Malinowski, *Coral Gardens and Their Magic;* Rappaport, *Pigs for the Ancestors.*

61. Hildebrand, "A Tale of Two Tuber Crops," esp. 275, Table 15.1.

62. See "Compositions." "Farmer rice varieties on the Upper Guinea coast will be wrongly understood if regarded as heritage varieties—selections mandated by localised cultural traditions. Here it will be argued, with supporting evidence from history and agronomy, that they are better understood as the products of resistance to slave-based commodification. As such, these small-farmer emancipatory innovations deserve a name. Here, they will be termed anti-commodities"; Richards, "Rice as Commodity and Anti-Commodity," 10–11.

63. Taking Saraiva's point that any systematic "tinkering with plant and animal life" is a form of biopolitics; Saraiva, *Fascist Pigs,* 12.

64. Eriksen, *Small Places, Large Issues.*

65. We take the title of this section from Kahn, *Always Hungry, Never Greedy.*

66. Uzendoski, "Manioc Beer and Meat," 883; Mosko, "The Fractal Yam," 693.

67. Malinowski, "The Primitive Economics of the Trobriand Islanders," 2; see also Malinowski, *Coral Gardens and Their Magic;* Malinowski, *Argonauts of the Western Pacific;* Mosko, "The Fractal Yam"; MacCarthy, "Playing Politics with Yams."

68. Pfaffenberger, "Symbols Do Not Create Meaning"; Kahn, *Always Hungry, Never Greedy.*

69. "Spheres of exchange intimate the disconnection of subsistence from wealth production, effectively inhibiting relations of domination, promoting egalitarian distribution

Notes to Pages 78–82   **263**

of livelihood resources"; Sillitoe, "Why Spheres of Exchange?" 1. For lack of space we omit the second Trobriand-Pacific sphere of prestige exchange, with its distinction and complementarity between male and female goods; Weiner, *Inalienable Possessions.*

70. Malinowski, *Argonauts of the Western Pacific,* 60.

71. Cook, "The Obsolete 'anti-Market' Mentality," 327.

72. Appadurai, *The Social Life of Things;* Norton, *Sacred Gifts, Profane Pleasures;* Bray, "Technological Transitions"; Fullilove, *The Profit of the Earth.*

73. Julian Steward and Marvin Harris are probably the most famous early proponents of cultural ecology, while Jared Diamond may be considered a spiritual heir; e.g., Steward, "The Concept and Method of Cultural Ecology"; Harris, *Cows, Pigs, Wars and Witches;* Diamond, *Collapse.* The field has strongly influenced today's nutritional anthropology, while also prompting a critical reaction expressed through the more recent field of political ecology.

74. Rappaport, *Pigs for the Ancestors;* Biersack, "The Sun and the Shakers, Again"; Filer, "Interdisciplinary Perspectives on Historical Ecology."

75. https://raifilm.org.uk/films/the-kawelka-ongkas-big-moka/ (accessed June 2022).

76. Although not referred to by Rappaport, this calculation inevitably evokes Henry A. Wallace's hog-corn price ratio, devised in 1915 as a measure for the profitability of hog raising; Saraiva and Slaton, "Statistics as Service to Democracy." Evidence of agricultural activity has been found in sites in the Highlands dated around 8000 B.C.E., making the Highlanders among the world's earliest farmers. Sweet potatoes are known to have reached Highland New Guinea from South America before Europeans penetrated the interior, gradually displacing the native taro; Filer, "Interdisciplinary Perspectives on Historical Ecology," 264, 263.

77. Diamond, *Collapse,* cited Filer, "Interdisciplinary Perspectives on Historical Ecology," 263.

78. Le Roy Ladurie, *Times of Feast, Times of Famine;* Arrighi, Hamashita, and Selden, *The Resurgence of East Asia.*

79. Balée, "The Research Program of Historical Ecology"; Trischler, "The Anthropocene." See "Actants" for a critique of such uses of the biological sciences.

80. Uzendoski, "Manioc Beer and Meat."

81. Uzendoski, "Manioc Beer and Meat," 885.

82. Rival, "Amazonian Historical Ecologies"; Rival and McKey, "Domestication and Diversity in Manioc."

83. See also Ford and Nigh, *The Maya Forest Garden.*

84. Viveiros de Castro, "Perspectival Anthropology," 4, 6. See also Kohn, *How Forests Think.*

85. Descola, "Le jardin de Colibri," 80.

86. Rival and McKey, "Domestication and Diversity in Manioc," 1124; Daly and Shepard, "Magic Darts and Messenger Molecules."

87. Norton, "The Chicken or the Iegue," 29, 30. On anthropophagy, see "Compositions," "Citrus in the Ruins," and Saraiva, "Anthropophagy and Sadness."

88. See Deleuze and Guattari, *A Thousand Plateaux,* on rhizomatic theories (nonlinear, nondendritic, not seeking ultimate causes, and so forth); Mosko, "The Fractal Yam," discusses the isomorphism of yam growth and Trobriand understanding of kinship and social bonds.

264 Notes to Pages 82–89

89. On intersecting approaches to the historicity and resilience of tuber societies in Amazonia, see Uzendoski, "Making Amazonia." The first documented florescence of moka exchanges in colonial Highland New Guinea in the 1930s was succeeded by a new impulse postindependence, with the expansion of commercial coffee growing and the advent of parliamentary democracy; Strathern and Stewart, "Ceremonial Exchange," 243. Yam and kula culture are still vigorous in the Trobriands (Mosko, "The Fractal Yam"; Kuehling, "We Die for Kula"), though concerns are growing about population pressure and soil depletion; MacCarthy, "Playing Politics with Yams."

90. Liu, *Tea War*.

91. Naturalization was the term used by Bentinck, chairman of the Tea Commission of 1834, arguing for the introduction of tea to British India; see Liu, "The Birth of a Noble Tea Country," 80. On "skill and science" see Walker, "Memorandum," 11.

92. Gardella, *Harvesting Mountains*. The historical exception was a brief period in the eleventh century when tea was a state monopoly; Smith, *Taxing Heaven's Storehouse*.

93. On the East India Companies of Europe see Berg, *The Age of Manufactures;* Ellis, Coulton, and Mauger, *Empire of Tea*.

94. Ball, *An Account of the Cultivation;* Fortune, *Three Years' Wanderings;* Fortune, *A Journey to the Tea Countries*.

95. A project notably associated with Joseph Banks; Browne, "Biogeography and Empire."

96. Ross, "The Plantation Paradigm," and see "Times," "The Social Life of Cocoa."

97. Sharma, "British Science, Chinese Skill and Assam Tea"; Sharma, *Empire's Garden*.

98. Meegahakumbura et al., "Indications for Three Independent Domestication Events."

99. C. A. Bruce, superintendent of tea, details the transition from gardening wild tea trees to domesticating them and bringing them into plots on the estate, deploying a combination of Assamese and Chinese techniques; Bruce, "Report on the Manufacture of Tea," 468; Bray, "Translating the Art of Tea," 120–21. Darjeeling teas retained greater affinities to Chinese flavor and production systems; Besky, *The Darjeeling Distinction*.

100. Like the coffee estates established by James Hill, an ambitious English planter, in El Salvador in the 1900s, the Assam tea estates were "always a work in progress, always groaning to life and threatening to sputter out." Sedgewick, "Against Flows," 157.

101. Assamese refused to work on the plantations, so British tea planters went in search of sources of more "docile" labor, strongly supported by the colonial government, which introduced a sequence of labor laws over the decades to ensure adequate supplies of and control over indentured workers. This labor regime and its political impact have been a key focus of postcolonial research on tea; Breman, *Labour Migration;* Behal, "Coolie Drivers or Benevolent Paternalists?"; Nitin Varma, "Producing Tea Coolies?"

102. Behal, "Coolie Drivers or Benevolent Paternalists?"

103. See "Actants," "Seeing Like an Elephant."

104. See "Actants," "Cinchona." On frontier zones as interhuman and interspecies warzones, see Nichter, "Of Ticks, Kings, Spirits"; Biggs, *Quagmire*.

105. Arnold, *The Tropics and the Traveling Gaze*.

106. Besky, *The Darjeeling Distinction,* is particularly good on chains of value creation in the tea industry.

107. Classically set out in Mintz, *Sweetness and Power*. The rise of consumption studies as the key to interpreting global history has produced a flood of studies of tea consump-

Notes to Pages 89–96   **265**

tion in Britain, including Macfarlane and Macfarlane, *Green Gold;* Ellis, Coulton, and Mauger, *Empire of Tea;* Hanser, "Teatime in the North Country," provides an unusual local vignette.

108. Before independence, some nationalists opposed tea drinking as condoning colonial oppression; Lutgendorf, "Making Tea in India."

109. Gardella, *Harvesting Mountains;* Menzies, "Ancient Forest Tea"; Zhang, *Puer Tea.*

110. Again, among a flood of recent publications in Chinese and in Western languages, see Smith, *Taxing Heaven's Storehouse;* Hinsch, *The Rise of Tea Culture in China.*

111. For the technical history of these innovations in processing, see Huang, *Fermentations and Food Science.*

112. Gardella, *Harvesting Mountains;* Liu, "The Two Tea Countries."

113. Gardella, *Harvesting Mountains,* 59; 61, Table 7; 62, Table 8. The streamlined clippers, whose rigging allowed them to sail fast without relying on monsoon winds, were able to deliver new teas fresh from the pre-monsoon harvest.

114. Gardella, 164, Table 22; 11, Table 3; 163, quoting a 1925 British observer.

115. E.g., Matthee, "From Coffee to Tea."

116. Matthee, "From Coffee to Tea," 229.

117. Robisheaux, "Microhistory and the Historical Imagination"; Laveaga, "Largo Dislocare."

118. Levi, "Microhistoria e historia global," 28.

119. Subrahmanyam, "Connected Histories."

120. See the discussion of the "Great Divergence" debate in "Times," as well as in Conrad, *What Is Global History?* 42; Levi, "Microhistoria e historia global," 27 and 33; Hahn, review of *Empire of Cotton.*

121. E.g., Raj, "Introduction"; Norton, *Sacred Gifts, Profane Pleasures;* Andrade, "A Chinese Farmer, Two African Boys, and a Warlord."

122. Norton, *Sacred Gifts, Profane Pleasures,* 4.

123. Sedgewick, "Against Flows," 143.

124. Puig de la Bellacasa, "Making Time for Soil"; Tsing, *The Mushroom at the End of the World;* Hartigan, "Plants as Ethnographic Subjects."

125. Despite our foray into Amerindian interspecies ontologies, this chapter foregrounds humans and human work as makers of places. We reserve a more systematic reflection on interspecies coalitions and struggles for chapter 4, "Actants," even though plants themselves are now increasingly recognized as place makers by scientists, social scientists, and the general public.

126. Conrad, *What Is Global History?* 69–70.

CHAPTER 3. SIZES

1. See "Rice" in "Times," and "Muddy Waters" later in this chapter.

2. Chambers and Mingay, *The Agricultural Revolution,* 173.

3. https://www.ers.usda.gov/data-products/ag-and-food-statistics-charting-the-essentials/farming-and-farm-income/ (accessed 3 August 2019); MacDonald, Korb, and Hoppe, "Farm Size," 4.

4. USDA and National Agricultural Statistics Service, "Farms and Land in Farms, 2018 Summary," 7.

266 Notes to Pages 96–101

5. See for example FAO, "Family Farming Knowledge Platform," or the recent World Bank agribusiness initiative for smallholder producers; World Bank, "Agribusiness."

6. E.g., Massey, *For Space; Rangan and Kull, "What Makes Ecology 'Political'?"; Sassen, Deciphering the Global.*

7. Trends in farm size have served as one key criterion for assessing at what point the Agricultural Revolution took place in Britain; see Overton, *Agricultural Revolution in England.* Or see the debates about farm size and economic involution in early modern China outlined in "Times."

8. Kron, "Agriculture, Roman Empire," and "Compositions," "Worker Cooperatives."

9. Curtin, *The Rise and Fall of the Plantation Complex; Follett et al., Plantation Kingdom.*

10. Ross, "The Plantation Paradigm"; Dove, "Plants, Politics, and the Imagination"; see also "The Social Life of Cocoa" in "Times," and "Tea" later in this chapter.

11. Marling consisted of digging lime or chalk into heavy soils to improve the texture; see for instance Markham, *Farwell to Husbandry.*

12. Markham, *A Way to Get Wealth.* See Drayton, *Nature's Government,* 51–54, on how property, scale, and improvement were linked in the discourses of science and political economy in early modern England.

13. Overton, *Agricultural Revolution in England,* summarizes the copious literature on the processes that transformed English farming.

14. Chambers and Mingay, *The Agricultural Revolution;* Overton, *Agricultural Revolution in England;* Allen, "The Agricultural Revolution."

15. Maxby, *A New Instruction;* Markham, *A Way to Get Wealth;* Hartlib, *His Legacy of Husbandry.*

16. The striking similarities between the cultivation methods and principles of horse-hoeing husbandry advocated by Tull and the principles and practices of northern Chinese tillage systems, described in "Muddy Waters" later in this chapter, suggest that Tull, like other European agronomists of the period, was aware of the accounts of Chinese farming recently published by Jesuit observers; see Bray, *Agriculture,* 558–61.

17. Hobsbawm and Rudé, *Captain Swing.* Drayton, *Nature's Government,* explains how the ideology of improvement through enlightened estate farming and management at scale permeated British colonial policy. Arnold, "Agriculture and 'Improvement' in Early Colonial India," shows that these principles did not easily translate where "native" farming systems were already in place, but the case was different for supposedly unoccupied lands, such as those opened up for tea estates, as we show later in this chapter.

18. Slicher van Bath, *The Agrarian History of Western Europe,* 239.

19. Chambers and Mingay, *The Agricultural Revolution,* 3; Slicher van Bath, *The Agrarian History of Western Europe,* 304.

20. See "Times" on "industrious revolution" in Japan and China.

21. Fussell, "Low Countries' Influence"; Overton, *Agricultural Revolution in England;* on "industrious revolution" see "Rice" in "Times."

22. Allen, "Tracking the Agricultural Revolution."

23. Overton, *Agricultural Revolution in England;* Allen, "Tracking the Agricultural Revolution"; Allen, "The Agricultural Revolution."

24. Young, *A Course of Experimental Agriculture;* Huang, *The Peasant Family;* Landes, *The Wealth and Poverty of Nations;* Mokyr, *The Lever of Riches;* Mokyr, *The Enlightened Economy.*

Notes to Pages 101–104 **267**

25. Peasant grievances against aristocratic landlords helped trigger the French Revolution of 1789. The propertied classes in Britain feared with some reason that the new proletarians, rural and urban, would follow the French example. Signs of revolt were ruthlessly and violently suppressed.

26. Kron, "The Much Maligned Peasant." Not surprisingly, the language and treatment reserved for agricultural laborers were still less obliging. Young was an honorable exception: he generally expressed compassion and understanding for the plight of the rural poor. Hardin, "The Tragedy of the Commons," remains extraordinarily influential in economic thought—the award of the Nobel Prize for Economics to Elinor Ostrom in 2009 for demonstrating how common property could be successfully managed (Ostrom, *Governing the Commons*) caused some astonishment.

27. Toynbee, *Lectures on the Industrial Revolution in England,* 88. Young was Toynbee's main source for the condition and history of British agriculture.

28. Toynbee, *Lectures on the Industrial Revolution in England;* Prothero, Lord Ernle, *Pioneers and Progress;* Overton, *Agricultural Revolution in England,* 3–4; "A weapon ready forged" in "Compositions."

29. Bridger, "The Heirs of Pasha"; Landsberger, "Iron Women and Foxy Ladies." https://chineseposters.net/themes/tractor-girls.php (accessed 5 August 2019).

30. Fitzgerald, "Blinded by Technology," 461–62. Henry Ford played a key role in the drive to industrialize, selling thousands of tractors to the USSR in the 1920s and setting up the first Soviet tractor factory in 1924; Smith, *Works in Progress,* 8.

31. See Smith, *Works in Progress,* for a nuanced account of the failures and successes of Soviet agricultural planning. For more on collectivization and the scaling-up ambitions of the Soviet Great Break of 1928–1930, see "Breeding" in "Reproductions."

32. Hamilton, "Agribusiness, the Family Farm," 577.

33. See also "Rice" in "Times." The earlier Green Revolution in Mexico was more overtly productivist and pro-capitalist, targeting not peasant maize farms but the large wheat farms of the northern states. This was the technological package subsequently exported to Punjab to launch a Green Revolution there; Laveaga, "Largo Dislocare"; Harwood, "Was the Green Revolution Intended to Maximise Food Production?"

34. Fischer, "Why New Crop Technology Is Not Scale-Neutral."

35. Lipton, *Why Poor People Stay Poor;* Harwood, "Was the Green Revolution Intended to Maximise Food Production?"

36. Schumacher, *Small Is Beautiful.*

37. Richards, *Indigenous Agricultural Revolution;* Harwood, *Europe's Green Revolution and Others Since.*

38. Harwood, *Europe's Green Revolution and Others Since,* 141–42.

39. Conway, *The Doubly Green Revolution.*

40. http://www.fao.org/family-farming/decade/en/ Much research has been devoted recently to repeasantization; see for instance Dominguez, "Repeasantization in the Argentina of the 21st Century," and other publications posted on the FAO Family Farming Knowledge Platform, http://www.fao.org/family-farming/detail/en/c/340001/ (accessed 10 June 2019).

41. Nygard, "Seeds of Agribusiness," 26.

42. Friedmann, "World Market, State, and Family Farm"; McLelland, "Social Origins of Industrial Agriculture."

268 Notes to Pages 106–117

43. Whyte, "Introduction," gives an astute and prescient introduction to the complicated social impact of these reforms.
44. "Times," "The Life and Times of the Tobacco Plant."
45. Morgan, "The Labor Problem," 610.
46. Menard, Carr, and Walsh, "A Small Planter's Profits."
47. Galenson, "The Settlement and Growth of the Colonies," 139–40.
48. Craven, *Soil Exhaustion*, 30–39, quotation p. 31.
49. Hening, *The Statutes at Large*, Act V of 1629, 142–43; Morgan, *American Slavery, American Freedom*.
50. See "Times," "The Life and Times of the Tobacco Plant."
51. This offers an interesting parallel with Indian tea varieties, also bred and cultivated to produce the largest possible leaves; see "Tea" later in this chapter.
52. Menard, *Sweet Negotiations*, 4; Brown, *Good Wives, Nasty Wenches*.
53. Richter, *Before the Revolution*, 346–47.
54. Thomas W. Crowder to William Gray, 18 October 1846, William Gray Papers, Virginia Historical Society, Richmond, Va.
55. Woodman, *New South–New Law*.
56. Hahn, *Making Tobacco Bright*.
57. Waltz Maynor, 12 March 2002, oral history interview, in the possession of the author; Hahn, *Making Tobacco Bright*.
58. Hahn, *Making Tobacco Bright*.
59. Finger, *The Tobacco Industry in Transition*.
60. Beck, "Capital Investment Replaces Labor"; Beck, "The Labor Squeeze."
61. For an overview of the global history of coffee mostly from a commodity-chain perspective, see Clarence-Smith and Topik, *The Global Coffee Economy*. For an alternative way of writing global narratives by following plant pathologies, see McCook, *Coffee Is Not Forever*.
62. See "Compositions," "Citrus in the Ruins."
63. Topik and Clarence-Smith, "Introduction," 2.
64. See Matthee, "From Coffee to Tea"; Prange, " 'Measuring by the Bushel' "; Clarence-Smith, "The Spread of Coffee Cultivation."
65. Gago, "Robusta Empire."
66. Topik and Clarence-Smith, "Introduction," 15. See also "Times," "The Social life of Cocoa."
67. McCook, *Coffee Is Not Forever;* Ameha, "Significance of Ethiopian Coffee Genetic Resources." See also "Actants" on nonhuman agents.
68. Saraiva, *Fascist Pigs*, 144–55.
69. Quoted in Saraiva, *Fascist Pigs*, 149.
70. Schaeffer, "Coffee Unobserved."
71. Geoffroy, "La diffusion du café au Proche-Orient arabe."
72. Keall, "The Evolution of the First Coffee Cups."
73. Tuchscherer, "Coffee in the Red Sea."
74. McCann, *People of the Plow*, 53.
75. Ficquet, "Le rituel du café."
76. McCann, *People of the Plow;* Koehler, *Where the Wild Coffee Grows*.
77. McCann, *People of the Plow*, 178.

Notes to Pages 117–132 **269**

78. This is a similar process to the advance of Ghana's cocoa frontier through abusa agreements; see "Times," "Cocoa."
79. McCann, *People of the Plow,* 173–83.
80. Similarly, cotton workers in Portuguese Angola could only afford the time to grow manioc (cassava), not traditional food grains; see "Compositions," "A weapon ready forged."
81. Hauser, *Tea;* Walker, "Memorandum," 11.
82. Scott, *Seeing Like a State,* 262–305.
83. The Java tea plantations were pioneered by the expert Dutch tea taster and merchant J. J. L. L. Jacobson, who imported Chinese seeds, workers, and methods to establish the first tea estate in 1826; Jacobson, *Handboek.*
84. Robertson, "Oral History."
85. Sharma, " 'Lazy' Natives"; Nitin Varma, "Producing Tea Coolies?"
86. Bray, "Translating the Art of Tea."
87. Sharma, " 'Lazy' Natives," 1309.
88. See Bray, "Translating the Art of Tea," on the rocky road to mechanization. For an account of the early machinery, motive-power sources and workshops see Antrobus, *A History of the Assam Company,* 289–304.
89. Although not in China's internal and other export markets; see "Places." On the transformation of British tastes from green to black tea see Ellis, Coulton, and Mauger, *Empire of Tea;* Rappaport, *A Thirst for Empire.*
90. Gupta, "The History of the International Tea Market."
91. Lutgendorf, "Making Tea in India," 15. Between 1929 and 1932 the price of tea at London auctions fell to half the value it was a decade earlier; Gupta, "The History of the International Tea Market," Figure 1.
92. Wittfogel, *Oriental Despotism.* Worster, "Hydraulic Society in California,' "cheekily applies Wittfogel's ideas to twentieth-century California, where the U.S. Bureau of Reclamation played a role equivalent to that of the imperial Bureau of Public Works (*gongbu*).
93. This section draws primarily on Bray, *The Rice Economies.*
94. An illustrated summary of these technologies can be found in Bray, *The Rice Economies,* 68–100. See Lansing, *Priests and Programmers,* on the sophistication and efficiency of the Balinese water-regulation system organized through temples.
95. Chen Fu, *Nongshu,* sec. 1, p. 2.
96. Marks, *Tigers, Rice, Silk, and Silt,* 53.
97. In 2005 UNESCO declared the Jiangnan "Rice-Fish" system a GIAHS (Globally Important Agricultural Heritage System); the "Huzhou Mulberry-Dyke and Fish Pond System," described by Chen Fu, was given GIAHS status in 2017; http://www.fao.org/giahs/giahsaroundtheworld/designated-sites/asia-and-the-pacific/en/ (accessed 4 January 2021), and see "Reproductions," "Reclaiming Waste."
98. See "Times," "Rice."
99. See "Times," "Millet in China."
100. Jia Sixie, *Qimin yaoshu,* 44. See Bray, "Agriculture."
101. Xia Weiying, *Lüshi chunqiu,* 27.
102. King, *Farmers of Forty Centuries;* Diffloth, *Les nouveaux systèmes de culture.*
103. There is a huge literature, from Japanese theories of tight- versus loose-knit societies (Bray, *The Rice Economies;* Ishii, *Thailand: A Rice-Growing Society*) to recent considerations of the

270   Notes to Pages 132–140

group or gender identities, positive or negative, produced by working on water in different circumstances (Linares, "When Jola Granaries Were Full"; Hawthorne, "The Cultural Meaning of Work").

104. For examples of studies by archaeologists, historians, and anthropologists see Leach, *Pul Eliya;* Turner and Harrison, "Prehistoric Raised-Field Agriculture in the Maya Lowlands"; Li, *Agricultural Development in Jiangnan, 1620–1850;* Shah, "Telling Otherwise"; Morrison, "Archaeologies of Flow."

105. Hamilton, "Agribusiness, the Family Farm," 577.

106. Thanks to Alina Cucu for this observation.

CHAPTER 4. ACTANTS

1. Malinowski, *Coral Gardens and Their Magic,* 63. In *How Natives Think* (1910) the philosopher Lucien Lévy-Bruhl proposed that human societies progress from a primitive mindset, which does not follow logic or distinguish between the supernatural and reality, to the modern, logical mindset that resists mystical explanations of how the world works.

2. https://www.nrcs.usda.gov/wps/portal/nrcs/detailfull/national/soils/health/?cid= nrcs142p2_053860 (accessed June 2022).

3. Coupaye, "Ways of Enchanting," 447.

4. Latour, "On Actor-Network Theory," 373, emphases in original.

5. Latour, *Reassembling the Social,* 130.

6. Saraiva, *Fascist Pigs.* "Introduction," n. 80.

7. Gómez, *The Experiential Caribbean;* de Luna, *Collecting Food, Cultivating People;* Mukharji, "Occulted Materialities."

8. Quoted in Tully, *The Devil's Milk,* 86.

9. See, namely, Taussig, *Shamanism, Colonialism, and the Wild Man;* Pineda Camacho, *Holocausto en el Amazonas.* The novelist Mario Vargas Llosa has dealt masterfully with the topic in two novels: Vargas Llosa, *La casa verde;* Vargas Llosa, *El sueño del celta.*

10. Hecht, *The Scramble for the Amazon.*

11. Davis, *Late Victorian Holocausts.*

12. The anthropologist Manuela Carneiro da Cunha offers an original description of the intricate credit scheme that connects the tapper in the forest with myriad intermediaries located in the many branches of the Amazon River, all the way up to the British financial system. Cunha, *Cultura com aspas.*

13. Casement, *The Amazon Journal.*

14. Quoted in Tully, *The Devil's Milk,* 97.

15. Taussig, *Shamanism, Colonialism, and the Wild Man;* Mitchell, *Roger Casement;* Goodman, *The Devil and Mr. Casement.*

16. Hochshild, *King Leopold's Ghost.*

17. Conrad, *Heart of Darkness.*

18. Taussig, "Culture of Terror—Space of Death—Casement, Roger."

19. Taussig, "Culture of Terror—Space of Death—Casement, Roger," 479.

20. Grandin, *Fordlandia;* Garfield, *In Search of the Amazon;* Dean, *Brazil and the Struggle for Rubber.*

21. McCook, "Global Rust Belt."

Notes to Pages 140–150 **271**

22. Ross, *Ecology and Power.*
23. Brockway, *Science and Colonial Expansion: The Role of the British Royal Botanic Gardens;* Drayton, *Nature's Government;* Galeano, *Las venas abiertas de América Latina,* 118–21.
24. Bonneuil, "Mettre en ordre et discipliner les tropiques"; Aso, *Rubber and the Making of Vietnam.*
25. Ross, *Ecology and Power.*
26. Tully, *The Devil's Milk.*
27. Stoler, *Carnal Knowledge and Imperial Power;* Stoler, *Capitalism and Confrontation.*
28. Ross, *Ecology and Power.*
29. Ross, "Developing the Rain Forest," 208, quoting Bauer, *The Rubber Industry.*
30. Dove, "Smallholder Rubber."
31. Cunha, *Cultura com aspas.*
32. Hecht, *The Scramble for the Amazon.*
33. Hecht, "The Last Unfinished Page of Genesis," 62.
34. Hecht, "The Last Unfinished Page of Genesis," 60.
35. Hecht and Cockburn, *The Fate of the Forest;* Revkin, *The Burning Season;* Souza, *O empate contra Chico Mendes.*
36. Cunha, *Cultura com aspas.*
37. For a critical assessment of such narratives see Philip, "Imperial Science Rescues a Tree."
38. Deb Roy, *Malarial Subjects.*
39. Headrick, *The Tools of Empire: Technology and European Imperialism in the Nineteenth Century;* Curtin, "The End of the 'White Man's Grave.' "
40. This point is developed in a sophisticated manner in Deb Roy, *Malarial Subjects.*
41. Crawford, *The Andean Wonder Drug.*
42. Estrella, "Ciencia ilustrada y saber popular."
43. Newson, *Life and Death in Early Colonial Ecuador;* McNeill, *Mosquito Empires.*
44. Crawford, *The Andean Wonder Drug,* 31–32.
45. Crawford, *The Andean Wonder Drug,* 31–32; Newson, *Life and Death in Early Colonial Ecuador,* 55–58.
46. Gómez, *The Experiential Caribbean.*
47. Crawford, *The Andean Wonder Drug.*
48. Crawford, *The Andean Wonder Drug;* Puig-Samper, "El oro amargo."
49. Nieto, *Remedios para el imperio;* Frías, *Tras El Dorado vegetal;* Marcaida and Pimentel, "Green Treasures and Paper Floras"; Puerto, *La ilusión quebrada;* Lafuente, "Enlightenment in an Imperial Context."
50. For a critical overview of the dark legend thesis, see Pimentel and Pardo-Tomás, "And Yet, We Were Modern."
51. Bouza, *Corre manuscrito;* Cañizares-Esguerra, "Bartolomé Inga's Mining Technologies."
52. Crawford, *The Andean Wonder Drug;* Puig-Samper, "El oro amargo"; Frías, *Tras El Dorado vegetal;* Bleichmar, *Visible Empire.*
53. For a critique of such tendencies see Saraiva, "A relevância da história das ciências."
54. Drayton, *Nature's Government,* 206–11.
55. Goss, *The Floracrats.*
56. Goss, "Building the World's Supply of Quinine."

272 Notes to Pages 150–159

57. In spite of the chemists' success in 1944, only in 2001 was quinine fully synthesized. During World War II, the United States organized a new major effort to develop cinchona plantations in South America; Cuvi, "The Cinchona Program (1940–1945)."

58. For a similar approach to indigo, see Kumar, *Indigo Plantations and Science.*

59. In Eduardo Kohn's *How Forests Think,* for example, Amazonian "forests" consist not of plants (which figure in only two pages of the book) but of jaguars, monkeys, were-jaguars, and prospectors; they are the grounds for hunting, not gathering or gardening. In this literature plants fade into a general background of habitat. "The implication is that plants are too far from us to trouble our beliefs in the same way that animals can. A cat staring at Derrida is disconcerting in a way that a geranium is not"; Dove, "Plants, Politics, and the Imagination," S309.

60. Trautmann, *Elephants and Kings;* Kistler, *War Elephants;* Nossov and Dennis, *War Elephants;* Ison, "War Elephants."

61. Trautmann, *Elephants and Kings,* 46.

62. In 1171, "several hundred wild elephants ate the rice plants" in one coastal region of South China; Marks, *Tigers, Rice, Silk, and Silt,* 42. The classic longue durée study of climatic and human contributions to the disappearance of China's elephants is Elvin, *The Retreat of the Elephants.*

63. Trautmann, *Elephants and Kings,* 286.

64. Lahiri, *The Great Indian Elephant Book.*

65. Sivasundaram, "Trading Knowledge."

66. Weatherstone, "Historical Introduction," 11.

67. The geographers and topographers of the Raj also depended on the elephants to "see" the world for them. See Baker, "Trans-Species Colonial Fieldwork."

68. Antrobus, *A History of the Assam Company,* 224.

69. Shell, "When Roads Cannot Be Used," 66.

70. Trautmann, *Elephants and Kings,* 489.

71. Orwell, "Shooting an Elephant."

72. Locke, "Explorations in Ethnoelephantology," 87.

73. Nossov and Dennis, *War Elephants,* 8.

74. Münster, "Working for the Forest," 431.

75. Münster, "Working for the Forest," 435–36.

76. Nossov and Dennis, *War Elephants,* 8.

77. van Schendel, "Geographies of Knowing, Geographies of Ignorance."

78. Shell, "Elephant Convoys beyond the State."

79. Scott, *The Art of Not Being Governed.*

80. "The Boll Weevil Convention," 2, quoted in Baker and Hahn, *The Cotton Kings,* 75–76.

81. Eltis, Morgan, and Richardson, "Agency and Diaspora in Atlantic History."

82. Callon, *The Laws of the Markets;* Callon, Yuval, and Muniesa, *Market Devices.*

83. Beckert, *Empire of Cotton,* 201.

84. Baptist, *The Half Has Never Been Told;* Olmstead and Rhode, "Cotton, Slavery, and the New History of Capitalism."

85. Russell, *Evolutionary History.*

86. Baker and Hahn, *The Cotton Kings,* chap. 4, "Cornering Cotton."

87. Wallace, *Agricultural Prices,* 13.

Notes to Pages 161–172   273

88. Lange, Olmstead, and Rhode, "The Impact of the Boll Weevil"; Giesen, *Boll Weevil Blues.*
89. Woodman, *New South—New Law;* Robins, *Cotton and Race.*
90. Baker and Hahn, "Cotton."
91. Saraiva and Slaton, "Statistics as Service to Democracy."
92. Gilbert, *Planning Democracy.*
93. Daniel, *Breaking the Land.*
94. MacKenzie, *An Engine, Not a Camera.*
95. Serres, "Science and the Humanities."
96. Serres, "Science and the Humanities," 12.
97. Khomami, "Apocalypse Wow."
98. Malm, "The Origins of Fossil Capital," 17.
99. Mitchell, *Carbon Democracy,* 14.
100. Camargo and Pimenta de Castro, *Portugal em chamas.*
101. Haraway, "Anthropocene, Capitalocene"; Moore, "The Capitalocene, Part I."
102. Esser, "Eucalyptus Globulus."
103. Pyne, *Burning Bush.*
104. Radich and Alves, *Dois séculos da floresta em Portugal.*
105. Bennett, "A Global History of Australian Trees"; Tyrrell, *True Gardens of the Gods;* Beattie, "Imperial Landscape of Health"; Silva-Pando and Pino-Pérez, "Introduction of Eucalyptus into Europe."
106. On forests and fascism, see Brüggemeier, Cioc, and Zeller, *How Green Were the Nazis?;* Armiero and von Hardenberg, "Green Rhetoric in Blackshirts"; Saraiva, "Fascist Modernist Landscapes."
107. See also the section on cotton and manioc in Mozambique in "Compositions."
108. The best account of these processes is the novel by Ribeiro, *When the Wolves Howl.*
109. The proliferation of eucalyptus in other countries of the Global South, such as Chile and Brazil, in the second half of the twentieth century is also connected to the use of the tree in paper-pulp production.
110. Russell, "Coevolutionary History," 1515; Russell, *Greyhound Nation.*
111. LeCain, *The Matter of History.*
112. Gómez, "Caribbean Stones and the Creation of Early-Modern Worlds," 16.
113. Gómez, *The Experiential Caribbean,* 3, xvii–xix.
114. de Luna, "Inciteful Language," 47; de Luna, "Compelling Vansina," 172.
115. Gille, "Actor Networks, Modes of Production, and Waste Regimes," 1060.
116. Haraway, *The Companion Species Manifesto;* Haraway, *When Species Meet.*
117. Raffles, *Insectopedia,* 4.

CHAPTER 5. COMPOSITIONS

1. *Suoshan nongpu* (Account of the agriculture of Suo Mountain), quoted Bray, *Agriculture,* 1984, 506.
2. Bray and Métailié, "Who Was the Author of the *Nongzheng quanshu?*" Xu is famous today as a polymath statesman who "served as Grand Secretary of the empire, led an astronomical reform, translated Western scientific books [including Euclid's *Elements*], renovated the army, compiled an important treatise on agriculture, and was a Christian convert"; Jami, Engelfriet, and Blue, "Introduction," 1.

274 Notes to Pages 172–180

3. We find a curious parallel in George Washington Carver's recuperation of Southern swamps; see "Reproductions," "Wastings."

4. Xu Guangqi, *Nongzheng quanshu*, 1299; 1299–1309 for the full locust-control study.

5. By the 1590s sweet potatoes had been quite widely adopted in South China (see later in this chapter) but were still regarded with suspicion in the Yangtze region.

6. The proliferation of famine food (*jiuhuang*) treatises after 1400 is discussed in Needham and Lu, "The Esculentist Movement." On how agrarian policies and definitions evolved, see von Glahn, *Economic History*. On the statecraft dimensions of Xu's farming model and how he saw its contributions to the economy and the defense of the nation, see Bray and Métailié, "Who Was the Author of the *Nongzheng Quanshu?*"

7. Bray and Métailié, "Who Was the Author of the *Nongzheng Quanshu?*" 338.

8. On Qing policies toward risk management and attention to marginal zones as part of the broader cropscape see Marks, "It Never Used to Snow," and the other studies in Elvin and Liu, *Sediments of Time*.

9. Bubandt and Tsing, "Feral Dynamics of Post-Industrial Ruin," 6.

10. Tsing, Mathews, and Bubandt, "Patchy Anthropocene," S186.

11. The discussion of Hercule Florence's watercolor follows Marquese, "Exilio escravista."

12. Schwartz, *Segredos internos;* Alencastro, *O trato dos viventes;* Curtin, *The Rise and Fall of the Plantation Complex.*

13. Dean, *With Broadax and Firebrand;* Pádua, *Um sopro de destruição.*

14. Marquese, "Exilio escravista."

15. Marquese, "Capitalismo, escravidão e a economia."

16. Matos, *Café e ferrovias.*

17. Lévi-Strauss, *Tristes tropiques*, 93.

18. Saraiva, "Anthropophagy and Sadness."

19. For a similar dynamic in the Rio de Janeiro area see Pereira, *Cana, café e laranja.*

20. Hasse, *A laranja no Brasil.*

21. Pereira, *Cana, café e laranja;* Saraiva, "Anthropophagy and Sadness"; Hasse, *A laranja no Brasil.*

22. Salaman, *The History and Social Influence of the Potato.* Salaman was not a professional historian; his emphasis on the social dimensions of crop botany derived from long-term experience as director of the Potato Virus Research Institute at Cambridge; Berry, "Plants Are Technologies."

23. Salaman, *The History and Social Influence of the Potato,* 206, emphasis added.

24. McNeill, "How the Potato Changed the World's History," 67.

25. Spary, *Feeding France;* Saraiva, *Fascist Pigs;* Earle, "Food, Colonialism and the Quantum of Happiness"; Earle, "Promoting Potatoes in Eighteenth-Century Europe"; Earle, *Feeding the People.*

26. Karasch, "Manioc," 186.

27. Thanks to the popularity of fries and chips, today there is a huge global trade in white potatoes, exported almost entirely in processed form; other tubers like cassava have gained global markets primarily as animal feed or industrial starch (FAO, *World Food and Agriculture*).

28. Mazumdar, *Sugar and Society.*

29. Ho, "The Introduction of American Food Plants into China"; the sweet potato also followed an overland route into China through Yunnan, in the southwest.

Notes to Pages 180–184 **275**

30. Xu Guangqi planted experimental gardens and wrote a treatise on the sweet potato as early as the 1590s (Xu Guangqi, *Nongzheng quanshu,* 688–95).

31. Cheung, "A Desire to Eat Well."

32. On tea as a smallholder industry in China see "Places." On sugar see Mazumdar, *Sugar and Society;* Daniels, *Agro-Industries;* Marks, *Tigers, Rice, Silk, and Silt;* Sabban, "L'industrie sucrière." In around 1640 Japan imported almost three thousand tons of Chinese sugar, transported by Chinese ships, and about one thousand tons of Chinese powdered sugar went to Amsterdam. Seeing the rich profits to be made, the Dutch sponsored sugar cultivation and manufacture in Taiwan, which started exporting sugar to Europe in 1636, and in Batavia, where sugar began to replace pepper after 1650; Mazumdar, *Sugar and Society,* 80–86.

33. Mazumdar, *Sugar and Society,* 100–105.

34. Barickman, *A Bahian Counterpoint;* Carney and Rosomoff, *In the Shadow of Slavery.*

35. See for example Alpern, "Exotic Plants of Western Africa"; McCann, "Maize and Grace."

36. On farinha and cassava cultivation along the Angola coast, first documented in 1608, see Karasch, "Manioc," 183–84; von Oppen, "Cassava, 'the Lazy Man's Food'?" 19. On the introduction of cassava to Mozambique by its governor in 1768 see Bastião, "Entre a Ilha e a Terra: Processos de construção do continente fronteiro à Ilha de Moçambique (1763–c. 1802)."

37. On cassava in the formation and expansion of the Lunda Empire in the Congo Basin and Upper Zambezi, see von Oppen, "Cassava, 'the Lazy Man's Food'?" Von Oppen suggests that environmental conditions, climatic uncertainty, and frequent conflict were likely factors in the initial Lunda adoption of cassava and explains how by the nineteenth century local cassava cultivation integrated the region into long-distance trade, provisioning caravans transporting "slaves, ivory, beeswax and wild rubber for export" (von Oppen, 28).

38. Carter et al., *Introduction and Diffusion of Cassava in Africa;* Juhé-Beaulaton, "De l'igname au manioc dans le golfe de Guinée"; Bradbury et al., "Geographic Differences in Patterns of Genetic Differentiation among Bitter and Sweet Manioc (*Manihot esculenta* subsp. *esculenta*; *Euphorbiaceae*)"; Domingos, "Na pista da mandioca colonial e pós-colonial." On railroads and the spread of cassava in West Africa see Iwuagwu, "The Spread of Cassava."

39. Isaacman, "Peasants, Work and the Labor Process"; Domingos, "Na pista da mandioca colonial e pós-colonial." The classic in this field, documenting the interdependence of mining, migrant labor, and feminized subsistence farming, is Richards, *Land, Labour and Diet in Northern Rhodesia.*

40. Salaman, *The History and Social Influence of the Potato,* 101; Earle, *The Body of the Conquistador;* Domingos, "Na pista da mandioca colonial e pós-colonial," 332.

41. Engels, *The Condition of the Working Class in England in 1844,* 88–89, emphasis added.

42. Barickman, "A Bit of Land, Which They Call Roça"; Carney and Rosomoff, *In the Shadow of Slavery.* Tuber and other cash crops sometimes enabled escaped slaves and other groups resisting colonial encroachment to evade the authorities. In Mozambique, for example, it was claimed that soon after the Portuguese introduced manioc, in the late eighteenth century, unruly "cafres" used the crop to set up autonomous zones from which they traded gold and ivory; Domingos, "Na pista da mandioca colonial e pós-colonial," 326.

43. Mintz, *Tasting Food, Tasting Freedom,* 43.

276 Notes to Pages 184–188

44. Hazareesingh and Maat, *Local Subversions of Colonial Cultures.*

45. Spary, *Feeding France;* Earle, *Feeding the People.*

46. Smith, *The Wealth of Nations,* vol. 1, 161–62; Young, *A Tour in Ireland,* vol. 2, 32.

47. McNeill argues that the adoption of potatoes was an innovation spearheaded by monarchs like Frederick the Great, primarily in response to famines and to wartime pillaging of standing crops; McNeill, "How the Potato Changed the World's History." Earle counters that potatoes were widely grown but had simply attracted little favor from elites; the change was due in large measure to new ideas about food and governance; Earle, "Promoting Potatoes in Eighteenth-Century Europe."

48. Curtler, *A Short History of English Agriculture.*

49. Spary, *Feeding France.*

50. Earle, *Feeding the People,* 5–6.

51. See Fussell, review of *The History and Social Influence of the Potato,* 263, on enclosures, farm wages and the shift to potatoes.

52. This despite the efforts of the National Agricultural Labourers' Union, founded by Joseph Arch in 1872.

53. *The Labourers' Friend,* n.s., 86 (1851), 113, quoted Burchardt, "Land and the Laborer," 682; Leivers, "The Provision of Allotments in Derbyshire Industrial Communities."

54. Interspecies synergies are a principal focus of recent anthropological work on the dynamics of "landscapes" in the "patchy anthropocene" (discussed further later in this chapter); Tsing, Mathews, and Bubandt, "Patchy Anthropocene."

55. James C. Scott argues that these practices of sorting and standardization, essential to the domestication of cereals, also domesticated people as well as plants, molding the forms and institutions of state systems; Scott, *Against the Grain.* We return to weeds later in this chapter.

56. Commercial U.S. bee operators may own more than eighty thousand hives, rented out for a succession of crops across the country and throughout the year.

57. Thompson, "The Second Agricultural Revolution," 65.

58. Thompson, "The Second Agricultural Revolution"; Thirsk, *Alternative Agriculture;* Harwood, *Europe's Green Revolution and Others Since;* and see "Reproductions," "Crop Diversity and Pure Lines."

59. We return to this trend in "Wasting," the final section of "Reproductions."

60. Legumes, including pulses ("small beans" in classical Chinese) and soybeans ("great beans"), were known to increase soil fertility and improve its texture. We now know that this is because the nodules that form on the root systems of legumes contain *Rhizobia,* nitrogen-fixing bacteria.

61. As discussed in "Times," the hardy foxtail millet (*Setaria italica*) was the chief food staple in North China. Panicled or broomcorn millet (*Panicum miliaceum*) was also popular but less productive. Glutinous varieties of all cereals were used for brewing, but panicled millet was considered to make the best wines or beers.

62. Jia Sixie, *Qimin yaoshu,* 111.

63. King, *Farmers of Forty Centuries;* Ford and Nigh, *The Maya Forest Garden.*

64. Mol, *The Logic of Care;* Puig de la Bellacasa, " 'Nothing Comes without Its World.' "

65. Haraway, *When Species Meet;* van Dooren, "Invasive Species in Penguin Worlds."

66. Ortiz, *Cuban Counterpoint,* 6–7, emphases added. And see "Orientations."

67. Ortiz, *Cuban Counterpoint,* 60, 303–4.

68. "Plantations create monocrops to make it possible for coerced and alienated labor—and more recently, machines—to tend crops without the care that farming otherwise requires"; Tsing, Mathews, and Bubandt, "Patchy Anthropocene," S189.

69. Puig de la Bellacasa, "Making Time for Soil," 699, 700, 703; Hartigan, "Plants as Ethnographic Subjects."

70. Both discussed in "Times." Tsai, "Farming Odd Kin in Patchy Anthropocenes," discusses a contemporary instance of the duck-snail-fish-rice collective.

71. What follows is based on Ford and Nigh, *The Maya Forest Garden*. In milpa "'slashing' is equivalent to coppicing, pollarding, and pruning" (Ford and Nigh, 18).

72. Landon, "The 'How' of the Three Sisters."

73. Ford and Nigh, *The Maya Forest Garden*, 121, 112–13.

74. See "Reproductions," "Wastings"; Radio Zapatista, "Los rostros (no tan) ocultos del mal llamado 'Tren Maya.' "

75. Bray, *Agriculture*, 1984, 429–33.

76. Bray, "Agriculture," 2019.

77. White, "Fallowing, Crop Rotation, and Crop Yields in Roman Times."

78. Kron, "Agriculture, Roman Empire," 217.

79. Kron, "Agriculture, Roman Empire," 217–19.

80. Slicher van Bath, *The Agrarian History of Western Europe*, 282.

81. Feudal claims to grazing were a prominent item in the *Cahiers de doléances* collected just before the 1789 Revolution; e.g., https://books.openedition.org/irhis/927?lang=en

82. Still common practice in Spain and Catalunya.

83. Brisebarre, *Bergers des Cévennes;* Daugstad, Mier, and Peña-Chocarro, "Landscapes of Transhumance in Norway and Spain."

84. We use "corn" here as the generic term for a region's staple grains. In medieval and early modern Europe these included wheat, barley, rye, oats, and the mixed crops of cereals and pulses (maslin) that were frequently planted to reduce the risk of harvest failure. When the English encountered American maize they called it "Indian corn."

85. Thompson, "The Second Agricultural Revolution," 64.

86. Slicher van Bath, *The Agrarian History of Western Europe*, 281.

87. Slicher van Bath, *The Agrarian History of Western Europe*, 296, 284.

88. Chambers and Mingay, *The Agricultural Revolution*, 54–76.

89. Allen, "The Agricultural Revolution," 60.

90. The class relations underpinning the New Husbandry are less appealing today. On the impact of enclosures and the exploitation of farmworkers, see for instance Devine, *The Scottish Clearances.*

91. Thompson, "The Second Agricultural Revolution," 65.

92. Quoted Clark and Foster, "Ecological Imperialism and the Global Metabolic Rift," 322, 316, 315.

93. Standard plant patents (for commercial hybrids, for instance) allow purchasers to reuse seed as long as they don't circulate or sell it. On the battles around GM crops, Roundup, and Monsanto see Bray, "Genetically Modified Foods."

94. Beinart and Middleton, "Plant Transfers in Historical Perspective: A Review Article," 17–18. Oats and rye are the classic examples; Harlan and de Wet, "Some Thoughts about Weeds." See also Beinart and Wotshela, *Prickly Pear*, 3, on "why a wild and sometimes invasive plant from Mexico remained important to African women."

95. Dove, "Plants, Politics, and the Imagination," S310.

96. Dove, "Plants, Politics, and the Imagination," S311, Figure 1.

97. Fullilove, *The Profit of the Earth*, 2017, 151.

98. Dove, "Obituary: Harold C. Conklin," 3.

99. Dove, "Plants, Politics, and the Imagination," S314, quoting tropical agronomists.

100. U.S. Department of the Interior, Definitions Subcommittee of the Invasive Species Advisory Committee, "Invasive Species Definition Clarification and Guidance."

101. For rats as an invasive species, see McNeill, "Of Rats and Men."

102. Vieyra-Odilon and Vibrans, "Weeds as Crops."

103. Morita, "Multispecies Infrastructure," 748–49. The classic work on smallholder experimental seed breeding, often involving crossing cultivars with wild or feral varieties, is Richards, *Indigenous Agricultural Revolution*.

104. Kaplan, "Historical and Ethnobotanical Aspects of Domestication in Tagetes." *Tagetes erecta, lucida,* and *patula* are the species most commonly cultivated.

105. Neher, "The Ethnobotany of Tagetes," 321; Vasudevan, Kashyap, and Sharma, "Tagetes."

106. Neher, "The Ethnobotany of Tagetes," Table 1, 318–21.

107. Kaplan, "Historical and Ethnobotanical Aspects of Domestication in Tagetes," 201.

108. Kaplan, "Historical and Ethnobotanical Aspects of Domestication in Tagetes," 200–201.

109. Hyde, "Cultivated Power," 173, 328.

110. Herbert, *Flora's Empire*, 2–6; Goody, *The Culture of Flowers*, 327–46.

111. Neher, "The Ethnobotany of Tagetes," 321.

112. Curry, "Making Marigolds."

113. Šivel et al., "Lutein Content in Marigold Flower," 521.

114. Lim, "Tagetes erecta."

115. See Uekötter, *Comparing Apples, Oranges, and Cotton,* for global examples, and Bonneuil and Fressoz, *The Shock of the Anthropocene,* 170–79, chap. 8, "The Phronocene," for European cases of this debate.

116. Moore, "The Capitalocene Part II."

117. Scott, *Against the Grain;* Fullilove, *The Profit of the Earth,* 2017.

118. Ortiz, *Cuban Counterpoint,* 102–3, xli.

119. Letter to Malinowski, 9 April 1940, quoted Santí, "Towards a Reading of Fernando Ortiz's Cuban Counterpoint," 10, emphases added.

120. Norton, *Sacred Gifts, Profane Pleasures.*

121. Fitzgerald, "Blinded by Technology"; Smith, *Works in Progress.*

122. Li, *Land's End;* Dove, "Plants, Politics, and the Imagination"; Abazue et al., "Oil Palm Smallholders and Its Sustainability Practices in Malaysia"; Pakiam, Khor, and Chia, "Johor's Oil Palm Industry."

123. Meillassoux, *Maidens, Meal, and Money;* Palat, "Dependency Theory"; Dove, "Plants, Politics, and the Imagination," S319.

124. Tsing, Mathews, and Bubandt, "Patchy Anthropocene"; Bonneuil and Fressoz, *The Shock of the Anthropocene;* Haraway, "Anthropocene, Capitalocene"; LeCain, "Against the Anthropocene: A Neo-Materialist Perspective."

125. Bonneuil and Fressoz, *The Shock of the Anthropocene;* Haraway, "Anthropocene, Capitalocene"; LeCain, "Against the Anthropocene: A Neo-Materialist Perspective."

Notes to Pages 207–214 **279**

CHAPTER 6. REPRODUCTIONS

1. *The Palm Tree* (770 C.E.), translation after Poitou, *Spain and Its People,* 506.
2. As we saw in "Times," date palm cultivation was in fact mostly done by reproducing offshoots, not seeds.
3. Watson, "The Arab Agricultural Revolution and Its Diffusion, 700–1100"; Decker, "Plants and Progress"; Avni, "Early Islamic Irrigated Farmsteads and the Spread of Qanats in Eurasia," 329.
4. For a strong argument for the historiographical benefits of integrating history of technology perspectives into such projects as the history of biology, see Berry, "Historiography of Plant Breeding and Agriculture."
5. This section presents a shortened version of an argument fully developed in Saraiva, "Breeding Europe."
6. For a detailed description of the vault and its functions and purposes see Fowler, "The Svalbard Global Seed Vault."
7. For critical histories of the urge to conserve biodiversity, see Fenzi and Bonneuil, "From 'Genetic Resources' to 'Ecosystems Services' "; Curry, *Endangered Maize.*
8. For the problems with the use of this term when referring to crop diversity see Ash, "Plants, Patents and Power."
9. Plucknett and Smith, *Gene Banks and the World's Food,* 8–12.
10. For an informed discussion of the challenges facing Europe concerning the erosion of its traditional agricultural diversity see Veteläinen, Negri, and Maxted, *European Landraces.*
11. Vellvé, *Saving the Seed,* 53–59.
12. Similar attention to the technologies of seedbanks can be found in Curry, "From Working Collections to the World Germplasm"; Fullilove, *The Profit of the Earth.* Seed-saver networks, in contrast, typically rely on "paper bags, jars, an ice-cream tub and a pencil for labelling" as the "essential tools for the trade"; Turner, "Plotting the Future."
13. Gayon and Zallen, "The Role of the Vilmorin Company"; Bonneuil, "Mendelism, Plant Breeding and Experimental Cultures."
14. Landraces are currently defined as dynamic populations of cultivated plants with historical origins, distinct identities, and lack of formal crop improvement. They are often genetically diverse, locally adapted, and associated with traditional farming systems; see Hammer and Diederichsen, "Evolution, Status and Perspectives."
15. Bonneuil, "Mendelism, Plant Breeding and Experimental Cultures," 17.
16. Vellvé, *Saving the Seed,* 30–31.
17. Lehmann, "Collecting European Land-Races."
18. For a global history of such expeditions see Flitner, *Sammler, Räuber und Gelehrte.*
19. Lokustov, *Vavilov and His Institute;* Pringle, *The Murder of Nikolai Vavilov.*
20. Lokustov, *Vavilov and His Institute,* 82–83.
21. Lokustov, *Vavilov and His Institute,* 84–90.
22. Lokustov, *Vavilov and His Institute,* 85.
23. Flitner, "Genetic Geographies."
24. He was arrested and charged with espionage in 1940 and died in prison of malnutrition in 1943; Joravsky, *The Lysenko Affair.*

280   Notes to Pages 214–224

25. Roll-Hansen, *The Lysenko Effect*. For a general view of the Soviet organization of scientific research see Krementsov, *Stalinist Science*.

26. Harris, "Vavilov's Concept of Centers of Origin."

27. Lafuente and Valverde, "The Emergence of Early Modern Commons."

28. Harwood, "The Fate of Peasant-Friendly Plant Breeding."

29. Saraiva, "Breeding Europe," 194.

30. Baur, "Die Bedeutung der primitiven Kulturrassen"; Flitner, *Sammler, Räuber und Gelehrte.*

31. Kater, *Das Ahnenerbe der SS.*

32. On these institutions see Deichmann, *Biologists under Hitler,* 214–18 and 258–64; Gausemeier, "Genetics as a Modernization Program."

33. Quoted by Susanne Heim in Elina, Heim, and Roll-Hansen, "Plant Breeding on the Front," 167.

34. Knüpffer, "The Balkan Collections 1941–42 of Hans Stubbe."

35. Saraiva, *Fascist Pigs*; Heim, *Kalorien, Kautschuk, Karrieren.*

36. For example Kloppenburg, *First the Seed*. For a critical view of Green Revolution literature, see Kumar et al., "Roundtable."

37. Curry, "From Working Collections to the World Germplasm."

38. Saraiva, "Breeding Europe."

39. Ferments were also made from sprouting barley, steamed millets or rice, soybeans, or the mash left from brewing.

40. Jia Sixie, *Qimin yaoshu,* 358, translated Huang, *Fermentations and Food Science,* 170–71.

41. Huang, *Fermentations and Food Science,* 376–77.

42. Francks, "Consuming Rice," 152; Francks, *The Japanese Consumer.*

43. Morris-Suzuki, *The Technological Transformation of Japan,* 32.

44. Lee, "The Microbial Production of Expertise," 174.

45. Walker, "Commercial Growth and Environmental Change in Early Modern Japan"; Francks, "Consuming Rice"; Victoria Lee, "The Microbial Production of Expertise."

46. Cwiertka, *Modern Japanese Cuisine.*

47. Ohnuki-Tierney, *Rice as Self.*

48. Shurtleff and Aoyagi, "History of Kikkoman."

49. Lee, "Mold Cultures," 233–34.

50. Lee, "The Microbial Production of Expertise." The fact that Japanese brewers had traditionally thought of their work with molds as a form of interspecies collaboration "helped to shape a relatively autonomous and lasting scientific tradition of seeing microbes as living workers as much as pathogens in Japan"; "Mold Cultures," 231.

51. In 2011 Kikkoman scientists, working with three public institutes, sequenced the genome of their *kōji;* https://www.kikkoman.com/en/news/2011news/05.html (accessed 16 November 2020).

52. https://www.oishisojapan.com/home/2018/6/28/yamaroku-soy-sauce (accessed 16 November 2020).

53. Pereira, *O Douro e o vinho do Porto: De Pombal a João Franco;* Jacquinet, "Technological, Institutional and Market Structure Changes as Evolutionary Processes." The earliest sources date back to the mid-seventeenth century. One important documented change was the evolution of the bottle, which took its final shape between

about 1800 and 1820 (Jacquinet, 191–92). Most of the technical information from early sources deals with cultivation and pressing techniques.

54. Martins, *Tudo sobre o vinho do Porto.*

55. Duguid, "Networks and Knowledge," 520.

56. Marquis of Villa Maior, 1876, quoted by Domingues and Sotto Mayor, *Douro à la carte,* 86.

57. Andrade Martins, *Memória do vinho do Porto;* Barreto, "O vinho do Porto e a intervenção do Estado."

58. Pereira, "O vinho do Porto," 185–91.

59. Castello Branco, *O vinho do Porto, processo d'uma bestialidade inglesa,* 10.

60. Macedo, *A situação económica no tempo de Pombal;* Pereira, *Livre câmbio e desenvolvimento económico.*

61. Macedo, *Projectar e construir a nação.*

62. Although the technical procedures differ, many famous brands of champagne, sherry, or whisky also use blending of wines or liquors from several years or provenances to ensure homogeneity.

63. The exception is vintage ports. The bottles are labeled with their year and place of origin (usually a single *quinta*). These fine ports, which are not blended, will be sold at high prices as *vintage port* identified by the year of the harvest

64. Capela, *O vinho para o preto,* 24.

65. Correia, *A industrialização da castanha de cajú,* 27.

66. Gille, "Actor Networks, Modes of Production, and Waste Regimes"; Gille, *From the Cult of Waste to the Trash Heap of History.*

67. Quoted Penvenne, *Women, Migration and the Cashew Economy,* 34.

68. Thevet, *Les singularitez de la France antarctique,* 318–19. Thevet's account of cannibalism was one of several that inspired Montaigne's essay on the subject.

69. Correia, *A industrialização da castanha de cajú,* 21.

70. Among those arguing the case of soil-erosion control are Morton, "The Cashew's Brighter Future," in 1961, and, in 2008, Asogwa, Hammed, and Ndubuaku, "Integrated Production and Protection Practices of Cashew (*Anacardium occidentale*) in Nigeria." The criticism of anachronism comes from Johnson, "The Botany, Origin, and Spread of the Cashew," 5.

71. Meaney-Leckie, "The Cashew Industry of Ceará, Brazil," 318; Blazdell, "The Mighty Cashew," 221–22 and Table 1.

72. Johnson, "The Botany, Origin, and Spread of the Cashew," 5–6; Correia, *A industrialização da castanha de cajú,* 45.

73. Morton, "The Cashew's Brighter Future," 68.

74. Deepa, "Industrial Crisis and Women Workers: A Study of Cashew Processing in Kerala," 34, 35.

75. Cantrell, *Cashew Nuts,* 1.

76. Cantrell, *Cashew Nuts,* 22.

77. Langley, *Century in Malabar,* 58; Cantrell, *Cashew Nuts,* 1–2.

78. Langley, *Century in Malabar,* 56; Abeyagunawardena, "Lessons for the Cashew Industry"; Blazdell, "The Mighty Cashew," 222.

79. Lindberg, *Modernization and Effeminization in India,* 28; Harilal et al., "Power in Global Value Chains," 14.

282 Notes to Pages 233–241

80. Harilal et al., "Power in Global Value Chains," 14.

81. Langley, *Century in Malabar,* 54, quoted Lindberg, *Modernization and Effeminization in India,* 33.

82. Lindberg, *Modernization and Effeminization in India*; Harilal et al., "Power in Global Value Chains"; Penvenne, *Women, Migration and the Cashew Economy.*

83. Penvenne, *Women, Migration and the Cashew Economy,* 40.

84. Harilal et al., "Power in Global Value Chains," 12; Meaney-Leckie, "The Cashew Industry of Ceará, Brazil," 320.

85. E.g., Deepa, "Industrial Crisis and Women Workers: A Study of Cashew Processing in Kerala"; Lindberg, *Modernization and Effeminization in India*; Harilal et al., "Power in Global Value Chains"; Penvenne, "Seeking the Factory for Women"; Penvenne, *Women, Migration and the Cashew Economy.* Penvenne also published her study as a Portuguese open-access translation, dedicated to the Mozambican women who contributed so much to her research; Penvenne, *Tarana.*

86. Hersey, *My Work Is That of Conservation.*

87. Hersey, *My Work Is That of Conservation,* 126.

88. For discussion of the global significance of the Tuskegee Institute see Zimmerman, *Alabama in Africa.* On the significance of George Washington Carver's example for black technical education in the United States see Slaton, "George Washington Carver Slept Here."

89. Du Bois, *The Souls of Black Folk,* 46.

90. Du Bois, *The Souls of Black Folk,* 117.

91. Carver, *How to Build Up Worn Out Soils,* 4–5.

92. Address at the Atlanta Exposition, 1895.

93. Rossiter, *The Emergence of Agricultural Science;* Ferleger, "Uplifting American Agriculture"; Whayne, "Black Farmers and the Agricultural Cooperative Extension Service."

94. Finlay, "Old Efforts at New Uses." Today the chemurgy project lives on as "green" research on transforming crop waste into industrial "bio-resources"; see Mgaya et al., "Cashew Nut Shell."

95. Finlay, "Old Efforts at New Uses," 34.

96. "Ford Shows Auto Built of Plastic," *New York Times,* 14 August 1941.

97. Katznelson, *Fear Itself,* 86.

98. Du Bois in the April 1934 issue of his journal *Crisis* quoted Kendi, *Stamped from the Beginning,* 339.

99. In Joseph Heller's caricature of the policy, "[Major Major's father's] specialty was alfalfa, and he made a good thing out of not growing any. The government paid him well for every bushel of alfalfa he did not grow. The more alfalfa he did not grow, the more money the government gave him, and he spent every penny he didn't earn on new land to increase the amount of alfalfa he did not produce"; Heller, *Catch-22,* 86.

100. Bennet and Pryor, *This Land We Defend,* 80; Maher, "A New Deal Body Politic."

101. FAO, *The State of the World's Biodiversity;* http://www.fao.org/giahs/en/ (accessed 22 February 2019).

102. Scott, *The Art of Not Being Governed;* FAO, *World Food and Agriculture,* vii.

103. FAO, *World Food and Agriculture.*

104. The classic critique here is Boserup, *Woman's Role in Economic Development.*

Notes to Pages 241–247 **283**

105. FAO, *The State of the World's Biodiversity*, 373. On the gendered expectations of participatory plant breeding, see Galié, "Empowering Women Farmers."
106. Harwood, *Europe's Green Revolution and Others Since*, 141–42.
107. China currently has fifteen GIAHS sites, more than any other nation, with five more under consideration; Japan comes second with eleven sites.
108. Bray, "The Craft of Mud-Making."
109. Schmalzer, *Red Revolution, Green Revolution;* Perry, "From Mass Campaigns to Managed Campaigns."
110. Schneider, "Dragon Head Enterprises"; Luo, Andreas, and Li, "Grapes of Wrath."
111. Zhang, Chen, and Vitousek, "An Experiment for the World"; Xue et al., "Rural Reform in Contemporary China."
112. Chang, "Environing at the Margins," 4–5.
113. Third World Network, https://www.twn.my/title2/susagri/2017/sa598.htm (accessed 21 November 2020).
114. Guo, García-Martín, and Plieninger, "Recognizing Indigenous Farming Practices for Sustainability."
115. http://www.fao.org/giahs/giahsaroundtheworld/designated-sites/asia-and-the-pacific/wannian-traditional-rice-culture/detailed-information/en/ (accessed 21 November 2020).
116. Fletcher, "The Time Is Ripe for Rice-Fish Culture."
117. Agricultural Heritage, https://www.agriculturalheritage.com/fao-giahs-programme-2/ (accessed 23 November 2020). On the political contradictions inherent in a century of projects to conserve biodiversity through seeds and their farming systems on different scales, see Fenzi and Bonneuil, "From 'Genetic Resources' to 'Ecosystems Services.' "
118. Harrell, "China's Tangled Web of Heritage," on the ambiguities of heritage preservation.
119. *Resistencia autónoma*, first-grade textbook for the course "La libertad según l@s Zapatistas," https://radiozapatista.org/?page_id=20294 (accessed June 2022); Hernández, Perales, and Jaffee, " 'Without Food There Is No Resistance' "; "Los rostros (no tan) ocultos."
120. Bray, *Technology and Gender*; Edgerton, *The Shock of the Old;* Slaton, *Reinforced Concrete;* Saraiva, *Fascist Pigs*; Jones-Imhotep, *The Unreliable Nation.*
121. To cite just two influential publications from this huge field, see Strathern, *Reproducing the Future;* Clarke and Haraway, *Making Kin Not Population.* For a survey of the politics of procreative technologies in modern and contemporary East Asia, see Bray, "Introduction."
122. Bray, *Technology and Gender*, 212–25; Hahn, *Making Tobacco Bright*, 2011, 129–47; Saraiva, *Fascist Pigs*, 21–42.
123. de Luna, *Collecting Food, Cultivating People*, 1.
124. A cropscape-based approach to race and class formation echoed later by Williams, *Capitalism and Slavery;* Mintz, *Sweetness and Power;* Sharma, " 'Lazy' Natives, Coolie Labour, and the Assam Tea Industry"; and many others.
125. Du Bois, *Black Reconstruction.* On the Black radical tradition see Robinson, *Black Marxism;* Jenkins and Leroy, *Histories of Racial Capitalism.*

EPILOGUE

1. In the sense of *sala polivalent*—the Catalan or Iberian term for a multifunctional space where many sports can be played.
2. Conrad and Osterhammel, *An Emerging Modern World;* Parker, *Global Crisis;* Beckert, *Empire of Cotton.*
3. This point about the problematic politics of historiography has been highlighted by global historians themselves. See, for example, Conrad, *What Is Global History?* 214–19.
4. Subrahmanyam, *Faut-il universaliser l'histoire?*
5. White, *Metahistory.*
6. Chen, "The Case of Bingata"; Shen, "Cultivating China's Cinchona"; Norton, *Sacred Gifts, Profane Pleasures;* Gómez, *The Experiential Caribbean;* de Luna, *Collecting Food, Cultivating People;* Green, *A Fistful of Shells.*
7. Smith, "Amidst Things," 853.
8. The first published fruits of this collective can be found at http://www.technologystories .org/category/no-1-the-republic-of-plants/ (accessed 14 July 2021).
9. "Recipes for Resilience", http://www.caribbeanfood4climate.com/ (accessed 7 June 2022); NRAS (Network of Rural and Agrarian Studies), http://www. ruralagrarianstudies.org/ (accessed 7 June 2022); Tsing, *The Mushroom at the End of the World.*
10. Chatterjee, "Our Past as Our Future."

Bibliography

Abazue, C. M., A. C. Er, A. S. A. Ferdous Alam, and Halima Begum. "Oil Palm Smallholders and Its Sustainability Practices in Malaysia." *Mediterranean Journal of Social Sciences* 6, no. 54 (2015): 482–88. https://doi.org/10.5901/mjss.2015.v6n6s4p482.

Abeyagunawardena, Chandani Dias. "Lessons for the Cashew Industry." *Daily News,* 17 March 2003. http://archives.dailynews.lk/2003/03/17/bus04.html.

Akrich, Madeleine. "A Gazogene in Costa Rica: An Experiment in Techno-Sociology." In *Technological Choices,* edited by Pierre Lemonnier, 289–337. London: Routledge, 1993.

Alder, Ken. "Thick Things: Introduction." *Isis* 98, no. 1 (1 March 2007): 80–83. https://doi.org/10.1086/512832.

Alencastro, Luiz Felipe de. *O trato dos viventes: Formação do Brasil no Atlântico Sul, séculos XVI e XVII.* São Paulo: Companhia das Letras, 2000.

Allen, Robert C. "The Agricultural Revolution." In *The British Industrial Revolution in Global Perspective,* edited by Robert C. Allen, 57–79. Cambridge: Cambridge University Press, 2009.

———. "Tracking the Agricultural Revolution in England." *Economic History Review* LII, no. 2 (1999): 209–35.

Alpern, Stanley B. "Exotic Plants of Western Africa: Where They Came From and When." *History in Africa* 35, no. 1 (2008): 63–102. https://doi.org/10.1353/hia.0.0018.

Ameha, Mesfin. "Significance of Ethiopian Coffee Genetic Resources to Coffee Improvement." In *Plant Genetic Resources of Ethiopia,* edited by J. M. M. Engels, J. G. Hawkes, and Melaku Worede, 354–60. Cambridge: Cambridge University Press, 1991.

286 Bibliography

Andrade, Tonio. "A Chinese Farmer, Two African Boys, and a Warlord: Toward a Global Microhistory." *Journal of World History* 21, no. 4 (2010): 573–91.

Andrade Martins, Conceição. *Memória do vinho do Porto.* Lisbon: Instituto de Ciências Sociais, University of Lisbon, 1990.

Antrobus, H. A. *A History of the Assam Company, 1839–1953.* Edinburgh: T. and A. Constable, 1957.

Appadurai, Arjun. *Modernity at Large: Cultural Dimensions of Globalization.* Public Worlds, vol. 1. Minneapolis: University of Minnesota Press, 1996.

——, ed. *The Social Life of Things: Commodities in Cultural Perspective.* Cambridge: Cambridge University Press, 1986. http://dx.doi.org/10.1017/CBO9780511819582.

Armiero, Marco, and Wilko Graf von Hardenberg. "Green Rhetoric in Blackshirts: Italian Fascism and the Environment." *Environment and History* 19, no. 3 (2013): 283–311.

Arnold, David. "Agriculture and 'Improvement' in Early Colonial India: A Pre-History of Development." *Journal of Agrarian Change* 5, no. 4 (2005): 505–25. https://doi.org/10.1111/j.1471-0366.2005.00110.x.

——. *The Tropics and the Traveling Gaze: India, Landscape, and Science, 1800–1856.* Culture, Place, and Nature. Seattle: University of Washington Press, 2006.

Arrighi, Giovanni, Takeshi Hamashita, and Mark Selden, eds. *The Resurgence of East Asia: 500, 150 and 50 Year Perspectives.* Routledge, 2003.

Asante, Winston Adams, Emmanuel Acheampong, Edward Kyereh, and Boateng Kyereh. "Farmers' Perspectives on Climate Change Manifestations in Smallholder Cocoa Farms and Shifts in Cropping Systems in the Forest-Savannah Transitional Zone of Ghana." *Land Use Policy* 66 (2017): 374–81. https://doi.org/10.1016/j.landusepol.2017.05.010.

Ash, Lindsay. "Plants, Patents and Power: Reconceptualizing the Property Environment in Seeds in the 19th and 20th Centuries." M.A. thesis, University of Vienna and Leipzig University, 2009.

Aso, Michitake. *Rubber and the Making of Vietnam: An Ecological History, 1897–1975.* Chapel Hill: University of North Carolina Press, 2018.

Asogwa, E. U., L. A. Hammed, and T. C. N. Ndubuaku. "Integrated Production and Protection Practices of Cashew (*Anacardium occidentale*) in Nigeria." *African Journal of Biotechnology* 7, no. 25 (2008).

Austen, Ralph A. *Trans-Saharan Africa in World History.* Oxford: Oxford University Press, 2010.

Avni, Gideon. "Early Islamic Irrigated Farmsteads and the Spread of Qanats in Eurasia." *Water History* 10, no. 4 (2019): 313–38. https://doi.org/10.1007/s12685-018-0225-6.

Bairoch, Paul. *Economics and World History: Myths and Paradoxes.* Chicago: University of Chicago Press, 1993.

Baker, Bruce E., and Barbara Hahn. "Cotton." *Essential Civil War Curriculum* (blog), n.d. Accessed 7 April 2018.

——. *The Cotton Kings: Capitalism and Corruption in Turn-of-the-Century New York and New Orleans.* Oxford: Oxford University Press, 2016.

Baker, Julian. "Trans-Species Colonial Fieldwork: Elephants as Instruments and Participants in Mid-Nineteenth Century India." In *Conflict, Negotiation, and Coexistence,* edited by Piers Locke and Jane Buckingham, 115–36. Oxford: Oxford University Press, 2016. https://doi.org/10.1093/acprof:oso/9780199467228.003.0006.

Balée, William. "The Research Program of Historical Ecology." *Annual Review of Anthropology* 35 (2006): 75–98.

Ball, Samuel. *An Account of the Cultivation and Manufacture of Tea in China: Derived from Personal Observation with Remarks on the Experiments Now Making for the Introduction of the Culture of the Tea Tree in Other Parts of the World.* London: Longman, 1848.

Banaji, Jairus. "Islam, the Mediterranean and the Rise of Capitalism." *Historical Materialism* 15, no. 1 (2007): 47–74.

Baptist, Edward E. *The Half Has Never Been Told: Slavery and the Making of American Capitalism.* New York: Basic Books, 2014.

Barickman, B. J. *A Bahian Counterpoint: Sugar, Tobacco, Cassava, and Slavery in the Recôncavo, 1780–1860.* Stanford: Stanford University Press, 1998.

———. " 'A Bit of Land, Which They Call Roça': Slave Provision Grounds in the Bahian Recôncavo, 1780–1860." *Hispanic American Historical Review* 74, no. 4 (1994): 649–87. https://doi.org/10.2307/2517495.

Barreto, António. "O vinho do Porto e a intervenção do Estado." *Análise social* 24, no. 100 (1988): 373–90.

Bastião, Maria Paula Pereira. "Entre a Ilha e a Terra: Processos de construção do continente fronteiro à Ilha de Moçambique (1763–c. 1802)." M.A. thesis, Faculty of Social Sciences and Humanities, New University of Lisbon, 2013. https://run.unl.pt/handle/10362/11344.

Bauer, P. T. *The Rubber Industry: A Study in Competition and Monopoly.* London: Plastics and Rubber Institute, 1948.

Baur, E. "Die Bedeutung der primitiven Kulturrassen und der wilden Verwandten unserer Kulturpflanzen für die Pflanzenzüchtung." *Jahresbericht Deutsche Landwirtschaft Gesellschaft* 29 (1914): 104–9.

Beattie, James. "Imperial Landscapes of Health: Place, Plants and People between India and Australia, 1800s–1900s." *Health and History* 14, no. 1 (2012): 100–120.

Beck, John. "Capital Investment Replaces Labor." *Flue-Cured Tobacco Farmer,* March 1968, 6–7.

———. "The Labor Squeeze." *Flue-Cured Tobacco Farmer,* June 1968, 20–21.

Beckert, Sven. *Empire of Cotton: A Global History.* New York: Random House, 2014.

Behal, Rana P. "Coolie Drivers or Benevolent Paternalists? British Tea Planters in Assam and the Indenture Labour System." *Modern Asian Studies* 44, no. 1 (2010): 29–51. https://doi.org/10.1017/S0026749X09990059.

Behm, Amanda, Christienna Fryar, Emma Hunter, Elisabeth Leake, Su Lin Lewis, and Sarah Miller-Davenport. "Decolonizing History: Enquiry and Practice." *History Workshop Journal* 89 (2020): 169–91. https://doi.org/10.1093/hwj/dbz052.

Beinart, William, and Karen Middleton. "Plant Transfers in Historical Perspective: A Review Article." *Environment and History* 10, no. 1 (February 2004): 3–29.

Beinart, William, and Luvuyo Wotshela. *Prickly Pear: The Social History of a Plant in the Eastern Cape.* Johannesburg: Wits University Press, 2011.

Bender, Barbara. "Landscapes on-the-Move." *Journal of Social Archaeology* 1, no. 1 (2001): 75–89. https://doi.org/10.1177/146960530100100106.

288 Bibliography

———. "Theorising Landscapes, and the Prehistoric Landscapes of Stonehenge." *Man* 27, no. 4 (1992): 735–55. https://doi.org/10.2307/2804172.

Bennet, Hugh Hammond, and William Clayton Pryor. *This Land We Defend*. New York: Longmans, Green, 1942.

Bennett, Brett M. "A Global History of Australian Trees." *Journal of the History of Biology* 44, no. 1 (2011): 125–45.

Bennett, Jane. *Vibrant Matter: A Political Ecology of Things*. Durham, NC: Duke University Press, 2010.

Berg, Maxine. *The Age of Manufactures, 1700–1820: Industry, Innovation and Work in Britain*. 2nd ed. Routledge, 1994.

Bergson, Henri. *Creative Evolution*. Mineola, NY: Dover, 1998.

Berlan, Amanda. "Child Labour and Cocoa: Whose Voices Prevail?" *International Journal of Sociology and Social Policy* 29, nos. 3–4 (2009): 141–51. https://doi.org/10.1108/01443330910947516.

Berry, Dominic J. "Historiography of Plant Breeding and Agriculture." In *Handbook of the Historiography of Biology*, edited by Michael R. Dietrich, Mark E. Borrello, and Oren Harman, 499–525. Historiographies of Science. Cham: Springer International, 2021. https://doi.org/10.1007/978-3-319-90119-0_27.

———. "Plants Are Technologies." In *Histories of Technology, the Environment and Modern Britain*, edited by John Agar and Jacob Ward, 161–85. London: UCL Press, 2018. https://www.uclpress.co.uk/collections/history/products/87840.

Besky, Sarah. *The Darjeeling Distinction: Labor and Justice on Fair-Trade Tea Plantations in India*. Berkeley: University of California Press, 2013.

Biersack, Aletta. "The Sun and the Shakers, Again: Enga, Ipili, and Somaip Perspectives on the Cult of Ain: Part Two." *Oceania* 81, no. 3 (November 2011): 225–43.

Biggs, David. "Promiscuous Transmission and Encapsulated Knowledge: A Material-Semiotic Approach to Modern Rice in the Mekong Delta." In *Rice: Global Networks and New Histories*, edited by Francesca Bray, Peter A. Coclanis, Edda L. Fields-Black, and Dagmar Schäfer, 118–37. Cambridge: Cambridge University Press, 2015.

———. *Quagmire: Nation-Building and Nature in the Mekong Delta*. Seattle: University of Washington Press, 2011.

Black, John, Nigar Hashimzade, and Gareth Myles. *A Dictionary of Economics*. Oxford: Oxford University Press, 2012.

Blain, Marc-A. "Le rôle de la dépendance externe et des structures sociales dans l'économie frumentaire du Canada et de l'Argentine (1880–1930)." *Revue d'histoire de l'Amérique française* 26, no. 2 (1972): 239–70.

Blazdell, P. "The Mighty Cashew." *Interdisciplinary Science Reviews* 25, no. 3 (2000): 220–26.

Bleichmar, Daniela. *Visible Empire. Botanical Expeditions and Visual Culture in the Spanish Enlightenment*. Chicago: Chicago University Press, 2012.

Bloch, Marc. *Apologie pour l'histoire, ou, Métier d'historien*. Cahiers des Annales 3. Paris: Armand Colin, 1949.

———. *Les caractères originaux de l'histoire rurale française*. Paris: Belles Lettres, 1931.

Blue, Gregory. "China and Western Social Thought in the Modern Period." In *China and Historical Capitalism: Genealogies of Sinological Knowledge*, edited by Timothy Brook and Gregory Blue, 57–109. Cambridge: Cambridge University Press, 1999.

"The Boll Weevil Convention." *Southern Mercury*. 12 November, 1903.

Bonneuil, Christophe. "Mendelism, Plant Breeding and Experimental Cultures: Agriculture and the Development of Genetics in France." *Journal of the History of Biology* 39, no. 2 (2006): 281–308.

———. "Mettre en ordre et discipliner les tropiques: Les sciences du végétal dans l'empire français 1870–1940." Ph.D. dissertation, Paris 7, 1997.

Bonneuil, Christophe, and Jean-Baptiste Fressoz. *The Shock of the Anthropocene: The Earth, History and Us*. Translated by David Fernbach. London: Verso Books, 2015.

Boserup, Ester. *Woman's Role in Economic Development*. London: Allen and Unwin, 1970.

Bouza, Fernando. *Corre manuscrito: Una historia cultural del Siglo de Oro*. Madrid: Marcial Pons, 2001.

Bradbury, E. Jane, Anne Duputié, Marc Delêtre, Caroline Roullier, Alexandra Narváez-Trujillo, Joseph A. Manu-Aduening, Eve Emshwiller, and Doyle McKey. "Geographic Differences in Patterns of Genetic Differentiation among Bitter and Sweet Manioc (*Manihot esculenta* Subsp. *esculenta*; Euphorbiaceae)." *American Journal of Botany* 100, no. 5 (2013): 857–66. https://doi.org/10.3732/ajb.1200482.

Braudel, Fernand. *Civilisation matérielle et capitalisme (XVe–XVIIIe siècle)*. 3 vols. Paris: Armand Colin, 1967.

———. *Civilization and Capitalism, 15th–18th Century. Volume I: The Structures of Everyday Life*. Translated by Siân Reynolds. London: William Collins, 1981.

———. *Civilization and Capitalism, 15th–18th Century. Volume II: The Wheels of Commerce*. Translated by Siân Reynolds. London: William Collins, 1982.

———. *Civilization and Capitalism, 15th–18th Century. Volume III: The Perspective of the World*. Translated by Siân Reynolds. London: William Collins, 1984. http://archive.org/details/BraudelFernandCivilizationAndCapitalism.

Bray, Francesca. "Agriculture." In *The Six Dynasties 220–581*, edited by Albert E. Dien and Kenneth Knapp, 2:355–73. *Cambridge History of China*. Cambridge: Cambridge University Press, 2019.

———. "The Craft of Mud-Making: Cropscapes, Time, and History." *Technology and Culture* 61, no. 2 (2020): 645–61. https://doi.org/10.1353/tech.2020.0056.

———. "Feeding the Farmers, Feeding the Nation: The Long Green Revolution in Kelantan, Malaysia." In *Handbook of Food and Anthropology*, edited by James L. Watson and Jakob A. Klein, 173–99. London: Bloomsbury, 2016.

———. "Genetically Modified Foods: Shared Risk and Global Action." In *Revising Risk: Health Inequalities and Shifting Perceptions of Danger and Blame*, edited by Barbara Herr Harthorn and Laury Oakes, 185–207. Westport, CT: Praeger, 2003.

———. "Health, Wealth, and Solidarity: Rice as Self in Japan and Malaysia." In *Moral Foods: The Construction of Nutrition and Health in Modern Asia*, edited by Angela Ki Che Leung and Melissa L. Caldwell, 23–46. Honolulu: University of Hawaii Press, 2019.

———. "Instructive and Nourishing Landscapes: Natural Resources, People and the State in Late Imperial China." In *The Wealth of Nature: How Natural Resources Have Shaped Asian History, 1600–2000*, edited by Greg Bankoff and Peter Boomgaard, 205–26. London: Palgrave Macmillan, 2007.

———. "Introduction." In *Gender, Health, and History in Modern East Asia*, edited by Angela Ki Che Leung and Izumi Nakayama. Hong Kong: Hong Kong University Press, 2017.

290   Bibliography

———. *The Rice Economies: Technology and Development in Asian Societies*. Berkeley: University of California Press, 1994. (1st ed. 1986.)

———. *Science and Civilisation in China: Volume 6, Biology and Biological Technology, Part 2, Agriculture*. Cambridge: Cambridge University Press, 1984.

———. "Science, Technique, Technology: Passages between Matter and Knowledge in Imperial Chinese Agriculture." *British Journal for the History of Science* 41, no. 3 (2008): 319–44. https://doi.org/10.1017/S0007087408000873.

———. "Technological Transitions." In *Cambridge History of the World, Volume 6, Part 1, The Construction of a Global World, 1400–1800 C.E.*, edited by Merry Wiesner-Hanks, Jerry H. Bentley, and Sanjay Subrahmanyam, 76–106. Cambridge: Cambridge University Press, 2015.

———. *Technology and Gender: Fabrics of Power in Late Imperial China*. Berkeley: University of California Press, 1997.

———. *Technology, Gender and History in Imperial China: Great Transformations Reconsidered*. London: Routledge, 2013.

———. "Translating the Art of Tea: Naturalizing Chinese Savoir Faire in British Assam." In *Entangled Itineraries: Materials, Practices, and Knowledges across Eurasia*, edited by Pamela H. Smith, 99–137. Pittsburgh: University of Pittsburgh Press, 2019.

Bray, Francesca, Barbara Hahn, John Bosco Lourdusamy, and Tiago Saraiva. "Cropscapes and History: Reflections on Rootedness and Mobility." *Transfers* 9, no. 1 (2019): 20–41. https://doi.org/10.3167/TRANS.2019.090103.

Bray, Francesca, and Georges Métailié. "Who Was the Author of the *Nongzheng Quanshu?*" In *Statecraft and Intellectual Renewal in Late Ming China: The Cross-Cultural Synthesis of Xu Guangqi (1562–1633)*, edited by Catherine Jami, Peter Engelfriet, and Gregory Blue, 322–59. Leiden: Brill, 2001.

Bray, Francesca, and A. F. Robertson. "Sharecropping in Kelantan, Malaysia." In *Research in Economic Anthropology*, edited by George Dalton, 3:209–44. Greenwich, CT.: JAI Press, 1980.

Breman, Jan. *Labour Migration and Rural Transformation in Colonial India*. Amsterdam: Free University Press, 1990.

Bridger, Sue. "The Heirs of Pasha: The Rise and Fall of the Soviet Woman Tractor Driver." In *Gender in Russian History and Culture*, edited by Linda Edmondson, R. W. Davies, and E. A. Rees, 194–211. Studies in Russian and East European History and Society. London: Palgrave Macmillan, 2001. https://doi.org/10.1057/9780230518926.

Brisebarre, Anne-Marie. *Bergers des Cévennes*. Espace des hommes. Nancy: Berger-Levrault, 1979.

Brockway, Lucile. *Science and Colonial Expansion: The Role of the British Royal Botanic Gardens*. New York: Academic Press, 1979.

Brook, Timothy. "Capitalism and the Writing of Modern History in China." In *China and Historical Capitalism: Genealogies of Sinological Knowledge*, edited by Timothy Brook and Gregory Blue, 110–57. Cambridge: Cambridge University Press, 1999.

Brown, Kathleen M. *Good Wives, Nasty Wenches, and Anxious Patriarchs: Gender, Race, and Power in Colonial Virginia*. Chapel Hill: Omohundro Institute of Early American History and University of North Carolina Press, 1996.

Browne, Janet. "Biogeography and Empire." In *Cultures of Natural History*, edited by Nicholas Jardine, James A. Secord, and Emma C. Spary, 305–21. Cambridge: Cambridge University Press, 1996.

Bruce, C. A., Superintendent of Tea Culture. "Report on the Manufacture of Tea, and on the Extent and Produce of the Tea Plantations in Assam: Transactions of the Agricultural and Horticultural Society of India, Vol. VII." Report to the British Parliamentary Tea Committee. London, 1839.

Brüggemeier, Franz-Josef, Mark Cioc, and Thomas Zeller, eds. *How Green Were the Nazis? Nature, Environment, and Nation in the Third Reich.* Athens: Ohio University Press, 2005.

Bubandt, Nils, and Anna Tsing. "Feral Dynamics of Post-Industrial Ruin: An Introduction." *Journal of Ethnobiology* 38, no. 1 (2018): 1–7. https://doi.org/10.2993/0278-0771-38.1.001.

Burchardt, Jeremy F. S. "Land and the Laborer: Potato Grounds and Allotments in Nineteenth-Century Southern England." *Agricultural History* 74, no. 3 (2000): 667–84.

Burke, Peter. "The Annales in Global Context." *International Review of Social History* 35, no. 3 (1990): 421–32. https://doi.org/10.1017/S0020859000010063.

Callon, Michel. "Some Elements of a Sociology of Translation: Domestication of the Scallops and the Fishermen of St Brieuc Bay." *Sociological Review* 32, no. 1 suppl. (1984): 196–233. https://doi.org/10.1111/j.1467-954X.1984.tb00113.x.

———, ed. *The Laws of the Markets.* Oxford: Blackwell, 1998.

Callon, Michel, Millo Yuval, and Fabian Muniesa. *Market Devices.* Malden: Blackwell, 2007.

Camargo, João, and Paulo Pimenta de Castro. *Portugal em chamas: Como resgatar as florestas.* Lisbon: Bertrand, 2018.

Canales, Jimena. *The Physicist and the Philosopher: Einstein, Bergson and the Debate That Changed Our Understanding of Time.* Princeton: Princeton University Press, 2015.

Canet, Gerardo, and Erwin Raisz. *Atlas de Cuba.* Cambridge, MA: Harvard University Press, 1949.

Cañizares-Esguerra, Jorge. "Bartolomé Inga's Mining Technologies: Indians, Science, Cyphered Secrecy, and Modernity in the New World." *History and Technology* 34, no. 1 (2018): 61–70.

———, ed. *Entangled Empires: The Anglo-Iberian Atlantic, 1500–1830.* Philadelphia: University of Pennsylvania Press, 2018.

Cantrell, Georgia. *Cashew Nuts.* Washington, DC: War Food Administration, Office of Marketing Services, 1945.

Capela, José. *O vinho para o preto: Notas e textos sobre a exportação do vinho para África.* Porto: Afrontamento, 1973.

Carney, Judith A. *Black Rice: The African Origins of Rice Cultivation in the Americas.* Cambridge, MA: Harvard University Press, 2001.

Carney, Judith A., and Richard Nicholas Rosomoff. *In the Shadow of Slavery: Africa's Botanical Legacy in the Atlantic World.* Berkeley: University of California Press, 2009.

Carter, S., L. Fresco, P. Jones, and J. Fairbairn. *Introduction and Diffusion of Cassava in Africa: IITA Research Guide, No. 49.* Ibadan, Nigeria: IITA (International Institute of Tropical Agriculture), 1997. https://biblio1.iita.org/handle/20.500.12478/3918.

Carver, George Washington. *How to Build Up Worn Out Soils.* Alabama: Tuskegee Institute, 1905.

Casale, Giancarlo. *The Ottoman Age of Exploration.* New York: Oxford University Press, 2010.

Casement, Roger. *The Amazon Journal of Roger Casement*. Edited by Angus Mitchell. London: Anaconda, 1997.

Castello Branco, Camillo. *O vinho do Porto, processo d'uma bestialidade inglesa, exposição a Thomas Ribeirlo*. Porto: Livraria Lella-Chardron, 1903.

Chambers, J. D., and G. E. Mingay. *The Agricultural Revolution 1750–1880*. London: B. T. Batsford, 1966.

Chang, Chia-ju. "Environing at the Margins: *Huanjing* as a Critical Practice." In *Chinese Environmental Humanities: Practices of Environing at the Margins*, edited by Chia-ju Chang, 1–32. Cham: Springer International, 2019. https://doi.org/10.1007/978-3-030-18634-0_1.

Charbonnier, Julien. "La maîtrise du temps d'irrigation au sein des oasis alimentées par des aflâj." *Revue d'ethnoécologie* 4 (2013). http://ethnoecologie.revues.org/1471.

Chatterjee, Ashoke. "Our Past as Our Future: Weaving Tomorrow at Chirala." *Asia InCH: Thinkers, Creators, Makers, Doers* (blog), December 2018. https://asiainch.org/article/our-past-as-our-future-weaving-tomorrow-at-chirala/.

Chatterjee, Indrani. "Connected Histories and the Dream of Decolonial History." *South Asia: Journal of South Asian Studies* 41, no. 1 (2018): 69–86. https://doi.org/10.1080/00856401.2018.1414768.

Chaudhuri, Kirti (K. N.). "O imperio na economia mundial." In *Historia da expansao portuguesa*, edited by Kirti (K. N.) Chaudhuri and Francisco Bethencourt, 248–73. Lisbon: Circulo de Leitores, 1998.

———. *Trade and Civilisation in the Indian Ocean: An Economic History from the Rise of Islam to 1750*. Cambridge: Cambridge University Press, 1985.

Chen, BuYun. "The Case of Bingata: Trafficking Textile Art and Technique across the East China Sea." In *Knowledge in Translation: Global Patterns of Scientific Exchange, 1000–1800 CE*, edited by Patrick Manning and Abigail Owen, 117–33. Pittsburgh: University of Pittsburgh Press, 2018.

Chen Fu. *Nongshu* (Agricultural treatise). Beijing: Zhonghua, 1956. (1st ed. 1149.)

Chen, Ruikun, Ayako Shimono, Mitsuko Aono, Nobuyoshi Nakajima, Ryo Ohsawa, and Yosuke Yoshioka. "Genetic Diversity and Population Structure of Feral Rapeseed (*Brassica Napus* L.) in Japan." *PLOS ONE* 15, no. 1 (16 January 2020): e0227990. https://doi.org/10.1371/journal.pone.0227990.

Cheung, Sui-Wai. "A Desire to Eat Well: Rice and the Market in Eighteenth-Century China." In *Rice: Global Networks and New Histories*, edited by Francesca Bray, Peter A. Coclanis, Edda L. Fields-Black, and Dagmar Schäfer, 84–98. Cambridge: Cambridge University Press, 2015.

Clarence-Smith, William Gervase. "The Spread of Coffee Cultivation in Asia, from the Seventeenth to the Early Nineteenth Century." In *Le commerce du café avant l'ère des plantations coloniales: Espaces, réseaux, sociétés (XVe–XIXe siècle)*, edited by Michel Tuchscherer, 371–84. Cairo: IFAO, 1997.

Clarence-Smith, William Gervase, and Steven Topik, eds. *The Global Coffee Economy in Africa, Asia and Latin America, 1500–1989*. Cambridge: Cambridge University Press, 2003.

Clark, Brett, and John Bellamy Foster. "Ecological Imperialism and the Global Metabolic Rift: Unequal Exchange and the Guano/Nitrates Trade." *International Journal of Comparative Sociology* 50, nos. 3–4 (2009): 311–34. https://doi.org/10.1177/0020715209105144.

Clarke, Adele E., and Donna Jeanne Haraway, eds. *Making Kin Not Population.* Chicago: Prickly Paradigm Press, 2018.

Cohen, Deborah. *Braceros: Migrant Citizens and Transnational Subjects in the Postwar United States and Mexico.* Chapel Hill: University of North Carolina Press, 2011.

Conrad, Joseph. *Heart of Darkness.* New York: Signet Classics, 1997. (1st ed. 1899.)

Conrad, Sebastian. *What Is Global History?* Princeton: Princeton University Press, 2016.

Conrad, Sebastian, and Jürgen Osterhammel. *An Emerging Modern World, 1750–1850.* Cambridge, MA: Belknap Press of Harvard University Press, 2018.

Conway, Gordon. *The Doubly Green Revolution: Food for All in the Twenty-First Century.* Ithaca, NY: Cornell University Press, 1999.

Cook, Scott. "The Obsolete 'Anti-Market' Mentality: A Critique of the Substantive Approach to Economic Anthropology." *American Anthropologist* 68, no. 2 (1966): 323–45.

Cooper, Frederick. *Africa since 1940: The Past of the Present.* Cambridge: Cambridge University Press, 2002.

Cornejo-Polar, Antonio. "Mestizaje, transculturación y heterogeneidad." *Revista de critica literaria latinoamericana* 40 (1994): 368–71.

Coronil, Fernando. "Introduction to the Duke University Press Edition." In *Cuban Counterpoint: Tobacco and Sugar,* by Fernando Ortiz, ix–lvii. Translated by Harriet de Onís. Durham, NC: Duke University Press, 1995.

Correia, António Balbino Ramalho. *A industrialização da castanha de cajú.* Lourenço Marques: Direcção dos Serviços de Economia e Estatística Geral da Provincia de Mocambique, 1963. https://agris.fao.org/agris-search/search.do?recordID=US201300095623.

Coupaye, Ludovic. "Ways of Enchanting: *Chaînes opératoires* and Yam Cultivation in Nyamikum Village, Maprik, Papua New Guinea." *Journal of Material Culture* 14, no. 4 (2009): 433–58. https://doi.org/10.1177/1359183509345945.

Craven, Avery Odelle. *Soil Exhaustion as a Factor in the Agricultural History of Virginia and Maryland, 1606–1860.* Champaign: University of Illinois Press, 1926.

Crawford, Matthew James. *The Andean Wonder Drug: Cinchona Bark and Imperial Science in the Spanish Atlantic, 1630–1800.* Pittsburgh: University of Pittsburgh Press, 2016.

Critz, José Morilla, Alan L. Olmstead, and Paul W. Rhode. " 'Horn of Plenty': The Globalization of Mediterranean Horticulture and the Economic Development of Southern Europe, 1880–1930." *Journal of Economic History* 59, no. 2 (1999): 316–52.

Cronon, William. *Nature's Metropolis: Chicago and the Great West.* New York: W. W. Norton, 1991.

Crosby, Alfred W. *The Columbian Exchange: Biological and Cultural Consequences of 1492.* Westport, CT: Greenwood, 1972.

———. *Ecological Imperialism: The Biological Expansion of Europe, 900–1900.* 2nd ed. Cambridge: Cambridge University Press, 2004. (1st ed. 1986.)

Cunha, Manuela Carneiro da. *Cultura com aspas e outros ensaios.* São Paulo: UBU, 2017.

Curry, Helen Anne. *Endangered Maize: Industrial Agriculture and the Crisis of Extinction.* Berkeley: University of California Press, 2022.

———. "From Working Collections to the World Germplasm Project: Agricultural Modernization and Genetic Conservation at the Rockefeller Foundation." *History and Philosophy of the Life Sciences* 39, no. 2 (2017).

———. "Making Marigolds: Colchicine, Mutation Breeding, and Ornamental Horticulture, 1937–1950." In *Making Mutations: Objects, Practices, Contexts,* edited by Luis Campos and Alexander von Schwerin, 259–84. Berlin: Max Planck Institute for the History of Science, 2010.

Curry-Machado, Jonathan. *Cuban Sugar Industry: Transnational Networks and Engineering Migrants in Mid-Nineteenth Century Cuba.* New York: Palgrave Macmillan, 2011.

Curtin, Philip. " 'The End of the' White Man's Grave"? Nineteenth-Century Mortality in West Africa." *Journal of Interdisciplinary History* 21, no. 1 (1990): 63–88.

———. *The Rise and Fall of the Plantation Complex: Essays in Atlantic History.* Studies in Comparative World History. Cambridge: Cambridge University Press, 1990.

Curtler, W. H. R. *A Short History of English Agriculture.* Oxford: Clarendon Press, 1909. http://www.gutenberg.org/files/16594/16594-h/16594-h.htm.

Cuvi, Nicolás. "The Cinchona Program (1940–1945): Science and Imperialism in the Exploitation of a Medicinal Plant." *Dynamis* 31, no. 1 (2011): 183–206. https://doi.org/10.4321/S0211-95362011000100009.

Cwiertka, Katarzyna Joanna. *Modern Japanese Cuisine: Food, Power and National Identity.* London: Reaktion Books, 2014.

Dale, Stephen Frederic. *The Orange Trees of Marrakesh: Ibn Khaldun and the Science of Man.* Cambridge, MA: Harvard University Press, 2015. http://www.hup.harvard.edu/catalog.php?isbn=9780674967656.

Daly, Lewis, and Glenn Shepard. "Magic Darts and Messenger Molecules: Toward a Phytoethnography of Indigenous Amazonia." *Anthropology Today* 35, no. 2 (2019): 13–17. https://doi.org/10.1111/1467-8322.12494.

Daniel, Pete. *Breaking the Land: The Transformation of Cotton, Tobacco, and Rice Cultures since 1880.* Champaign: University of Illinois Press, 1986.

Daniels, Christian. *Science and Civilisation in China: Volume VI, Biology and Biological Technology, Part 3: Agro-Industries: Sugarcane Technology.* Cambridge: Cambridge University Press, 1996.

Daston, Lorraine. *Things That Talk: Object Lessons from Art and Science.* Cambridge, MA: Zone Books, 2002.

Daugstad, Karoline, Margarita Fernández Mier, and Leonor Peña-Chocarro. "Landscapes of Transhumance in Norway and Spain: Farmers' Practices, Perceptions, and Value Orientations." *Norsk Geografisk Tidsskrift—Norwegian Journal of Geography* 68, no. 4 (2014): 248–58. https://doi.org/10.1080/00291951.2014.927395.

Davis, Mike. *Late Victorian Holocausts: El Niño Famines and the Making of the Third World.* London: Verso, 2002.

Davis, Natalie Zemon. "Decentering History: Local Stories and Cultural Crossings in a Global World." *History and Theory* 50, no. 2 (2011): 188–202.

Dean, Warren. *Brazil and the Struggle for Rubber: A Study in Environmental History.* Cambridge: Cambridge University Press, 1987.

———. *With Broadax and Firebrand: The Destruction of the Brazilian Atlantic Forest.* Berkeley: University of California Press, 1995.

Deb Roy, Rohan. *Malarial Subjects: Empire, Medicine and Nonhumans in British India, 1820–1909.* Cambridge: Cambridge University Press, 2017.

Decker, Michael. "Plants and Progress: Rethinking the Islamic Agricultural Revolution." *Journal of World History* 20, no. 2 (2009): 187–206.

Deepa, G. L. "Industrial Crisis and Women Workers: A Study of Cashew Processing in Kerala." Ph.D. dissertation, Jawaharlal Nehru University, 1994.

Deichmann, Ute. *Biologists under Hitler.* Cambridge, MA: Harvard University Press, 1996.

DeLanda, Manuel. *A Thousand Years of Nonlinear History.* Cambridge, Mass: MIT Press, 1997.

Deleuze, Gilles, and Félix Guattari. *A Thousand Plateaux: Capitalism and Schizophrenia.* Translated by Brian Massumi. Minneapolis: University of Minnesota Press, 1987.

de Luna, Kathryn M. *Collecting Food, Cultivating People: Subsistence and Society in Central Africa.* Yale Agrarian Studies. New Haven: Yale University Press, 2016. https://yalebooks.yale.edu/book/9780300218534/collecting-food-cultivating-people/.

———. "Compelling Vansina: Contributions to Early African History." *History in Africa* 45 (2018): 161–73.

———. "Inciteful Language: Knowing and Naming Technology in South Central Africa." *History and Technology* 34, no. 1 (2018): 41–50.

Demiriz, Yıldız. "Tulips in Ottoman Turkish Culture and Art." In *The Tulip: The Symbol of Two Nations,* edited by Michiel Roding and Hans Theunissen, 57–75. Utrecht and Istanbul: M.Th. Houtsma Stichting and Turco-Dutch Friendship Association, 1993.

Descola, Philippe. *Beyond Nature and Culture.* Chicago: University of Chicago Press, 2013.

———. "Le jardin de Colibri: Procès de travail et catégorisations sexuelles chez les Achuar de l'Équateur." *Homme* 23, no. 1 (1983): 61–89. https://doi.org/10.3406/hom.1983.368343.

Devine, T. M. *The Scottish Clearances.* London: Penguin, 2019. https://www.penguin.co.uk/books/305/305334/the-scottish-clearances/9780141985930.html.

de Vries, Jan. "Industrious Peasants in East and West: Markets, Technology, and Family Structure in Japanese and Western European Agriculture." *Australian Economic History Review* 51, no. 2 (2011): 107–19. https://doi.org/10.1111/j.1467-8446.2011.00331.x.

———. *The Industrious Revolution: Consumer Behavior and the Household Economy, 1650 to the Present.* New York: Cambridge University Press, 2008.

Diamond, Jared. *Collapse: How Societies Choose to Fail or Succeed.* New York: Viking, 2005.

———. *Guns, Germs and Steel: The Fate of Human Societies.* New York: W.W. Norton, 1997.

Diffloth, Paul. *Les nouveaux systèmes de culture: Dry-farming: Méthodes chinoise et russe, système Jean—système Devaux.* Paris: Librairie Beillière, 1917.

Domingos, Nuno. "Na pista da mandioca colonial e pós-colonial: Das formas de representação do global." In *Estudos sobre a globalização,* edited by D. R. Curto, 319–51. Lisbon: Edições 70, 2016.

Domingues, Álvaro, and João Paulo Sotto Mayor. *Douro à la carte.* Edições de Risco, 2009.

Dominguez, Diego. "Repeasantization in the Argentina of the 21st Century." *Psicoperspectivas: Individuo y sociedad* 11 (2012): 134–57.

Dooren, Thom van. "Invasive Species in Penguin Worlds: An Ethical Taxonomy of Killing for Conservation." *Conservation and Society* 9 (n.d.): 286–98.

Dove, Michael R. "Obituary: Harold C. Conklin (1926–2016)." *American Anthropologist* 119, no. 1 (2017): 174–77.

Bibliography

————. "Plants, Politics, and the Imagination over the Past 500 Years in the Indo-Malay Region." *Current Anthropology* 60, no. S20 (2019): S309–20. https://doi.org/10.1086/702877.

————. "Smallholder Rubber and Swidden Agriculture in Borneo: A Sustainable Adaptation to the Ecology and Economy of the Tropical Forest." *Economic Botany* 47, no. 2 (1993): 136–47. https://doi.org/10.1007/BF02862016.

Drayton, Richard. *Nature's Government: Science, Imperial Britain, and the "Improvement" of the World*. New Haven: Yale University Press, 2000.

Drayton, Richard, and David Motadel. "Discussion: The Futures of Global History." *Journal of Global History* 13, no. 1 (2018): 1–21. https://doi.org/10.1017/S1740022817000262.

Du Bois, W. E. B. *Black Reconstruction in America 1860–1880*. New York: Harcourt Brace, 1935.

————. *The Souls of Black Folk*. New York: Penguin, 2018. (1st ed. 1903.)

Duguid, Paul. "Networks and Knowledge: The Beginning and End of the Port Commodity Chain, 1703–1860." *Business History Review* 79, no. 3 (2005): 493–526. https://doi.org/10.1017/s0007680500081423.

Dunn, Ross E. "The Trade of Tafilalt: Commercial Change in Southeast Morocco on the Eve of the Protectorate." *African Historical Studies* 4, no. 2 (1971): 271–304.

Earle, Rebecca. *The Body of the Conquistador: Food, Race and the Colonial Experience in Spanish America, 1492–1700*. Cambridge: Cambridge University Press, 2012. https://doi.org/10.1017/CBO9780511763359.

————. "The Columbian Exchange." In *The Oxford Handbook of Food History*, edited by Jeffrey M. Pilcher, 341–57. Oxford: Oxford University Press, 2012. https://doi.org/10.1093/oxfordhb/9780199729937.013.0019.

————. *Feeding the People: The Politics of the Potato*. Cambridge: Cambridge University Press, 2020.

————. "Food, Colonialism and the Quantum of Happiness." *History Workshop Journal* 84 (2017): 170–93. https://doi.org/10.1093/hwj/dbx046.

————. "Promoting Potatoes in Eighteenth-Century Europe." *Eighteenth-Century Studies* 51, no. 2 (2017): 147–62. https://doi.org/10.1353/ecs.2017.0057.

Edgerton, David. *The Shock of the Old: Technology and Global History since 1900*. Reprint ed. London: Profile, 2008.

Elina, Olga, Susanne Heim, and Nils Roll-Hansen. "Plant Breeding on the Front: Imperialism, War, and Exploitation." *Osiris* 20 (2005): 161–79.

Ellis, Markman, Richard Coulton, and Matthew Mauger. *Empire of Tea: The Asian Leaf That Conquered the World*. London: Reaktion Books, 2015.

Eltis, David, Philip Morgan, and David Richardson. "Agency and Diaspora in Atlantic History: Reassessing the African Contribution to Rice Cultivation in the Americas." *American Historical Review* 112, no. 5 (2007): 1329–58.

Elvin, Mark. *The Pattern of the Chinese Past: A Social and Economic Interpretation*. Stanford: Stanford University Press, 1973.

————. *The Retreat of the Elephants: An Environmental History of China*. New Haven: Yale University Press, 2006.

Elvin, Mark, and Ts'ui-jung Liu, eds. *Sediments of Time: Environment and Society in Chinese History*. Cambridge: Cambridge University Press, 1998.

Engels, Friedrich. *The Condition of the Working Class in England in 1844.* London: S. Sonnenschein, 1892.

Eriksen, Thomas Hylland. *Small Places, Large Issues: An Introduction to Social and Cultural Anthropology.* London: Pluto Press, 1995.

Erimtan, Can. *Ottomans Looking West? The Origins of the Tulip Age and Its Development in Modern Turkey.* London: I. B. Tauris, 2010.

Esser, Lora L. "Eucalyptus globulus." In *Fire Effects Information System.* Rocky Mountain Research Station, Fire Sciences Laboratory: U.S. Department of Agriculture, Forest Service, 1993. https://www.fs.fed.us/database/feis/plants/tree/eucglo/all.html.

Estrella, Eduardo. "Ciencia ilustrada y saber popular en el conocimiento de la quina en el siglo XVIII." In *Saberes andinos: Ciencia y tecnología en Bolivia, Ecuador y Perú,* ed. Marcos Cueto, 35–57. Lima: Instituto de Estudios Peruanos, 1995.

FAO. "Family Farming Knowledge Platform." Accessed 4 January 2021. http://www.fao.org/family-farming/home/en/.

———. *FAO Statistical Pocketbook, World Food and Agriculture, 2015.* Rome: FAO, 2015.

———. *Perennial Crops for Food Security. Proceedings of the FAO Expert Workshop.* Rome: FAO, 2014. http://archive.org/details/PerennialCropsForFoodSecurityProceedings OfTheFAOExpertWorkshop.

———. *The State of the World's Biodiversity for Food and Agriculture.* Edited by J. Bélanger and D. Pilling. Rome: FAO, 2019. http://www.fao.org/3/CA3129EN/CA3129 EN.pdf.

Farmer, B. H. *Green Revolution? Technology and Change in Rice-Growing Areas of Tamil Nadu and Sri Lanka.* London: Macmillan, 1977.

Fenzi, Marianna, and Christophe Bonneuil. "From 'Genetic Resources' to 'Ecosystems Services': A Century of Science and Global Policies for Crop Diversity Conservation." *Culture, Agriculture, Food and Environment* 38, no. 2 (2016): 72–83. https://doi.org/10.1111/cuag.12072.

Ferleger, Lou. "Uplifting American Agriculture: Experiment Station Scientists and the Office of Experiment Stations in the Early Years after the Hatch Act." *Agricultural History* 64, no. 2 (1990): 5–23.

Ficquet, Éloi. "Le rituel du café, contribution musulmane à l'identité nationale éthiopienne." In *O Islão na África Subsariana,* edited by A. C. Gonçalves, 159–65. Porto: Centro de Estudos Africanos da Universidade do Porto, 2004. https://ler.letras.up.pt/uploads/ficheiros/6912.pdf.

Filer, Colin. "Interdisciplinary Perspectives on Historical Ecology and Environmental Policy in Papua New Guinea." *Environmental Conservation* 38, no. 2 (2011): 256–69. https://doi.org/10.1017/S0376892910000913.

Finger, William R. *The Tobacco Industry in Transition.* Washington, DC: Lexington Books, 1981.

Finlay, Mark R. "Old Efforts at New Uses: A Brief History of Chemurgy and the American Search for Biobased Materials." *Journal of Industrial Ecology* 7, nos. 3–4 (2004): 33–46.

Fischer, Klara. "Why New Crop Technology Is Not Scale-Neutral—A Critique of the Expectations for a Crop-Based African Green Revolution." *Research Policy* 45, no. 6 (2016): 1185–94. https://doi.org/10.1016/j.respol.2016.03.007.

298 Bibliography

Fitzgerald, Deborah. "Blinded by Technology: American Agriculture in the Soviet Union, 1928–1932." *Agricultural History* 70, no. 3 (1996): 459–86.

———. *Every Farm a Factory: The Industrial Ideal in American Agriculture.* Yale University Press, 2003. http://www.jstor.org/stable/j.ctt1nprsq.

Flemming, Højlund. "Date Honey Production in Dilmun in the Mid 2nd Millennium BC: Steps in the Technological Evolution of the Madbasa." *Paléorient* 16, no. 1 (1990): 77–86.

Fletcher, Rob. "The Time Is Ripe for Rice-Fish Culture." The Fish Site, 14 December, 2018. https://thefishsite.com/articles/the-time-is-ripe-for-rice-fish-culture.

Flitner, Michael. "Genetic Geographies. A Historical Comparison of Agrarian Modernization and Eugenic Thought in Germany, the Soviet Union and the United States." *Geoforum* 34, no. 2 (2003): 175–85.

———. *Sammler, Räuber und Gelehrte: Pflanzengenetische Ressourcen zwischen deutscher Biopolitik und internationaler Entwicklung 1890–1994.* Frankfurt: Campus, 1995.

Flynn, Dennis O., and Arturo Giráldez. "Born with a 'Silver Spoon': The Origin of World Trade in 1571." *Journal of World History* 6, no. 2 (1995): 201–21.

Follett, Richard, Sven Beckert, Peter A. Coclanis, and Barbara M. Hahn. *Plantation Kingdom: The American South and Its Global Commodities.* Baltimore: Johns Hopkins University Press, 2016.

Ford, Anabel, and Ronald Nigh. *The Maya Forest Garden: Eight Millennia of Sustainable Cultivation of the Tropical Woodlands.* Walnut Creek, CA: Left Coast Press, 2016.

Fortune, Robert. *A Journey to the Tea Countries of China and India.* London: John Murray, 1852.

———. *Three Years' Wanderings in the Northern Provinces of China, Including a Visit to the Tea, Silk and Cotton Countries.* London: John Murray, 1847.

Fowler, Cary. "The Svalbard Global Seed Vault: Securing the Future of Agriculture." The Global Crop Diversity Trust, 2008. https://www.researchgate.net/publication/273757294_Svaldbard_Global_Seed_Vault.

Francks, Penelope. "Consuming Rice: Food, 'Traditional' Products and the History of Consumption in Japan." *Japan Forum* 19, no. 2 (2007): 147–68. https://doi.org/10.1080/09555800701330030.

———. "Rice and the Path of Economic Development in Japan." In *Rice: Global Networks and New Histories,* edited by Francesca Bray, Peter A. Coclanis, Edda L. Fields-Black, and Dagmar Schäfer, 318–34. Cambridge: Cambridge University Press, 2015.

———. *Technology and Agricultural Development in Pre-War Japan.* New Haven: Yale University Press, 1984.

———. *The Japanese Consumer: An Alternative Economic History of Modern Japan.* Cambridge: Cambridge University Press, 2009.

Frank, André Gunder. *ReOrient: Global Economy in the Asian Age.* Berkeley: University of California Press, 1998.

Frías, Marcelo. *Tras El Dorado vegetal: José Celestino Mutis y la real expedición botánica del Nuevo Reino de Granada (1783–1808).* Seville: Diputación de Sevilla, 1994.

Friedmann, Harriet. "World Market, State, and Family Farm: Social Bases of Household Production in the Era of Wage Labor." *Comparative Studies in Society and History* 20, no. 4 (1978): 545–86. https://doi.org/10.1017/S001041750001255X.

Friesen, Gerald. *The Canadian Prairies: A History*. University of Toronto Press, 1987.

Fullilove, Courtney. *The Profit of the Earth: The Global Seeds of American Agriculture*. Chicago: University of Chicago Press, 2017.

Fussell, G. E. "Low Countries' Influence on English Farming." *English Historical Review* 74, no. 293 (1959): 611–22.

———. Review of *The History and Social Influence of the Potato,* by R. N. Salaman. *English Historical Review* 65, no. 255 (1950): 262–63.

Gago, Maria do Mar. "Robusta Empire: Coffee, Scientists and the Making of Colonial Angola (1898–1961)." Ph.D. dissertation, University of Lisbon, 2018.

Galeano, Eduardo. *Las venas abiertas de América Latina*. Mexico: Siglo XXI, 1971.

Galenson, David W. "The Settlement and Growth of the Colonies: Population, Labor and Economic Development." In *The Cambridge Economic History of the United States,* edited by Hugh Rockoff, Stanley Engerman, and Robert Gallman, 1:135–207. Cambridge: Cambridge University Press, 1996.

Galié, Alessandra. "Empowering Women Farmers: The Case of Participatory Plant Breeding in Ten Syrian Households." *Frontiers: A Journal of Women Studies* 34, no. 1 (2013): 58–92. https://doi.org/10.5250/fronjwomestud.34.1.0058.

Gallo, Ezequiel. *La pampa gringa: La colonización agrícola en Santa Fe 1870–1895*. Buenos Aires: Edhasa, 1983.

Gambino, Megan. "Alfred W. Crosby on the Columbian Exchange." *Smithsonian Magazine*, October 4, 2011. https://www.smithsonianmag.com/history/alfred-w-crosby-on-the-columbian-exchange-98116477/.

Garber, Peter M. *Famous First Bubbles: The Fundamentals of Early Manias*. Cambridge, MA: MIT Press, 2000.

Gardella, Robert. *Harvesting Mountains: Fujian and the China Tea Trade, 1757–1937*. Berkeley: University of California Press, 1994.

Garfield, Seth. *In Search of the Amazon: Brazil, the United States and the Nature of a Region*. Durham, NC: Duke University press, 2013.

Gausemeier, Bernd. "Genetics as a Modernization Program." *Historical Studies in the Natural Sciences* 40, no. 4 (2010): 429–56.

Gauthier-Pilters, H., and A.I. Dagg. *The Camel, Its Evolution, Ecology, Behaviour, and Relationship to Man*. Chicago: University of Chicago Press, 1981.

Gayon, Jean, and Doris T. Zallen. "The Role of the Vilmorin Company in Promotion and Diffusion of the Experimental Science of Heredity in France, 1840–1929." *Journal of the History of Biology* 31, no. 2 (1998): 241–62.

Geertz, Clifford. *Agricultural Involution: The Process of Ecological Change in Indonesia*. Berkeley: University of California Press, 1963.

Gelderblom, Oscar, Abe de Jong, and Joost Jonker. "The Formative Years of the Modern Corporation: The Dutch East India Company VOC, 1602–1623." *Journal of Economic History* 73, no. 4 (2013): 1050–76.

Geoffroy, Éric. "La diffusion du café au Proche-Orient arabe par l'intermédiaire des soufis: Mythe et réalité." In *Le commerce du café avant l'ère des plantations coloniales: Espaces, réseaux, sociétés (XVe–XIXe siècle)*, edited by Michel Tuchscherer, 7–15. Cairo: IFAO, 2001.

Giesen, James C. *Boll Weevil Blues: Cotton, Myth, and Power in the American South*. Chicago: University of Chicago Press, 2011.

Gilbert, Jess. *Planning Democracy: Agrarian Intellectuals and the Intended New Deal.* New Haven: Yale University Press, 2015.

Gille, Zsuzsa. "Actor Networks, Modes of Production, and Waste Regimes: Reassembling the Macro-Social." *Environment and Planning A: Economy and Space* 42, no. 5 (2010): 1049–64. https://doi.org/10.1068/a42122.

———. *From the Cult of Waste to the Trash Heap of History: The Politics of Waste in Socialist and Postsocialist Hungary.* Bloomington: Indiana University Press, 2007. http://ebookcentral.proquest.com/lib/ed/detail.action?docID=334267.

Godinho, Vitorino Magalhães. *Os descobrimentos e a economia mundial.* Lisbon: Presença, 1983.

Goldgar, Anne. *Tulipmania: Money, Honor, and Knowledge in the Dutch Golden Age.* Chicago: University of Chicago Press, 2007.

Gómez, Pablo F. "Caribbean Stones and the Creation of Early-Modern Worlds." *History and Technology* 34, no. 1 (2 January 2018): 11–20. https://doi.org/10.1080/07341512.2018.1516849.

———. *The Experiential Caribbean: Creating Knowledge and Healing in the Early Modern Atlantic.* Chapel Hill: University of North Carolina Press, 2017. http://ebookcentral.proquest.com/lib/ed/detail.action?docID=4821057.

Goodman, Jordan. *The Devil and Mr Casement: One Man's Struggle for Human Rights in South America's Heart of Darkness.* London: Verso, 2009.

Goody, Esther N. *Parenthood and Social Reproduction: Fostering and Occupational Roles in West Africa.* Cambridge: Cambridge University Press, 1982.

Goody, Jack. *The Culture of Flowers.* Cambridge: Cambridge University Press, 1993.

———. *The Theft of History.* Cambridge: Cambridge University Press, 2006. http://hdl.handle.net/2027/heb.31043.

Goss, Andrew. "Building the World's Supply of Quinine: Dutch Colonialism and the Origins of a Global Pharmaceutical Industry." *Endeavour* 38, no. 1 (2014): 8–18.

———. *The Floracrats: State-Sponsored Science and the Failure of the Enlightenment in Indonesia.* Madison: University of Wisconsin Press, 2011.

Grandin, Greg. *Fordlandia: The Rise and Fall of Henry Ford's Forgotten Jungle City.* Metropolitan, 2009.

Green, Toby. *A Fistful of Shells: West Africa from the Rise of the Slave Trade to the Age of Revolution.* London: Allen Lane, 2019.

Grist, D. H. *Rice.* London: Longman, 1975.

Gros-Balthazard, Muriel, Claire Newton, Sarah Ivorra, MargaretaTengberg, Jean-Christophe Pintaud, and Jean-Frédéric Terral. "Origines et domestication du palmier dattier (*Phoenix dactylifera* L.): État de l'art et perspectives d'étude." *Revue d'ethnoécologie* 4 (2013). https://doi.org/10.4000/ethnoecologie.1524.

Guo, Tianyu, María García-Martín, and Tobias Plieninger. "Recognizing Indigenous Farming Practices for Sustainability: A Narrative Analysis of Key Elements and Drivers in a Chinese Dryland Terrace System." *Ecosystems and People* 17, no. 1 (2021): 279–91. https://doi.org/10.1080/26395916.2021.1930169.

Gupta, Bishnupriya. "The History of the International Tea Market, 1850–1945." In *EH.Net Encyclopedia,* edited by Robert Whaples. EH.net, March 16, 2008. https://eh.net/?=international+tea+market.

Haffner, Jeanne. *The View from Above: The Science of Social Space.* Cambridge, MA: MIT Press, 2013.

Hahn, Barbara M. *Making Tobacco Bright: Creating an American Commodity, 1617–1937.* Baltimore: Johns Hopkins University Press, 2011. https://jhupbooks.press.jhu.edu/content/making-tobacco-bright.

———. Review of *Empire of Cotton: A Global History,* by Sven Beckert, and *The Half has Never Been Told: Slavery and the Making of American Capitalism,* by Edward E. Baptist. *Agricultural History* 89, no. 3 (2015): 482–86.

Hahn, Barbara, Tiago Saraiva, Paul W. Rhode, Peter Coclanis, and Claire Strom. "Does Crop Determine Culture?" *Agricultural History* 88, no. 3 (2014): 407–39. https://doi.org/10.3098/ah.2014.088.3.407.

Hamilton, Shane. "Agribusiness, the Family Farm, and the Politics of Technological Determinism in the Post-World War II United States." *Technology and Culture* 55, no. 3 (2014): 560–90.

Hammer, Karl, and Axel Diederichsen. "Evolution, Status, and Perspectives for Landraces in Europe." In *European Landraces: On-Farm Conservation, Management and Use,* edited by V. Veteläinen, V. Negri, and N. Maxted, 23–44. Rome: Biodiversity International, 2009.

Hammers, Roslyn L. *Pictures of Tilling and Weaving: Art, Labor and Technology in Song and Yuan China.* Hong Kong: Hong Kong University Press, 2011.

Hanser, Jessica. "Teatime in the North Country: Consumption of Chinese Imports in North-East England." *Northern History* 49, no. 1 (2012): 51–74. https://doi.org/10.1179/174587012X13230354351627.

Haraway, Donna. "Anthropocene, Capitalocene, Plantationocene, Chthulucene: Making Kin." *Environmental Humanities* 6, no. 1 (2015): 159–65.

———. *The Companion Species Manifesto: Dogs, People, and Significant Otherness.* Chicago: Prickly Paradigm Press, 2003.

———. *When Species Meet.* Minneapolis: University of Minnesota Press, 2007.

Hardin, Garrett. "The Tragedy of the Commons." *Science,* n.s., 162 (1968): 1243–48.

Harilal, K. N., Nazneen Kanji, J. Jeyaranjan, Mindul Eapen, and P. Swaminathan. "Power in Global Value Chains: Implications for Employment and Livelihoods in the Cashew Nut Industry in India." London: International Institute for Environment and Development, 2006. https://www.researchgate.net/publication/45795971_Power_in_global_value_chains_implications_for_employment_and_livelihoods_in_the_cashew_nut_industry_in_India.

Harlan, Jack R., and J. M. J. de Wet. "Some Thoughts about Weeds." *Economic Botany* 19, no. 1 (1965): 16–24.

Harrell, Stevan. "China's Tangled Web of Heritage." In *Cultural Heritage Politics in China,* edited by Tami Blumenfield and Helaine Silverman, 285–94. New York: Springer, 2013. https://doi.org/10.1007/978-1-4614-6874-5_15.

Harris, D. R. "Vavilov's Concept of Centers of Origin of Cultivated Plants: Its Genesis and Its Influence on the Study of Agricultural Origins." *Biological Journal of the Linnean Society* 39, no. 1 (1990): 7–16.

Harris, Marvin. *Cows, Pigs, Wars and Witches: The Riddles of Culture.* London: Hutchinson, 1975.

Hartigan, John. "Plants as Ethnographic Subjects." *Anthropology Today* 35, no. 2 (2019): 1–2. https://doi.org/10.1111/1467-8322.12491.

Hartlib, Samuel. *Samuel Hartlib, His Legacy of Husbandry Wherein Are Bequeathed to the Common-Wealth of England, Not Onely Braband and Flanders, but Also Many More*

302 Bibliography

Outlandish and Domestick Experiments and Secrets (of Gabriel Plats and Others) Never Heretofore Divulged in Reference to Universal Husbandry. London: Richard Wodnothe, 1665.

Harvey, John H. "Turkey as a Source of Garden Plants." *Garden History* 4, no. 3 (1976): 21–42.

Harwood, Jonathan. *Europe's Green Revolution and Others Since: The Rise and Fall of Peasant-Friendly Plant Breeding.* London: Routledge, 2012.

———. "The Fate of Peasant-Friendly Plant Breeding in Nazi Germany." *Historical Studies in the Natural Sciences* 40, no. 4 (2010): 569–603.

———. "The Green Revolution as a Process of Global Circulation: Plants, People and Practices." *Historia Agraria* 75 (2018): 37–66.

———. "Was the Green Revolution Intended to Maximise Food Production?" *International Journal of Agricultural Sustainability* 17, no. 4 (2019): 312–25. https://doi.org/10.1080/14735903.2019.1637236.

Hasse, Geraldo. *A laranja no Brasil 1500–1987.* São Paulo: Duprat Iobe, n.d.

Hauser, I. L. *Tea: Its Origin, Cultivation, Manufacture and Use.* Chicago: Rand, McNally, 1890.

Hawthorne, Walter. "The Cultural Meaning of Work: The 'Black Rice Debate' Reconsidered." In *Rice: Global Networks and New Histories,* edited by Francesca Bray, Peter A. Coclanis, Edda L. Fields-Black, and Dagmar Schäfer, 279–90. Cambridge: Cambridge University Press, 2015.

Hayami, Akira. "The Industrious Revolution." *Look Japan* 38, no. 436 (1992): 8–10.

———. *Japan's Industrious Revolution: Economic and Social Transformations in the Early Modern Period.* Studies in Economic History. Tokyo: Springer Japan, 2015.

Hazareesingh, Sandip, and Harro Maat, eds. *Local Subversions of Colonial Cultures: Commodities and Anti-Commodities in Global History.* London: Palgrave Macmillan, 2016.

Headrick, Daniel. *The Tools of Empire: Technology and European Imperialism in the Nineteenth Century.* New York: Oxford University Press, 1981.

Hecht, Gabrielle. *Being Nuclear: Africans and the Global Uranium Trade.* Cambridge, MA: MIT Press, 2014.

Hecht, Susanna. "The Last Unfinished Page of Genesis: Euclides Da Cunha and the Amazon." *Novos Cadernos NAEA,* 11, no. 1 (2009): 43–69.

———. *The Scramble for the Amazon and the Lost Paradise of Euclides Da Cunha.* Chicago: Chicago University Press, 2013.

Hecht, Susanna, and Alexander Cockburn. *The Fate of the Forest: Developers, Destroyers, and Defenders of the Amazon.* Chicago: University of Chicago Press, 2010.

Heim, Susanne. *Kalorien, Kautschuk, Karrieren: Pflanzenzüchtung und landwirtschaftliche Forschung in Kaiser-Wilhelm-Instituten, 1933–1945.* Göttingen: Wallstein, 2003.

Heller, Joseph. *Catch-22.* New York: Simon and Schuster, 1999. (1st ed. 1961.)

Henderson, Georg L. *California and the Fictions of Capital.* Philadelphia: Temple University Press, 2003.

Hening, William Waller. *The Statutes at Large: Being a Collection of All the Laws of Virginia, from the First Session of the Legislature, in the Year 1619.* Vol. 1. Richmond, VA: Samuel Pleasants, Junior, Printer to the Commonwealth, 1809.

Herbert, Eugenia W. *Flora's Empire: British Gardens in India.* Philadelphia: University of Pennsylvania Press, 2012.

Hernández, Carol, Hugo Perales, and Daniel Jaffee. " 'Without Food There Is No Resistance': The Impact of the Zapatista Conflict on Agrobiodiversity and Seed Sovereignty in Chiapas, Mexico." *Geoforum,* September 12, 2020. https://doi.org/10.1016/j.geoforum.2020.08.016.

Hersey, Mark. *My Work Is That of Conservation: An Environmental Biography of George Washington Carver.* Athens: University of Georgia Press, 2011.

Hildebrand, Elisabeth A. "A Tale of Two Tuber Crops: How Attributes of Enset and Yams May Have Shaped Prehistoric Human-Plant Interactions in Southwest Ethiopia." In *Rethinking Agriculture: Archaeological and Ethnoarchaeological Perspectives,* edited by Tim Denham, Jose Iriarte, and Luc Vrydaghs, 273–98. Walnut Creek, CA: Left Coast Press, 2007.

Hill, Polly. *Migrant Cocoa-Farmers of Southern Ghana: A Study in Rural Capitalism.* Cambridge: Cambridge University Press, 1963.

Hill, R. D. "Back to the Future! Thoughts on Ratoon Rice in Southeast and East Asia." In *Perennial Crops for Food Security: Proceedings of the FAO Expert Workshop,* edited by FAO, 362–75. Rome: FAO, 2014.

———. "The Cultivation of Perennial Rice, an Early Phase in Southeast Asian Agriculture?" *Journal of Historical Geography* 36, no. 2 (2010): 215–23. https://doi.org/10.1016/j.jhg.2009.09.001.

Hinsch, Bret. *The Rise of Tea Culture in China: The Invention of the Individual.* London: Rowman and Littlefield, 2015.

Ho, Ping-Ti. "Early-Ripening Rice in Chinese History." *Economic History Review* 9, no. 2 (1956): 200–218. https://doi.org/10.2307/2591742.

———. "The Introduction of American Food Plants into China." *American Anthropologist* 57, no. 2 (1955): 191–201.

Hobsbawm, E. J., and George F. E. Rudé. *Captain Swing.* London: Lawrence and Wishart, 1969.

Hochschild, Adam. *King Leopold's Ghost: A Story of Greed, Terror, and Heroism in Colonial Africa.* Boston: Houghton Mifflin, 1999.

Huang, H. T. *Science and Civilisation in China, Volume 6, Part 5, Fermentations and Food Science.* Cambridge: Cambridge University Press, 2000. http://www.cambridge.org/es/academic/subjects/history/history-science-and-technology/science-and-civilisation-china-volume-6-part-5.

Huang, Philip C. C. *The Peasant Family and Rural Development in the Yangzi Delta, 1350–1988.* Stanford: Stanford University Press, 1990.

Hyde, Elizabeth. "Cultivated Power: Flowers, Culture, and Politics in Early Modern France." Ph.D. dissertation, Harvard University, 1998. http://search.proquest.com/docview/304434769/abstract/63144603A75A4C00PQ/1.

Irwin, Robert. *Ibn Khaldun: An Intellectual Biography.* Princeton: Princeton University Press, 2018.

———. "Toynbee and Ibn Khaldun." *Middle Eastern Studies* 33, no. 3 (1997): 461–79.

Isaacman, Allen. "Peasants, Work and the Labor Process: Forced Cotton Cultivation in Colonial Mozambique 1938–1961." *Journal of Social History* 25, no. 4 (1992): 815–55.

Ishii, Yoneo, ed. *Thailand: A Rice-Growing Society.* Honolulu: University Press of Hawai'i, 1978.

Bibliography

Ison, David. "War Elephants: From Ancient India to Vietnam." *Warfare History Network*, 2016. https://warfarehistorynetwork.com/2016/10/11/history-of-war-elephants-from-ancient-india-to-vietnam/.

Iwuagwu, Obi. "The Spread of Cassava (Manioc) in Igboland, South-East Nigeria: A Reappraisal of the Evidence." *Agricultural History Review* 60, no. 1 (2012): 60–76.

Jacobson, J. J. L. L. *Handboek voor de kultuur en fabrikatie von thee*. Batavia: ter Landsdrukkerij, 1843.

Jacquinet, Marc. "Technological, Institutional and Market Structure Changes as Evolutionary Processes: The Case of the Port Wine Sector (1680–1974)." Ph.D. dissertation, Technical University of Lisbon, 2006. http://search.proquest.com/docview/2018648959/?pq-origsite=primo.

Jami, Catherine, Peter Engelfriet, and Gregory Blue. "Introduction." In *Statecraft and Intellectual Renewal in Late Ming China: The Cross-Cultural Synthesis of Xu Guangqi (1562–1633)*, edited by Catherine Jami, Peter Engelfriet, and Gregory Blue, 1–15. Leiden: Brill, 2001.

Jáuregui, Carlos A. *Canibalia: Canibalismo, calibanismo, antropogagia cultural y consumo en América Latina*. Madrid: Iberoamericana, 2008.

Jenkins, Destin, and Justin Leroy, eds. *Histories of Racial Capitalism*. New York: Columbia University Press, 2021.

Jia Sixie. *Qimin yaoshu jiaoshi* (Annotated edition of *Qimin yaoshu*, Essential techniques for the common people, completed ca. 540.) Edited by Miao Qiyu and Miao Guilong. Beijing, Agriculture Press, 1982.

Johnson, D. "The Botany, Origin, and Spread of the Cashew *Anacardium occidentale* L." *Journal of Plantation Crops* 1, no. 1–2 (1973): 1–7.

Jones-Imhotep, Edward. *The Unreliable Nation: Hostile Nature and Technological Failure in the Cold War*. Cambridge, MA: MIT Press, 2017.

Joravsky, David. *The Lysenko Affair*. Cambridge, MA: Harvard University Press, 1970.

Juhé-Beaulaton, Dominique. "De l'igname au manioc dans le golfe de Guinée: Traite des esclaves et alimentation au royaume du Danhomè (XVIIe–XIXe siècle)." *Afriques: Débats, méthodes et terrains d'histoire* 05 (2014). https://doi.org/10.4000/afriques.1669.

Kahn, Miriam. *Always Hungry, Never Greedy: Food and the Expression of Gender in a Melanesian Society*. Cambridge: Cambridge University Press, 1986.

Kaplan, Lawrence. "Historical and Ethnobotanical Aspects of Domestication in Tagetes." *Economic Botany* 14, no. 3 (1960): 200–202. https://doi.org/10.1007/BF02907950.

Karababa, Eminegül. "Marketing and Consuming Flowers in the Ottoman Empire." *Journal of Historical Research in Marketing* 7, no. 2 (2015): 280–92.

Karasch, Mary. "Manioc." In *The Cambridge World History of Food*, edited by Kenneth F. Kiple and Kriemhild Coneè Ornelas, 1:181–87. Cambridge: Cambridge University Press, 2000.

Kater, Michael. *Das Ahnenerbe der SS: 1935–1945. Ein Beitrag zur Kulturpolitik des Dritten Reiches*. Munich: Oldenbourg, 1997.

Katznelson, Ira. *Fear Itself: The New Deal and the Origins of Our Time*. New York: Liveright, 2013.

Keall, Edward J. "The Evolution of the First Coffee Cups." In *Le commerce du café avant l'ère des plantations coloniales: Espaces, réseaux, sociétés (XVe–XIXe siècle)*, edited by Michel Tuchscherer, 35–50. Cairo: IFAO, 2001.

Kendi, Ibram X. *Stamped from the Beginning: The Definitive History of Racist Ideas in America.* New York: Bold Type Books, 2016.

Khomami, Nadia. "Apocalypse Wow: Dust from Sahara and Fires in Portugal Turn UK Sky Red." *Guardian,* October 16, 2017, sec. "UK News." https://www.theguardian.com/uk-news/2017/oct/16/apocalypse-wow-saharan-dust-and-iberian-fires-turn-uk-skies-red.

King, F.H. *Farmers of Forty Centuries, or, Permanent Agriculture in China, Korea and Japan.* Madison, WI: Mrs. F. H. King, 1911.

Kistler, John. *War Elephants.* Lincoln: University of Nebraska Press, 2007.

Kloppenburg, Jack Ralph. *First the Seed: The Political Economy of Plant Biotechnology.* Ithaca: Cornell University Press, 1985.

Knudsen, Michael Helt, and Jytte Agergaard. "Ghana's Cocoa Frontier in Transition: The Role of Migration and Livelihood Diversification." *Geografiska Annaler: Series B, Human Geography* 97, no. 4 (2015): 325–42. https://doi.org/10.1111/geob.12084.

Knüpffer, H. "The Balkan Collections 1941–42 of Hans Stubbe in the Gatersleben Gene Bank." *Czech Journal of Genetics and Plant Breeding* 46 (2010): 27–33.

Ko, Dorothy. *The Social Life of Inkstones: Artisans and Scholars in Early Qing China.* Seattle: University of Washington Press, 2018.

Koehler, Jeff. *Where the Wild Coffee Grows: The Untold Story of Coffee from the Cloud Forests of Ethiopia to Your Cup.* New York: Bloomsbury, 2017.

Kohn, Eduardo. *How Forests Think: Toward an Anthropology beyond the Human.* Berkeley: University of California Press, 2013.

Kreike, Emmanuel. *Recreating Eden: Land Use, Environment and Society in Southern Angola and Northern Namibia.* Portsmouth, NH: Heinemann, 2004.

Krementsov, Nikolai. *Stalinist Science.* Princeton: Princeton University Press, 1997.

Krige, John, ed. *How Knowledge Moves: Writing the Transnational History of Science and Technology.* Chicago: University of Chicago Press, 2019. https://www.press.uchicago.edu/ucp/books/book/chicago/H/bo34094209.html.

Kron, J. Geoffrey. "Agriculture, Roman Empire." In *The Encyclopedia of Ancient History,* edited by Roger S. Bagnall, Kai Brodersen, Craige B. Champion, Andrew Erskine, and Sabine R. Huebner, 217–22. Abingdon: Blackwell, 2013.

———. "The Much Maligned Peasant: Comparative Perspectives on the Productivity of the Small Farmer in Classical Antiquity." In *People, Land, and Politics: Demographic Developments and the Transformation of Roman Italy 300 BC–AD 14,* edited by Luuk de Ligt and Simon Northwood, 71–119. Leiden: Brill, 2008. http://ebookcentral.proquest.com/lib/ed/detail.action?docID=467730.

Krueger, R. R. "Date Palm Status and Perspective in the United States." In *Date Palm Genetic Resources and Utilization: Volume 1: Africa and the Americas,* edited by Jameel M. Al-Khayri, Shri Mohan Jain, and Dennis V. Johnson, 447–85. Dordrecht: Springer Netherlands, 2015.

Kuehling, Susanne. " 'We Die for Kula'—An Object-Centred View of Motivations and Strategies in Gift Exchange." *Journal of the Polynesian Society* 126, no. 2 (2017): 181–208. https://doi.org/10.15286/jps.126.2.181-208.

Bibliography

Kumar, Prakash. *Indigo Plantations and Science in Colonial India.* Cambridge: Cambridge University Press, 2012. https://doi.org/10.1017/CBO9781139150910.

Kumar, Prakash, Timothy Lorek, Tore C. Olsson, Nicole Sackley, Sigrid Schmalzer, and Gabriela Soto Laveaga. "Roundtable: New Narratives of the Green Revolution." *Agricultural History* 91, no. 3 (2017): 397–422. https://doi.org/10.3098/ah.2017.091.3.397.

Lafuente, Antonio. "Enlightenment in an Imperial Context: Local Science in the Late Eighteenth-Century Hispanic World." *Osiris* 15 (2000): 155–73.

Lafuente, Antonio, and Nuria Valverde. "The Emergence of Early Modern Commons: Technology, Heritage and Enlightenment." *HoST—Journal of History of Science and Technology* 2 (2008): 13–42.

Lahiri, Dhriti K. Choudhury. *The Great Indian Elephant Book: An Anthology of Writings on Elephants in the Raj.* New Delhi: Oxford University Press, 1999.

Landes, David S. *The Wealth and Poverty of Nations: Why Some Are So Rich and Some So Poor.* W. W. Norton, 1999.

Landon, Amanda J. "The 'How' of the Three Sisters: The Origins of Agriculture in Mesoamerica and the Human Niche." *Nebraska Anthropologist* 23 (2008): 110–24.

Landsberger, Stefan R. "Chinese Propaganda Posters." https://chineseposters.net/

Lange, Fabian, Alan L. Olmstead, and Paul W. Rhode. "The Impact of the Boll Weevil 1892–1932." *Journal of Economic History* 69, no. 3 (2009): 685–718.

Langley, W. K. M, ed. *Century in Malabar: The History of Pierce Leslie & Co., Ltd., 1862–1962.* Madras: Madras Advertising Co. on behalf of Peirce Leslie & Co., 1962.

Lansing, J. Stephen. *Priests and Programmers: Technologies of Power in the Engineered Landscape of Bali.* Princeton: Princeton University Press, 1991.

Latour, Bruno. "On Actor-Network Theory: A Few Clarifications." *Soziale Welt* 47, no. 4 (1996): 369–81.

———. *Reassembling the Social: An Introduction to Actor-Network-Theory.* Clarendon Lectures in Management Studies. Oxford: Oxford University Press, 2005.

———. *We Have Never Been Modern.* Cambridge, MA: Harvard University Press, 1993.

Laveaga, Gabriela Soto. "Largo Dislocare: Connecting Microhistories to Remap and Recenter Histories of Science." *History and Technology* 34, no. 1 (2018): 21–30. https://doi.org/10.1080/07341512.2018.1516850.

Le Roy Ladurie, Emmanuel. *Times of Feast, Times of Famine: A History of Climate since the Year 1000.* Translated by Barbara Bray. London: George Allen and Unwin, 1972.

Leach, Edmund. *Pul Eliya, a Village in Ceylon: A Study of Land Tenure and Kinship.* Cambridge: Cambridge University Press, 1961.

LeCain, Timothy J. "Against the Anthropocene. A Neo-Materialist Perspective." *International Journal for History, Culture and Modernity* 3, no. 1 (2015): 1–28. https://doi.org/10.18352/hcm.474.

———. *The Matter of History: How Things Create the Past.* Cambridge: Cambridge University Press, 2017. https://doi.org/10.1017/9781316460252.

Lee, Seung-Joon. *Gourmets in the Land of Famine: The Culture and Politics of Rice in Modern Canton.* Stanford: Stanford University Press, 2011.

Lee, Victoria. "Mold Cultures: Traditional Industry and Microbial Studies in Early Twentieth-Century Japan." In *New Perspectives on the History of Life Sciences and Agriculture,* edited by Denise Phillips and Sharon Kingsland, 231–52. Archimedes. Cham: Springer International, 2015. https://doi.org/10.1007/978-3-319-12185-7_12.

————. "The Microbial Production of Expertise in Meiji Japan." *Osiris* 33, no. 1 (2018): 171–90. https://doi.org/10.1086/699405.

Lehmann, Christian O. "Collecting European Land-Races and Development of European Gene Banks—Historical Remarks." *Kulturpflanz* 29, no. 1 (1981): 29–40.

Leivers, Clive. "The Provision of Allotments in Derbyshire Industrial Communities." *Family and Community History* 12, no. 1 (1 May 2009): 51–64. https://doi.org/10.1179/175138109X437353.

Lemonnier, Pierre, ed. *Technological Choices: Transformation in Material Cultures since the Neolithic*. London: Routledge, 1993.

Lesnaw, Judith A., and Said A. Ghabrial. "Tulip Breaking: Past, Present, and Future." *Plant Disease* 84, no. 10 (October 2000): 1052–60.

Levi, Giovanni. "Microhistoria e historia global." *Historia crítica* 69 (2018): 21–35.

Lévi-Strauss, Claude. *Tristes tropiques*. New York: Penguin, 2012. (1st ed. 1955.)

Li, Bozhong. *Agricultural Development in Jiangnan, 1620–1850*. London: Macmillan, 1998.

Li, Tania Murray. *Land's End: Capitalist Relations on an Indigenous Frontier*. Durham, NC: Duke University Press, 2014.

————. "What Is Land? Assembling a Resource for Global Investment." *Transactions of the Institute of British Geographers* 39, no. 4 (1 October 2014): 589–602. https://doi.org/10.1111/tran.12065.

Lightfoot, Dale R., and James A. Miller. "Sijilmassa: The Rise and Fall of a Walled Oasis in Medieval Morocco." *Annals of the Association of American Geographers* 86, no. 1 (1996): 78–101.

Lim, T. K. "Tagetes erecta." In *Edible Medicinal and Non-Medicinal Plants: Volume 7, Flowers*, edited by T. K. Lim, 432–47. Dordrecht: Springer Netherlands, 2014. https://doi.org/10.1007/978-94-007-7395-0_26.

Linares, Olga F. "When Jola Granaries Were Full." In *Rice: Global Networks and New Histories*, edited by Francesca Bray, Peter A. Coclanis, Edda L. Fields-Black, and Dagmar Schäfer, 229–44. Cambridge: Cambridge University Press, 2015.

Lindberg, Anna. *Modernization and Effeminization in India: Kerala Cashew Workers since 1930*. Copenhagen: NIAS Press, 2005.

Lipton, Michael. *Why Poor People Stay Poor: A Study of Urban Bias in World Development*. Canberra: ANU Press, 1977.

Liu, Andrew B. *Tea War: A History of Capitalism in China and India*. New Haven: Yale University Press, 2020.

————. "The Birth of a Noble Tea Country: On the Geography of Colonial Capital and the Origins of Indian Tea." *Journal of Historical Sociology* 1 (2010): 73. https://doi.org/10.1111/j.1467-6443.2009.01360.x.

————. "The Two Tea Countries: Competition, Labor, and Economic Thought in Coastal China and Eastern India, 1834–1942." Ph.D. dissertation, Columbia University, 2015. http://search.proquest.com/docview/1655360271/abstract/DE3C42FEF233404FPQ/1.

Locke, Piers. "Explorations in Ethnoelephantology: Social, Historical, and Ecological Intersections between Asian Elephants and Humans." *Environment and Society: Advances in Research* 4 (2013): 79–97.

Lokustov, Igor C. *Vavilov and His Institute: A History of the World Collection of Plant Genetic Resources in Russia*. Rome: International Plant Resources Genetic Institute, 1999.

308 Bibliography

Lombard, Pierre. "Du rythme naturel au rythme humain: Vie et mort d'une technique traditionnelle, le qanat." In *Rites et rythmes agraires,* edited by Marie-Claire Cauvin, 69–86. Lyon: Maison de l'Orient et de la Méditerranée, Jean Pouilloux, 1991.

Luo, Qiangqiang, Joel Andreas, and Yao Li. "Grapes of Wrath: Twisting Arms to Get Villagers to Cooperate with Agribusiness in China." *China Journal* 77 (21 September 2016): 27–50. https://doi.org/10.1086/688344.

Lutgendorf, Philip. "Making Tea in India: Chai, Capitalism, Culture." *Thesis Eleven* 113, no. 1 (2012): 11–31.

Lydon, G. *On Trans-Saharan Trails: Islamic Law, Trade Networks and Cross-Cultural Exchange in Nineteenth-Century Western Africa.* Cambridge: Cambridge University Press, 2009.

MacCarthy, Michelle. "Playing Politics with Yams: Food Security in the Trobriand Islands of Papua New Guinea." *Culture, Agriculture, Food and Environment* 34, no. 2 (2012): 136–47.

MacDonald, James M., Penni Korb, and Robert A. Hoppe. "Farm Size and the Organization of U.S. Crop Farming." USDA Economic Research Service, 2013. https://doi.org/10.22004/ag.econ.262221.

Macedo, Jorge Borges de. *A situação económica no tempo de Pombal: Alguns aspectos.* 2nd ed. Lisbon: Moraes, n.d.

Macedo, Marta. *Projectar e construir a nação: Engenheiros, ciência e território em Portugal no século XX.* Lisbon: Imprensa de Ciências Sociais, 2012.

———. "Standard Cocoa: Transnational Networks and Technoscientific Regimes in West African Plantations." *Technology and Culture* 57, no. 3 (2016): 557–85.

Macfarlane, Alan, and Iris Macfarlane. *Green Gold: The Empire of Tea.* New ed. London: Ebury Press, 2004.

MacKenzie, Donald. *An Engine, Not a Camera: How Financial Models Shape Markets.* Cambridge, MA: MIT Press, 2008.

Magee, Peter. *The Archaeology of Prehistoric Arabia.* Cambridge: Cambridge University Press, 2014. https://doi.org/10.1017/CBO9781139016667.

Maher, Neil M. "A New Deal Body Politic: Landscape, Labor, and the Civilian Conservation Corps." *Environmental History* 7, no. 3 (2002): 435–61. https://doi.org/10.2307/3985917.

Malinowski, Bronisław. *Argonauts of the Western Pacific: An Account of Native Enterprise and Adventure in the Archipelagoes of Melanesian New Guinea.* Studies in Economics and Political Science, No. 65. London: G. Routledge, 1922.

———. *Coral Gardens and Their Magic.* London: George Allen and Unwin, 1935.

———. "The Primitive Economics of the Trobriand Islanders." *Economic Journal* 31, no. 121 (1921): 1–16. https://doi.org/10.2307/2223283.

Malm, Andreas. "The Origins of Fossil Capital: From Water to Steam in the British Cotton Industry." *Historical Materialism* 21, no. 1 (2013): 15–68. https://doi.org/10.1163/1569206X-12341279.

Marcaida, José Ramón, and Juan Pimentel. "Green Treasures and Paper Floras: The Business of Mutis in New Granada (1783–1808)." *History of Science* 52, no. 3 (2014): 277–96. https://doi.org/10.1177/0073275314546967.

Markham, Gervase. *Markhams Farwell to Husbandry or, The Inriching of All Sorts of Barren and Sterill Grounds in Our Kingdome, to Be as Fruitfull in All Manner of Graine,*

Pulse, and Grasse as the Best Grounds Whatsoeuer Together with the Anoyances, and Preseruation of All Graine and Seede, from One Yeare to Many Yeares. London: Roger Jackson, 1620.

———. *A Way to Get Wealth.* London: Nicholas Oakes for John Harrison, 1631.

Marks, Robert B. " 'It Never Used to Snow': Climatic Variability and Harvest Yields in Late-Imperial South China, 1650–1850.' " In *Sediments of Time: Environment and Society in Chinese History,* edited by Mark Elvin and Ts'ui-jung Liu, 411–46. Cambridge: Cambridge University Press, 1998.

———. *Tigers, Rice, Silk, and Silt: Environment and Economy in Late Imperial South China.* Studies in Environment and History. Cambridge: Cambridge University Press, 1998.

Marquese, Rafael de Bivar. "Capitalismo, escravidão e a economia cafeeira do Brasil no longo século XIX." *Saeculum* 29 (July/December 2013): 289–321.

———. "Exílio escravista: Hercule Florence e as fronteiras do açúcar e do café no Oeste paulista (1830–1879)." *Anais do Museu Paulista* 24, no. 2 (2016): 11–51.

Martins, João Paulo. *Tudo sobre o vinho do Porto: Os sabores e as histórias.* Lisbon: Dom Quixote, 2000.

Massey, Doreen. *For Space.* London: Sage, 2005.

Matos, Odilon Nogueira. *Café e ferrovia: A evolução ferroviária de São Paulo e o desenvolvimento da cultura cafeeira.* São Paulo: Alfa-Omega Sociologia e Politica, 1990.

Matthee, Rudi. "From Coffee to Tea: Shifting Patterns of Consumption in Qajar Iran." *Journal of World History* 7, no. 2 (1996): 199–230.

Maxby, Edward. *A New Instruction of Plowing and Setting of Corne, Handled in Manner of a Dialogue between a Ploughman and a Scholler.* London: Felix Kynghow, 1601.

Mazumdar, Sucheta. *Sugar and Society in China: Peasants, Technology, and the World Market.* Cambridge, MA: Harvard University Press, 1998.

McCann, James C. "Maize and Grace: History, Corn, and Africa's New Landscapes, 1500–1999." *Comparative Studies in Society and History* 43, no. 2 (2001): 246–72.

———. *People of the Plow: An Agricultural History of Ethiopia, 1800–1990.* Madison: University of Wisconsin Press, 1995.

McCook, Stuart. *Coffee Is Not Forever: A Global History of the Coffee Leaf Rust.* Athens: Ohio University Press, 2019.

———. "Global Rust Belt: *Hemileia vastatrix* and the Ecological Integration of World Coffee Production since 1850." *Journal of Global History* 1, no. 2 (July 2006): 177–95. https://doi.org/10.1017/S174002280600012X.

McCusker, John J. "The Demise of Distance: The Business Press and the Origins of the Information Revolution in the Early Modern Atlantic World." *American Historical Review,* April 2005, 295–321.

McLelland, Gary Michael. "Social Origins of Industrial Agriculture: Farm Dynamics in California's Period of Agricultural Nascence." *Journal of Peasant Studies* 24, no. 3 (1997): 1–24.

McNeill, J. R. *Mosquito Empires: Ecology and War in the Greater Caribbean, 1620–1914.* Cambridge: Cambridge University Press, 2010.

———. "Of Rats and Men: A Synoptic Environmental History of the Island Pacific." *Journal of World History* 5, no. 2 (1994): 299–349.

McNeill, William H. "How the Potato Changed the World's History." *Social Research* 66, no. 1 (1999): 67–83.

Meaney-Leckie, Anne. "The Cashew Industry of Ceará, Brazil: Case Study of a Regional Development Option." *Bulletin of Latin American Research* 10, no. 3 (1991): 315–24. https://doi.org/10.2307/3338673.

Meegahakumbura, M. K., M. C. Wambulwa, K. K. Thapa, M. M. Li, M. Möller, J. C. Xu, J. B. Yang, et al. "Indications for Three Independent Domestication Events for the Tea Plant (*Camellia sinensis* (L.) O. Kuntze) and New Insights into the Origin of Tea Germplasm in China and India Revealed by Nuclear Microsatellites." *PLOS ONE* 11, no. 5 (2016): e0155369. https://doi.org/10.1371/journal.pone.0155369.

Meillassoux, Claude. *Maidens, Meal, and Money: Capitalism and the Domestic Community.* Themes in the Social Sciences. Cambridge: Cambridge University Press, 1981.

Menard, Russell R. *Sweet Negotiations: Sugar, Slavery, and Plantation Agriculture in Early Barbados.* Charlottesville: University of Virginia Press, 2006.

Menard, Russell R., Lois Green Carr, and Lorena S. Walsh. "A Small Planter's Profits: The Cole Estate and the Growth of the Early Chesapeake Economy." *William and Mary Quarterly* 40, no. 2 (1983): 171–96.

Menocal, María Rosa. *The Ornament of the World: How Muslims, Jews, and Christians Created a Culture of Tolerance in Medieval Spain.* New York: Back Bay Books, 2002.

Menzies, Nicholas K. "Ancient Forest Tea." In *The Social Lives of Forests: Past, Present, and Future of Woodland Resurgence,* edited by Susanna B. Hecht, Kathleen D. Morrison, and Christine Padoch, 239–48. Chicago: University of Chicago Press, 2014. http://chicago.universitypressscholarship.com/view/10.7208/chicago/9780226024134.001.0001/upso-9780226322667.

Méry, Sophie. "The First Oases in Eastern Arabia: Society and Craft Technology in the 3rd Millennium BC at Hili, United Arab Emirates." *Revue d'ethnoécologie,* no. 4 (2013). https://doi.org/10.4000/ethnoecologie.1631.

Mgaya, James, Ginena B. Shombe, Siphamandla C. Masikane, Sixberth Mlowe, Egid B. Mubofu, and Neerish Revaprasadu. "Cashew Nut Shell: A Potential Bio-Resource for the Production of Bio-Sourced Chemicals, Materials and Fuels." *Green Chemistry* 21, no. 6 (2019): 1186–1201. https://doi.org/10.1039/C8GC02972E.

Mintz, Sidney W. *Sweetness and Power: The Place of Sugar in Modern History.* New York: Viking, 1985.

———. *Tasting Food, Tasting Freedom: Excursions into Eating, Culture, and the Past.* Boston: Beacon Press, 1996.

Mitchell, Angus. *Roger Casement: 16 Lives.* New York: O'Brian Press, n.d.

Mitchell, Don. "Battle/Fields: Braceros, Agribusiness, and the Violent Reproduction of the California Agricultural Landscape during World War II." *Journal of Historical Geography* 36, no. 2 (1 April 2010): 143–56. https://doi.org/10.1016/j.jhg.2010.01.003.

Mitchell, Timothy. *Carbon Democracy: Political Power in the Age of Oil.* London: Verso, 2011.

Mokyr, Joel. *The Enlightened Economy: An Economic History of Britain 1700–1850.* New Haven: Yale University Press, 2009.

———. *The Lever of Riches: Technological Creativity and Economic Progress.* New York: Oxford University Press, USA, 1992.

Mol, Annemarie. *The Logic of Care: Health and the Problem of Patient Choice.* London: Routledge, 2008.

Molina, Natalia. *How Race Is Made in America: Immigration, Citizenship, and the Historical Power of Racial Scripts.* Berkeley: University of California Press, 2014.

Moon, David. *The American Steppes: The Unexpected Russian Roots of Great Plains Agriculture, 1870s–1930s.* Cambridge: Cambridge University Press, 2020.

———. *The Plough That Broke the Steppes: Agriculture and Environment on Russia's Grasslands, 1700–1914.* Oxford: Oxford University Press, 2013.

Moore, Jason W. "The Capitalocene, Part I: On the Nature and Origins of Our Ecological Crisis." *Journal of Peasant Studies* 44, no. 3 (2017): 594–630. https://doi.org/10.1080/03066150.2016.1235036.

———. "The Capitalocene, Part II: Accumulation by Appropriation and the Centrality of Unpaid Work/Energy." *Journal of Peasant Studies* 45, no. 2 (2018): 237–79. https://doi.org/10.1080/03066150.2016.1272587.

Morgan, Edmund S. *American Slavery, American Freedom.* New York: W. W. Norton, 1975.

———. "The Labor Problem at Jamestown, 1607–18." *American Historical Review* 76, no. 3 (1971): 595–611.

Morita, Atsuro. "Multispecies Infrastructure: Infrastructural Inversion and Involutionary Entanglements in the Chao Phraya Delta, Thailand." *Ethnos* 87, no. 4 (2017): 738–57.

Morrison, Kathleen D. "Archaeologies of Flow: Water and the Landscapes of Southern India Past, Present, and Future." *Journal of Field Archaeology* 40, no. 5 (2015): 560–80. https://doi.org/10.1179/2042458215Y.0000000033.

Morris-Suzuki, Tessa. *The Technological Transformation of Japan: From the Seventeenth to the Twenty-First Century.* Cambridge: Cambridge University Press, 1994.

Morton, Julia. "The Cashew's Brighter Future." *Economic Botany* 15, no. 1 (1961): 57–78.

Mosko, Mark S. "The Fractal Yam: Botanical Imagery and Human Agency in the Trobriands." *Journal of the Royal Anthropological Institute* 15, no. 4 (2009): 679–700.

Mukharji, Projit Bihari. "Occulted Materialities." *History and Technology: Special Issue: Thinking with the World: Histories of Science and Technology from the "Out There"* 34, no. 1 (2018): 31–40. https://doi.org/10.1080/07341512.2018.1516851.

Münster, Ursula. "Working for the Forest: The Ambivalent Intimacies of Human—Elephant Collaboration in South Indian Wildlife Conservation." *Ethnos* 81, no. 3 (26 May 2016): 425–47. https://doi.org/10.1080/00141844.2014.969292.

Neal, Larry D., and Marc D. Weidenmier. "Crises in the Global Economy from Tulips to Today." In *Globalization in Historical Perspective,* edited by Michael D. Bordo, Alan M. Taylor, and Jeffrey G. Williamson, 473–514. Chicago: University of Chicago Press, 2003. http://www.nber.org/chapters/c9596.

Needham, Joseph. *Science and Civilisation in China: Volume IV, Physics and Physical Technology, Part 1: Physics.* Cambridge: Cambridge University Press, 1962.

Needham, Joseph, and Gwei-Djen Lu. "The Esculentist Movement in Mediaeval Chinese Botany; Studies on Wild (Emergency) Food Plants." *Archives internationales d'histoire des sciences* 21 (1968): 225–48.

Neher, Robert Trostle. "The Ethnobotany of Tagetes." *Economic Botany* 22, no. 4 (1968): 317–25. https://doi.org/10.1007/BF02908126.

Newson, Linda. *Life and Death in Early Colonial Ecuador.* Norman: University of Oklahoma Press, 1995.

Nichter, Mark. "Of Ticks, Kings, Spirits, and the Promise of Vaccines." In *Paths to Asian Medical Knowledge,* edited by Charles Leslie and Allan Young, 224–53. Berkeley: University of California Press, 1992.

Nieto, Mauricio. *Remedios para el imperio: Historia natural y la apropiación del Nuevo Mundo.* Bogotá: Instituto Colombiano de Antropología e Historia, 2000.

Nitin Varma, M. A. "Producing Tea Coolies? Work, Life and Protest in the Colonial Tea Plantations of Assam, 1830s–1920s." Doctoral dissertation, Humboldt University, 2011.

Norton, Marcy. *Sacred Gifts, Profane Pleasures: A History of Tobacco and Chocolate in the Atlantic World.* Ithaca, NY: Cornell University Press, 2008.

———. "Tasting Empire: Chocolate and the European Internalization of Mesoamerican Aesthetics." *American Historical Review* 111, no. 3 (June 2006): 660–91.

———. "The Chicken or the Iegue: Human-Animal Relationships and the Columbian Exchange." *American Historical Review* 120, no. 1 (2015): 28–60. https://doi.org/10.1093/ahr/120.1.28.

Nossov, K., and Peter Dennis. *War Elephants.* New Vanguard 150. Oxford: Osprey, 2008.

Nuñez, José Jesús Reyes. "A Forgotten Atlas of Erwin Raisz: 'Atlas de Cuba.'" In *Progress in Cartography,* edited by Georg Gartner, Markus Jobst, and Haosheng Huang, 289–304. Cham: Springer International, 2016. https://doi.org/10.1007/978-3-319-19602-2_18.

Nygard, Travis Earl. "Seeds of Agribusiness: Grant Wood and the Visual Culture of Grain Farming, 1862–1957." Ph.D. dissertation, University of Pittsburgh, 2009. http://search.proquest.com/docview/304978243/abstract/B36B7C4113F64701PQ/1.

Ohnuki-Tierney, Emiko. *Rice as Self: Japanese Identities Through Time.* Princeton: Princeton University Press, 1994.

Olmstead, Alan L., and Paul W. Rhode. "Adapting North American Wheat Production to Climatic Challenges, 1839–2009." *Proceedings of the National Academy of Sciences* 108, no. 2 (2011): 480–85. https://doi.org/10.1073/pnas.1008279108.

———. "Biological Globalization: The Other Grain Invasion." In *The New Comparative Economic History: Essays in Honor of Jeffrey G. Williamson,* edited by Timothy J. Hatton, Kevin H. O'Rourke, and Alan M. Taylor, 115–40. Cambridge, MA: MIT Press, 2007.

———. "Cotton, Slavery, and the New History of Capitalism." *Explorations in Economic History* 67, no. 1 (January 2018): 1–17.

———. "The Evolution of California Agriculture, 1850–2000." In *California Agriculture: Dimensions and Issues,* edited by Jerome B. Siebert, 1–23. Berkeley: University of California Press, 2003.

———. "The Red Queen and the Hard Reds: Productivity Growth in American Wheat, 1800–1940." *Journal of Economic History* 62, no. 4 (December 2004): 929–66.

Olsson, Jan. "Trading Places: Griffith, Patten and Agricultural Modernity." *Film History* 17, no. 1 (2005). http://www.jstor.org/stable/3815468.

O'Rourke, Kevin H. "The European Grain Invasion, 1870–1913." *Journal of Economic History* 57, no. 4 (1997): 775–801.

Ortíz, Fernando. *Cuban Counterpoint: Tobacco and Sugar.* Translated by Harriet de Onís. New York: A. A. Knopf, 1947.

Orwell, George. "Shooting an Elephant." In *The Collected Essays, Journalism and Letters of George Orwell*, 1:235–42. New York: Harcourt, Brace and World, 1968. https://www.orwellfoundation.com/the-orwell-foundation/orwell/essays-and-other-works/shooting-an-elephant/.

Ostrom, Elinor. *Governing the Commons: The Evolution of Institutions for Collective Action*. Canto Classics. Cambridge: Cambridge University Press, 2015. (1st ed. 1990.)

Overton, Mark. *Agricultural Revolution in England: The Transformation of the Agrarian Economy 1500–1850*. Cambridge: Cambridge University Press, 1996.

Pádua, José Augusto. *Um sopro de destruição: Pensamento político e crítica ambiental no Brasil escravista, 1786–1888*. Rio de Janeiro: Jorge Zahar, 2002.

Pakiam, Geoffrey K., Yu Leng Khor, and Jeamme Chia. "Johor's Oil Palm Industry: Past, Present and Future." In *Johor: Abode of Development?* edited by Francis E. Hutchinson and Serina Rahman, 73–106. Singapore: ISEAS, 2020.

Palat, Ravi. "Dependency Theory and World-Systems Analysis." In *A Companion to Global Historical Thought*, edited by Prasenjit Duara, Viren Murthy, and Andrew Sartori, 369–83. Basingstoke: Palgrave Macmillan, 2014.

———. *The Making of an Indian Ocean World-Economy, 1250–1650—Princes, Paddy Fields, and Bazaars*. Basingstoke: Palgrave Macmillan, 2015. //www.palgrave.com/gb/book/9781137542199.

Park, Choong-Hwan. "Nongjiale Tourism and Contested Space in Rural China." *Modern China* 40, no. 5 (2014): 519–48. https://doi.org/10.1177/0097700414534160.

Parker, Geoffrey. *Global Crisis: War, Climate Change, and Catastrophe in the Seventeenth Century*. New Haven: Yale University Press, 2013.

Pearse, Andrew. *Seeds of Plenty, Seeds of Want: Social and Economic Implications of the Green Revolution*. Oxford: Clarendon Press, 1980.

Penvenne, Jeanne Marie. "Seeking the Factory for Women: Mozambican Urbanization in the Late Colonial Era." *Journal of Urban History* 23, no. 3 (1997): 342–80.

———. *Tarana: Mulheres, migração e a economia do caju no sul de Moçambique 1945–1975* (Women, Migration and the Cashew Economy in Southern Mozambique 1945–1975). Translated by António Roxo Leão. Woodbridge, Suffolk: James Currey, 2019.

———. *Women, Migration and the Cashew Economy in Southern Mozambique 1945–1975*. Woodbridge, Suffolk: James Currey, 2015. http://doi.org/10.2307/j.ctvt6rjn7.

Pereira, Gaspar Martins. *O Douro e o vinho do Porto: De Pombal a João Franco*. Porto: Afrontamento, 1991.

———. "O vinho do Porto: Entre o artesanato e a agroindústria." " *Revista da Faculdade de Letras, História, Porto* 6 (2005): 185–92.

Pereira, Miriam Halpern. *Livre câmbio e desenvolvimento económico (Free Trade and Economic Development: Portugal in the Second Half of XIX Century)*. Lisbon: Sa. de Costa, 1971. https://agris.fao.org/agris-search/search.do?recordID=US201300486043.

Pereira, Waldick. *Cana, café & laranja: História econômica de Nova Iguaçu*. Rio de Janeiro: Fundação Getúlio Vargas / SEEC, 1977.

Perry, Elizabeth J. "From Mass Campaigns to Managed Campaigns: 'Constructing a New Socialist Countryside.' " In *Mao's Invisible Hand*, edited by Sebastian Heilmann and Elizabeth J. Perry, 30–61. Leiden: Brill, 2020.

314 Bibliography

Pfaffenberger, Bryan P. "Symbols Do Not Create Meanings—Activities Do: Or, Why Symbolic Anthropology Needs the Anthropology of Technology." In *Anthropological Perspectives on Technology*, edited by Michael B. Schiffer, 77–86. Albuquerque: University of New Mexico Press, 2001.

Philip, Kavita. "Imperial Science Rescues a Tree: Global Botanic Networks, Local Knowledge and the Transcontinental Transplantation of Cinchona." *Environment and History* 1, no. 2 (1995): 173–200.

Pimentel, Juan, and José Pardo-Tomás. "And Yet, We Were Modern. The Paradoxes of Iberian Science after the Grand Narratives." *History of Science* 55, no. 2 (2017): 133–47.

Pineda Camacho, Roberto. *Holocausto en el Amazonas: Una historia social de la casa Arana.* Bogota: Planeta, 2000.

Plevin, Rebecca. "Palmeros—the 'Special Ops' of Farmworkers—Are Increasingly Rare, Threatening the Coachella Valley Date Industry." *Desert Sun,* March 16, 2018. https://eu.desertsun.com/story/news/2018/03/15/palmero-shortage-threatens-coachella-valley-date-farming-legacy/374254002/.

Plucknett, Donald L., and Nigel J. H. Smith. *Gene Banks and the World's Food.* Princeton: Princeton University Press, 1987.

Poitou, Eugene. *Spain and Its People: A Record of Recent Travel.* London: T. Nelson and Sons, 1873.

Pomeranz, Kenneth. *The Great Divergence: China, Europe, and the Making of the Modern World Economy.* Princeton: Princeton University Press, 2000.

Popenoe, Paul B. *Date Growing in the Old World and the New.* Altadena, CA: West India Gardens, 1913.

Postel, Charles. *The Populist Vision.* Oxford: Oxford University Press, 2007.

Prange, Sebastian R. " 'Measuring by the Bushel': Reweighing the Indian Ocean Pepper Trade." *Historical Research* 84, no. 224 (2011): 212–35. https://doi.org/10.1111/j.1468-2281.2010.00547.x.

Pringle, Peter. *The Murder of Nikolai Vavilov: The Story of Stalin's Persecution of One of the Great Scientists of the Twentieth Century.* New York: Simon and Schuster, 2008.

Prothero, R.E. Lord Ernle. *The Pioneers and Progress of British Farming.* London: Longmans, 1888.

Puerto, Javier. *La ilusión quebrada: Botánica, sanidad y política científica en la España Ilustrada.* Madrid: Consejo Superior de Investigaciones Científicas, 1988.

Puig de la Bellacasa, Maria. "Making Time for Soil: Technoscientific Futurity and the Pace of Care." *Social Studies of Science* 45, no. 5 (1 October 2015): 691–716. https://doi.org/10.1177/0306312715599851.

———. " 'Nothing Comes Without Its World': Thinking with Care." *Sociological Review* 60, no. 2 (2012): 197–216.

Puig-Samper, Miguel Ángel. "El oro amargo: La protección de los quinares americanos y los proyectos de estanco de la quina en Nueva Granada." In *El bosque ilustrado: Estudios sobre la política forestal española en América,* edited by Manuel Lucena, 219–40. Madrid: Instituto Nacional para la Conservación de la Naturaleza-Instituto de la Ingeniería de España, 1991.

Pyne, Stephen. *Burning Bush: A Fire History of Australia.* Seattle: University of Washington Press, 1991.

Radich, Maria Carlos, and António Alberto Monteiro Alves. *Dois séculos da floresta em Portugal.* Lisbon: CELPA-Associação da Indústria Papeleira, 2000.

Radio Zapatista. "Los rostros (no tan) ocultos del mal llamado 'tren maya,' " 10 October 2020. https://radiozapatista.org/?p=35469&lang=en.

Raffles, Hugh. *Insectopedia.* New York: Vintage, 2011.

———. " 'Local Theory': Nature and the Making of an Amazonian Place." *Cultural Anthropology* 14, no. 3 (1999): 323–60.

Raj, Kapil. "Introduction: Circulation and Locality in Early Modern Science." *British Journal for the History of Science* 43, no. 4 (2010): 513–17. https://doi.org/10.1017/S0007087410001238.

Rangan, Haripriya, and Christian A. Kull. "What Makes Ecology 'Political'? Rethinking 'Scale' in Political Ecology." *Progress in Human Geography* 33, no. 1 (2009): 28–45. https://doi.org/10.1177/0309132508090215.

Rappaport, Erika. *A Thirst for Empire: How Tea Shaped the Modern World.* Princeton: Princeton University Press, 2019.

Rappaport, Roy A. *Pigs for the Ancestors: Ritual in the Ecology of a New Guinea People.* New Haven: Yale University Press, 1967.

Revkin, Andrew. *The Burning Season: The Murder of Chico Mendes and the Fight for the Amazon Rain Forest.* Washington, DC: Island Press, 1990.

Rheinberger, Hans-Jörg. *Toward a History of Epistemic Things: Synthesizing Proteins in the Test Tube.* Stanford: Stanford University Press, 1997.

Ribeiro, Aquilino. *When the Wolves Howl.* New York: Macmillan, 1963.

Richards, A. I. *Land, Labour and Diet in Northern Rhodesia: An Economic Study of the Bemba Tribe.* Oxford: Oxford University Press, 1939.

Richards, Paul. *Indigenous Agricultural Revolution: Ecology and Food Production in West Africa.* Boulder, CO: Westview, 1985.

———. "Rice as Commodity and Anti-Commodity." In *Local Subversions of Colonial Cultures: Commodities and Anti-Commodities in Global History,* edited by Sandip Hazareesingh and Harro Maat, 10–28. London: Palgrave Macmillan, 2016.

Richter, Daniel K. *Before the Revolution: America's Ancient Pasts.* Cambridge, MA: Harvard University Press, 2011.

Rival, Laura. "Amazonian Historical Ecologies." *Journal of the Royal Anthropological Institute* 12 (2006): S79–94.

Rival, Laura, and Doyle McKey. "Domestication and Diversity in Manioc (*Manihot esculenta* Crantz ssp. *esculenta*, Euphorbiaceae)." *Current Anthropology* 49, no. 6 (2008): 1119–28. https://doi.org/10.1086/593119.

Robertson, A. F. *The Dynamics of Productive Relationships: African Share Contracts in Comparative Perspective.* Cambridge: Cambridge University Press, 1987.

Robertson, A. S. "Oral History of Tea Planting in South India." Oral History Archive. Cambridge: Centre for South Asian Studies, 1976.

Robertson, Emma. *Chocolate, Women and Empire: A Social and Cultural History.* Manchester: Manchester University Press, 2009.

Robins, Jonathan E. *Cotton and Race Across the Atlantic: Britain, Africa, and America, 1900–1920.* Rochester: University of Rochester Press, 2016.

Robinson, Cedric J. *Black Marxism: The Making of the Black Radical Tradition.* Chapel Hill: University of North Carolina Press, 2000. (1st ed. 1983.)

316 Bibliography

Robisheaux, Thomas. "Microhistory and the Historical Imagination: New Frontiers." *Journal of Medieval and Early Modern Studies* 47, no. 1 (2017): 1–6. https://doi.org/10.1215/10829636-3716554.

Roll-Hansen, Nils. *The Lysenko Effect: The Politics of Science.* New York: Humanity Books, 2005.

Rood, Daniel B. *The Reinvention of Atlantic Slavery: Technology, Labor, Race, and Capitalism in the Greater Caribbean.* Oxford: Oxford University Press, 2017.

Ross, Corey. "Developing the Rain Forest: Rubber, Environment and Economy in Southeast Asia." In *Economic Development and Environmental History in the Anthropocene: Perspectives on Asia and Africa,* edited by Gareth Austin, 199–218. London: Bloomsbury, 2017.

———. *Ecology and Power in the Age of Empire: Europe and the Transformation of the Tropical World.* Oxford University Press, 2017.

———. "The Plantation Paradigm: Colonial Agronomy, African Farmers, and the Global Cocoa Boom, 1870s–1940s." *Journal of Global History* 9, no. 1 (2014): 49–71. https://doi.org/10.1017/S1740022813000491.

Rossiter, Margaret W. *The Emergence of Agricultural Science: Justus Liebig and the Americans, 1840–1880.* Princeton: Princeton University Press, 1975.

Rothstein, Morton. "Centralizing Firms and Spreading Markets: The World of International Grain Traders, 1846–1914." *Business and Economic History* 17 (1988): 103–13.

Ruggles, D. Fairchild. *Gardens, Landscape, and Vision in the Palaces of Islamic Spain.* University Park: State University of Pennsylvania Press, 2000.

Russell, Edmund. "Coevolutionary History." *American Historical Review* 119, no. 5 (2014): 1514–28. https://doi.org/10.1093/ahr/119.5.1514.

———. *Evolutionary History: Uniting History and Biology to Understand Life on Earth.* Cambridge: Cambridge University Press, 2011.

———. *Greyhound Nation: A Coevolutionary History of England, 1200–1900.* Cambridge: Cambridge University Press, 2018. https://doi.org/10.1017/9781139049269.

Sabban, Françoise. "L'industrie sucrière, le moulin à sucre et les relations sino-portugaises aux XIVe-XVIIIe siècles." *Annales histoire, sciences sociales* 49, no. 4 (1994): 817–62.

Saha, Madhumita, and Sigrid Schmalzer. "Green-Revolution Epistemologies in China and India: Technocracy and Revolution in the Production of Scientific Knowledge and Peasant Identity." *BJHS Themes* 1 (2016): 145–67. https://doi.org/10.1017/bjt.2016.2.

Saito, Osamu. "An Industrious Revolution in an East Asian Market Economy? Tokugawa Japan and Implications for the Great Divergence." *Australian Economic History Review* 50, no. 3 (2010): 240–61. https://doi.org/10.1111/j.1467-8446.2010.00304.x.

Salaman, R. N. *The History and Social Influence of the Potato.* Cambridge: Cambridge University Press, 1949.

Salzmann, Ariel. "The Age of Tulips: Confluence and Conflict in Early Modern Consumer Culture (1550–1730)." In *Consumption Studies and the History of the Ottoman Empire, 1550–1922: An Introduction,* edited by Donald Quataert, 83–106. Albany: State University of New York Press, 2000.

Sanders, Elizabeth. *Roots of Reform: Farmers, Workers, and the American State, 1877–1917.* Chicago: University of Chicago Press, 1999.

Santí, Enrico Mario. "Towards a Reading of Fernando Ortiz's *Cuban Counterpoint.*" *Review: Literature and Arts of the Americas* 37, no. 1 (2004): 6–18. https://doi.org/10.1080 /0890576042000239500.

Saraiva, Tiago. "A relevância da história das ciências para a história global." In *Estudos sobre a globalização,* edited by Diego Ramada Curto, 297–318. Lisbon: Edições 70, 2016.

———. "Anthropophagy and Sadness: Cloning Citrus in São Paulo in the Plantationocene Era." *History and Technology* 34, no. 1 (2018): 89–99. https://doi.org/10.1080/07 341512.2018.1516877.

———. "Breeding Europe: Crop Diversity, Gene Banks, and Commoners." In *Cosmopolitan Commons: Sharing Resources and Risks across Borders,* edited by Neil Disco and Eda Kranakis, 185–212. Cambridge, MA: MIT Press, 2013.

———. *Cloning Democracy: Californian Oranges and the Making of the Global South.* Cambridge, MA: MIT Press, forthcoming.

———. "Fascist Modernist Landscapes: Wheat, Dams, Forests, and the Making of the Portuguese New State." *Environmental History* 21, no. 1 (2015): 54–75.

———. *Fascist Pigs: Technoscientific Organisms and the History of Fascism.* Cambridge, MA: MIT Press, 2016. https://muse.jhu.edu/book/48402.

———. "The Scientific Co-Op: Cloning Oranges and Democracy in the Progressive Era." In *New Materials: Towards a History of Consistency,* edited by Amy Slaton, 119–50. Philadelphia: University of Pennsylvania Press, 2019.

Saraiva, Tiago, and Amy Slaton. "Statistics as Service to Democracy: Experimental Design and the Dutiful American Scientist." In *Technology and Globalisation,* edited by David Pretel and Lino Camprubi, 217–55. Cham: Palgrave Macmillan, 2018.

Sassen, Saskia, ed. *Deciphering the Global: Its Scales, Spaces and Subjects.* London: Routledge, 2013.

Schaeffer, Charles. "Coffee Unobserved: Consumption and Commoditization of Coffee in Ethiopia before the Eighteenth Century." In *Le commerce du café avant l'ère des plantations coloniales: Espaces, réseaux, sociétés (XVe–XIXe siècle),* edited by Michel Tuchscherer, 23–34. Cairo: IFAO, 2001.

Schama, Simon. *The Embarrassment of Riches: An Interpretation of Dutch Culture in the Golden Age.* New York: Alfred A. Knopf, 1987.

Scheele, Judith. "Traders, Saints, and Irrigation: Reflections on Saharan Connectivity." *Journal of African History* 51, no. 3 (2010): 281–300.

Schendel, Willem van. "Geographies of Knowing, Geographies of Ignorance: Jumping Scale in Southeast Asia." *Environment and Planning D: Society and Space* 20, no. 6 (2002): 647–68. https://doi.org/10.1068/d16s.

Schiebinger, Londa. *Plants and Empire: Colonial Bioprospecting in the Atlantic World.* Cambridge, MA: Harvard University Press, 2004. http://www.hup.harvard.edu/ catalog.php?isbn=9780674025684&content=reviews.

Schmalzer, Sigrid. "Layer upon Layer: Mao-Era History and the Construction of China's Agricultural Heritage." *East Asian Science, Technology and Society* 13, no. 3 (2019): 413–41.

———. *Red Revolution, Green Revolution: Scientific Farming in Socialist China.* Chicago: University of Chicago Press, 2016.

Schneider, Mindi. "Dragon Head Enterprises and the State of Agribusiness in China." *Journal of Agrarian Change* 17, no. 1 (2017): 3–21. https://doi.org/10.1111/ joac.12151.

Bibliography

Schumacher, E. F. *Small Is Beautiful: Economics as if People Mattered.* New York: Harper and Row, 1973.

Schwartz, Stuart B. *Segredos internos: Engenhos e escravos na sociedade colonial 1550–1835.* São Paulo: Companhia das Letras, 1988.

Scott, James C. *Against the Grain: A Deep History of the Earliest States.* New Haven: Yale University Press, 2017.

———. *Seeing Like a State: How Certain Schemes to Improve the Human Condition Have Failed.* Yale Agrarian Studies. New Haven: Yale University Press, 1998. http://ebookcentral.proquest.com/lib/ed/detail.action?docID=3420352.

———. *The Art of Not Being Governed: An Anarchist History of Upland Southeast Asia.* New Haven: Yale University Press, 2010.

Sedgewick, Augustine. "Against Flows." *History of the Present* 4, no. 2 (2014): 143–70. https://doi.org/10.5406/historypresent.4.2.0143.

Seekatz, Sarah. "America's Arabia: The Date Industry and the Cultivation of Middle Eastern Fantasies in the Deserts of Southern California." Ph.D. dissertation, University of California, Riverside, 2014. https://escholarship.org/uc/item/02r8x22x.

Serres, Michel. "Science and the Humanities: The Case of Turner." Translated by Catherine Brown and William Paulson. *SubStance* 26, no. 2 (1997): 6–21. https://doi.org/10.2307/3684693.

Service, Elman R. *Primitive Social Organization: An Evolutionary Perspective.* New York: Random House, 1962.

Shah, Eshah. "Telling Otherwise: A Historical Anthropology of Tank Irrigation in South India." *Technology and Culture* 49, no. 2 (2008): 658–74.

Sharma, Jayeeta. "British Science, Chinese Skill and Assam Tea: Making Empire's Garden." *Indian Economic and Social History Review* 43, no. 4 (2006): 429–55.

———. *Empire's Garden: Assam and the Making of India.* New Delhi: Permanent Black, 2012.

———. " 'Lazy' Natives, Coolie Labour, and the Assam Tea Industry." *Modern Asian Studies* 43, no. 6 (2009): 1287–1324.

Shell, Jacob. "Elephant Convoys beyond the State: Animal-Based Transport as Subversive Logistics." *Environment and Planning D: Society and Space* 37, no. 5 (2019): 905–23. https://doi.org/10.1177/0263775818805491.

———. "When Roads Cannot Be Used: The Use of Trained Elephants for Emergency Logistics, Off-Road Conveyance, and Political Revolt in South and Southeast Asia." *Transfers* 5, no. 2 (2015): 62–80.

Sheller, Mimi. "The New Mobilities Paradigm for a Live Sociology." *Current Sociology* 62, no. 6 (2014): 789–811.

Shen, Yubin. "Cultivating China's Cinchona: The Local Developmental State, Global Botanic Networks and Cinchona Cultivation in Yunnan, 1930s–1940s." *Social History of Medicine* 34, no. 2 (2021): 577–91.

Shiba, Yoshinobu. *Commerce and Society in Sung China.* Translated by Mark Elvin. Ann Arbor: Michigan University Press, 1970.

Shurtleff, William, and Akiko Aoyagi. "History of Kikkoman." SoyInfo Center, 2004. https://www.soyinfocenter.com/HSS/kikkoman.php.

Siegelbaum, Lewis. "The Odessa Grain Trade: A Case Study in Urban Growth and Development in Tsarist Russia." *Journal of European Economic History* 9, no. 1 (1980): 113–51.

Sillitoe, Paul. "Why Spheres of Exchange?" *Ethnology* 45, no. 1 (2006): 1–23.

Silva-Pando, F. J., and R. Pino-Pérez. "Introduction of Eucalyptus into Europe." *Australian Forestry* 79, no. 4 (2016): 283–91.

Sivasundaram, Sujit. "Trading Knowledge: The East India Company's Elephants in India and Britain." *Historical Journal* 48, no. 1 (March 2005): 27–63. https://doi.org/10.1017/S0018246X04004212.

Šivel, M., Stanislav Kracmar, Miroslav Fišera, Borivoj Klejdus, and Vlastimil Kubáň. "Lutein Content in Marigold Flower (*Tagetes erecta* L.) Concentrates Used for Production of Food Supplements." *Czech Journal of Food Sciences* 32 (2014): 521–25. https://doi.org/10.17221/104/2014-CJFS.

Slaton, Amy. "George Washington Carver Slept Here: Racial Identity and Laboratory Practice at Iowa State College." *History and Technology* 17, no. 4 (2001): 353–74.

———. *Reinforced Concrete and the Modernization of American Building, 1900–1930.* Baltimore: Johns Hopkins University Press, 2001.

Slicher van Bath, B. H. *The Agrarian History of Western Europe, A.D. 500–1850.* Translated by Olive Ordish. London: Edward Arnold, 1963.

Smith, Adam. *An Inquiry into the Nature and Causes of the Wealth of Nations.* 2 vols. London: W. Strahan and T. Cadell, 1776. http://hdl.handle.net/1842/1455.

Smith, Jenny Leigh. *Works in Progress: Plans and Realities on Soviet Farms, 1930–1963.* New Haven: Yale University Press, 2014. http://doi.org/10.12987/yale/9780300200690.001.0001.

Smith, Kate. "Amidst Things: New Histories of Commodities, Capital, and Consumption." *Historical Journal* 61, no. 3 (2018): 841–61.

Smith, Pamela H. "Nodes of Convergence, Material Complexes, and Entangled Itineraries." In *Entangled Itineraries: Materials, Practices, and Knowledges across Eurasia*, edited by Pamela H. Smith, 5–24. Pittsburgh: University of Pittsburgh Press, 2019.

Smith, Paul J. *Taxing Heaven's Storehouse: Horses, Bureaucrats, and the Destruction of the Sichuan Tea Industry, 1074–1224.* Cambridge, MA: Harvard University Press, 1991.

Smith, Thomas C. *The Agrarian Origins of Modern Japan.* Stanford: Stanford University Press, 1959.

Souza, Márcio. *O empate contra Chico Mendes.* São Paulo: Marco Zero, 1990.

Spary, E. C. *Feeding France: New Sciences of Food, 1760–1815.* Cambridge: Cambridge University Press, 2014.

Steward, J. H. "The Concept and Method of Cultural Ecology." In *International Encyclopedia of the Social Sciences,* edited by D. L. Sills, 337–44. New York: Macmillan, 1968.

Stoler, Ann Laura. *Capitalism and Confrontation in Sumatra's Plantation Belt, 1870–1979.* 2nd ed. Ann Arbor: University of Michigan Press, 1995.

———. *Carnal Knowledge and Imperial Power: Race and the Intimate in Colonial Rule.* Berkeley: University of California Press, 2002.

Strathern, Andrew, and Pamela J. Stewart. "Ceremonial Exchange: Debates and Comparisons." In *A Handbook of Economic Anthropology,* 2nd ed., edited by James G. Carrier, 239–56. Northampton, MA: Edward Elgar, 2012.

Strathern, Marilyn. *Reproducing the Future: Essays on Anthropology, Kinship and the New Reproductive Technologies.* Manchester: Manchester University Press, 1992.

Bibliography

Subrahmanyam, Sanjay. "Connected Histories: Notes towards a Reconfiguration of Modern Eurasia." In *Beyond Binary Histories: Re-Imagining Eurasia to c. 1830,* edited by Victor Lieberman, 289–316. Ann Arbor: University of Michigan Press, 1999.

———. *Faut-il universaliser l'histoire? Entre dérives nationalistes et identitaires.* Paris: CNRS, 2020.

———. *The Portuguese Empire in Asia 1500–1700: A Political and Economic History.* London: Longman, 1993.

Sugihara, Kaoru. "The East Asian Path of Economic Development: A Long-Term Perspective." In *The Resurgence of East Asia: 500, 150 and 50 Year Perspectives,* edited by Giovanni Arrighi, Takeshi Hamashita, and Mark Selden, 78–113. London: Routledge, 2003.

Swaminathan, M. S. *Sustainable Agriculture: Towards an Evergreen Revolution.* Delhi: Konark, 1996. https://www.cabdirect.org/cabdirect/abstract/19971802735.

Taussig, Michael. " 'Culture of Terror—Space of Death—Casement, Roger: Putumayo Report and the Explanation of Torture.' " *Comparative Studies in Society and History* 26, no. 3 (1984): 467–97.

———. *Shamanism, Colonialism, and the Wild Man: A Study in Terror and Healing.* Chicago: University of Chicago Press, 1987.

Tengberg, Margareta. "Beginnings and Early History of Date Palm Garden Cultivation in the Middle East." *Journal of Arid Environments* 86 (2012): 139–47.

Thevet, André. *Les singularitez de la France antarctique.* Edited by Paul Gaffarel. Paris: Maisonneuve, 1878. (1st ed. 1557.)

Thirsk, Joan. *Alternative Agriculture: A History: From the Black Death to the Present Day.* Oxford University Press, 2000. http://www.oxfordscholarship.com/view/10.1093/acprof:oso/9780198208136.001.0001/acprof-9780198208136.

Thompson, E. P. "Time, Work-Discipline, and Industrial Capitalism." *Past and Present* 38 (1967): 56–97.

Thompson, F. M. L. "The Second Agricultural Revolution, 1815–1880." *Economic History Review* 21, no. 1 (1968): 62–77. https://doi.org/10.2307/2592204.

Tilley, Christopher. *A Phenomenology of Landscape: Places, Paths and Monuments.* Explorations in Anthropology. Oxford: Berg, 1994.

Topik, Steven C., and Allen Wells. *Global Markets Transformed, 1870–1945.* Cambridge, MA: Belknap Press of Harvard University Press, 2012.

Topik, Steven, and William Gervase Clarence-Smith. "Introduction: Coffee and Global Development." In *The Global Coffee Economy in Africa, Asia and Latin America, 1500–1989,* edited by William Gervase Clarence-Smith and Steven Topik, 1–20. Cambridge: Cambridge University Press, 2003.

Toynbee, Arnold. *Lectures on the Industrial Revolution in England: Popular Addresses, Notes and Other Fragments.* Cambridge: Cambridge University Press, 2011. (1st ed. 1887.)

Trautmann, Thomas R. *Elephants and Kings: An Environmental History.* Chicago: University of Chicago Press, 2015.

Trischler, Helmuth. "The Anthropocene: A Challenge for the History of Science, Technology, and the Environment." *NTM Zeitschrift für Geschichte der Wissenschaften, Technik und Medizin* 24, no. 3 (2016): 309–35. https://doi.org/10.1007/s00048-016-0146-3.

Tsai, Yen-Ling. "Farming Odd Kin in Patchy Anthropocenes." *Current Anthropology* 60, no. S20 (2019): S342–53. https://doi.org/10.1086/703414.

Tsing, Anna Lowenhaupt. "More-Than-Human Sociality: A Call for Critical Description." In *Anthropology and Nature,* edited by Kirsten Hastrup, 27–42. Abingdon: Routledge, 2014.

———. *The Mushroom at the End of the World: On the Possibility of Life in Capitalist Ruins.* Princeton: Princeton University Press, 2015. https://press.princeton.edu/titles/10581.html.

Tsing, Anna Lowenhaupt, Andrew S. Mathews, and Nils Bubandt. "Patchy Anthropocene: Landscape Structure, Multispecies History, and the Retooling of Anthropology: An Introduction to Supplement 20." *Current Anthropology* 60, no. S20 (2019): S186–97. https://doi.org/10.1086/703391.

Tuchscherer, Michel. "Coffee in the Red Sea Area from the Sixteenth to the Nineteenth Century." In *The Global Coffee Economy in Africa, Asia, and Latin America, 1500–1989,* edited by William Gervase Clarence-Smith and Steven Topik, 50–66. Cambridge University Press, 2003.

Tully, John. *The Devil's Milk: A Social History of Rubber.* New York: New York University Press, 2011.

Turner, Alexander. "Plotting the Future: The 'Seed Guardians' Bringing Variety to UK Gardens." *Guardian,* 19 January 2021, sec. "Environment." https://amp.theguardian.com/environment/2021/jan/19/plotting-the-future-the-seed-guardians-bringing-variety-to-uk-gardens-aoe.

Turner, B. L., and Peter D. Harrison. "Prehistoric Raised-Field Agriculture in the Maya Lowlands." *Science* 213, no. 4506 (1981): 399–405.

Tyrrell, Ian R. *True Gardens of the Gods: Californian-Australian Environmental Reform, 1860–1930.* Berkeley: University of California Press, 1999.

Uekötter, Frank, ed. *Comparing Apples, Oranges, and Cotton: Environmental Histories of the Global Plantation.* Frankfurt-on-Main: Campus, 2014.

Urry, John. "The Sociology of Space and Place." In *The Blackwell Companion to Sociology,* edited by Judith R. Blau, 3–15. Oxford: Blackwell, 2001.

U.S. Department of the Interior, Definitions Subcommittee of the Invasive Species Advisory Committee. "Invasive Species Definition Clarification and Guidance," 27 April 2006. https://www.doi.gov/sites/doi.gov/files/uploads/isac_definitions_white_paper_rev.pdf.

USDA and National Agricultural Statistics Service. "Farms and Land in Farms, 2018 Summary," April 2019. Available at https://www.nass.usda.gov.

Uzendoski, Michael A. "Making Amazonia: Shape-Shifters, Giants, and Alternative Modernities." *Latin American Research Review* 40, no. 1 (2005): 223–36.

———. "Manioc Beer and Meat: Value, Reproduction and Cosmic Substance Among the Napo Runa of the Ecuadorian Amazon." *Journal of the Royal Anthropological Institute* 10, no. 4 (2004): 883–902. https://doi.org/10.1111/j.1467-9655.2004.00216.x.

Vargas Llosa, Mario. *El sueño del celta.* Madrid: Alfaguara, 2013.

———. *La casa verde.* Madrid: Alfaguara, 2013. (1st ed. 1966.)

Vasudevan, Padma, Suman Kashyap, and Satyawati Sharma. "Tagetes: A Multipurpose Plant." *Bioresource Technology* 62, no. 1 (1 October 1997): 29–35. https://doi.org/10.1016/S0960-8524(97)00101-6.

Vaught, David. "Transformations in Late Nineteenth-Century Rural California." In *A Companion to California History*, edited by William Deverell and David Igler, 215–29. Chichester: Wiley-Blackwell, 2008.

Veblen, Thorstein. *The Theory of the Leisure Class*. New York: Macmillan, 1899.

Vellvé, Renée. *Saving the Seed. Genetic Diversity and European Agriculture*. London: GRAIN/Earthscan, 1992.

Verschuer, Charlotte von, and Wendy Cobcroft. *Rice, Agriculture, and the Food Supply in Premodern Japan*. London: Routledge, 2016. https://www.routledge.com/Rice-Agriculture-and-the-Food-Supply-in-Premodern-Japan/Verschuer-Cobcroft/p/book/9781138885219.

Veteläinen, V., V. Negri, and N. Maxted, eds. *European Landraces: On-Farm Conservation, Management and Use*. Rome: Biodiversity International, 2009.

Vidal de La Blache, Paul. "Les conditions géographiques des faits sociaux." *Annales de géographie* 11, no. 55 (1902): 13–23.

Vieyra-Odilon, Leticia, and Heike Vibrans. "Weeds as Crops: The Value of Maize Field Weeds in the Valley of Toluca, Mexico." *Economic Botany* 55, no. 3 (1 July 2001): 426–43. https://doi.org/10.1007/BF02866564.

Viraphol, Sarasin. *Tribute and Profit: Sino-Siamese Trade, 1652–1853*. Cambridge, MA: Harvard University Press, 1997.

Viveiros de Castro, Eduardo. "Exchanging Perspectives: The Transformation of Objects into Subjects in Amerindian Ontologies." *Common Knowledge* 25, nos. 1–3 (2019): 21–42. https://doi.org/10.1215/0961754X-7299066.

———. "Perspectival Anthropology and the Method of Controlled Equivocation." *Tipití: Journal of the Society for the Anthropology of Lowland South America* 2, no. 1 (2004): 3–22.

von Falkenhausen, Lothar. *Suspended Music: Chime-Bells in the Culture of Bronze Age China*. Berkeley: University of California Press, 1993.

von Glahn, Richard. *The Economic History of China: From Antiquity to the Nineteenth Century*. Cambridge: Cambridge University Press, 2016. https://doi.org/10.1017/CBO9781139343848.

von Oppen, Achim. "Cassava, 'the Lazy Man's Food'? Indigenous Agricultural Innovation and Dietary Change in Northwestern Zambia (ca. 1650–1970)." *Food and Foodways* 5, no. 1 (1991): 15–38. https://doi.org/10.1080/07409710.1991.9961989.

Walker, Brett L. "Commercial Growth and Environmental Change in Early Modern Japan: Hachinohe's Wild Boar Famine of 1749." *Journal of Asian Studies* 60, no. 2 (2001): 329–51. https://doi.org/10.2307/2659696.

Walker, John. "Memorandum." In *The Measures Adopted for Introducing the Cultivation of the Tea Plant within the British Possessions in India*, edited by Sir William Bentinck, 10–11. British Parliamentary Papers. London, 1834.

Wallace, Henry A. *Agricultural Prices*. Des Moines, IA: Wallace, 1920. https://catalog.hathitrust.org/Record/001887625.

Watson, Andrew M. "The Arab Agricultural Revolution and Its Diffusion, 700–1100." *Journal of Economic History* 34, no. 1 (March 1974): 8–35. https://doi.org/10.1017/S0022050700079602.

Watts, Sydney. "Food and the Annales School." In *The Oxford Handbook of Food History*, edited by Jeffrey M. Pilcher, 3–18. Oxford: Oxford University Press, 2012. https://doi.org/10.1093/oxfordhb/9780199729937.013.0001.

Weatherstone, J. "Historical Introduction." In *Tea: Cultivation to Consumption,* edited by K. C. Willson and M. N. Clifford, 1–24. Dordrecht: Springer Science and Business Media, 2012.

Weber, Max. *The Protestant Ethic and the Spirit of Capitalism.* Translated by Talcott Parsons. New York: Charles Scribner's Sons, 1930.

Weiner, Annette B. *Inalienable Possessions: The Paradox of Keeping-While-Giving.* Berkeley: University of California Press, 1992.

Wells, Miriam J. *Strawberry Fields: Politics, Class, and Work in California Agriculture.* Ithaca, NY: Cornell University Press, 1996.

Whatmore, Sarah. "Materialist Returns: Practising Cultural Geography in and for a More-Than-Human World." *Cultural Geographies* 13, no. 4 (2006): 600–609.

Whayne, Jeannie M. "Black Farmers and the Agricultural Cooperative Extension Service: The Alabama Experience, 1945–1965." *Agricultural History* 72, no. 3 (1998): 523–51.

White, Hayden. *Metahistory: The Historical Imagination in Nineteenth-Century Europe.* Baltimore: Johns Hopkins University Press, 2014. (1st ed. 1973.)

White, Kenneth D. "Fallowing, Crop Rotation, and Crop Yields in Roman Times." *Agricultural History* 44, no. 3 (1970): 281–90.

Whyte, Martin King. "Introduction: Rural Economic Reforms and Chinese Family Patterns." *China Quarterly* 130 (1992): 317–22. https://doi.org/10.1017/S0305741000040741.

Williams, Eric. *Capitalism and Slavery.* Chapel Hill: University of North Carolina Press, 1944.

Williams, Raymond. *The Country and the City.* London: Chatto and Windus, 1973.

Willis, F. Roy. "The Contribution of the 'Annales' School to Agrarian History: A Review Essay." *Agricultural History* 52, no. 4 (1978): 538–48.

Wittfogel, Karl A. *Oriental Despotism: A Comparative Study in Total Power.* New Haven: Yale University Press, 1957.

Woodman, Harold D. *New South—New Law: The Legal Foundations of Credit and Labor Relations in the Postbellum Agricultural South.* Walter Lynwood Fleming Lectures in Southern History. Baton Rouge: Louisiana State University Press, 1995.

World Bank. "Agribusiness." Text/HTML. World Bank. Accessed 4 January 2021. https://www.worldbank.org/en/topic/agribusiness.

Worster, Donald. "Hydraulic Society in California: An Ecological Interpretation." *Agricultural History* 56, no. 3 (1982): 503–15.

Xia Weiying. *Lüshi Chunqiu Shangnong deng sipian jiaoshi* (The four chapters on agriculture in the *Lüshi Chunqiu* emended and explained). Beijing: Zhonghua Editions, 1956.

Xu Guangqi. *Nongzheng quanshu* (Complete treatise on agricultural administration). Edited by Shi Shenghan. Shanghai: Guji Press, 1979. (1st ed. 1639.)

Xue, Yongji, KuoRay Mao, Nefratiri Weeks, and Jingyi Xiao. "Rural Reform in Contemporary China: Development, Efficiency, and Fairness." *Journal of Contemporary China* 30, no. 128 (2021): 266–82. https://doi.org/10.1080/10670564.2020.1790902.

Young, Arthur. *A Course of Experimental Agriculture: Containing an Exact Register of All the Business Transacted During Five Years on Near Three Hundred Acres of Various Soils.* Dublin: J. Exshaw, 1771.

———. *A Tour in Ireland; with General Observations on the Present State of That Kingdom, Made in the Years 1776, 1777, and 1778 and Brought down to the End of 1779.* 2 vols. Dublin: Whitestone, 1780.

324 Bibliography

Zarrilli, Adrián Gustavo. "Capitalism, Ecology, and Agrarian Expansion in the Pampean Region, 1890–1950." *Environmental History* 6, no. 4 (2001): 561–83.

Zhang, Fusuo, Xinping Chen, and Peter Vitousek. "An Experiment for the World." *Nature* 497, no. 7447 (May 2013): 33–35. https://doi.org/10.1038/497033a.

Zhang, Jinghong. *Puer Tea: Ancient Caravans and Urban Chic.* Seattle: University of Washington Press, 2014.

Zimmerman, Andrew. *Alabama in Africa: Booker T. Washington, the German Empire, and the Globalization of the New South.* Princeton: Princeton University Press, 2010.

Index

Page numbers in italic indicate illustrations.

Abd al-Rahman, 32–33, 37, 207
abusa, 50–52
actants: and the cropscape, 13–25;
    elephants as, 151–56; eucalyptus as,
    165–71; nonhuman, 2–4, 92, 140, 143,
    146, 174; and structuralist anthropol-
    ogy, 80–82
actor-network theory (ANT), 17, 134–71
agency, 3, 13–20, 80, 148, 184, 187, 197,
    214, 222, 234; entangled, 155–56;
    interspecies, 156, 186–89. *See also*
    actants: non-human
agricultural involution, 42–54, 181
agricultural revolutions, 98–102, 131
agroecology, 15, 202, 241–43
agronomy: 9–10, 43, 47, 53, 55, 98–102,
    186–87, 191, 196, 202, 240–44; in
    China, 11, 130–31, 134–45, 173; and
    plantation paradigm, 202
Ahnenerbe, 215

Akan, 50–51. *See also* Ghana
Akrich, Madeleine, 17
al-Andalus, 31–34
Algeria, 32, 33, 132, 145
All-Union Institute of Plant Industry
    (VIR), 212–15
altermundialistas, 195, 243
Amazon(ia), 24, 76–82, 85, 94, 137–44,
    146, 170, 195
Amerindians, 80–82, 137–39, 144–58,
    229–31
Amsterdam, 60–69, 85, 89, 113–15, 149
Andalusia, 192, 207. *See also* al-Andalus
Andes, 18, 76, 144–51, 170, 178–79
Angola, 18, 114, 145
Annales school, 3–6, 11, 25, 57, 76, 178,
    205, 208
Anthropocene, 20, 39, 79, 136, 164–68,
    202–9
anthropology, 20, 75–83, 134–36, 169–70

326 Index

Appadurai, Arjun, 78
Arab: civilization, 32; expansion into North Africa, 26, 29, 31; merchants, 30–31; scholars, 32
Arabian Peninsula, 26–27, 29
Arana, Julio César, 137–43
archaeology, 5–6, 27–8, 116, 191, 243
Aristotle, 12
Assam, 2, 83–90, *87, 119,* 120–24, 154–56
assemblages, 3–6, 17–18, 57, 127–28, 169, 194, 205, 249
Atlas de Cuba, 7, 7–10, 21
Aztecs, 2, 197–99, 204

bacteria, 188–89, 218
Bakewell, Robert, 99, 193
Balkans, 213–15
Baluchistan, 27, 33
Banya merchants, 114, 116
barley, 27, 56, 189, 197, 209, 212, 218–19; spring, 173; winter, 40, 128. *See also* fermentation
beans. *See* three sisters
beer, 218–19; cashew, 229; manioc, 76, 80–81. *See also* cassava
bees, 13, 187, 191
Bellacasa, María Puig de la, 189
Bender, Barbara, 5
Bergson, Henri, 25
Berlan, Amanda, 52
Bilbo, Theodore, 239
biodiversity, 103, 144, 146, 187, 189, 196, 210, 240–41
biopolitics and biopower, 76, 179
Bloch, Marc, 4
botany, 75, 80, 120–23, 148–49, 178, 212, 231; botanical gardens, 32, 63–65, 86–88, 214. *See also* Kew Gardens; plant hunters
Brabant, 100, 192
Branco, Camillo Castello, 225
brands and branding, 67, 89, 111, 220–21, 224–26
Braudel, Fernand, 11, 14, 25, 58
Brazil, 113–14, 166–67, 174–84; and cashews, 229–33, *230;* and coffee, 113–15, 167; historians of, 11; and

marigolds, 198; and port, 227; and rubber, 137–44; and sugar, 31, 76. *See also* São Paulo
bread, 14, 54, 69–73, 178, 185, 192, 218, 229
breeding, plant, *210,* 211–16, 241
brewing, 41, 53, 218–23, 241, 253
Britain, 15, 99–102, 134, 137, 185, 232–33; and cinchona-quinine, 144–51, 170; and elephants, 153–56; and Industrial Revolution (cotton and potatoes), 102, 158, 160, 164–66, 178, 184–85; and New Husbandry, 99–100, 192–94, 203; Parliament of, 88, 99; and port, 224–25, 227; and rubber, 137–39; and tea, 2, 17, 83, 88–91, 93, 118–25; and tobacco, 107–9. *See also* East India Company: British; Kew Gardens
Bruce, Charles, 154
Bubandt, Nils, 205
Burpee, David, 200

cacao: cultural significance in pre-Columbian Americas, 17, 91, 197, 204; in milpa gardens, 190; and plantations in São Tomé, 48. *See also* cocoa
Cadiz, 146
Cairo, 30, 113–16
Calcutta, 88, 91
California, 167, 187; and dates, 23–26, 33–37, 57, 209; and wheat, 71
camels, 29–31, 189
Canet, Gerardo, *7,* 7–11, 21
cannibals, 81, 139, 229
capitalism, 11, 202, 233; and alternatives, 44–45, 78, 94, 191; and cocoa, 51; and coffee, 177–78; and colonialism, 138–39, 245; European, 30–37; 60–69; 75, 92, 98–101, 120, 125, 167–68; 194; expanding, 166; industrial, 16, 44, 166, 169, 178–86; and international capital, 11, 24, 72, 157, 204; Islamic, 16, 30–37, 63–69; Japanese, 44; and overproduction, 163, 177, 234, 238; and sugar, 56; U.S., 11, *22,* 109, 237; and wheat, 70–75

Capitalocene, 166–67. *See also* Anthropocene

care, 2, 51, 132, 172–74, 188–90, 202–6, 233–34, 245; and chemicals, 194; and breeding, 211, 243–45; theory of, 188; and water, 28, 125–30. *See also* love; weeds

Caribbean, 11, 14, 18, 50, 81, 113–14, 181–82, 185; and cashews, 231; experiential, 146, 149. *See also* colonialisms; Cuba; plantations

Carver, George Washington, 3, 11, 208, 228, 235–40, *236*

Casement, Roger, 138–43

cashews, 21, 208, 227–34, *230*, 245; as anti-commodity, 228–29; in Brazil, 229–33; in India, 228–34; and technological innovation, 231–33. *See also* gender

cassava, 2, 8, 12, 24, 52, 76–82, 143–44, 178–82. *See also* Mozambique

Catholicism, 15, 33, 134, *183*, 199

cattle and livestock, 18, 128, 169, 184–87, 193, 202; cows, 79; donkeys and mules, 29, 55, 117, 131, 175, 235, 242, 245; horses, 99, 131, 151; water buffalo, 46, 127–28, 242. *See also* mixed farming; pigs; sheep/shepherds

Caxoeira plantation, 11, 174–76, *176*

cereals, 39, 103, 130, 173, 180, 186, 203, 233; and crop rotations, 192–93; and dates, 27, 189; distinct from tubers, 75–76, 182; domestication/reproduction, 13, 37, 56; and enclosures, 99; fermented, 218; yields, 47, 192–93, 209. *See also* bread; millets; rice; wheat

Ceylon, 89, 124, 140, 149, 232

chemicals, 47, 186, 226, 228; agricultural, 200. *See also* fertilizers: chemical; Green Revolution; pests; quinine; weeds

chemurgy, 238–39

Chen Fu, 127

Chicago, 14, 69–75, *71*, 94, 162

China, 30, 95–97, 133, 179–81, 192, 200–203, 241–44, 249; agricultural treatises of, 192; historians of, 43, 101, 125, 179, 241; imperial state and agriculture, *54*, 126, *201;* industrious revolution, 45, 179; junk trade of, 181; and locusts, 172; Maoist, 56, 106; Opium Wars, 43, 97, 181; and Oriental Despotism, 42; overseas labor migration, 140–41; People's Republic of, 102, 106; and polyculture, 187–92; and soy, 218–20; and water, 125–32, *129. See also* Jiangnan; millets; rice; silk and silkworms; tea (in China)

chinampas, 240

cinchona, 11, 18, 86, *150,* 169–70, 223; and Andean healers, 145–6; and Dutch Empire, 149–51; and the history of knowledge, 144–45, 150–51; as quinine, 149–51; and Spanish imperial botany, 146–49

civilization, 37–38, 56–57, 68, 178, 184, 207, 226–29, 234, 251; Arabian, 28–32; Asian, 42–45; Chinese, 52–56; cradles of, 29; ecological, 242; hydraulic, 125; ideas of, 26, 56–57, 75, 81, 85, 139; Maya, 191; and tea, 125. *See also* nomads; wilderness/wildness

civil wars: Chinese, 97; U.S., 109–12, 158–60, 235, 246

climate change, 20, 28–29, 103, 164–66. *See also* Anthropocene

Clusius, Carolus, 61, 65

coalitions, 3, 156, 174, 203–4, 218, 250; interspecies, 186–90

cocoa, 12, *49,* 57; *abusa* (sharecropping/ smallholding), 50–52; Akan lineages, 50, 52; forest farming, 48, 50, 52; in Ghana, 48–52; labor migration, 51–52; life cycle (tree, farm, family), 50–52. *See also* frontiers

coevolution, 140, 169, 188

coffee, 8, 48, 113–18, 149, 182, 240; in Brazil, 140, 167, 175–78, *176,* 203; in Ethiopia, 17, 97, 106, 113–18, 125; interlocking cultivation systems, 115–18; Islamic culture of, 67, 116; Italian Fascism and, 115–17; in Yemen, 115–16

328 Index

coffeehouses and coffee shops, 67, 114–16
Colombia, 114, 148, 170
colonialisms, 113, 138–39, 145, 169, *217*;
   settler, 48, 72–75, 89, 107–8, 115, 195,
   204, 231–34
Columbian Exchange, 2, 14–15, 26,
   80–82, 146
Columella, 98, 192
commercial cropping, 8, 30, 33–35, 38,
   41, 74, 83–91, 99, 103, 130, 160, 167,
   173, 178–81, 192–95, 200, 234. *See also*
   monocropping
commodities, 3–23, 60, 76, 98, 137, 155,
   163, *176,* 239; anti-commodities, 76,
   184, 228; cashew, 228–32; chains, 97,
   113–14, 133, 174; cinchona-quina-
   quinine, 145–51; coffee, 113–14, 167,
   177–78; dates, 30, 35; global history
   and, 13–18, 67, 76, 92; para-commodities, 76, 80, 83, 180–81, 184–85;
   potatoes, 184–85; rubber, 140–44, 196;
   scientific, 147; tea, 83–89, 124, 133;
   tulips, 60–62, 67; and weeds, 173;
   wheat, *71,* 72, 76–80. *See also* futures
   contracts, exchanges, and traders;
   plantations; standardization
Congo, 114, 138–40, 145
connected history, 208, 216
Conrad, Joseph, 139
Conrad, Sebastian, 93
Constantinople, 192. *See also* Istanbul
contrapunteo, 188, 202–6
Coronil, Fernando, 10
cotton, 2–3, 8–11, 40–41, 126, 138, 143,
   160, 173, 180–86, 190–94, 228,
   235–39, 246–47; and boll weevil, 13;
   and brokers, exchanges, and futures
   trading, 62, 157–64, *158*
credit, 30, 103, 109–12, 114, 138, 143,
   160–62
Creoles, 137, 141
creolization, 10
Cronon, William, 70
crop rotations, 1, 55, 98–99, 131, 184–86,
   191–94, 203, 218. *See also* scientific
   farming

cropscape, definition, 4–11
Crosby, Alfred W., 14. *See also* Columbian
   Exchange
Cuba, *7,* 7–11, 21, 38, 188–89, 203–4
Cunha, Euclides da, 143
cycles, 12, 20, 97, 103, 134, 172, 191,
   193; historical, 31–32; human-plant
   life, 48–52, 57, 162; pig ritual, 79–82;
   reproductive, 12, 37–39, 39–47, 106,
   109, 118, 245

Damascus, 32–33, 207
Darjeeling, 86–88
dates/date palms: in Al-Andalus, 32–33,
   207; in Arabia, 26–29; in California,
   33–37; and camels, 29–30; and
   capitalism, 29–31, 33–37; domestication of, 26–29; and oases, 27–31, 35;
   and Orientalism, *34,* 35–36; plant
   hunters and plant scientists, 33–35; and
   trans-Saharan trade, 29–31
debt, 138–43, 162, 235
decolonial critique/decolonizing history, 2,
   12, 15, 21, 247
Descola, Philippe, 81
determinism, 3, 28, 72, 90–91, 121, 132,
   142–44; crop/seed, 15, 42–48, 188;
   technological, 103, 159–62
development, 14–17, 39, 63, 167–68, 219,
   241–44; economists, 48; theories of, 17,
   42–44, 98–103, 202–4, 241–44; tubers
   and, 75, 94, 135; and wine, 226
de Vries, Jan, 44
Diamond, Jared, 79
diffusion, 27, 182, 198
domestication, 13, 19, 26–28, 37–39, 56,
   80–85, 151–56, 174, 188. *See also* weeds
Douro, 223–27
Dove, Michael, 195
dryland farming, 130–32
Du Bois, W. E. B., 11, 235, 239, 246

Earle, Rebecca, 185
earthworms, 19, 23, 135
East India Company: British, 2, 83;
   Dutch, 62–63, 113

Index 329

ecology, 78–79, 169, 174, 203–5, 241–44
Ecuador, 80, 145–46
efficiency, 28, 96, 98–99, 103, 120, 191, 197, 202, 242; camel, 29; market, 162; soil, 189
Egypt, 33, 98, 125, 192
elephants, 3, 22, *152*, 195, 231, 248; and nonhuman agency, 155–57; and tea plantations, 151–56; war elephants, 151–53; and Zomia, 156–57
eleusine, 118
Elvin, Mark, 43
Engels, Friedrich, 184
environmentalism, 96, 104, 144, 194, 243. *See also* care; history: environmental
essentialism, 25, 37, 56, 169, 221; seed or genetic, 209–17, 246
Ethiopia, 17, 97, 113–8, 125, 212–15
eucalyptus, 12, 19, 88, 136, 196; and fire, 165–66; and history of the Anthropocene, 164–71; and paper pulp, 167–68; in Portugal, 165–68
Euphrates, 32–33, 207
Eurocentrism, 16, 31, 68
exceptionalism, 15; of Chicago, 71; of the Douro region of Portugal, 225; Japanese, 45; Western, 15
extraction, 43, 56, 99, 137–44, 200, 205, 231–34, 240; labor, 93, 180

falaj, 28–30
fallowing, 4, 107, 184, 191–92. *See also* crop rotations
famine, 48, 173, 178, 180, 184
FAO. *See* U.N. Food and Agriculture Organization (FAO)
farming systems, 15, 48, 103, 202–6, 240–44. *See also* agroecology
fascism, 115, 167, 238, 246
FDA. *See* Food and Drug Administration (FDA)
fear, 142, 149, 161. *See also* care; love; violence
fermentation, 3, 219–20, 245; of cashews, 229; of cocoa, 51; ferment cake, 218–19, 221; of tea, 90; of wine, 225

Ferreira, Dona Antónia Adelaide, 225–26
fertilizers, 43, 50, 53, 109–12, 117, 131, 134, 193–94; animal and vegetal, 128, 186–87, 191, 237, 242; chemical, 42, 46, 103, 187–88, 216, 226, 237
flagelados, 138, 143
Flanders, 100, 192
Florence, Hercule, 174–78, *176*
flowers, culture of, 65, 199
fodder, 153, 186, 192, 196. *See also* cattle and livestock
food: packing, 232; processing, 182, 200, 223; quality, 232; regulation, 223; sovereignty, 96, 103, 243–44; for wageworkers, 226
Food and Drug Administration (FDA), 232
foraging, 47, 80, 153, 192, 196, 231, 237; animals, 153–55, 195. *See also* weeds
Ford Motor Company, Fordism, and Henry Ford, 97, 140, 143, 238
forests, 167–68, 175; cinchona, 144–51; clearing, 121, 153, 167, 175–77, *176;* cocoa, 48–52; coffee, 115–18; and elephants, 153–57; fallow cropping, 48–52; fires, 165–68, 175–77, 190; gardening, 3, 56, 80, 117–18, 189–90, 196, 198; management, 190; national, 167; reafforestation, 196; rubber, 137–44; tea, 85. *See also* foraging
Forrester, James, 225–26
fossil fuels, 165–66, 187. *See also* Anthropocene; climate change
France, 8, 68, 101, 114, 175, 197, 227; and bread, 185; empire, 15, 18, 38, 117, 141, 175; merchants from, 72, 113; pharmacists/plant breeders/scientists from, 145, 211; and potatoes, 185–86; and tulips, 66–68; and wine, 224, 227. *See also* Annales school
freedom, 15, 109, 125, 156, 184–85, 215, 235–37
frontiers, 41, 104, 106, 108, 143–44, 146; cocoa, 3, 12, 21, 48–51, *49*, 57; coffee, 177; tea, 154; wheat, 72–74

330 Index

Fuchs, Leonhart, 198
fungus, 140, 143, 189
futures contracts, exchanges, and traders, 4, 60–66, 69–74, 157–64, *158*

gardens, 2–6, 27, 47, 52, 114, 195, 203; botanical and imperial, 32, 63, 88, 140, 144–59, 214; cassava, tubers, and yams, 2, 19, 52, 60, 79–80, 179–80; coffee, 113; formal, 199; and magic, 77, 134–35; middle-class culture and, 200; and nostalgia, 31–33, 199; provision and vegetable, 40, 79–82, 173, 177, 179–85, 198, 203; royal, 65, 68, 207; tea, 2, 22, 83–94, 121–22, 154–55; walled, 6, 60–61. *See also* forests: gardening; Kew Gardens
gathering, 47, 56, 82, 115, 139
Geertz, Clifford, 42–43
General Foods Corporation, 232
Germany, 14, 72–74, 103, 114, 209–17, 238
gender, 38, 42, 80, 141, 233–34, 241, 247
Gengzhi tu, 41, *201*
Ghana, 3, 21, 31, 48–52, *49, 57*
Gille, Zsuzsa, 170, 228
Globally Important Agricultural Heritage Systems, xiii, 209, 228, 240–46. *See also* heritage
Goa, 231
gold, 30–31, 167, 175
Gómez, Pablo, 136, 169–70
Graz, 215
grazing, 40, 122, 192–96. *See also* cattle and livestock; sheep/shepherds
Great Depression, 124, 163, 177, 239
Great Migration, 161
Green Revolution, 4, 15–19, 39, 57, 130, 241; and plant breeding, 216–17; and rice, 45–46, 197; and scale, 103–4, 202
Gujarat, 114

Haiti, 113–15, 175
hands, 9, 33, 138–40, 188, 219, 229–31, 233
Haraway, Donna, 171, 188

Harrell, Stevan, 244
Hawqal, Ibn, 30
Hayami, Akira, 44
herbalists, 146, 195, 198
heritage: and biodiversity, 240–41; in China, 241–44; and GIAHS, 241, 243; and Zapatistas, 244–45. *See also* food: sovereignty; millets
Hill, Polly, 48
Himmler, Heinrich, 216
Hinduism, 196–204
history: of capitalism, 11, 22, 31, 44, 60–66, 78, 157, 169; of climate, 79; coevolutionary, 18, 169; cultural, 21, 135, 164; economic, 21, 61–67, 72, 91–92, 100–102, 108, 157, 162, 204; environmental, 18, 20, 79, 103, 158, 164, 175, 249; global, 20, 79; of knowledge, 144, 148, 170; national, 74, 143, 208; of science, 20, 135, 169, 208; of technology, x, 6, 13, 23, 92, 135, 157, 164, 169, 208–10, 245, 249; teleology, Whig history, 169. *See also* metahistory; microhistory
horticulture, 5, 132, 188, 201
Hungary, 228
hunting, 47, 80–81, 153
hydrology/hydroelectrics, 87, 132, 168

imagination: and agricultural revolution, 102; failure of, 144, 237; historical, 23, 82; milpa, 196; plantation, 202; and reproduction, 246; and weeds, 195
Inca, 179, 182
indentured laborers, 85, 89, 93, 107, 114, 121–22, 141, 181
India, 2, 22, 30–31, 42, 44–5, 101, 141, 153, 215; British East India Company, 2, 88; and cashews, 228–34; and cinchona, 144–51; and coffee, 113–16, 118; colonial, 167; and Dutch East India Company, 62; and elephants, 151–57; and eucalyptus, 166; and marigolds, 199–200; Mughal, 156, 199; and tea, 17, 83–92, *87,* 97, 118–24, *119. See also* Assam; cashews; cinchona;

East India Company; elephants; Green
Revolution; Kerala; marigolds;
medicine, Ayurvedic; tea (in India)
Indonesia, 62, 140, *150,* 165, 195–96, 204.
See also Java; Sumatra
Industrial Revolution (British), 44, 84,
101–2, 158, 164, 178–79, 185, 193
industrious revolution: in China, 179–81;
in Europe, 44; in Japan, 44
intentionality, 92, 136, 153, 168
invasive species, 19, 37, 196
Iran, 27–28, 91, 114, 213–15
Iraq, 27, 33
Ireland, 22, 75–76, 101, 165, 178–86
IRRI and IR8, 45–47, 197, 223. *See also*
Green Revolution
irrigation, 125, 127, 208, 242; and dates,
28–30, 35–36; and Green Revolution,
103; and rice, 46
Istanbul, 60–69, *64,* 89, 116
Italian empire in East Africa, 115–17

Japan, 15, 90–91, 101, 125–6, 130,
169, 199, 220–22; empire, 44, 90–91,
141, 150, 221; Meiji period, 42–44;
national diet, 221; and rice, 39–45, 55,
197; and soy sauce, 218–23,
222
Java, 42, 113–16, 121, 128, 141, 144,
149–51, *150,* 196
Jefferies, William, 232
Jiangnan, 40–41, 95, 127–31, 181,
242

Kangra, 86
Kansas, 14, 74
Kerala, 88, 232–33
Kew Gardens, 88, 140, 144, 148–49
Khaldun, Ibn, 11, 31–32, 37
Kikkoman, 221–23
kinship, 76, 93, 117
Ko, Dorothy, 18
kok-saghyz. *See* breeding, plant; rubber
Kollam. *See* Quilon
Korea, 168, 221
kulaks, *105,* 106, 133

labor: cheap, 182, 184, 233; Chinese
contract, 193; and coolies, 141, 142,
180; and proletariat, 36, 99, 102, 221;
and subaltern workforces, 180; unions,
233; wage labor, 51, 114, 180, 205,
233. *See also* slavery and enslaved
peoples
Lâle Devri, 2, 67–68
landlordism, 180
land property regimes: allotments, 111–12,
185–86, 203; collectivization, 106, 133,
213; commons, 167, 209–12; sharecropping, 46, 50, 109–11, 117, 160,
235–37, 239
landraces, 211–13, 215, 223, 244–45
landscape, 4–6, 14–15, 121, 169, 175,
188; heritage, 57, 208; industrial/
monocrop, 16, 39, 168, 174, 179, 204;
nonhuman change to, 154, 166
latifundia, 98
Latour, Bruno, 135. *See also* actants;
actor-network theory; assemblages
Lee, Victoria, 222
Lenin Academy of Agricultural Science,
214
Leningrad, 213–14
Leopold II, 138–39
Levi, Giovanni, 92
Li, Tania Murray, 6
Liebig, Justus von, 193. *See also* fertilizers;
soil
Liverpool, 8, 157, 159
locusts, 4, 171–73
longue durée. *See* Annales school
love, 2, 13, 33, 66–68, 88, 155, 188, 207.
See also care; violence
Luna, Kathryn de, 136, 170, 246

Madrid, 147, 223
magic, 134–35; fermentation as, 218;
healers, 18, 145–46, 151
mahouts, 153–56
maize, 19, 50, 55–56, 75, 182, 187, 191,
194–98; and coffee, 118; in Cuba, 8; in
Portugal, 224; and rubber, 143; in the
Soviet Union, 213

332 Index

malaria, 86, 128, 141–50, 167. *See also* cinchona; mosquitoes

Malaysia, 46, 142, 204

Malinowski, Bronisław, 76–78, 134

Manchuria, 221

manioc. *See* cassava

manufacturing, 42, 130, 145, 219–20; of agricultural products, 42–45, 111, 238; as model for agriculture, 124, 193. *See also* Industrial Revolution; industrious revolution

manure, 79, 131, 187, 192–93, 237, 245. *See also* cattle and livestock; fertilizers; sheep/shepherds

Maoism, 55–56, 106, 242

marginal land, 161, 173, 179, 180

marigolds, 2, 12, 21, 174, 204, 251; as crop and weed, 198, and gardening, 200; and religion, 197–200

markets, 4, 46, 66, 78, 96, 181, 208, 250; and agricultural revolution, 99–103; and brands, 221, 224; for cinchona, 147–49; for coffee, 114–17, 177; for dates, 35–37; defined, 159; and heritage, 242; as part of the cropscape, 20–21; in Poland post 1989, 133; for ratoons, 38; for rice, 41, 45, 180; for rubber, 136–43; for seeds, 211; and slavery, 138; as social engine, 164; surplus, 41–43, 192–93; for tea, 17, 60, 83–85, 88–93, 120, 123–24; theories of, 78; for tobacco, 57, 106–7; types of, 78, 159; for wheat, 69–75, 94, 180. *See also* commodities; Memphis Cotton Exchange; port wine; sugar; tulips

marshes, 41, 47, 127, 172, 191

Marx, Karl, 42, 125, 136, 186, 194, 250; cultural Marxism, 5

material culture, 5, 92, 146, 199

materiality, 3, 20, 70, 91, 248; and new materialism, 19–20, 136, 169

Mauss, Marcel, 78

Maya, 3, 191, 196

Mazumdar, Sucheta, 180–81

McCann, James C., 118

McKey, Doyle, 81

McNeill, William, 179

Mecca and Medina, 116

mechanization, 9, 35–36, 43, 84, *105*, 111–12, 122–25, 191. *See also* agricultural revolutions; bread; Green Revolution

medicinal plants, 55, 146–51, 167, 190, 195–200, 204, 231; tea as, 85, 90. *See also* cinchona; tobacco

medicine, Ayurvedic, 199

Mediterranean, 29–35, 98, 114–16, 207–8, 215, 225

Mekong, 127

melons, 187, 189, 191, 203

Memphis Cotton Exchange, *158*

Mendes, Chico, 144

Menelik II, 117

Mennonites, 14, 74–75

Mesoamerica, 160, 190–91

Mesopotamia, 27–28, 125

metahistory, 250

Mexico, 8, 17, 31, 35–36, 125, 132–33, 196, 198–200, 240; Gulf of, 160–61

microhistory, 23, 92–93, 132, 250

migrations, 6–14, 231; human, 10, 51–52, 74, 118, 138, 141–43, 161, 178–79, 203, 243; weevil, 160. *See also* Great Migration

millets: dryland farming techniques, 130–31, 241–42; hardy species, 53; historical dynamics, 52–56, 57; metaphor of government, 53; "orphan crops," 55; revival, 55, 241–42; significance, 53, 54; staple cereals of early North China, 52; symbol of Chinese civilization, 52–53, *54*

milpa, 17, 190–91, 196, 198, 201–2, 206, 240–41. *See also* forests: gardening

Mintz, Sidney, 11, 56

missions/missionaries (Christian), 82, 134, 145–46, 199, 204

Mississippi, 159, 239

mixed farming, 55, 173, 192–93, 203

mocha, 113–16

modernization, 15, 39, 43–45, 102, 221, 234; alternatives to, 92, 250; in China,

106, 242; theories of, 42; in Turkey, 67–69. *See also* Green Revolution; microhistory

Mongolia, 213

monocropping, 16, 114, 118, 140–42, 161, 168, 174, 197, 211–12, 235; of cereals, 180. *See also* plantations; weeds

Monsanto, 194, 206

Morrill Act, 111

mosquitoes, 18, 86, 146, 151

motion, types of (Aristotelian), 12

Mozambique, 2, 227–34; cotton-manioc complex, 182

mulberries, 40, 127

multicropping, 43, 114, 128, 142, 191–92. *See also* crop rotations

Munnar, 86–88

Mussolini, Benito, 115

mutuality, 2, 19, 60, 109, 144, 153–55, 171, 186, 205. *See also* assemblages; coalitions; domestication

Namibia, 18

Narkomzem, 214

Nazi, 22, 186, 208–17, *217, 238*, 245

Netherlands, 60–68, 209; and chinchona, 149–51, *150;* and empire, 15, 31, 113, 116, 121, 170, 175, 195; and rubber, 141–42, 144. *See also* Amsterdam; East India Company: Dutch; Java

New Husbandry, 99–100, 192–94, 203

New Orleans, 159

New York, 69, 72, 114, 177, 238

Nicaragua, 114

Niger, 171–72

Nilgiris, 86, 149

nomads, 14, 26, 31–32, 229; and settled peoples, 29, 57, 72–75

Norfolk, Coke of, 99

North Africa, 26–27, 29, 31, 33–35, 113, 192, 212

North Carolina, 97, 107–13, *110,* 125

North Carolina Agricultural and Mechanical College, 111

North Carolina State University, 112

Norton, Marcy, x, 81–82, 92

oases, 3, 23, 26–37, 57, 189

oats, 197, 209

O'Connell, Daniel, 22, *183*

Odessa, 71–74, *71*

odor, 2, 147, 197–98

Olmstead, Alan L., 73

ontologies, 5, 75–81, 134–36, 169–70, 178, 218, 245. *See also* anthropology

Opium Wars, 43, 97, 181

oranges, 1, 8, 21, 27, 33, 167, 203, 207; and ruins, 174–78, *176*

"orphan crops," 47, 55

Ortíz, Fernando, 9–11, 188–89, 203–4

Ottoman, 2, 200; and tulips, 17, 22, 60–69, *63, 70*

Palat, Ravi, 44

Papua New Guinea, 19, 78–79, 82, 135

Parmentier, Antoine-Auguste, 185

pastures, 153–54, 192, 193

patchiness, 16, 172–74, 184–85, 196, 202–5

patents, 100, 111–12, 194

peasant: agriculture, survival of, 48, 55, 69–72, 83, 180, 185, 201–2; farmers and family, 14, 72, 202, 220; movements, 96; threats to, 98–102

permaculture, 191

Peru, 31, 137–38, 143–48, 182, 193, 199–200, 214. *See also* Amazon(ia)

Peruvian Amazon Rubber Company, 137–38

pests, 121, 155, 187, 199, 211, 215, 237; and crops moving, 12; and history writing, 18, 20; and leaf blight, 140–42; and weeds, 194–97; weevils as, 160–64

Philippines, 114, 196

pigs, 41, 78–79, 136, 151. *See also* sweet potatoes

planning, 97, 102, 115, 132, 168, 201–2, 212–13, 226, 243

Plantationocene, *176*

plantation paradigm, 50, 89, 195, 202–5, 233

334 Index

plantations, 7, 9–18, 22, 24, 63, 98–99, 173, 177–84, 191, 195–96, 202–5, *217;* cashew, 233–37; cinchona and quinine, 145–51, *150;* citrus, 174–79; coffee, 82, 113–15, 174–79; and elephants, *152,* 154–55; elites, 175; eucalyptus, 167, 171; and port, 225–26; rubber, 22, 136–45, 216–17; in Southeast Asia, 143; sugar, 31, 56, 82, 174–79, 186, 188, 247; tea, 2, 22, 83–93, *119,* 121–25, 133; tobacco, 104, 107–11. *See also* colonialisms; violence; weeds

plant hunters, 26, 34–35, 85, 140, 198, 214–15

Pliny, 192

Poland, 133, 216

Polanyi, Karl, 78

political economy, 9–10, 53, 78, 99–101, 182–84, 188

pollination, 12, 35–36, 187–89, 191; and genetically modified crops, 194

pollution, 168, 177. *See also* Anthropocene; climate change

polyculture, 174, 186–91, 218. *See also* coalitions; three sisters

Porto, xiii, 224–26

Portugal, 165, 166–68, 199, 224–27, 245; and empire, 2, 31, 175, 199, 227–28, 228–34, 245; and slavery, 2, 31, 182. *See also* cashews; Porto; port wine

port wine, 3, 218, 223–27, 245; and blending, 226–27; connoisseurs, 227; in the Douro Valley, 223–26; and the regulatory state, 224–25; types of, 226–27

postcolonial critique, 14–15, 21, 89, 98, 156, 195

post-humanism, 13, 19–20, 135, 174

potatoes, 14, 22, 75, 143, 178–86, *183,* 215; as source of public happiness, 184. *See also* cassava; sweet potatoes; tubers; yams

Potosí, 147

prices: as historical actor, 157–64, 169. *See also* capitalism; commodities; futures contracts, exchanges, and traders

Protestantism, 66, 139

Prothero, R. E., 102

Quilon, 232–33

quinine, 18, 145, 149–51, *150. See also* cinchona

race, racialism, and racism, 21, 99, 120, 136, 141, 163, 194, 208; and the Black radical tradition, 246–47; and capitalism, 22; and plantation management, 85–89; in plants, 212–15; and soil, 235–40; and waste, 228

Raffles, Hugh, 59, 171

railroads, 14, 69–74, *71,* 155, 159, 165, 167, 177–78, 226

Raj, Kapil, 23

ratoons, 38–39, 47, 108

rats, 196

Refik, Ahmed, 67–68

Regel, Robert, 212

religion, 21, 68, 86, 197–200, 204, 218

Reynolds, R. J., 112

rhizomes, 1, 6, 12, 26, 58, 82

Rhode, Paul W., 73

rice, 12, 22, 39–47, 57–58, 103, 187, 196–97, 226; in China, 40–42; in Japan, 42–44; in Malaysia, 46; "rice as self," 40, 45; South India, 44; and soy sauce, 219–21; in wet, 45, 126–30, 191. *See also* IRRI and IR8; rice life cycles

rice life cycles: Champa quick-ripening varieties, 40; human manipulations of, 39–40, 47; IRRI "miracle rices," 45–47; multicropping, 40, 43, 128; ratoon rices, 39, 47–48; single-crop, 39; transplanting, 40; upland (dry) rice, 47. *See also* rice

rinderpest, 117

Rival, Laura, 80–82

Rockefeller Foundation, 104, 216

Rome and Roman Empire, 29, 32, 98–100, 151, 192, 203, 208, 213

rootedness, 1–6, 20–23, 29–33, 43–44, 50, 62, 187, 224, 249

Ross, Corey, 195

Index **335**

Roundup, 194

rubber, 82, 157, 169–70, 179, 195; agency and violence, 136–44; ersatz, 22, 216–17, *217;* plantations, 15, 22, 182, 195–96; tappers, 137, 144

ruins, 26, 31–33, 126, 166, 203, 206, 224, 227–28, 235; in Brazil, 174–78; in California, 33–37; financial, 69, 178

Rusafa, 32–33, 207

Russell, Edmund, 169

Russia, 18, 71–75, *71,* 93, 212

rye, 197, 209

Saadabad, 68

Salaman, R. N., 178–79, 186

Sahara, 3, 23, 26–31, 57, 114, 165

sake, 220–21

Salvador, Vicente, 229

sandy soils, 41, 111, 178, 229, 235

São Paulo, 11, 113, 167, 174–78, *176,* 203

São Tomé and Príncipe, 48

Schmalzer, Sigrid, 55

Schumacher, E. F., 103

science and technology studies (STS), 18, 164; feminist, 188

scientific farming, 99, 101, 120, 184–86

Scott, James C., 10, 22, 53, 56, 156, 202

Sedgewick, Augustine, 92

seeds, 200, 207, 209–17

Serres, Michel, 164–68

settler, 29, 75, 108, 204; white settler, 48, 72, 89, 195

shade trees, 27–29, 48–50, 88, 117, 186, 190, 233. *See also* dates/date palms

Shanghai, 173

sharecropping. *See under* land property regimes

sheep/shepherds, 151, 163, 167, 193

Sicily, 192

silk and silkworms, 1, 40–41, 67, 95, 127, 169, 173, 181, 189, 220–21; Bursa, 67

Silk Road, 62

silver, 1, 31, 42, 179–80; quina as, 147–51

size, 12–21, 54, 70, 79, 142, 202–4; and "big is better," 97–98; bonanza farms, 104; in East Asia, 95–96; and English

Agricultural Revolution, 98–102; of farm, 39, 83, 193; politics of scale, 96, 101–2; and "small is beautiful," 103–4, 106

slash-and-burn. *See* swidden agriculture

slavery and enslaved peoples, 9, 14, 18, 38, 48, 56, 81, 98, 146, 160; of African origin, 175; in Brazil, 175–77; and cassava, 181–82; and coffee, 113–14; and cotton in the U.S., 235–37; and dates, 30–31; and history writing, 246–47; and Nazis, 216; and sugar, 188; and tobacco in Virginia, 106–9

smallholding, 100–104, *105, 110,* 114, 179, 191, 195, 202–5; in Africa, 2, 234; in China, 90, 97, 131, 181, 242; and cocoa, 50–52; and coffee, 116–18; in Cuba, 8–9; in Europe, 98–101; and rubber, 142, 195; and tea, 90; and tobacco, 108–9

Smith, Adam, 184

Smith, Pamela, 17

Smith, Thomas C., 43

soil: erosion, 28, 131, 142, 167, 177, 194, 231, 235–40; and conservation, 239–40; and sharecroppers 235–37, 239–40. *See also* Carver, George Washington

songs, 2, 233–34, 244

sorghum, 2, 182

Southeast Asia, 45, 137, 140–43, 145, 151–56, 196, 205

Soviet Union, 102–6, *105,* 133, 204–17, 245

soy and soybeans, 106, 187, 194, 203, 218–23; as fuel, 238; sauce, 218–23, *222*

Spain, 15, 98, 147, 207, 215; and cinchona 145–51; empire, 26, 38, 92, 175, 179, 182, 204, 223; and marigolds, 197–99

Stalin, Joseph, 105, 213–14

standardization, 38, 65, 69–75, 187, 209, 232

Stoler, Ann Laura, 141–42

subaltern, 14, 180, 251

subsistence, 8, 14, 55, 102, 113, 153, 195, 240; and cashews, 229; and cocoa, 51; ratoon rice as, 47; tubers, 60, 76–78, 180

336 Index

Sudan, 30, 115–16

Sufis, 116

sugar, 15, 82, 89, 113, 120, 179, 186, 203; beet, 194; in Brazil, 31, 76, 138–43, 175–78, *176;* in the Caribbean, 11, 56; in China, 126–27, 180–82; in Cuba, *7,* 8–11, 21, 188; in fermentation, 218; in India, 155; in Mozambique, 228; in Portugal, 224–25, and reproduction of whiteness, 247; in Spain, 207; and weeds, 195–96

Suleiman the Magnificent, 63, 116

Sumatra, 140–41

surveyors/surveying, 143, 154, 212–13

Svalbard Global Seed Vault, 3, 208–10, 240

sweet potatoes, 78–79, 237; in China, 173, 179, 180–81; as "coarse food," 180; as engines of world history, 178–80; and pigs, 78–79, 173

swidden (slash-and-burn) agriculture, 16, 79, 142–44, 190–91, 240

sword grass, 195–96

Taiwan, 44, 90–91, 221

Tamils, 141

Tasmania, 166. *See also* eucalyptus

taste, 3, 15, 21, 147, 250; and cashews, 208, 229; and coffee, 113; and port wine, 223–26; and soy sauce, 221; and tea, 89–93, 120, 123; and tulips, 60–69

Tatars, 14, 74–75, 93

Taussig, Michael, 139–42

tea (in China), 83–84, 89–91; British market, 83–84, 90–91; and East India Company, 83; Fujian, 84, 89–91; green teas for Chinese market, 89; merchant middlemen, 84; oolong tea for American market, 90; smallholder production, 90, 97; Taiwan, 90; tea clippers, 90; tea regions, 89

tea (in India): anticolonial symbol, 122; Assam, 2–3, 83, 86; Assam tea plants, 85, 120, 123–24; black tea, 89, 120, 123–4; branding, 89; changing British tastes, 89, 90, 123–24; Chinese tea

bushes become "weeds," 3, 85, 120, 123; companies and shareholders, 120, 121, 124; Darjeeling, 86–88; East India Company, 2, 83–85, 88; engineers, 122–23; estates (gardens), 84, 86, *119;* industrial ideals, 120; labor discipline, 85–86, 121–23; managers, 86, 89; manual work and tools, 121–23; mechanization and machines, 120, 123–24; Munnar, 86, 87; Nilgiris, 86; pests and threats, 86; plantation model, 84, 88, 120, 121; power sources and fuel, 87–88, 122–23; racial hierarchies, 85, 120; transplantation of Chinese tea, 2, 83. *See also* cinchona; elephants; indentured laborers

teff, 118

terroir, 223–24, 243

texture, 10, 59, 147

Thevet, André, 229–31, *230*

three sisters (maize, beans, and squash), 19, 190

Tian Shan Mountains, 216

tillage, 131–32, 188, 194

Tilley, Christopher, 5

timber, 40, 82, 90, 131, 155. *See also* cashews; eucalyptus; forests

tobacco: bright, 111; burgesses, 38, 107; chemical fertilizers, 111–12; credit, 109, 112; in Cuba, 8–11, 38, 188, 203; enslaved labor, 38, 107–9, 112; and facts of the plant, 37–39, 57, 108; inspection laws, 108; markets, 107, 111–12; mechanization, 112–13; in milpa gardens, *190;* oscillations in farm size, 106–13; and patriarchy, 38, 107; sharecropping, 109–12, *110;* smallholding, 9; standardization and quality control, 38, 111–12, 203; and transculturation, 204; in Virginia and North Carolina, 38–39, 107–12, 188; as weed, 37

Townshend, "Turnip," 99, 102

tractors, 46, 102, *105,* 187, 191, 242

transculturation, 10–11, 203–6

transhumance, 193

transportation, 69–73, 87, 108, 114, 117, 122, 137, 177–82, 208, 242. *See also* railroads

Travancore, 233

Trobriand(er)s, 60, 76–79, *77,* 84–85, 93, 134

Tsing, Anna Lowenhaupt, 174, 205

tubers, 24, 56, 85, 94, 174, 233; in Africa, 182–83; in Amazonia, 80–82; in the Andes, 178, 182; as anti-commodities and para-commodities, 76, 83, 180, 185; as engines of world history, 178–86; exchange and reciprocity, 76–78; and gender, 77, 79–80; moral associations, 184–86; in Mozambique, 2, 182–83; in New Guinea Highlands, 78–79, 135; small-scale societies, 76; and social theory, 75–83; Trobriand Islands, 76–78, *77,* 134. *See also* cassava; potatoes; sweet potatoes; yams

tulips, 11, 16–17, 22, 199; bulbs and offsets, 61, 63; and capitalisms, 61, 62–63, 66–67; in the Dutch Republic, 60; and history recentered, 67–69, 93–94, in Istanbul, 17, 63–66, *64;* markets, 60, 61, 63, 66–67; Ottoman flower trade, 65–66. *See also* Istanbul; Lāle Devri; Ottoman

Tull, Jethro, 99, 102, 131

Tunisia, 32, 33

Tupi, 229–30, *230*

Turner, J. M. W., 164–66

turnips, 184, 192

Tuskegee Institute, 235–39

Ucururi, 137

Ukraine, 72–74, 216–17, *217. See also* Odessa

U.N. Food and Agriculture Organization (FAO), xiii, 47, 96, 104, 240–44

United States, 3, 9, 11, 22; and cotton, 157–64; and dates, 33–37; and farm size, 96; federal government, 162; as importer, 90–91, 177, 232; and marigolds, 200; soil and race, 235–40;

and tobacco, 13, 38–39, 107–12; and wheat, 69–74

USDA. *See* U.S. Department of Agriculture (USDA)

U.S. Department of Agriculture (USDA), 14, 26, 33–35, 104, 111–12, 163, 239–40

Vansina, Jan, 169

Vavilov, Nikolai I., 212–16

Veblen, Thorstein, 66

Versailles, 68

Via Campesina, 205

Victoria, Roche, 232

Vidal de La Blache, Paul, 4

Vienna, 61, 65, 215

Vietnam, 40, 45, 106, 114, 140–41

Vilmorin Company, 211

violence, 10, 68, 93, 97, 104, 108, 203; and care, 188; and class, 133; and domestication, 56; in moving crops, 13, 19; and plantations, 48, 122, 175; and rubber, 136–44; and weeding, 194; wheat frontiers, 73–74. *See also* care; love

Virginia, 38–39, 97, 107–12, 125, 160, 188, 203

Virginia Company, 107

Vitapack, 232

VOC. *See* East India Company: Dutch

Wallace, Henry, 159, 163

Wangjinzhuang, 55, 242–43

Washington, Booker T., 235–40, *236*

waste, 208–9, 218, 227–29, 232–34, 235–40, 246; gleaning, 203; household, 79; and soil, 235–40; toxic, 228

water, 207; dryland farming techniques, 130–32; farm scale, 130, 132; field scale, 130; hydraulic society, 125; irrigation and drainage, 129, *129;* moisture conservation, 131–32, 187–88; water management, 125; wet-rice farming techniques, 127–30, *129*

Wayanad, 86

338 Index

Weber, Max, 42, 66

weeds, 13, 21, 53, 186, 208, 237, 248, 250; and Chinese agronomy, 130–31, 173–74; and exclusion, 194–98; and moving crops, 1–2; and pests, 161, 187, 194; tobacco as, 37

weevils, 8, 13, 21, 157–64, 237

West Virginia, 73

wheat, 1–3, 22, 60, 62, 85, 89, 98, 187, 191, 203, 209; in the Americas, 13–18, 69–70, 73, 93; in Arabia, 27; in China, 40, 55, 127–28, 218; domestication, 56; in Ethiopia, 118; and fermentation, 104, 195, 218, 238; in Ireland, 76, 181; in Rome, 98; in the Soviet Union, 102; varieties of, 14, 69, 72–75, 128, 209–15, 246; as waste, 238. *See also* wheat frontiers

wheat frontiers, *71;* in Argentina and Canada, 71–73; in Chicago and the US West, 69–72, *70, 85;* grain elevators, 70, 72; Odessa and Russian steppes, 71–72; railways, 69, 70, *71,* 72; standardization and grading, 72–73; Tatars and Mennonites, 74–75; violence, 14, 73–75, 93, 195

wilderness/wildness, 117–18, 121, 137–39, 143–44, 151–56, 172–73, 212–14, 245. *See also* breeding, plant; foraging; weeds

Williams, Raymond, 5

wine, 98, 192, 219, 227–29, 231–32, 234, 242. *See also* port wine

Wittfogel, Karl, 42, 125

Xu Guangqi, 3, 11, *129,* 172–74, 200–202

yams, 3, 19, 24, 51–52, 60, 76–78, *77,* 134–35, 180–82

Yangtze, 40, 53, 89, 126–27, 246

yeasts, 218, 222

Yemen, 113–16

Young, Arthur, 101–2, 184

Zapatistas, 191, 244

Zomia, 47, 156, 202